M000240175

Rebellion in the Ranks

ANNO REGNI

GEORGII III.

REGIS

Magnæ Britanniæ, Franciæ, & Hiberniæ,

DECIMO SEXTO.

At the Parliament begun and holden at *Weſtminſter,* the Twenty-ninth Day of *November, Anno Domini* 1774, in the Fifteenth Year of the Reign of our Sovereign Lord GEORGE the Third, by the Grace of God, of *Great Britain, France,* and *Ireland,* King, Defender of the Faith, *&c.*

And from thence continued, by ſeveral Prorogations, to the Twenty-fixth Day of *October,* 1775; being the Second Seſſion of the Fourteenth Parliament of *Great Britain.*

LONDON:

Printed by CHARLES EYRE and WILLIAM STRAHAN, Printers to the King's moſt Excellent Majeſty. 1776.

The Acts of Parliament passed betweeen November 29, 1774 and October 26, 1775, and printed in 1776. This document included the Mutiny Act. (*William L. Clements Library*)

Rebellion in the Ranks

Mutinies of the American Revolution

JOHN A. NAGY

WESTHOLME
Yardley

Westholme Publishing, LLC

Eight Harvey Avenue

Yardley, Pennsylvania 19067

Visit our Web site at www.westholmepublishing.com

First Printing: November 2007

10 9 8 7 6 5 4 3 2 1

ISBN: 978-1-59416-055-4

(ISBN 10: 1-59416-055-4)

Printed in United States of America

To Ida Marie Nagy, Jennifer Ann Nagy, and Lisa Marie Nagy. Thank you for you encouragement, help, and patience.

Contents

Maps

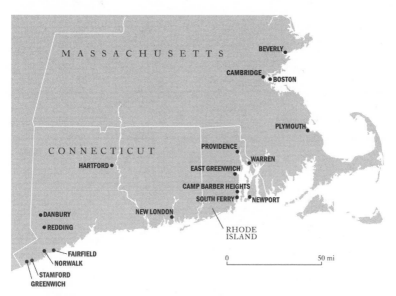

Map 1. New England.

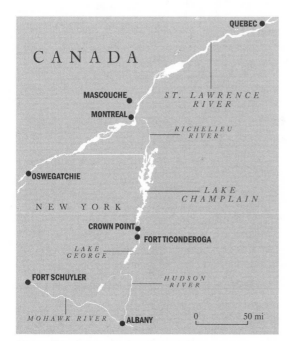

Map 2. Upper New York and Canada.

Map 3. Pennsylvania and Virginia.

Map 4. The Carolinas.

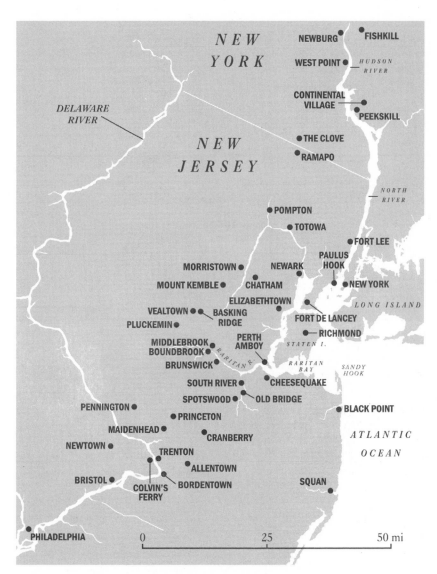

Map 5. New Jersey and lower New York.

Map 6. Staten Island, lower New York, and northern New Jersey.

Map 7. Great Britain.

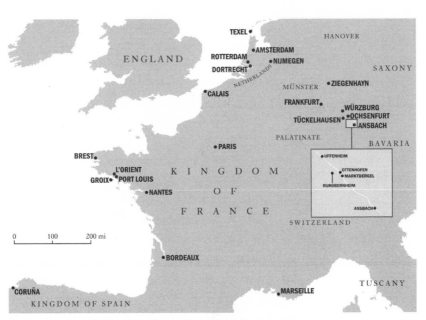

Map 8. France, Germany, Netherlands, and northern Spain.

Introduction

THE WORD MUTINY USUALLY CONJURES up the image of one of the Hollywood versions of a mutiny such as the *Mutiny on the Bounty* (1935 and 1962) with Captain William Bligh and Lieutenant Fletcher Christian or the adaptation of Herman Wouk's novel the *Caine Mutiny* (1954) with Lieutenant Commander Philip Francis Queeg. Hollywood history has led us to think that mutinies are strictly a naval event, but this is not true. Groups of men, usually armed, acting in defiance of authority happened both on land and at sea. The history of mutinies could probably be traced back to the first organized military units. It seems that someone in any organized group is always going to be dissatisfied with how the group is run especially when they have no input into its operation.

During the American Revolution, mutiny was a charge in 5.8 percent of all of the American courts martial.[1] This provides a very large universe from which to consider cases for inclusion. This book provides information on many mutinies, some of which are described for the first time. It is not, however, an exhaustive recount of every mutiny listed in official papers since the term was used to describe a variety of disciplinary problems from simple individual disobedience to actual armed insurrection. It is the latter that fall under the most rigorous definition of mutiny and merit the most attention. Some choices were obvious such as the Pennsylvania Line mutiny, the largest mutiny ever experienced by the United States military. Many cases of reported mutiny involve an individual soldier or small group of soldiers and are more correctly seen as cases of insubordination. For example, on August 28, 1777, fourteen soldiers from Colonel Christopher Greene's 1st Rhode Island Regiment laid down their arms and refused to do any duty because they had not received the clothing they had been promised. They were arrested and tried on September 2 at Peekskill, New York, but were found not guilty of mutiny but guilty of disorderly conduct.[2] Likewise, I consider switching sides as desertion rather than mutiny. But there are cases of individuals standing up to the authorities for the same reasons as large bodies of troops. On January 10, 1780, Ann Glover, widow of Sergeant Samuel Glover, petitioned the North Carolina General Assembly and told the story of her husband's mutiny. He had enlisted in 1775 in the 2nd North Carolina Regiment under Colonel Robert Howe and served three years out of the state before being returned. He was then under the command of Brigadier General James Hogun who had been made a brigadier general in the Continental Army on January 9, 1779. His unit was to go with the general to South Carolina. Samuel Glover spoke up and said they were owed twelve months back pay and were "suffering for want of subsistence which at that time was unjustly and cruelly withheld from them, a general clamor arose among the common soldiery and they called for their stipend allowed by Congress but it was not given them, although their just due." Sergeant Samuel Glover "stood forth in his own and their behalf and, unhappily for him, demanded their pay, refused to obey the command of his superior officer and would not march until they had justice done them."[3] Samuel Glover was executed in 1779 for his mutiny.[4]

Other records of disobedience reached the status of mutiny and were quelled with money, not force. On October 16, 1781, Brigadier General John Lacey of the Pennsylvania Militia left Camp Newtown in Bucks County, Pennsylvania. It was also happened to be the day of disbursing the militia. William Crispin, commissary general, was at his quarters when he heard the beating of the Rogues March. The tune was traditionally played when an undesirable was being sent out of camp. Normally the musicians would parade the individual in front of the regimental formation and then take him to the gate of the camp. Here he would be told never to return, and on many occasions, he was presented with a parting gift, a kick from the youngest drummer as he left.

As soon as Crispin heard the music, he knew there was going to be trouble. Captain Buskirk and Ensign Stiner of Colonel McVeagh's Battalion of Philadelphia County Militia arrived leading their company with fixed bayonets. Upon their arrival at Crispin's quarters, they demanded that three canteens be filled with alcoholic beverages for their three officers. They said it was needed "to carry them home." In the eighteenth century, a small supply of alcoholic drink was considered part of the military ration.

Crispin informed them that the liquor had already been dispensed to the battalion as ordered by General Lacey. He then produced Quartermaster

Davis's voucher for the liquor that was dispensed. The Philadelphians demanded the canteens be filled and if Crispin did not comply they swore they were going to go to the magazine and take what they wanted. Crispin forbade them to touch the magazine; if they did, it would be at their peril. Crispin called over Colonel McVeagh who had just arrived. In order to pacify the men, Colonel McVeagh gave them money out of his own funds so they could purchase liquor. Crispin informed General Lacey that he thought Captain Buskirk's and Ensign Stiner's had behaved in a manner unbecoming an officer and gentleman in the army. He formally filed a complaint against them and asked for a court martial.[5] No record of a court martial was found.

Lieutenant Colonel Philip Van Cortlandt of the 4th New York Regiment also controlled mutinous situations by spending his own money. In June 1775 at Newtown, New York, he guaranteed the men of Lieutenant Abraham Riker's company who were threatening to walk that he would buy them the clothes they were promised. At Albany, New York, that same year, Van Cortlandt had been paying recruits during their training. When he ran out of funds, 181 of the men left and the rest were preparing to join them. He went with the officers to the barracks and when they arrived they found a scene of total disorder. Van Cortlandt addressed the men, calmed the situation, and got volunteers who went and brought back the men who had already left. When the ranking officer Colonel Goose Van Schaick arrived, he pardoned them.[6]

Sometimes mutiny was listed in charges against soldiers, but the distinction between mutiny and disobedience is blurred. Without additional information, it can be difficult to ascertain. On August 2, 1777, for instance, Lieutenant Roger Moore and Ensign David Russel [Resco] of Captain Roger's company in Colonel Roger Enos's Connecticut Regiment were tried for mutiny, disobeying orders, and refusing to march and secure the post. Their court martial was held on the 19th at Peekskill, New York, with Colonel John Durkee of the 4th Connecticut Regiment as president. The court found them not guilty of mutiny but guilty of desertion. They were sentenced to death.[7] The court decided the prisoners, however, were objects of compassion and made such a recommendation to the commander in chief. Washington granted them his pardon. As was done with every pardon from death, the prisoners were reminded of the very atrocious nature of their crime and "Have by the Articles of War, subjected them to the punishment of *death*, that the remission of their punishment is a signal act of mercy by the Commander in

Chief, and demands a grateful return of fidelity, submission, obedience and active duty, in any future military service which he shall assign them."[8]

Prison mutinies such as uprisings onboard the prison ships and slave uprisings are not included in this book. Neither is the story of the chief conspirator in the plot to assassinate George Washington during the summer of 1776, Thomas Hickey, who happened to be one of the general's body guards, who was tried and executed, in part, for mutiny. His case is really one of an individual being caught receiving pay from the enemy and not one of active military revolt against authority. Near mutinies are not included either, such as when General Montgomery was going to move a light battery of guns within range of the Fort at St. John in Canada in 1775, and the men objected with obvious threats of mutiny. Montgomery changed his plans and the confrontation did not occur.

Finding information on some of the events turned out to be a challenge, and in the end even though a mutiny certainly occurred, there just was not enough source material. John Ingersoll a resident of Tuckahoe, Gloucester County, New Jersey, tells in his pension documents about entering in service aboard a boat commanded by Captain Enoch Willetts that sailed out of Great Egg Harbor, New Jersey, and when they entered Little Egg Harbor saw an unnamed English ship that had run aground. A few days earlier the crew had mutinied.[9] Additional cases include the June 1779 mutiny of the American troops under Colonel Theodorick Bland at the Albemarle Barracks just north of Charlottesville, Virginia, and the May 1783 desertion of fifty Maryland troops under Lieutenant Colonel Josiah Harmar at James Island, South Carolina. The State Records of North Carolina records that in July 1781 Colonel Guilford Dudley lost his entire command of Light Horse of the North Carolina Militia to mutiny except for one man. No further substantive references to any of these events has been found.[10]

I also encountered references to a mutiny in one secondary source but could not find another source to confirm that anything actually did happen. One such case is recorded in Alexander Garden's *Anecdotes of the Revolutionary War in America*. In it Gardner states that General Thomas Pinckney put down a mutiny at an early period of the war by walking amongst the mutineers and with one blow of his saber cut down the ringleader and ended the mutiny.[11] I was unable to find anything in manuscripts or print and when I questioned experts that I know on southern history in the American

Revolution found that no one had any knowledge of such an event actually happening.

After surveying examples of the two major causes of mutiny during the American Revolution among Continental and militia troops, command and control of soldiers and the lack of supplies, the book continues through the dark period of the Pennsylvania Line mutiny and other mutinies among Continental troops that it caused, a revolt of the officer corps, and the final defiance of troops fed up with the lack of pay and continued service despite the cessation of hostilities at war's end. The book closes with examples of naval mutinies from both sides, including the exploits of John Paul Jones, and mutinies among British and Hessian soldiers.

This book does assume that the reader has a basic knowledge of the key events and personalities of the American Revolution. The reader is encouraged to refer to the notes at the back of the book as they provide additional information on the events and their contexts.

The reader will no doubt observer two striking features of mutinies of the American Revolution: the large number of spies involved in information gathering on both sides regarding the state of troops and the fact that most mutinies of size occurred toward the end of the war, when the lack of clothing and food pushed men to the limits of their endurance. These are the stories of how much these men suffered for the cause of liberty. One man on picket duty only had his hat, a blanket, and his musket and not another article of clothing.[12] In another case in camp there was no meat of any kind for ten days while the men were on limited rations. Then on the next day, they were told there was going to be no food distributed that day.[13] There were risks for both sides in a mutiny, however, and the dangers were real. Two hundred New Hampshire Continental troops under Brigadier General Enoch Poor's command refused to cross the Hudson River in November 1777 until they got their ten months back pay and breeches. Trying to quell the mutiny, Second Captain Zacheriah Beal of the 3rd New Hampshire Regiment ran a soldier through with his sword. Before the soldier died, he fatally shot Beal.[14] Despite all these problems the Continental Army managed to survive and defeat the most powerful military force on the planet in its day.

1

Break Open the Guardhouse

MUTINIES OF COMMAND AND CONTROL

Since Concord and Lexington, the Continental Army had been following a winding, undulating, and cratered road of have and mostly have not. Mutiny had been the army's traveling companion since September 1775, when Washington advised Congress,

> It gives me great pain to be obliged to solicit the attention of the honorable Congress to the state of the army, in terms which imply the slightest apprehension of being neglected. But my situation is inexpressibly distressing to see the winter fast approaching upon a naked army, the time of their service within a few weeks of expiring, and no provision yet made for such important events. Added to this the military chest is totally exhausted. The paymaster has not a single dollar in hand. The Commissary General assures me he has strained his credit to the utmost for the subsistence of the army. The Quarter Master General is precisely in the same situation and the greater part of the army in a state not far from mutiny. . . . I know not to whom to impute this failure, but I am of opinion, if the evil is not immediately remedied and more punctuality observed in future, the army must absolutely break up.[1]

Mutiny was not a new concept for George Washington. His familiarity with the subject of mutinous troops began during his service as a young lieutenant colonel in the French and Indian War. At one point during that war, Washington's troops were destitute of clothing and he wrote "they are now naked and can't get credit for a hat, and are teasing the officers every day to furnish them with these and other necessaries."

On August 19, 1754, while Washington was at church, twenty-five of his soldiers assembled, and in front of their officers, they began leaving. They were quickly stopped and "imprisoned before the plot came to its full height."

Now, twenty-one years later, after the battles of Concord and Lexington, men were responding to the "Lexington alarm" and assembling around Boston and the British army. Congress found it had inherited an army and appointed George Washington its general. He would now be in charge of laying siege to Boston.

Washington left Philadelphia with General Charles Lee and traveled through the colonies of New Jersey, New York, and Connecticut, to Springfield, Massachusetts, where they were met by Dr. Benjamin Church and Moses Gill.[2] Church and Gill were given the honor of escorting the two generals on their trip through Massachusetts.[3] The group arrived at Cambridge at 2:00 p.m. on July 2.

The next morning the troops were assembled on the common and received George Washington as their commander in chief. Now the two former allies, Thomas Gage and George Washington, who twenty years earlier both served under General Edward Braddock in the French and Indian War, were enemies.

What Washington inherited could hardly be called an army. It was an assortment of angry farmers, tradesmen, laborers, and other locals who had decided to take up arms against the British. They resented the "Lobsterbacks," the soldiers who epitomized the might of King George. It was really a mob doing what it wanted, when it wanted, and how it wanted. Discipline was nonexistent, and when any large body of people assembles, rumors fill the void where there is a lack of information.

Abigail Adams wrote on July 25, 1775, to dear friend and husband John about the news she had heard that "an order has been given out in town that no person shall be seen to wipe their faces with a white handkerchief. The reason I hear is, that 'tis a signal of mutiny."[4]

Rumors of what was happening in the besieged city of Boston had made their way to Baltimore, Maryland. A broadside published on August 10, 1775, claiming to be an extract of a letter, dated August 4 from a gentleman in New York to a friend in Baltimore of undoubted veracity, said, "By express just arrived from Boston, we are informed the Lieutenant Governor of Canada is taken prisoner, General Gage is at the point of death, the people and soldiers in Boston die from 50 to 100 in a day, and the soldiers had a mutiny."[5] Any one of these events would have been a major story in and of itself, but whoever made it up chose to go whole hog. Rumors like these were not going to help the Continental officers get control of their troops. With their men believing the current situation would quickly end, and the war would be of short duration, it was difficult to stabilize the troops' morale and discipline.

Command and control was a problem for the officers of the fledgling American army with all the early military units, both continental and state. The men had banded together to get rid of a king and certainly did not want to acquire a group of military despots. The first mutiny of the American Revolutionary War occurred because of a lack of military control. An amalgam of soldiers was still being forged into an army. The Pennsylvania and Virginia riflemen who joined the army at Boston were among the most respected troops, despite the fact that their units were often the most obstreperous ones in camp. These men, many of whom came from beyond the Allegheny range and were known in some circles as "over the mountain men," lived on their own in the wilderness away from the restrictions of society and were as a group more reluctant to accept orders from anyone. Assigned to the outpost positions, they were exempt from the drudgery of guard and fatigue duty. This special status went to some of their heads. Troops stationed on Prospect Hill became unruly and insubordinate to a degree that was a cut above the unruly mob making up the siege. No one was going to tell them what they could or could not do. They had twice broken open the guard house to release companions who were confined for petty offenses. "Once when an offender was brought to the post to be whipped, it was with the utmost difficulty they were kept from rescuing him in the presence of all their officers. They openly damned them and behaved with great insolence. However, the colonel [William Thompson] was pleased to pardon the man and all remained quiet."[6]

On Sunday September 10, 1775, Third Lieutenant David Ziegler the adjutant of Colonel William Thompson's Pennsylvania Rifle Battalion confined a sergeant for neglect of duty and murmuring. Members of the sergeant's company were determined to set him free. Lieutenant Ziegler seized the ringleader of the coup, John Leaman, and placed him in jail.[7] Ziegler then went to report the incident to Colonel Thompson who had just finished dinner and was enjoying the company of some fellow officers. All of a sudden, they heard huzzaing and found the guard house had been broken open. Colonel Thompson and several of the officers acted quickly and recaptured Leaman from among the mutineers. In order to get him out of the area Thompson sent him to the jail at headquarters in Cambridge, about a mile away.

Camp was quiet for about twenty minutes before some men of Captain James Ross's notoriously ill-disciplined Company H swore to go to Cambridge and release the prisoner. The Lancaster County men were joined by other riflemen of Company H. The mutineers, now totaling thirty-two men with loaded rifles, marched off from Prospect Hill toward Cambridge. They were intent on freeing John Leaman.

Word was quickly sent to General George Washington, who immediately called out some five hundred armed men to protect the main jail. Colonel Daniel Hitchcock's 2nd Rhode Island Regiment and part of General Nathanael Greene's Brigade were ordered under arms.

The thirty-two mutineers had traveled about a half mile when they realized the size of the force assembled to oppose them at the main jail. They stopped their journey and took cover in the woods on a hill. Generals Greene, Lee, and Washington arrived on the scene.

Washington ordered the mutineers to ground their arms. They rapidly complied as they were facing overwhelming firepower. Washington then ordered Captain George Nagel's Berks County (Company G) Pennsylvania Riflemen to fix bayonets and surround the mutineers, which they quickly accomplished. Washington next ordered parts of Colonel Hitchcock's Rhode Island and Colonel Moses Little's Massachusetts Regiments also to fix their bayonets and surround the mutineers.[8] Two men were identified as the leaders of the mutiny and were bound. All the mutineers were marched back to camp. Twenty-six of them were turned over to the guardhouse at Prospect Hill and the other six were sent to the main guardhouse at Cambridge.[9]

The next day, to ensure that the remaining riflemen were kept busy and to dispel the idea that they were a privileged corps, Washington issued a general order. It read, "Colonel Thompson's Battalion of Riflemen posted upon Prospect Hill, to take their share of all duty of guard and fatigue, with the brigade they encamp with." They had lost their special work exemption. He also ordered "a general court martial to sit as soon as possible to try the men of that regiment, who are now prisoners in the main guard, and at Prospect Hill, and accused of *mutiny*."[10]

The general orders issued on September 11 instructed that a court martial of those charged with mutiny of Colonel Thompson's Battalion of Riflemen be conducted as soon as possible.[11] At seven o'clock in the morning on the 12th, a court martial composed of three field officers and ten captains convened, with Colonel John Nixon of Massachusetts presiding. Just months before, Nixon had been wounded at Bunker Hill.

The mutineers were convicted of disobedient and mutinous behavior. Because the possibility of the mutiny spreading still existed and a strong military authority had yet to be established, they were given a light sentence. They were fined twenty shillings, which was to be taken from their next month's pay and given to the hospital fund. John Leaman who instigated the mutiny was also sentenced to six days' imprisonment.[12]

Despite their value as good fighters, the "over the mountain men" would remain a discipline problem throughout the war.

WHILE THE SIEGE OF BOSTON CONTINUED, the Americans began their first major military operation. The Continental Army made a thrust into Canada at the end of 1775 in an attempt to remove the British threat from the north and possibly convince the Canadians to join the rebellion. The Americans aim was to take the fortress city of Quebec from which the British, like the French before them, governed Canada.

American armies were led by Colonel Benedict Arnold, driving north through Maine to Quebec, and Brigadier General Richard Montgomery, following Lake Champlain to Montreal and then on to Quebec. Montgomery took Montreal and then pushed on to Quebec where Arnold was already waiting for him.

On December 26, 1775, Montgomery made a plea for more troops to General Philip J. Schuyler. Schuyler commanded the Northern Department with its headquarters at Albany, New York. Schuyler sent a letter on December 30, along with copies of letters from Generals Montgomery and Wooster to Congress urging that large reinforcements be sent to Canada. The letters were read in Congress on January 6.[13] But by that time, the American assault on fortress Quebec had failed and Montgomery was dead. The American losses were 51 killed, 36 wounded, and 387 captured. The British lost 7 killed and 11 wounded in the nighttime battle.[14]

On January 8, 1776, Congress started issuing resolves. The 1st Pennsylvania Battalion under the command of Colonel Bull and the 2nd New Jersey Battalion under the command of Colonel William Maxwell were ordered to march immediately to Albany, New York. Once at Albany, they were to be put under the command of General Schuyler.[15] This was a complete turnaround for the Pennsylvanians who had been under orders to go south to Virginia where the weather was much more moderate.

On January 13, Schuyler made another appeal for troops to Washington.[16] Washington was having problems of his own keeping his army in the field. Many soldiers were leaving; few were arriving and staying. He responded to Schuyler, "Since the dissolution of the old army, the progress in raising recruits for the new has been so very slow and inconsiderable that five thousand militia have been called in for the defense of our lines. A great part of these are gone home again, and the rest induced to stay with the utmost difficulty and persuasion, though their going would render the holding of them truly precarious and hazardous, in case of an attack. In short I have not a man to spare."[17]

Washington called a war council to discuss the situation. A request was sent to Connecticut, Massachusetts, and New Hampshire for a regiment from each.[18] Regiments were sent from Connecticut under Colonel Charles Burrell, from Massachusetts under Colonel Elisha Porter, and from New Hampshire under Colonel Timothy Bedell.

On January 17, Philadelphia received word of the failed attempt to storm Quebec and the death of General Montgomery. It was somber news. Still, the companies of men of the 1st Pennsylvania Battalion began the trek to Canada, with each company to follow the other. Jonathan Jones's Company A left a cold and dreary Philadelphia that same month and began their march to Quebec where there was, unbeknown to them, six feet of snow on the ground. On the outskirts of Quebec on January 30, Caleb Haskill and the rest of a fourteen-man company in Colonel Livingston's Massachusetts Continental regiment refused guard duty. The mutineers were quickly tried, convicted, and fined, which ended their protest.[19]

Meanwhile 1st Pennsylvania Battalion passed through Germantown, Bethlehem, and Easton where they crossed the Delaware River. In New Jersey, they went by way of Oxford and Sussex Court House and on into New York at Goshen and Wallkill. From Goshen north they traveled by sled. They made this journey to Albany, New York, in just eleven days and reported to General Schuyler.

Some of the Pennsylvanian companies did not leave Philadelphia until much later, arriving at Albany in April.[20] On this journey their shoes, moccasins, and mittens were worn out. They would pause at Albany to regain their strength and be supplied with new dry goods. From here, north there would be wilderness except for some very small settlements and forts. They would have to be on their guard as there were hostile Indians who were fighting alongside the British. As in most wars, neutrals went extinct quickly. It was choose or be destroyed. The Indians, being in the middle of the two belligerents, had to take a side. Most chose the British army and King George in the hope of stopping or slowing the encroachment of the colonists.

It took several days to refit the Pennsylvanians and get supplies for the journey to far-off Quebec. Bread was baked for them at Forts George and Ticonderoga. Pork was being prepared for the expedition. They had to bring their food as little foraging could be done in the territory that lay ahead. In the relative comfort of Albany, they began to murmur about the privations on their trip from Philadelphia and that they had not been paid, and to speculate about the long cold journey that lay ahead.

As the days passed, thoughts of the approaching journey grew to nightmare proportions until Company F of the 1st Pennsylvania Battalion exploded in an open mutiny. The unit was commanded by Captain William Jenkins of Philadelphia. General Schuyler acted quickly, arresting the mutineers and holding a court martial on February 9, 1776, for the ringleaders Richard Casey, Brunt Debidie, John Fannan, William Henry, John King, Samuel Leslie, Michael McQuicken, and Patrick Queen. Colonel Goose Van Schaick of the 2nd New York regiment was president.

The men pleaded not guilty. After listening to testimony from the witnesses, the court decided that Casey, Debidie, Henry, and McQuicken were to receive thirty-nine lashes on their bare backs, Fannan, King, and Leslie would be whipped fifteen times, while Patrick Queen was judged not guilty. By the middle of February, the Pennsylvanians were once again traveling north.[21]

THE WILDERNESS FORTS THAT SUPPORTED the Continental efforts in the north despite their strategic importance, also felt the effects of mutiny. Fort Ticonderoga was the citadel of the north country of New York. It sits at the strategic location on Lake Champlain that protected the portage to Lake George. In 1755, it was the southernmost point of French Canada, marked by a small fort. The French abandoned the fort in 1759 during the French and Indian War. The British repaired and expanded the site and renamed it Fort Ticonderoga.

On May 9, 1775, in a clever raid, the Americans stormed the fort, capturing it from the small British garrison. In the winter of 1776, Colonel Henry Knox led an expedition that dragged cannons from both Fort Ticonderoga and Crown Point on sleds over the snow to Boston. The cannons were placed on Dorchester Heights, forcing the British evacuation of Boston.

Assigned to oversee Ticonderoga in early 1777, Colonel Anthony Wayne, who would soon be promoted to brigadier general, described the conditions at the great fort as a motley garrison of 1,000 men and boys and 850 militia of which "one third part are Albany Dutchmen who can not speak one word of English. 'Tis said that there is some consolation in hell itself." He described a scene of Major Michael Ryan parading the guard.

> If he order them to be silent they one and all begin to jabber Dutch, when he orders them to rest their firelocks, they lay them down on the ground butts and muzzles intermixed as being the most natural state of rest. When ordered to march, they make off in full speed to their respective huts. Ryan pursues and flogs them, gets a Dutch interpreter and perhaps in the course of three or four hours mounts a guard. However they answer one good purpose for after tattoo they suffer none to pass as perhaps the counter sign being of no use to them. Thus we go on.[22]

On February 9, 1777, Major Samuel Hay, of the 7th Pennsylvania Regiment and aide to General Anthony Wayne, went into the woods to check on the situation around the fort. Hay was shocked when he found fourteen or fifteen men sitting and warming themselves by a fire. They were a detachment under Captain Fitch of Colonel Seman's Regiment that had been sent to cut abatis for the defenses of the fort.[23] Without ordering any of his men to get to work, Captain Fitch responded that "the state had not sent them here to cut abatis but to keep guard and defend the garrison nor in his opinion was it necessary it should be cut." Major Hay responded by telling Captain Fitch that he "was both surprised and ashamed to hear an officer give such an answer especially before his soldiers that it was sufficient to break him."[24] No records of a court martial were found.

Two days later, on February 11, 1777, the men of Captain John Nelson's Rifle Company, who had originally reported to Colonel Wayne of the 4th Pennsylvania Battalion, were under arms with their packs on their backs and preparing to leave. This company, raised in January 1776, was intended to serve in Canada. It consisted of one captain, three lieutenants, four sergeants, four corporals, and seventy privates.[25]

The riflemen were getting their belongings together when news of their imminent departure was brought to Wayne's attention. When he arrived at their encampment he found the men assembled and beginning their march. When he inquired as to the cause of their action, they responded "in a tumultuous manner" to inform him their enlistments had expired the previous month and they "looked upon themselves as at liberty to go home."

Wayne ordered them to halt. He called for their leader to step out and speak for them, as he could not answer all of them at one time. A sergeant stepped forward from the ranks and when he did, Wayne put a loaded pistol to his chest threatening him. The sergeant sank to his knees and pleaded for his life. Wayne ordered all the men to lay down their arms. They immediately complied. Wayne addressed the men and convinced them to agree to remain until the 20th of the month. The mutineers disbursed and returned to duty.

The events of the day were not yet complete. Josiah Holida, of Captain Aaron Coe's Company in Colonel Timothy Robinson's Massachusetts Militia Regiment, attempted to incite the men to mutiny again. When Wayne confronted him, Holida tried to justify his mutinous conduct. Wayne chastised Holida for his insolence in front of the men and had him removed to the main guardhouse.

Later that day, Colonel Robinson reluctantly paid a visit to Wayne to inform him that a written complaint had been lodged against him and "he was sorry for it but was obliged to take notice of it." Colonel Robinson then handed Wayne the written complaint, dated the 11th, from Josiah Holida. He stated in his complaint that he had been confined and brought before Anthony Wayne for no just cause. On the 10th Wayne "shamefully beat and abused" him "contrary to the rules of good order and discipline and a breach of the law of god and man prejudicat[e] to the cause in which we are engaged."[26]

Wayne discovered that the complaint had been written by Captain Aaron Coe. He then summoned Captain Coe who acknowledged that he wrote the letter and knew the reason why his soldier, Josiah Holida, was struck and confined. Captain Coe then stated it was his "opinion that every soldier had a right to deliver his sentiments on every occasion without being punished." Wayne was flabbergasted and "ordered him in arrest as an abettor of the mutiny."[27]

That evening, a letter from thirty-six officers (three majors, ten captains, and twenty-three lieutenants) was given to Colonel Timothy Robinson concerning the arrest and planned transfer of Captain Coe to Albany for a court martial. They claimed that both Coe and Holida "may receive a fair and impartial trial on the grounds by court martial composed of officers of the militia from the state to which the offenders belong."[28]

The next day, Colonel Wayne, communicated the events of the mutiny to General Schuyler and said he wanted to send Coe and Holida to Albany for a court martial. Wayne stated that to try them there at Fort Ticonderoga by their own people would prove no good.[29] On the 16th, General Schuyler wrote back to Wayne that Captain Coe's conduct in justifying Holida was indeed criminal. However, he needed to have him tried at Fort Ticonderoga rather than at Albany. To hold the court martial at Albany would require much travel expense and lost time for the witnesses and the jury. Schuyler wrote out an order for a court martial to sit there, sent the warrant to Wayne, and allowed him to pick the judge advocate. Schuyler wanted a copy of the proceedings as soon as it was completed.[30]

The general order for the court martial of Captain Coe and Private Holida was issued on the 17th, with Colonel Francis Barber of Dayton's New Jersey regiment to be president. The rest of the court was to be composed of an equal number of Dayton's 3rd New Jersey and Simon's militia regiments.[31]

Three days later, General Schuyler realized that the articles of war required that courts martial for trial of militia be composed of officers of the same provincial corps as the offender. He then told Wayne if the orders had been issued to countermand them, or if the court had begun to dissolve it, replace it with one that complied with the articles of war.[32]

Wayne acknowledged General Schuyler's correspondence of the 16th and 19th, informing him that he had dropped the charges against Coe and Holida and released them from confinement. It seems that after spending some time under lock and key they had a change of heart and were "much humbled." Wayne believed that "upon the whole it will have a better effect than to have pushed it further as all the officers esteem it as an act of grace proceeding immediately from you and seem as sensible of the [leniency]. . . . They now do duty with [alacrity] and like a child when in dread of correction—promise never to err again."[33]

IN SOME CASES A MUTINY AGAINST AUTHORITY was a good thing. Nicholas Haussegger was commissioned a major on January 4, 1776, and a colonel on

July 17.[34] He was then was sent from the Northern Army to Philadelphia on September 11, 1776.[35]

On December 10, 1776, Haussegger in command of the German Battalion was stationed at Coryell's Ferry, New Jersey.[36] His assignment was to ensure that no intelligence was conveyed to the enemy and no person was to pass the Delaware River except by written order from the brigadier general in charge.[37]

The German Battalion was composed of Maryland and Pennsylvania German settlers. Colonel Haussegger had, at some point, contacted the British and made arrangements to change sides.

On January 4, 1777, Haussegger was leading his regiment as they came within a half mile of Princeton, which had been occupied by the British. He had intended to march his entire regiment into a trap. Major Ludowick Weltner, a Marylander, rode up and informed Haussegger that the city was still occupied. The two of them got into a heated discussion. Major Weltner countermanded Haussegger's orders and the regiment halted. As the two of them vehemently argued, the officers came to the head of the regiment to watch their commanding officers go at it.

Major Weltner said, "They shall not march until the town is reconnoitered and then we shall act according to circumstances."[38] Haussegger, insisting that he would reconnoiter the town himself, ordered ten men and Lieutenant Barnard Hubly to accompany him. Major Weltner ordered Hubly to remain with his platoon. Haussegger declared that this was a mutiny and he would have the major punished. They argued back and forth about the presence of the enemy.

Haussegger then took the ten men and marched into Princeton, where he went directly to the commanding Hessian officer, who had ordered all the troops to stay in their quarters and did not even have a sentinel at his own door. Haussegger surrendered himself and his men. The Hessian asked him where his regiment was. Haussegger said that "the Major had mutinied and usurped the command and even ordered an officer back to his place who he intended to have brought with him, and these ten men were all he could bring with him."[39]

The Hessian officer then pulled out a purse and poured some gold coins in his hand and told Haussegger to take what he wanted. A guard was ordered to take possession of the ten Americans. Haussegger then asked if he could have one of the men for a valet and was permitted to take a man by the name of Housman who was the younger brother of a butcher from York, Pennsylvania. They went to New York.[40]

Weltner's mutiny had saved his regiment from becoming prisoners of war. Haussegger was sent back from New York to Philadelphia on a parole to try and make an exchange that would allow him to return to active duty.[41]

In 1779, the British tried to pull a bit of chicanery by proposing to exchange the side-switching Haussegger for Dr. John Connolly, a Tory who had plotted to incite Indian attacks against settlers in the Ohio Territory. Washington was not to be outfoxed and prohibited the exchange.[42]

WHEN SIFTING THROUGH PERIOD DOCUMENTS, mutinies are often mentioned in passing but with no further details provided. In his journal, twenty-year-old Newport, Rhode Island, native Sergeant Jeremiah Greenman wrote that sometime during January 1779 at Warren, Rhode Island, while he was stationed there, part of the 2nd Rhode Island Regiment during the evening paraded under arms demanding their rights. When the general went on the parade ground, the men dispersed.[43] No further information about this mutiny has been found; however, it turns out that this same regiment was involved in several other mutinies in Rhode Island during that year that can shed light on the context of Greenman's comments.

On April 23 at around ten in the evening, most of the 2nd Rhode Island Regiment turned out under arms and took control of the artillery where they had been positioned. They were demanding to get paid. After about two hours, not having received any positive answers from the colonel in camp, they left. They were going to go to Providence to get satisfaction.

They marched to within two miles of the ferry to Providence and sent a message to General Horatio Gates, who had just taken over the command of the Northern Army in March. General John Glover, a former Marblehead, Massachusetts, fisherman and second in command, visited the men and encouraged them to believe that something would be done to address their grievances. Being satisfied with his response, they returned to Warren, arriving at nine the next morning, and disbanded. A committee was sent to Providence to make a complaint over their lack of pay. Later the committee reported to the men that they would be receiving some money by May 1.[44]

The 2nd Rhode Island Regiment again mutinied on the afternoon of July 24, 1779. Two thirds of the sergeants of conspired and ripped the bindings of their hats contrary to orders they were given in order to demonstrate their unhappiness, presumably over their pay. They were instructed to put them back on by next morning's guard mounting or they would be reduced to the ranks. Colonel Israel Angell received a mutinous letter written by a soldier named Hazzard and brought by one Twitchel. By eight o'clock on the 25th the sergeants had all their bindings back in place. Sergeant Jeremiah Greenman wrote in his journal "At roll call this evening" at Camp Barber's Heights the troops "behaved as well as here to fore [and] two of the mutineers deserted."[45]

Three days later, Sergeant Greenman wrote he was detached from the main body of men and was at South Ferry on the west side of Narragansett Bay opposite Conanicut Island. At 2:00 p.m. an express came from camp informing him that the bigger part of the 2nd Regiment had mutinied. His orders were to march immediately for camp with the men under his command except for three men who were to continue on post at South Ferry. Greenman says they marched back to camp as fast as they could. He arrived at 4:00 p.m. and fell in with his captain, William Humphrey of the 2nd Rhode Island Regiment. Captain Humphrey then set out after the mutineers, who had gone to East Greenwich to release from the guard a George Milliman who had been sentenced to death for mutinying. Captain Humphrey's men marched to within two miles of Greenwich when they were told that the mutineers were returning. They then started their return journey back to camp. Sergeant Greenman took his men and returned to South Ferry where he arrived at 2:00 a.m.[46]

On the 31st all the men had been given a pardon except George Milliman who was sent a prisoner in irons to Providence. On August 4, Major Thayer and Captain Coggeshall Olney and Ensign Wheaton went to Providence to provide evidence against Milliman. On August 8 Colonel Angell received an express from the adjutant general that he wanted eight noncommissioned officers and soldiers of Angell's 2nd Rhode Island Continental Regiment to provide evidence. On the 9th Lieutenant Colonel Jeremiah Olney went to Providence to attend the court martial.[47] George Milliman was sentenced to death but was not executed.[48]

GOOD FOOD AND CLOTHING ARE ALWAYS IMPORTANT to motivate soldiers and keep morale high, but money was the best way to retain control of the troops and the lack of it or disparity in pay were often sources of mutinous behavior. During the summer of 1776, Colonel Samuel Patterson, the owner of a grist mill on the Christiana River, led his Delaware Battalion of approximately five hundred men to Philadelphia to join the flying camp, a mobile strike force.

While in the City of Brotherly Love, two hundred of his men mutinied. The men had heard that Pennsylvania was paying its state troops more bounty money than they got. They laid down their arms and refused to go any farther unless they got the same deal as the Pennsylvanians. Patterson ordered his other men to fix bayonets. He then herded the malcontents down to boats waiting in the Delaware River. He threatened to send for Continental troops if they didn't cooperate. His strategy worked and the troops got back in line.

Patterson would complain that the men "from below," that is, Kent and Sussex Counties, Delaware, were "not fit for fatigue [duty], have no constitutions, and are always dissatisfied." He did say a few were "excessive good, others perhaps another day may be brave, not at present. In my opinion they had better have stayed at home."[49]

A couple of months later, Connecticut and Massachusetts had planned to issue additional pay to their soldiers in the field while other states had no such plans. Connecticut and Massachusetts did not end up issuing additional pay, and in November 1776, Washington told the Continental Congress this kind of inequity among the soldiers would unquestionably have brought about a mutiny.[50]

Inequity did bring about a mutiny in 1777, at Stamford, Connecticut, when one sergeant, one corporal, and thirteen privates from a group of fifty Connecticut militiamen divided between the towns of Fairfield, Norwalk, and Stamford refused to do their duty. Because of an order of Governor Jonathan Trumbull and the Council of Safety, their rations had been reduced to a level below those supplied to the Continental troops. The men insisted that because of a law passed by the state in December, they were entitled to the same pay and rations as the Continental troops and refused orders.

At Fairfield, Connecticut, native and Yale graduate Brigadier General Gold Selleck Silliman of the Connecticut militia told the men they were taking the wrong method to get relief of their grievance. Silliman told them to do their duty and make their representation to the governor and council. He volunteered to do it for them only if they all quietly did their duty. He wanted an answer by 9:00 p.m. otherwise, in the morning, he would "use proper measures to oblige them to do it."[51] In other words, he would force them into submission.

The men sent him a message that they would do their duty and asked him to make a representation to the governor for them. General Silliman sent a letter to Governor Trumbull, dated February 2, 1777, asking for a return to their usual allowance of rations and added that they also had no salt with which to preserve fresh provisions.[52] As quickly as it appeared, the mutiny was put down.

Discrepancies in pay among Continental troops also fostered mutinous behavior. Winter was passing at Fort Pitt, headquarters of the Western District of the Continental Army, when Captain John Finley, Deputy Judge Advocate, wrote to Brigadier General William Irvine on February 2, 1782, that the men were planning to mutiny over their not being paid. He recommended the use of force to keep the men in line.[53] On February 7, 1782, General Irvine wrote George Washington about conditions at the fort: "[there is] no cash to pay artifers, the troops in bad temper for want of pay; under very bad discipline; too long in one station as they have formed such connections as make them tenacious of the rights of citizens, while they at the same time retain all the vices of common soldiery."[54]

The 7th Virginia Regiment along with the 8th Pennsylvania Regiment occupied Fort Pitt.[55] The Virginians had gotten wind of some payments being made to the Pennsylvania troops and even to their Indian allies while they had not gotten any. They wrote to General Irvine,

> We have been at this post almost four years, and have been without pay two years and three months of this time; this undoubtedly your honor must be acquainted with. Your honor, likewise, saw when you first arrived here in what a deplorable condition we were, for want of clothing, almost naked, several days wanting provisions, in cold, open barracks with little fuel or fire—these extremities made us to utter things much to the prejudice of the character of soldiers; but that thing of murder, mutiny or desertion we abhor and disdain—it never was our real intentions, and we should look upon every one that has had that bad opinion of us to be our enemies. We have always been ready to exert ourselves in the service of our country, but more particularly, on these frontiers, entrusted to our charge. We are too sensible of the troubles and inconveniences (although there is but a handful of regular troops here) if this post should be evacuated. Though we have been upbraided by the country inhabitants for our fidelity—they calling us fools, cowards and a set of mean fellows for staying without our pay and just dues—yet we think more of honor than to listen to any advice than what is given to us by our officers.

It is reported amongst the soldiery that the officers of our regiment and the Indians have received pay; if it is so, we are sorry that the Indians should be in preference to us.[56] But this is news we cannot well credit. We are well assured your honor is too much of a soldier's friend.

We thought it very hard when the depreciation money was paid to the Pennsylvania line and none to the Virginia; and if the Indians have received pay, we think this harder.[57]

We are very sorry the country is not better able to pay the troops employed in its service; but we must need know and consider within our breasts, that when the war commenced the country was young and unprepared, and must of consequence be much in debt; but we hope it will overcome all in a short time, to our great joy and satisfaction, and we have no further reason to complain. We have nothing further to add, but remain your honor's most obedient and faithful soldiers of the 7th Virginia regiment.[58]

On April 30 a general court martial with Colonel John Gibson of the 7th Virginia Regiment presiding was held and John Phillips and Thomas Steed of the 7th Virginia were convicted of mutiny and attacking Lieutenant Samuel Bryson of the 2nd Pennsylvania Regiment. They were sentenced to death which was confirmed by General Irvine. Phillips and Steed sent a letter from the Fort Pitt Blockhouse on the 30th to General Irvine, "Your poor, unhappy, dying petitioners humbly beg of your honor's goodness to spare our lives for the space of some time longer that we may make our peace with Almighty God, we being in a bad situation to resign our mortality and change it to immortality. We hope and beg of your honor to grant us this request in this our last dying moments, and we hope the Almighty God will ever bless and requite your goodness hereafter. From your honor's sincere, penitent and humble petitioners." On May 2 Irvine issued orders that Phillips and Steed are to be executed tomorrow between 11:00 a.m. and noon. On the morning of the 3rd Irvine issued an order that "one subaltern, one sergeant, one drum and all the fifers in the garrison, twenty rank and file, properly armed and accoutered will attend the execution. Captain [Samuel] Brady [of the 3rd Pennsylvania Regiment] as officer of the day will see it performed. The party will parade at eleven o'clock." Irvine continued that he was "determined to keep up subordination and strict discipline" but because of his feelings of humanity he pardoned John Phillips. Steed was executed.[59]

WHILE TROOPS IN THE FIELD HAD NOT SEEN anything that resembled money in months, Congressmen were making sure they got their pay. The question was not whether a problem would arise but where.

The Connecticut Line troops were encamped at the "Connecticut Huts" on the east side of the North or Hudson River. Having not received pay, the men had hatched a plan for a mutiny for the morning of May 4, 1782, at the beating of reveille. Colonel Heman Swift heard about the plot on the morning of the 3rd. The conspirators had planned to meet that afternoon under the pretext of playing some ball.[60] Colonel Swift was required to attend a court martial that day but requested the other officers to observe the movements of the conspirators and find his informant and others who could be relied on to make other discoveries.

When Swift returned in the evening, he found that 150 people had been identified. He then tried to ascertain who the principals were. He immediately ordered 60 men from each regiment properly officered to parade and apprehended a number from whom he expected to obtain more information. After a long examination, he found that a mutiny committee from several regiments had been formed to develop a plan of action. When he questioned them, they acknowledged their participation on the mutiny committee. The plan called for the men to agree to sleep on their arms that night. "The reveille was to be at 4 o'clock next morning when they were to parade and somebody would appear to take command of them. They were then to march to Fishkill take possession of some fieldpieces draw their provisions and march to Hartford."[61]

Swift ordered out a large guard in front and behind the encampment, as well as sentinels posted close together, and ordered officers to walk in each regiment's campsite during the night. The night passed without any disturbance.

He and the officers who had been trying to unravel the plot had identified only privates as ringleaders. But they did not believe they were the instigators. They finally got the names of the instigators of the plot. The culprits were two sergeants of the 3rd Connecticut Regiment by the names of Gerred Bunce and Wyman Parker. Bunce was to have been their commander. Parker was deeply involved in the plot.

On May 5, Swift released all the soldiers who had been detained except for Sergeants Bunce, Parker, and a private by the name of Lud Gaylord. He sent those three men to the provost at West Point. He reported that he was

continuing the guard but everything seemed normal in camp. When the soldiers were interrogated, the only reason given for the plot was they wanted
their pay.[62]

On the morning of May 6, Colonel Swift sent his report off to George
Washington. Washington received Swift's report the same day and sent back
a response. He thanked Swift for his efforts and instructed him to apply to
Major General William Heath to appoint a court martial for the immediate
trial of the two sergeants who were the ringleaders and report their proceedings to back to him.[63]

A general court martial presided over by Colonel John Greaton of
Massachusetts was held on May 12 at West Point by order of Major General
William Heath. Sergeant Gerred Bunce and Wyman Parker of the 3rd
Connecticut Regiment and Lud Gaylord, soldier of the 1st Connecticut
Regiment, were tried. They were charged with endeavoring to excite a mutiny
in the Connecticut Line and also not revealing an intended mutiny to their
officers.

The court decided the charge of endeavoring to excite a mutiny in the
Connecticut Line was not supported against Sergeant Gerred Bunce and
found him not guilty.[64] In the case against Sergeant Wyman Parker, the court
also acquitted him of the charges against him.

The court martial decided that all the charges against Lud Gaylord were
true. He endeavored to excite a mutiny in the Connecticut Line, did not tell
his officers when he knew of a plot, and formed to carry it into execution, a
breach of the latter part of Article 4 Section 2d of the rules and Articles of
War. The Court with upward of two-thirds agreeing, sentenced Gaylord to
death. When Washington received the notice concerning Lud Gaylord's death
sentence, he approved it and ordered the execution for Monday, May 13.[65]
There would be no last-minute reprieve. Washington was having a hard time
keeping people in the ranks; despite Cornwallis's surrender, the war was not
over. He made an example of Gaylord, demonstrating the consequences of
mutiny.

Later, Washington explained to Robert Morris, Superintendent of
Finance, the situation in the field that existed because soldiers had not been
getting their pay while congressmen got theirs on time.

Minds soured by distresses are easily rankled; as a specimen of it, the privates of the Connecticut Line were the other day upon the eve of a gener-

al mutiny; the vigilance of the officers discovered it a few hours before they were to parade, and the ringleaders have been tried and executed; besides this, desertions are more prevalent than ever; by the last returns a greater number went off than ever did in the same space before, and tho' I know how much you have labored for the means of paying the army, and how inapplicable the remark is to you, 'till you are furnished with these, I cannot help adding, that it is very difficult if not impracticable to convince military men whose interests, feelings and wants are continually goading them, that people holding civil officers are better intitled to receive the wages of service punctually than they are. I mention these things, my Dear Sir, not so much because I think it in your power to afford redress, as because I think you should be acquainted with the temper that prevails.[66]

KEEPING CONTROL OVER THE TROOPS WHEN THEY DECIDED they had completed their contractual commitment was a difficult problem and remained a major source of friction between officers and enlisted men throughout the war. Once soldiers felt they had completed their duty, they felt no obligation to follow orders and believed they were entitled to go whenever they wanted. There was no incentive to stay for the pay, which was usually minimal, late, and in worthless paper money.

Early on New Year's Day 1780, about one hundred soldiers at West Point belonging to the Massachusetts regiments marched out of the snow-covered camp intending to go home. They had "slung their packs and went off with their arms and accoutrements." Having enlisted before January 1777 for a period of three years, they were of the opinion that their terms of enlistment expired on the first of the year. Major General William Heath wrote in his memoirs that he thought "many of them had months to serve before their three years' service was completed." As soon as General Heath was informed of the exodus, he sent Captain Bailey with one hundred men after the mutineers with the orders to "bring them back dead or alive."[67]

General Heath had been of the opinion that there was a conspiracy among the Massachusetts soldiers. He believed they were to rendezvous at Fishkill and proceed to Danbury, Connecticut. There, they were to be joined by men with like sentiments from French and Indian War veteran Brigadier General Enoch Poor's brigade. The mutineers would then march home together. Heath believed that disciplining a sergeant from Colonel Timothy Bigelow's

15th Massachusetts Regiment of Worcester County men caused some of the soldiers to change their minds. The sergeant in question had expressed negative sentiments a day or two earlier. He certainly received quick justice. He was confined, tried, sentenced to receive one hundred lashes, and reduced to the ranks. The sergeant's lashes were laid on in front of the Bigelow's brigade at evening roll call on New Year's Eve. Whether because of this harsh and public disciplinary measure or for some other reason, not one man from this brigade participated in the mutiny. However, a second group of mutineers, sixty men from Brigadier General John Glover's Brigade, left from the lines on New Year's Day. These men had not attended the New Year's Eve roll call because they were doing guard duty.

A detachment of General Poor's men and the Light Horse were immediately sent after this second group of mutineers. If the mutineers were able to escape and disburse, Heath had formulated a plan to write to the general assembly of the respective states requesting that they be arrested and returned to their units.

The first group of mutineers were unable to cross the Hudson River at West Point either in boats or on the ice. They then proceeded up along the west side of the Hudson River. Heath, not knowing how much distance the mutineers had on Captain Bailey and his corps, was afraid they would get through the snow to Fishkill before Bailey could intercept them. He sent an express rider with a message to the commanding officer of the regiment at Fishkill to be prepared to stop the men who had mutinied. Captain Bailey and his corps caught up with the men at New Windsor. The mutineers, who had been treading through deep snow in what was described as intense cold, did not put up a fight. January 2 brought another snow storm, but despite the four feet of snow on the ground, Captain Bailey brought the mutineers back to West Point on Monday the 3rd. Some of ringleaders were put under a close guard; the other soldiers were pardoned. But there was no word on the men from Brigadier General John Glover's Brigade.

At dusk on Monday, a fire had broken out on the outside of the southwest corner of the north redoubt on Constitution Island across from West Point. The fire was two feet below the parapet within the face, or outside, timbers. The fire was making its way toward the magazine that was in a bomb-proof end of the structure. The magazine contained ten barrels of gunpowder, boxes of ammunition, and one hundred barrels of salted provisions.

Heath singled out the efforts of Colonel David Lyman, his aide de camp, Lieutenant Colonel Ebenezer Sprout of the 12th Massachusetts, Captain Seth Drew of the 2nd Massachusetts, and an unnamed sergeant of the garrison of the redoubt for their conspicuous efforts in removing all the gunpowder and ammunition from the magazine. Through their efforts, along with Captain Walker's Company of Artillery and a sergeant's guard of infantry which had been posted in each redoubt, the fire was extinguished. Heath suspected, but could not prove, that the fire was intentional.[68]

General Enoch Poor. From a miniature drawn by General Thaddeus Kosciuszko. (*William L. Clements Library*)

The cold continued and reports of people freezing to death were heard in New York City on the 5th. It was not until Sunday the 9th that the wind changed directions and the bitter cold started to ease.[69]

On January 11 Heath received the news for which he was waiting. The mutineers from Brigadier General John Glover's Brigade had finally been "overtaken and secured" and were on their way back to camp. Eventually some of the mutineers were punished for their behavior. The men who had indeed fulfilled their commitments were honorably discharged.[70]

MUTINIES OF COMMAND AND CONTROL were not confined to the Northeast. Six weeks after the Battle of Bunker (Breed's) Hill, the South Carolina Committee of Safety sent William Henry Drayton, a weathy South Carolinian, and Reverend William Tennent, pastor of the Independent Church of Charles Town and a graduate of the College of New Jersey (Princeton) with a master's degree from Harvard, on a mission to the interior parts of the colony to explain to the people at large the nature of the unhappy public disputes between Great Britain and the American colonies. Their mission was to try to settle all political disputes between the people; to quiet their minds; and to persuade them to accept a general union in order to preserve themselves and their children from tyranny.

On August 2, 1775, Drayton and Tennent left the city of Charles Town (Charleston) by chaise at 6:00 a.m. They traveled to Middleton's Plantation at Goose Creek, about ten miles from Middleton Place on the Ashley River, and then continued on to Thomas Broughton's where they spent the night. Broughton's place, Mulberry Plantation, which was between Goose Creek and Monck's Corner, had been built in about 1714.

They were back on the road at six the next morning and dined at Martin's Tavern before spending the night at Captain William Fludd's, having covered thirty miles that day. Captain Fludd lived on the Santee River between Nelson's and Sumpter's New Ferry. They spent a terrible night there "owing to the noise of a maniac." Taverns, or ordinaries, tended to be noisy places with all the commotion of people trying to hear the latest gossip and news from those passing through the area. But private homes did not always offer greater quiet. As it was thought to be ungentlemanly to turn away travelers—whether friends, relatives, or merely casual acquaintances—a country house could be as noisy as a tavern.

The next morning, August 4, Drayton and Tennent set out at sunrise in a light drizzle making several stops on the way. They arrived at the home of Colonel William "Danger" Thomson.[71] Colonel Thomson was the commander of the South Carolina Rangers, later the South Carolina 3rd Regiment. His plantation, Belleville, was near the confluence of the Congaree and Wateree Rivers. Though the colonel was away, the family put them up for the night.

They got under way the next morning a little after daybreak. They left their chaise and continued with a good pair of horses lent to them by Mrs. Thomson. Reverend Tennent complained about the sixteen miles of bad steep and hilly roads, made all the more treacherous by the rain shower of the previous day. He claimed it was "the worst road I almost ever saw." Continuing on their mission, Drayton and Tennent rode to the house of a Mr. Patrick, who was a man of property among the "Dutch."[72] Mr. Patrick accompanied them for the next seven miles to a Colonel John Chestnut.

Colonel Chestnut was a partner of Colonel Joseph Kershaw of Camden, South Carolina, in the Chestnut and Kershaw Company, owner of the Granby trading house, later Fort Granby. At Colonel Chestnut's they also found a Lieutenant Dr. Charlton of Philadelphia, several militia officers, and two loyalist lawyers from North Carolina, Messrs. Benjamin Booth and John Dunn, who had been sent there as prisoners for stirring up the people of North Carolina. The two lawyers would be sent to the General Committee of the

South Carolina Provincial Congress at Charles Town where their future would be decided.

The assembled group discussed the situation in the area. The German "Dutch" were thought to be in fear of losing their lands if they opposed the king. Rumors were always flying about the countryside as to what the low country people were doing and how it was going to affect those in the backcountry. The current rumor was that the South Carolina Rangers were in the backcountry to destroy their property. Therefore, they were not turning out.

Drayton instructed Colonel Thomson to muster two Dutch companies in the neighborhood the following Wednesday. There had been problems in the past with Dutch captains disobeying orders to muster their men. The Dutch captains used the excuse that the extra musters could only be ordered by the governor.

In order to get to talk to these inhabitants, two Dutch clergymen were engaged to hold services and Drayton planned to be present. "We know in general," Drayton believed, "that an argument relating to money matters most readily catches a Dutchman's ear; we have declared that no non-subscriber [to the association in support of the revolution] in this settlement will be allowed to purchase at, or sell to this store or Charles Town."[73] Drayton also heard reports that he would not be allowed to speak in Colonel Thomas Fletchall's area on Fairforest Creek.[74] On this situation Drayton said, "We expect much trouble."

Drayton next visited the South Carolina Rangers, who were complaining about lack of provisions. Drayton discussed the situation with the men, assuring them that the public would do whatever it could to support them. Drayton told the hungry men about the noble cause in which they were involved. But words, no matter how eloquent, do not fill an empty stomach. The rangers were expected to go out and get their own food. Drayton told the men that the government could begin supplying the food but the expense would be deducted from their pay in the same manner as was done with the foot soldiers.

The men's grumbling turned to the subject of tents, or rather the lack of tents. Drayton's response was to tell them that "the British in American during the last war [the French and Indian War], not only generally used but preferred huts made of bushes." The men were not impressed. Drayton encouraged the men to pay the greatest obedience to their officers "as the only means by which they could become good soldiers."[75] The rangers were a group not known for their good behavior. Nonetheless, when Drayton and Tennent left the Congaree Creek encampment the situation was quiet.

Around midnight, an officer came from the camp, which was two miles from where Drayton and Tennent were staying. He informed them that a general mutiny had occurred in camp. "There was no longer any command or obedience; that the men were in an uproar at the idea of a deduction of their pay, for they had in general been promised provisions above their pay, and they were determined to quit the camp this morning and disband."[76]

That night, Colonel Thomson and Captain Kershaw stayed with Drayton and Tennent.[77] They agreed to wait until morning before taking any action. They were betting that the three captains and other officers in camp would get to the bottom of what was troubling the men and resolve the problem. On the morning of the 7th, they ordered the officers from the camp to come to them. Their bet paid off. During the course of the night the captains had successfully quelled the mutiny.

William Drayton and Reverend Tennent discussed the situation with the officers from the camp. They discovered three or four privates had instigated the mutiny. The men in question had volatile personalities. Unwise comments from some officers had destabilized an explosive situation. Captain Thomas Woodward of the South Carolina Rangers had apparently promised his men provisions above pay. First Lieutenant of the South Carolina Rangers Lewis Dutarque had made comments about "the cruelty of keeping encamped without tents."[78] Drayton believed that "from such sources, however, it was plain the discord of last night arose."[79]

The rangers were marched out of camp two miles to Congaree Store. Drayton, in front of the regiment, harangued them upon the discord of the previous night, attributing it to a few disorderly persons, who in the first instance, would by the colonel be passed over unnoticed in hopes such leniency would work a reformation in them. Drayton told them about the consequences if they did not straighten up and submit to authority. He warned them that if they deserted there would be a bounty placed on their heads and they would be hunted down and brought to Charles Town "dead or alive."[80]

AT WILLIAMSBURG, THE CAPITAL OF VIRGINIA, TROOPS were also being assembled for the war. One of these units that arrived in December 1775 was a company of mountain riflemen commanded by Captain George Gibson of

West Augusta, the name given to the disputed area with Pennsylvania that included Fort Pitt.[81] A reckless, insubordinate, and violent group opposed to any military authority, they were mockingly called "Gibson's Lambs." They were in camp just a short time before they staged a mutiny. The out-of-control mutineers alarmed the inhabitants of the city. They roamed aimlessly through the camp and threatened with death any officer who should presume to exercise authority over them.

An officer was sent to the quarters of Scottish-born Pennsylvania resident Colonel Hugh Mercer who immediately went to the barracks of the mutineers. Dr. Mercer, who was in his very late forties, ordered a general assembly of all the troops at Williamsburg. He then ordered them to disarm Captain George Gibson's company. The ringleaders were placed under a strong guard. Colonel Mercer, in the presence of the whole army, addressed the mutineers. He impressed on them their duties as citizen soldiers and the certainty of death if they continued to disobey their officers. "Gibson's Lambs" were silenced. The ringleaders were held in confinement then, after a sufficient time, were released back to their company.[82]

Major General Charles Lee also had difficulty with the soldiers assembling for duty. Reinforcements from Virginia were to meet him at Halifax, North Carolina, a short distance over the line from Virginia. At the end of May 1776, Lee was troubled by "the disorderly, mutinous and dangerous disposition of the 8th Regiment" of Virginia. In his correspondence of May 24 about the 8th Virginia, Lee said, "We have at length after infinite trouble got this banditti out of the town."[83]

The unit, composed primarily of German settlers from the Shenandoah Valley, was led by Colonel Peter Muhlenberg who had assumed command on March 1. Muhlenberg was born in Philadelphia. He graduated in 1763 from the College of Philadelphia, which would be seized by the state of Pennsylvania in 1779 because it was seen as a Tory bastion. It was the University of Pennsylvania, a state school, until 1791, when it went back to being a private institution.[84] Muhlenberg became a Lutheran clergyman in 1769. After moving to Woodstock in the Shenandoah Valley of Virginia where the majority of the residents were Anglican, he changed religions and was ordained an Anglican clergyman in London. He served as the chair of the Committee of Safety in Virginia's House of Burgesses in 1775 and as a member of Virginia's Provincial Convention in 1776.

Lee's letter telling all about the 8th Virginia's behavior was introduced into the Virginia convention by Edmund Pendleton. They promised to do something about the men's conduct.[85] General Lee, who had served with the British 44th and 103rd Regiments in the French and Indian War rising to the rank of lieutenant colonel, gave his unvarnished opinion of the situation with the back country troops.

> The spirit of desertion in these back country troops is so alarmingly great that I must submit it to the wisdom of the convention whether it is not of the utmost importance to devise some means to put a stop to it before it spreads, by enjoining the committees of the different counties to seize every soldier who can not produce an authentic discharge or pass and throw him into the county jail until he can be conveyed to the regiment to which he belongs or by some other means. But the convention are much better judges than I can possibly be of the proper method to be pursued. I can only affirm that unless some effectual method is devised and adopted it will be impossible for us to keep the field.

> The old countrymen [foreign born], particularly the Irish whom the officers have injudiciously enlisted in order to fill up their companies, have much contaminated the troops; and if more care is not taken on this head for the future the whole army will be one mass of disorder, vice, and confusion.[86]

Lee goes on to say, "I have so great reason to complain of the misconduct of this regiment [but] I must do the officers, particularly the field offices the justice to say that their conduct is in general very satisfactory." Lee closed the letter imploring that the convention "take this affair into their consideration and devise some means of stifling the evil before it gets too great a head."[87]

A large number of men from the back country who were Scotch Irish enlisted in the North Carolina Continentals, collected their bonus, and then went home. General Lee was still complaining about the behavior of the Irish soldiers. "Severity is necessary for an Irish soldiery. I am well acquainted with their dispositions, and know that the lenient measures and familiar manners adapted to the genius of your people only tend to inspire the Irish with the spirit of stubbornness and mutiny."[88]

Just as General Charles Lee had predicted, the situation did get out of control. At Wilmington, North Carolina, General John Ashe, in charge of the North Carolina Militia, and Brigadier General James Moore, head of the

North Carolina Continentals, had to contend with friction between their two groups. The militia men believed the continentals were not sharing in garbage details, and also thought that provisions and supplies were being preferentially given to the continentals. In short, they thought they were being treated unfairly. Ashe, raised at Rocky Point, a few miles northwest of Wilmington, was an experienced officer, having served as the senior captain and aide to a colonel of the North Carolina Militia in the French and Indian War. General Ashe, who had been the speaker of the Colonial Assembly from 1762 to 1765 and one of the leaders in opposition to the Stamp Act in North Carolina, wielded considerable influence.

On June 6, 1776, the day after the North Carolina Council of Safety, the new executive power of the province, first convened at Wilmington, General Ashe informed them of a mutiny among the militia from Bladen County. "There were a number of outlying malcontents in the county of Bladen, who were desirous of returning home and submitting to the Council." The council "agreed that all such persons concerned in the late insurrection, that should take an oath before the Chairman of the County or Town Committee, to submit to such order and regulation as might be made by the government of the Colony, and that when required, they would take up arms in defense thereof, might return to the peaceable enjoyment of their inhabitations."[89] Their solution to not being able to control the militia members and keep them in the field was to let them go home on the promise of future performance.

In July, it was the turn of the North Carolina Continentals who demanded pay and provisions. The event has been called the "unhappy mutiny." General Ashe took immediate action and used his militia to put down the insurrection of the continentals.

The Council of Safety sent their appreciation to General Ashe: "[we] applaud your conduct and that of the militia under your command for their readiness in assisting to quell the late mutiny among the regulars at Wilmington." The council members, as true politicians, wanted to believe "the unhappy tumult and confusion proceeded from an anxious desire among the soldiers of distressing the enemy and preventing their being supplied with any kind of provisions and not from any dislike or aversion to the service of their country."[90]

Diffusing mutinies through compromise ended up being a rather common occurrence. Joseph Graham enlisted in the 6th Regiment of the North Carolina Line under Colonel Archibald Lytle in Captain Christopher

Gooden's Company.[91] His contract called for him to serve nine months after they arrived at the place of rendezvous, which was to be Bladensburg in Maryland. His group assembled at Charlotte in Mecklenburg County near the South Carolina border where he lived. The officers who accompanied them on their march were Colonel William Lee Davidson of the 3rd, Major William Polk of the 9th, Henry Dickson (commonly called Hal Dickson), and Captain Smith Harris.

They marched out and had gotten as far as Moon Creek in Caswell County, North Carolina just south of Danville Virginia. Here, they received word that the British had evacuated Philadelphia and gone to New York. They were also told about the Battle of Monmouth that had occurred on June 28, 1778, and were informed that their services were no longer needed in the north. The men were concerned about what was going to happen to them. According to their enlistment, their time in service had not commenced as they had not gotten to Bladensburg, Maryland. They were uncertain when they would actually be in the army.

Amid this confusion, concern turned into words, then into a heated exchange, and finally into a riot. In the ensuing melee, officers broke swords and soldiers were injured. In an effort to restore order, a proposal was made that the soldiers take a furlough until the fall when their terms of service would commence. This would put their service after harvest time. Most of the men from the upland counties took the furlough agreement, Joseph Graham included.[92]

THE ULTIMATE AUTHORITY OVER THE COMMAND OF TROOPS between individual states and a central government touched upon one of the fundamental problems of American democracy before the Civil War and resulted in a number of mutinies, including one in South Carolina. In April 1779, General Benjamin Lincoln's forces were encamped at Purrysburg, South Carolina.[93] Purrysburg, Beaufort County, was founded in 1732 by settlers from Switzerland. It was about fifteen miles from the capital of Georgia on the banks of the Savannah River.

Lincoln was going to attack the British in Georgia with 4,000 soldiers, leaving General William Moutrie with 1,000 soldiers at Purrysburg to defend the post at Black Swamp. When the militiamen heard that Lincoln had planned to take them across the river into Georgia, they mutinied and refused to leave South Carolina. During the night, 400 militiamen fled and made a clean getaway. At the same time in Colonel Joseph Kershaw's South Carolina Militia a man deserted his post and behaved in an insolent manner to his captain. When the soldier was arrested, he grabbed a gun and threatened the life of the officer. Only the quick actions of the guard in overpowering him prevented him from carrying out his threat. Kershaw applied to General Lincoln for a court martial to rule on the soldier's escapade. Lincoln appointed Brigadier General Richard Richardson of the South Carolina Militia as president and other militia officers as members of the court martial.

When it came time for the militia officers to take the prescribed oath as stipulated by the Continental Congress, seven militia officers refused. They stated that militiamen were only responsible to state law. The situation was reported to General Lincoln who was surprised. Lincoln stated that the militiamen were being paid in continental pay, were subject to continental discipline, and if they were not under his command then they could leave whenever they chose "as he would furnish them with no more provision." A correspondence ensued in 1779 between Brigadier General William Moultrie and Colonel Pinckney over the issue and getting some changes in the state law.[94]

The relationship between the militia and the Continentals as well as between the states and the Continental Congress turned on the issue of states' rights versus a centralized government. Men considered themselves first Virginians, New Yorkers, or Pennsylvanians before they thought of themselves as Americans. This war was being waged to get rid of an autocrat, King George, and colonists were reluctant to replace King George with another ruler. The issue of states' rights versus the central government would ultimately lead to the Civil War.

2

Hungry, Naked, and Broke

MUTINIES OF DESTITUTION

*H*aving finished a frigid winter tour of guard duty at Morristown, New Jersey, in January 1780, a half-frozen Continental Army soldier returns to his hut at suppertime. Today his timing is good so he is hoping for a hot meal that consists of a watery soup made from melted snow, some dried beans, and the scraps of meat or fat from a bone. It's the same bone that has made a daily soak in the kettle for the last ten days. He and his messmates have not seen meat of any kind during that time. The camp cupboard is almost empty.

Because teamsters could not traverse the snow-covered roads, few provisions were available. When supplies did arrive they were not enough to fill the larder. The last meat that was distributed to the soldiers was from a horse that died of starvation. Most of the army's horses had been sent to where forage was available, and only a few were kept in camp for riding express and other duties. Some of the regiments had even taken to eating the forage set aside for these remaining horses.

Tonight's soup was supplemented just like yesterday and the day before with a firecake, a mixture of flour, water, and, if any was to be had, salt. Formed into a cake and baked on a rock or a griddle over the fire until blackened, the very hard and not very tasty biscuit would have acquired ashes from the fire into its composition as it baked.

Since the soldier had not been paid, he had no money to buy any food had it been available. When he did get money, it was in the heavily depreciated paper Continental dollars, which were almost worthless as soon as they were printed. He was unable to send money or goods home to his impoverished family. When starvation was added to the cold, the inactivity, and the lack of money it was often the breaking point that produced mutinies during the Revolutionary War.

As early as October 1776, in the wake of the loss of supplies of food and transports in the emergency evacuations of Long Island and New York City, Washington voiced his fears to Colonel Joseph Trumbull, commissary general of the Continental Army that the army would mutiny if not supplied with food.[1] Washington's dire forecast of mutiny due to the lack of money and supplies began occurring throughout the Continental Army during the following year, including his own. On December 19, 1777, months after the British had successfully occupied Philadelphia, the Continental Army marched from White Marsh, Pennsylvania, into their winter encampment at Valley Forge. There was not enough food in camp and the men would call this winter "the starving time." Washington wrote to Congress that mutiny had started on the evening of the 21st. The mutiny "with difficulty was suppressed by the spirited exertions of some officers."[2] Washington went on to relate how he was still very apprehensive about the situation as long as provisions were lacking.

On the afternoon of the 22nd, Washington received information that the enemy had left the city of Philadelphia in force and were advancing southwest towards Derby, Pennsylvania, apparently in hopes of foraging from that area. Washington said he "ordered the troops to be in readiness, that I might give every opposition in my power; when, behold! to my great mortification, I was not only informed, but convinced, that the men were unable to stir on account of provision, and that a dangerous mutiny had begun the night before."[3]

Brigadier General James Varnum of Rhode Island quoted Solomon to Washington, "Hunger will break through a stone wall." For three days his command had no bread and for two days they were entirely without any meat. When they had been offered beef, it was of such a vile quality that it could not be considered food. "The men must be supplied or they can not be commanded; the complaints are too ongoing to pass unnoticed. It is with pain that I mention this distress. I know it will make your Excellency unhappy. But, if you expect the exertions of virtuous principals while your troops are deprived of the essential necessities of life, your final disappointment will be great."[4]

The next day, on the 23rd, Washington wrote to the Continental Congress about the Commissary Department: "I am now convinced, beyond a doubt that unless some great and capital change suddenly takes place in that line, this Army must inevitably be reduced to one or other of these three things. Starve, dissolve, or disperse, in order to obtain subsistence in the best manner they can." He went on to say, "the men were unable to stir on account of provision, and that a dangerous mutiny begun the night before, and [which] with difficulty was suppressed by the spirited exertion's of some officers was still much to be apprehended on acct. of their want of this Article."[5]

Washington was forced to allow the men to go and try to collect provisions. The situation was so severe that "three or four days of bad weather would prove our destruction." Throughout the dark winter days of 1778 while the Continental Army was bivouacked at Valley Forge, the commanders feared a mutiny. At the end of January, Nathanael Greene observed that "our troops are naked; we have been upon the eve of starving and the army of mutinying. Our horses are dying by dozens every day for the want of forage, and the men getting sickly in their huts for the want of acids and soap to clean themselves."[6]

The conditions in camp did not improve and continued to be a burden on Washington as he was forced to deal with trifling matters. In February, the soldiers ran out of straw for bedding. Washington had to issue a general order on February 15 to deal with the problem. "The Commander in Chief anxious to have them furnished with every necessary to make them comfortable, desires the brigadiers and officers commanding brigades each to send out a party properly officered to procure straw and impress wagons to haul it to camp where they will deliver it to their respective Brigade Quarter-Masters who are to make an equal distribution thereof to the several regiments according to their numbers present."[7]

Their dire predictions unfortunately came to pass. Continental Congressman Francis Dana of Massachusetts, visiting Valley Forge in the middle of February 1778, described the mutiny.

> A great proportion of the soldiers are in a very suffering condition for want of necessary clothing, and totally unfit for duty; but even this evil would have been patiently endured had not another, irresistible in its nature, taken place, the want of provisions. . . . I yesterday mounted my horse and rode into camp and passed through several brigades, some of which were said to have been destitute of flour several days, enquiring separately of all the officers I knew, of different ranks, and am satisfied that by comparing their accounts I learnt the real state of these brigades: indeed the accounts were

not very different. For flour they had not suffered; but upon an average every regiment had been destitute of fish or flesh four days. On Saturday evening they received, some three-fourths and others one half pound of salted pork a man—not one day's allowance: nor have they assurance of regular supplies in future. We do not see from whence the supplies of meat are to come. The want of it will infallibly bring on a mutiny in the army.

Sunday morning, February 15, 1778, Colonel Brewer's regiment [the 12th Massachusetts] rose in a body and proceeded to General [John] Patterson's quarters. . . . They laid before him their complaints and threatened to quit the army. By a prudent conduct, he quieted them, but was under a necessity of permitting the men to go out of camp to purchase meat as far as their money would answer, to give them certificates for the other, and he would pay for it.[8]

The same spirit was rising in other regiments, but had been suppressed for the present by the prudence of some of their officers. But no prudence or management, without meat, could satisfy the hungry man. In plain terms, "'tis probable this army will disperse if the commissary department is so damnably managed."[9]

The same day as Dana was making his report and most likely in response to the mutiny of Colonel Brewer's troops, General Washington wrote, "The distress of this army for want of provisions is perhaps beyond anything you can conceive; and unless we strain every nerve to procure immediate relief, a general mutiny and dispersion is to be dreaded."

Because the Quartermaster and Commissary Departments were unable to supply the army, Washington took matters into his own hands. He requested Brigadier General William Smallwood of Maryland to assist Captain Lee in getting provisions from Dover, Delaware, and the Head of Elk (Elkton), Maryland, to Valley Forge for the relief of the soldiers there. "Every aid you can possibly afford him is demanded by the exigency of the occasion." Every morsel was needed and General Smallwood was told not to take any of the foodstuffs to support his troops as "no part of which can, without detriment, be spared from the use of this Camp."[10]

Governor George Clinton of New York was told of the dire situation at Valley Forge.

For some days past, there has been little less than a famine in camp. A part of the army has been a week without any kind of flesh, and the rest three or four days. Naked and starving as they are, we cannot enough admire the incomparable patience and fidelity of the soldiery, that they have not been ere this excited by their sufferings, to a general mutiny and dispersion. Strong symptoms, however, of discontent have appeared in particular instances; and nothing but the most active efforts every where can long avert so shocking a catastrophe.[11]

All the magazines or supply depots, of Delaware, Maryland, New Jersey, and Pennsylvania, combined, only held enough provisions to supply the army for a month. "When the fore mentioned supplies are exhausted, what a terrible crisis must ensue, unless all the energy of the continent is exerted to provide a timely remedy."[12]

A month later, Washington, overlooking the conduct of the 12th Massachusetts men, expressed how lucky he was that there was not a mutiny at Valley Forge.

> By death and desertion, we have lost a good many men since we came to this ground, and have encountered every species of hardship, that cold, wet, and hunger, and want of clothes were capable of producing; notwithstanding. And contrary to my expectations we have been able to keep the soldiers from mutiny or dispersion, although, in the single article of provisions, they have encountered enough to have occasioned one or the other of these in most other armies; as they have been (two or three times), days together, without provisions and once six days without any of the meat kind; could the poor horses tell their tale, it would be in a strain still more lamentable, as numbers have actually died from pure want.[13]

On May 13, 1778, General Anthony Wayne was at Mount Joy, Lancaster County, Pennsylvania when he described the status and condition of his troops to Richard Peters, secretary of war. Discipline had improved quickly but the men were much weaker and worse clothed than at the close of the last campaign at the end of 1777. Looking at the absolutely deplorable conditions of his men, Wayne was filled with rage.

> I hoped to be able to clothe the division under my command but the distresses of the other part of the troops belonging to this state were such as to beggar all description. Humanity obliged me to divide what would have in part clothed six hundred men among thirteen regiments which also being necessary in order to prevent mutiny and to put a stop to that spirit

of desertion, which has taken but too deep a root, and is not yet subsided. Our officers too are hourly offering in their resignations, especially those who have yet some property left. When or where it will end God knows. The pain I feel on the occasion is better felt than expressed. I am heartily tired of this way of life being the only general officer belonging to the state the whole line apply to me on every occasion. Their real wants are too many and too pressing to pass unheeded by, but yet I can't alleviate nor supply them.[14]

Wayne knew Peters had heard this same lament from many others who were also in desperate need of everything. He stressed to Peters that he was well aware that people tended to pay attention to "those subjects that lie nearest their hearts, or that give them most concern." This was his excuse for adding his voice to the multitude already talking to Peters.

I am not fond of danger, but I would most cheerfully agree to enter into action once every week in place of visiting each part of my encampment (which is my constant practice) and where objects strike my eye and ear, whose wretched condition beggars all description. The ball or bayonet could only pierce the body but such objects affect the mind and give the keenest wound to every feeling of humanity. For God's sake give us—if you can't give anything else—give us linen that we may be enabled to rescue the poor worthy fellows from the vermin which are now devouring them and which has emaciated and reduced numbers exactly to answer the description of Shakespeares apothecary.[15] Some hundreds we thought prudent to deposit some six foot under ground who have died of a disorder produced by a want of clothing. The whole army at present are sick of the same disorder, but the Pennsylvania line seem to be the most infected. A pointed and speedy exertion of Congress or appointing another Doctor may yet remove the disorder which once done I pledge my reputation we shall remove the enemy for I would much rather risque [risk] my life honor and the fate of America on our present force neatly and comfortably uniformed than on double their number covered with rags and crawling with vermin—but I am determined not to say an other word on the subject.[16]

WITH THE CONCLUSION OF THE 1778 CAMPAIGN capped by the British evacuation of Philadelphia and the American victory at Monmouth, New Jersey, Washington sent the army into its winter cantonments. Most of the brigades were to be in the Highlands of New York. Three brigades composed of

Connecticut and New Hampshire troops and 2nd Canadian Regiment known as both "Hazen's Regiment" and "Congress's Own Regiment" were to be posted in the vicinity of Danbury, Connecticut. They were to be under the command of sixty-year-old Major General Israel Putnam whom the soldiers nicknamed "Old Put."

Putnam was a wily old veteran of the French and Indian War and gave the famous instructions at the Battle of Bunker Hill (which was really fought at Breed's Hill), "Don't fire until you see the whites of their eyes." The troops were placed at Redding, Connecticut, to cover the magazines along the Connecticut River and be able to move quickly to protect the troops in the Highlands or the Connecticut coastal towns. General Putnam arrived at the camp around December 1 and established his headquarters in a farmhouse on Umpawaug Hill.

The appalling condition of the Connecticut men was a concern for General Samuel H. Parsons, a forty-one-year-old Harvard-educated lawyer. He had discussed the situation with General Washington who had personally assured him a supply of blankets, shirts, and small clothes would be provided. However, none of it ever arrived. Blankets were especially important when the army spent the night sleeping under the stars on the snow. The soldiers would first trample down the snow, then lop the tops off shrub pine and spread them on the ground. They would then spread out the blankets.[17]

Parsons, a nephew of the deputy governor of Connecticut, wrote Washington two days before Christmas reiterating their previous discussion on the subject and Washington's assurances that Parsons would be sent the badly need items. Parsons noted that his troops received nothing and most of the army's stockpile had been distributed. He reported that he had "eight hundred men that are totally destitute and many of them never had a blanket since their enlistment." Washington sent Parsons a copy of his order to Major Bigelow to furnish breeches, coats, and vests to his troops. But there were not enough supplies to meet demand. And what was sent couldn't be delivered because of bad road conditions.[18]

On December 27, General Parsons issued an order to the troops that "he has used every possible method to supply flour or bread to the brigade. Although a sufficiency of every article [of foodstuffs] necessary is at Danbury, the weather has been so extreme that it is impossible for teams to pass to that place . . . the soldiery, under the special circumstances caused by the severity of the season, will make themselves contented to that time." In other words they would have to starve until food could get through.

On fourteen of the previous twenty-two days, it either was bitterly cold, had rained, or had snowed.[19] On the 29th, Parsons ordered "half a pint of rum or brandy be delivered to each officer and soldier tomorrow." There had been a shortage of flour in New England at the time so they had to look to New York for their supplies. Parsons was having trouble maintaining guards at Horseneck because Mr. Leek at Bedford kept seizing the flour that was to supply them. He told General McDougall that if this practice did not desist the guards could not endure.[20]

General Israel Putnam published by C. Shepherd, London, on September 9, 1775. (*William L. Clements Library*)

Private Joseph Plumb Martin, who had arrived at the camp at Christmas, described the situation. They were busy building their winter huts that were ready in about a week. They "had nothing extraordinary, either of eatables or drinkables, to keep a new year or housewarming. Now came on the time again between grass and hay, that is, the winter campaign of starving."[21]

When the troops arrived at camp, the quartermaster of each regiment staked out the camp site marking the specific location of each hut. The huts were to be eight feet apart. The officers' huts were built sixteen feet to the rear of the soldiers' huts. The huts, built out of log dovetailed together, were at least six feet high and fourteen by sixteen feet. An officer from each regiment was to supervise his corps' hut construction. The quartermaster also marked out the associated wood lot and distributed tools for constructing the huts.

When the troops went into their winter quarters at Redding Ridge, they were underfed, poorly clothed, and financially impoverished. Many of the soldiers had left dependent wives, children, and parents behind when they joined the service. When the soldiers were paid it was in near worthless Continental currency. Once the job of building their huts and the construction of the camp was completed, the soldiers had more spare time to mull over their deplorable situation and realize just how cold and hungry they were.

Colonel Return Jonathan Meigs, writing on December 26, had predicted that the men would mutiny or desert. The soldiers had been constantly disappointed since they enlisted. The men no longer believed in the military's promises. Meigs could only remember one promise having been fulfilled by government and that was supplying the men with small amounts of pay. He acquainted Titus Hosmer, member of the Continental Congress and the Connecticut State Senate, of the shortages in clothing, food, and pay.

Meigs described the condition of his men, "Some now have neither shoes or stockings, a great number have no breeches or scarcely a substitute; linen overhauls [overalls] worn almost out are little better than nothing."[22] Some of his men had not had a blanket in eighteen months. The state had promised to reimburse soldiers at stipulated rates for blankets that they procured themselves but he had never been able to get any of the money that was owed to the men. Meigs warned that if the men mutinied, their grievances would be redressed. The men believed that whatever was done for them was in consequence of their mutiny thereby encouraging future mutinies.[23]

Morale was sinking fast. Samuel Richards, an officer of the Connecticut Line who had joined the service on May 4, 1775, described his feelings in his diary. "Winter quarters are generally supposed to give some repose to an army, the present gave us but little. Part of the time on short allowance or destitute; our clothes, worn out, our pay suspended for months beyond stipulated time and when received was in depreciated paper." He also complained, not surprisingly, about the severe weather and that there did not appear to be any "bright prospect before us of a speedy termination of the war."

The twenty-two-year-old also worried about dependents back home in Farmington, Connecticut, who could not fend for themselves: "We [are] spending the prime and vigor of our lives without laying any foundation for old age and those who had families unable to afford them anything for their present subsistence, those things kept our heads on a pillow of thorns rather than roses."[24] He certainly was not alone.

On December 30, the men of thirty-five-year-old General Jedidiah Huntington's Connecticut brigade assembled with their weapons. They were determined to march to Hartford and demand that the Connecticut legislature address their grievances. They had been suffering because of a lack of clothes and blankets and their pay was worthless. They demanded that arrangements with them be made good.

Old Put, apprised of their actions, mounted his horse and addressed the men from his saddle:

> My brave lads, whither are you going? Do you intend to desert your offi-
> cers, and to invite the enemy to follow you into the country? Whose cause
> have you been fighting and suffering so long in—is it not your own? Have
> you no property, no parents, wives, or children? You have behaved like men
> so far—all the world is full of your praises—and posterity will stand aston-
> ished at your deeds, but not if you spoil all at last. Don't you consider how
> much the country is distressed by the war, and that your officers have not
> been any better paid than yourselves? But we all expect better times, and
> that the country will do us ample justice. Let us all stand by one another,
> then, and fight it out like brave soldiers. Think what a shame it would be
> for Connecticut men to run away from their officers.[25]

When Putnam had finished his oration, he directed the acting major of the brigade to issue an order for the soldiers to shoulder arms, march to their reg-imental parades, and lodge arms. This was accomplished with promptness and good disposition. The chief instigators of the mutiny were placed under guard. During the night, the ringleader attempted to make his escape. The sentinel, who had also been involved in the mutiny, shot him dead on the spot.[26]

General Putnam considered mutiny an exceedingly delicate matter. On January 5, 1779, he notified General George Washington that nothing new concerning the disturbance in General Huntington's Brigade had occurred. He forwarded a petition with which he concurred for a pardon from the chief instigators of the mutiny who were being held under guard. Putnam indicat-ed that he would "do nothing rashly in the affair or take any alternative solu-tion until I have heard from you."[27]

On the 18th, Washington complimented Putnam for his efforts in quelling the mutiny and expressed his hope that the situation had been resolved. He gave his answer to Putnam's request for leniency by telling him what should be done in a mutinous situation.

> The conduct which a commanding officer is to observe, in cases of this
> kind in general, is to use every means for discovering the authors of the
> mischief, to inflict instant punishment on them, and reclaim the rest by
> clemency. The impression made on the minds of the multitude by the ter-
> ror of the example, and their inability to take any resolution when deprived
> of their ringleaders, are a sufficient security against farther attempts.

Humanity and policy unite in prescribing such limits to capital punishments, when the crime has been so general. With respect to the application in the present instance, and the doubt which arises from the foundation of complaints which the men have, it is to be observed that their mode of pursuing redress, is of so dangerous a tendency as to call for the exercise of wholesome severity; and tho' the circumstances may require it, to be tempered with more lenity than in ordinary cases, such a subversion of discipline and subordination cannot be passed unpunished. You will be best able to judge, from the degree of culpability of those in confinement, what measures ought to be taken respecting them, if there are any proper subjects for execution among them, it is to be regretted that the matter has suffered any delay. If the same causes should unluckily give birth to any future mutiny, the conduct abovementioned must be pursued; the severest and most summary example must be made of the leaders, while a representation is made to the rest, in firm and at the same time conciliatory language. That no measure compatible with our present circumstances is omitted for providing them, that mutiny will not only be ineffectual in procuring a remedy, but involve consequences infinitely worse than the evil complained of.[28]

On January 8, Washington, who was in Philadelphia at the time, wrote to Brigadier General Jedidiah Huntington, the son-in-law of Jonathan Trumbull, the governor of Connecticut. If the Board of War "does not see a probability of supplying you in any other manner, they will direct Major Bigelow to procure hats for the two Connecticut Brigades, which will put things into the proper train and take off any imputation of partiality."[29]

On the same day, Washington told Putnam that blankets, which were part of the grievance, had been ordered and a quick supply was expected. He reminded Putnam that the entire army had only half the number of blankets that were needed. General Samuel Holden Parsons's report of clothing for the troops at Redding was lost in the mails.

Washington wanted to know if the Connecticut troops were in a worse predicament than the rest of the army. If so, he wanted a report from Putnam so that he could get them to the same level. He reassured Putnam that it was his intention to treat the troops from all the states including Connecticut equally as to the distribution of clothing.[30]

While Washington was busy trying to put out the fire by supplying the needed blankets and clothes, the conditions for a mutiny among the Connecticut troops remained ripe.

Parsons was still having problems getting flour from New York to supply the troops. On January 2, he sent a letter to Governor Clinton of New York that "the Bedford Junto still refuses to suffer flour to come to this post. Are we to be sacrificed or is there a fixed design to sacrifice the officers commanding in this division?" Parsons complained that the troops were going to have to be moved if the constant supply interruptions continued. Three days later, he told General McDougall about having to withdraw the guards because provisions were not allowed to reach them.[31]

Joseph Plumb Martin wrote, "We settled in our winter quarters at the commencement of the New Year and went on in our old Continental Line of starving and freezing. We now and then got a little bad bread and salt beef (I believe chiefly horse-beef for it was generally thought to be such at the time). The month of January was very stormy, a good deal of snow fell, and in such weather it was mere chance if we got anything at all to eat."[32]

IN MAY 1780, FOLLOWING AN EVEN HARSHER WINTER, British spies had circulated the following document in the American camp at Morristown.

> Address to the soldiers of the Continental Army, 1780. The time is at length arrived, when all the artifices, and falsehoods of the Congress and of your commanders can no longer conceal from you, the misery of your situation; you are neither clothed, fed, nor paid; your numbers are wasting away by sickness, famine, nakedness, and rapidly so by the period of your stipulated services, being in general expired, this is then the moment to fly from slavery and fraud. I am happy in acquainting the old countrymen, that the affairs of Ireland are fully settled, and that Great Britain and Ireland are firmly united, as well from interest as from affection: I need not now tell you who are born in America, that you have been cheated and abused; and you are both sensible, that in order to procure your liberty you must quit your leaders, and join your real friends who scorn to impose upon you, and who will receive you with open arms; kindly forgiving all your errors. You are told that you are surrounded by numerous militia, this is also false associate then together, make use of your firelocks and join the British Army, where you will be permitted to dispose of yourselves as you please.[33]

Stories of the rations being distributed at other camps were the scuttlebutt of the day. A visitor from Bound Brook said, "We have nothing but Indian meal and that sour with salted beef in bad order [as] the teamsters having drawn out the brine to lighten their loads."[34]

It had been ten long days since the soldiers at Morristown had seen anything that looked like meat of any kind. Another season of starving had begun. Their rations had been cut. On May 25, they were suspended for the entire army at Morristown. There was going to be no food distributed that day.[35] That same morning, an unsigned letter was discovered in the rear of the Connecticut Brigade's encampment. It contained complaints of the lack of food and threatened that the troops would pillage the countryside to meet their needs.

Because a threatening letter had been found at the rear of the Connecticut huts, Washington decided on a show of force, which was to be carried out the next day, the 26th. Over the course of the past several months at Morristown, several courts martial had been held. Eleven soldiers had been convicted of desertion and sentenced to death, which sentences had been confirmed by Washington. The following is a list of the convictions:

A division Court Martial was held by order of Major General Lord Stirling with Colonel Matthias Ogden, of the 1st New Jersey Regiment, presiding at the encampment of the Jersey Brigade on February 24. Cornelius Nix, private in the 1st New Jersey Regiment was charged with "Deserting to the enemy twice, endeavoring to get there a third time and piloting a British prisoner of war into their lines." He was tried and found guilty of all the charges (except deserting twice) and sentenced to suffer death. The same court also heard the case of Emanuel Evans, a private in the 3rd New Jersey Regiment, who was charged with "Deserting to the enemy and taken in arms against the States." He was found guilty of the charges.[36]

Major General Lord Stirling ordered a Court Martial to be convened on March 30. Major Evan Edwards, of the 11th Pennsylvania Regiment was president. Coming before them that day was Thomas Brown a private in the 2nd New Jersey Regiment a repeat offender who was charged with "Desertion" and he pleaded guilty.[37]

Joseph Infelt and John Earhart, privates in the 10th Pennsylvania Regiment, were tried and found guilty of attempting to desert to the Enemy at a Division general court martial where of Lieutenant Colonel John Murray, of the 2nd Pennsylvania Regiment was the President.[38]

James Coleman of the 11th Pennsylvania Regiment was tried on April 29 at a Court Martial whereof Colonel Israel Shreve of the 2nd New Jersey Regiment was president for "Repeated Desertion Forgery and disposing of his Arms and Accoutrements." He pled guilty and was sentenced to suffer death.[39]

A Division General Court Martial with Lieutenant Colonel Commandant Frederick Weisenfels of the 4th New York Regiment as president was held on May 10, 1780. It heard the cases of Matthew Bell, a private in the 2nd and James Hanly of the 4th New York Regiments. They were tried for attempting to desert to the enemy with their arms and accoutrements. It also heard the case of Lancaster Lighthall of the 3rd New York Regiment who was tried for attempting to desert to the enemy but with another soldiers arms and accoutrements. Bell and Hanly were found guilty as charged. In Lighthall's case he was found guilty except for taking the arms and accoutrements of another soldier. The court ordered that all three of them to be shot to death.[40]

Corporal Thomas Clark of the 4th and Thomas Calvin of the 11th Pennsylvania Regiments were tried on May 13 with Major Reid presiding and found guilty of attempting to desert to the Enemy with their arms.[41]

Washington issued a general order on May 25 that instructed the camp color men from the Connecticut, New York, and Pennsylvania Brigades, under the direction of a sergeant, to dig graves that day for the eleven soldiers who were to be executed the following day. But the mutineers did not wait for Washington's big production.

The evening roll call had gone off without any excessive disorder. Colonel Return J. Meigs of the 6th Connecticut Regiment told his officers of the unsigned letter and instructed them to be watchful for any mutinous conduct. The officers and soldiers then returned to their huts. A half hour later the silence was broken by the beating of drums as elements of Colonels Meigs's 6th and Wyllys's 3rd Connecticut regiments marched under the direction of their sergeants with their weapons toward the right wing of the camp.[42] The mutineers expected other soldiers to join them.

Upon hearing the drums, all the offices came forth and asked what was happening. One of the ring-leading sergeants responded, "Their sufferings had become so great they could endure them no longer and were determined to quit the service and return home." He added that "from the commencement of the year they had received neither pay nor clothing, and now provisions faded."

Colonel Meigs, who was a favorite of the men, drew his sword and confronted the sergeant who had spoken for the group. Meigs had a history of courageous actions. He had accompanied Benedict Arnold on the expedition through the Maine wilderness to Canada. He led a raid on Sag Harbor, Long Island, during which he took ninety prisoners, destroyed twelve vessels, and did not lose a man. Congress was so appreciative of his accomplishments they voted him a sword.[43] He also served under General Wayne in the storming of Stony Point. Meigs commanded the sergeant to get back in the ranks and return with the rest of the men to their quarters. The sergeant, ignoring the command, leveled his gun with a fixed bayonet at Colonel Meigs. He told Meigs that they were determined and would not retreat from their plan to leave the army. During the scuffle Meigs was struck by one of the mutineers.

Only a long expostulation by the officers and the arrival of Colonels Walter Stewart of the 2nd and Thomas Craig of the 3rd Pennsylvania Regiments (who had been summoned by Colonel Meigs) kept additional soldiers on the right from joining the insurrectionists. The officers assured the men that if they would quietly return to their duty and their pressing wants were not supplied by a given day, they, the officers, would not attempt to stop them from leaving.[44]

The officers, backed by the Pennsylvania Line, then prevailed on the Connecticut troops to return to their huts. The men went to their tents but with a sullenness and gloom in their countenances, which clearly expressed that the mutinous temper was by no means subdued.[45] Several of the soldiers still attempted to leave and were arrested.

On Friday the 26th, Washington believed his show of force would help to discourage other disgruntled troops from revolting. At eleven o'clock in the morning, fifty men from each brigade with their officers turned out for what was expected to be a mass execution near the grand parade. They were formed in a square around the eleven condemned men. Three were from New Jersey; three more, from New York; and five, from Pennsylvania. Three were to be shot while eight were to be hanged.

According to Dr. James Thatcher of a Massachusetts Regiment who was an eyewitness, the men were brought to the place of execution in carts. The eight men to be hung stood on tall ladders "with halters round their necks, their coffins before their eyes, their graves open to their view, and thousands of spectators bemoaning their awful doom."

The ceremonies began as usual with Reverend William Rogers who was pastor of the First Baptist Church of Philadelphia and the Brigade Chaplain of the Pennsylvania troops. He chastised the men for their misdeeds and urged them to repent. Their eyes were then blindfolded. "At this awful moment while their fervent prayers are ascending to heaven, an officer comes forward and reads a reprieve for seven of them by the Commander-in-Chief. They hear their names read off one by one and for the three men waiting to be shot. The chaplain reminded them of the gratitude they owed the Commander-in-Chief, for his clemency towards them, and the only return in their power to make, was a life devoted to the faithful discharge of their duty."

The eighth man on the scaffold sentenced to be hanged was James Coleman of the 11th Pennsylvania Regiment. He had to go through the agonizing pain of hearing all the other names read but his. He was a man of unusual talents. He had forged "a number of discharges by which he and more than a hundred soldiers had left the army. He appeared to be penitent and behaved with uncommon fortitude and resolution." While on General Sullivan's expedition against the six Indian nations of New York State, he and another soldier of the 11th Pennsylvania Regiment had gotten separated at Lake Canandaigua.[46] They spent seven days in the wilderness trying to catch up with the main army that was on the march, subsisting on the hearts and livers of two dead horses that the army had left behind and whatever else they found in the forest.

Before his ladder was turned and his existence ended, "he addressed the soldiers, desired them to be faithful to their country and obedient to their officers." He "advised the officers to be punctual in their engagements to the soldiers and give them no cause to desert. He examined the halter and told the hangman the knot was not made right, and that the rope was not strong enough, as he was a heavy man. Having adjusted the knot and fixed it round his own neck, he was swung off instantly. The rope broke and he fell to the ground, by which he was very much bruised. He calmly ascended the ladder and said: 'I told you the rope was not strong enough. Do get a stronger one.' Another being procured, he was launched into eternity."[47]

By midday, all was apparently quiet. A Mr. Stevenson, an officer in the Pennsylvania Line, which was camped nearby, came and spent the day with the Connecticut troops.[48] Samuel Richards suspected that he was sent over to spy on them and report what they were doing.[49]

Washington correctly placed the blame for the mutiny on the lack of provisions. He realized how desperate the situation was and sent out letters the next day requesting supplies of meat and pleaded for every effort to bring an end to the deplorable conditions. He knew that until the hunger abated the situation could flare up at any time.

Washington told Henry Champion, deputy commissary for purchases, and Governor Jonathan Trumbull of Connecticut, "We are in a situation of extremity for want of meat. The Troops on several days have been entirely destitute of any, and for a considerable time past they have been at best at half, at quarter, at an eighth allowance of this essential article." This distress had produced a mutiny the previous night in the Connecticut line.[50] Additionally, he told Trumbull, "The men have borne their distress with a firmness and patience never exceeded, and every possible praise is due the officers for encouraging them to it, by precept, by exhortation, by example. But there are certain bounds, beyond which it is impossible for human nature to go. We are arrived at these." He iterated that it was only through the exertions of the officers that the entire corps was not involved in the mutiny.[51]

Several days later, Washington could still see the evil face of mutiny in the corps. He told Joseph Reed, president (governor) of Pennsylvania, "There is such a combination of circumstances to exhaust the patience of the soldiery that it begins at length to be worn out and we see in every line of the army, the most serious features of mutiny and sedition."[52] Washington was concerned that all of the Continental Army lines would mutiny.

Washington never missed a chance to unburden his troubles to Congress. Like the song that never ends, he once again told them of the truly depressing state of affairs with the army's supply situation and how two regiments of the Connecticut Line mutinied under arms and but for the timely actions by some of their officers it might have spread throughout the corps. He stated they had "a determination to return home, or at best to gain subsistence at the point of the bayonet. . . . They are in as great distress at West Point. . . . The Garrison of Fort Schuyler had . . . only a month's supply on hand, and that there was no more provision to send them."[53]

THE CONNECTICUT LINE MUTINY, ALONG WITH the capture of Charles Town, South Carolina, in May 1780, was thought at British Headquarters in New York to have demoralized the American will to continue the war or at least caused them to drop their guard.

Acting on this presumption, under the command of the Hessian General Baron Wilhelm von Knyphausen, approximately 6,000 Crown forces attempted an invasion of New Jersey on June 23, 1780. The goal was to capture Hobart Gap in the Watchung Mountains and then push on through to the Continental Army headquarters at Morristown. The invasion force crossed over from Staten Island to Elizabethtown. They were confronted with significant, unanticipated resistance from American Continental and local militia units at Springfield, New Jersey. The American forces, informed of the intentions of the Crown forces by one of George Washington's spies, held off the British attack. The invading army returned to Staten Island without accomplishing its mission.

AT THE SAME TIME THE BRITISH WERE contemplating an invasion of New Jersey, in June 1780, thirty-one men of Colonel Goose Van Schaick's 1st New York Regiment at Fort Schuyler left over the lack of pay and clothing, primarily shirts, and took their weapons with them. It was believed that the men were going to join the British at Oswegatchie (now Ogdensburg) on the Saint Lawrence River.

General Washington understood the importance of Fort Schuyler to the defense, not only to western New York, but the whole continent.[54] The Oneida Carrying Place was the western access to the Mohawk River, which is the backdoor to Albany and the Hudson River. If the British army succeeded in taking Fort Schuyler it could travel east down the Mohawk River and attack Albany. This is what Lieutenant Colonel Barry St. Ledger failed to accomplish as his part of the British Saratoga campaign in 1777.

Lieutenant Abraham Hardenbergh went after the mutineers with a group of friendly Oneida Indians. Fifteen of the mutineers had crossed the Grand River. On the evening of the second day of the pursuit, Lieutenant Hardenbergh and the Oneidas caught up with the remaining sixteen mutineers just as they were about to cross the Grand River. The mutineers commenced firing against Lieutenant Hardenbergh, who returned fire. Hardenberg and the Oneida Indians killed thirteen of the sixteen on this side of the river. The fifteen that had already passed the river escaped.[55]

The security of the western part of the state of New York depended on holding the post of Fort Schuyler. After the mutiny, Washington told General Robert Howe at West Point,

> I shall not be easy until I have thrown a handsome supply of provision into
> it. You will therefore be pleased instantly to send up one hundred barrels

of flour to Albany addressed to Colonel Van Schaick, who will forward it, and should His Excellency Governor Clinton call upon you for one hundred barrels of beef, you will deliver it to his order or send it up to Albany if required. This will be wanted for the garrison of the fort also, and must therefore be of sound and good quality. Should it be called for, give the commissary strict orders to have it inspected and put in the best order for keeping, before it is removed. I shall continue sending up flour to you as fast as teams can be procured to transport it.[56]

That same day, Washington wrote Governor George Clinton that he was concerned with the "dissatisfaction and spirit of desertion" that he found prevailing in Colonel Goose Van Schaick's 1st New York Regiment.

After the mutiny he wanted the unit removed form Fort Schuyler but was unable to replace them with Continentals. He asked Clinton to send at least three hundred men who were raised by the state for frontier service as the replacements. They were to take with them the provisions he was sending to the fort. The fort was to remain under the command of forty-year-old Schenectady native Lieutenant Colonel Cornelius van Dyck of the 1st New York Regiment.[57]

Washington also wrote to Colonel Van Schaick at Albany and told him of his request to Governor Clinton to relieve the fort. The men being relieved were to be sent to the main army. He said he felt for the men. They should "not tarnish by an unbecoming or unsoldierly conduct, the honor and character of perseverance which they have justly acquired."

The lack of pay and food was not unique to Fort Schuyler. Because of the significance of Fort Schuyler, Washington had General Howe ship another one hundred barrels of flour from West Point to Albany. He had previously ordered a hundred barrels of beef from Colonel Peter Gansevoort of Albany who was in charge of the 3rd New York Regiment. He told Van Schaick to get the beef and flour moved to the fort as soon as possible, using the replacements as an escort and to instruct Colonel van Dyck to supplement the salted barrel beef with fresh meat whenever possible. He was also releasing shoes from the Continental stockpile at New Windsor for Van Schaick's men.[58] Washington was determined not to lose Fort Schuyler to the British.

3

Firecake and Water

THE DIFFICULTY OF SUPPLY

*O*n February 22, 1775, the Massachusetts Provincial Congress appointed one of its members, John Pigeon, as the commissary to supply its troops. He began carrying out their orders by assembling magazines at Concord and Worcester with ordnance and foodstuffs to supply 15,000 men.

On March 15, Captain James Barrett was assigned to protect the magazines and have sufficient teams and vehicles in place to move the magazine if necessary. The Americans had been busy preparing for the day when they might have to defend themselves.

Military supplies for both the British and Continental forces were a concern even before the fighting began. King George III ordered William Legge and Lord Dartmouth, who was the secretary of state for the colonies, to instruct the fifty-four-year-old Major General Thomas Gage, who was acting royal governor and in charge of the British army at Boston, to take action against the Massachusetts malcontents.

Gage replaced Thomas Hutchinson as royal governor of Massachusetts. The prevailing theory in London was if Gage, who had been in Boston since May 1774, took preemptive action quickly, the rebels would not have time to gather a large force to oppose British rule or to get their military supplies together. The idea was to nip this whole rebellion in the bud. Some selective pruning would cut away the disease.

Lord Dartmouth stated that the decision to act "must be left to your own discretion to be executed or not, as you shall, upon weighing all the circumstances, think most advisable." Being a consummate politician, he then took away that choice when he said, "the Government of this country must act with firmness and decision. You will be on your guard, and on no account suffer the people, at least of the town of Boston, to assemble themselves in arms on any pretence whatever, either of town guards or militia duty."[1]

On April 14, 1775, General Gage received Dartmouth's letter of instructions. Gage had in his employ Newport-born, Boston-raised, and London-trained Dr. Benjamin Church as a spy. Dr. Church had been, since 1772, in the employment of Royal Governor Hutchinson as a paid informant.

Dr. Church was a skilled surgeon and one of the leading men of Massachusetts Whig politics. He traveled in the same circles of power with John and Samuel Adams, John Hancock, and Dr. Joseph Warren. He was a member of the North Caucus, Long Room Club, Boston Committee of Correspondence, the Massachusetts Provincial Assembly, and the Committee of Safety, sometimes its chairman. Paul Revere said Dr. Church "appeared to be a high son of liberty."[2]

Dr. Church had advised General Gage of the American supplies stored at Concord, Massachusetts. On April 15, Church reported that the Massachusetts Provincial Congress was sending embassies to the other New England colonies to discuss the formation of an army to oppose the Crown forces. Gage knew he had to take immediate action. If he removed or destroyed the military stores at Concord, it would remove from the rebels their much-needed war supplies, thus complying with his instructions from Lord Dartmouth.

To undertake this operation, General Gage chose Lieutenant Colonel Francis Smith of the 10th Regiment of Foot. Smith was a twenty-eight-year veteran near retirement who was cautious, overweight, self-indulgent, and slow. On Tuesday April 18, Gage informed Smith that he had received intelligence that a quantity of small arms, ammunition, provisions, and tents had been collected at Concord for the avowed purpose of raising and supporting the rebellion against his majesty.[3] Gage provided him with a "draught of Concord, on which is marked, the houses, barns, and which contain the above military stores."[4] In view of the extensive detail on the Concord map, they could only have been supplied by someone with intimate knowledge of John Pigeon's activities.

Gage had tried to keep his plan secret. He told Hugh Earl Percy of his plan and instructed him to tell no one. After his meeting with General Gage, Percy, when passing a group of Bostonians, was chided about the soldiers who were going after the rebel cannons at Concord. Percy immediately returned to Gage and informed him that his secret was out. Gage was flabbergasted and told Lord Percy he had only told one other person about the plan.

Dr. Joseph Warren had received intelligence from several sources that something was in the works. He was told of overhearing conversations from sailors and a report that the navy had placed their ships' longboats in the water.[5] This was a sign that the king's troops would soon be moving across the bay. He went to his confidential informant who was well coupled with the British high command. The informant told him there were sizable units of British regulars on the move who were to seize Samuel Adams and John Hancock at Lexington and burn the military stores at Concord.[6] Because of this intelligence, Adams and Hancock were able to depart before the British arrived in Lexington.

The source of this information was none other than Mrs. Margaret Kemble Gage, the beautiful New Jersey–born wife of British Major General Thomas Gage.[7] She had once said, "she hoped her husband would never be the instrument of sacrificing the lives of her countryman."[8] Gage had been devoted to her. But after the Battles of Concord and Lexington, he sent his wife of seventeen years to England on board the *Charming Nancy* while he stayed in America. Their relationship was never the same again.[9]

ON APRIL 19, 1775, THE FIRST SHOTS OF THE American Revolution were fired at Lexington and the outnumbered American militia retreated off the green. It would later be called the "shot heard 'round the world.'"

The British army advanced to the North Bridge at Concord where three to four hundred Minutemen blocked their path. Another skirmish took place with both sides taking casualties. The British troops, unable to take the bridge, fell back and began their retreat to Boston.

As the British army marched back to Boston, more Minutemen from the surrounding towns arrived and kept up a constant barrage along the route from behind stone walls, trees, and houses. Bullets buzzed like bees around the heads of the British. It was a withering fire. A few shots from behind a fence on the right would be followed by a few more from the farmhouse on the left. The soldiers would march a bit and more shots would come from the trees. Each volley would require the British soldiers to charge after the shooters who then just ran away. It was an exhausting retreat. They were making their way in yards but had miles to go back to Boston.

British reinforcements under the command of Hugh Earl Percy left Boston at 9:00 a.m., arriving at Lexington about 2:00 p.m. to rescue Lt. Colonel Smith and his corps who were almost out of ammunition. The British made a tactical withdrawal of their forces back to Charlestown, being harassed all the way.[10] No strategic weapons had been captured. The Minutemen then encircled Boston to keep the Redcoats bottled up and busy in Boston and out of the countryside.

War fever seized the country. News of the victory at Concord and Lexington raced from city to city down the continent More Minutemen and militia from several states joined the forces already assembled at Boston.

When George Washington took command on July 3, 1775, of the approximately 17,000 men surrounding Boston and the British Army, he had no idea what lay ahead. He did not inherit anything resembling an army. It was an undisciplined rabble of short-term enlistees. They were clothed in a multitude of outfits even within the same unit.

It was impossible to identify the officers from the enlisted men. Many were farmers, some of whom did not have weapons while others had weapons that were relics from the French and Indian War—weapons that might explode if actually fired. Others were backwoodsmen who lived off of what they shot. They were deficient in everything including hygiene. It was an army unlike any ever fielded by a country. It had no supply system and very little organization.

On June 15, the Continental Congress passed a resolution calling for a quartermaster general who was to be paid eighty dollars a month. The quartermaster general would oversee the Quartermaster Department, which was responsible for supply activities to furnish all camp equipment and tents. When the army went into winter quarters, it was also to provide whatever articles were need for sheltering the soldiers. However, Congress did not bother to appoint anyone to the position. Two months later on August 14, Washington turned to his aides-de-camp and appointed Major Thomas Mifflin. He was a thirty-one-year-old Philadelphia merchant. In December, Congress fixed the rank of the quartermaster general as a colonel in the Continental Army. At Cambridge, Joseph Trumbull, son of Jonathan Trumbull, governor of Connecticut, had been commissary for the

Connecticut troops and impressed Washington, who recommended him for the same position in the Continental Army. Congress agreed and appointed Trumbull to the position of commissary general of stores and provisions for the Continental Army.[11] The Commissary Department was responsible for procuring food and forage.

At first, Mifflin's and Trumbull's jobs were straightforward. The men were to supply the three stationary divisions of the army encamped at Roxbury, Prospect, and Winter Hills, Massachusetts, and the main body at Cambridge. Mifflin also set up two field offices, one at Roxbury and the other to service both Prospect and Winter Hills. Mifflin assembled a staff of nineteen assistants at his headquarters at Cambridge who either did paperwork or supervised others in the field. One of the superintendents supervised the work of fifty carpenters while two others supervised the stable and the granary.

Trumbull established four issuing stores, each headed by a storekeeper. The stores at Cambridge and Roxbury each issued provisions to two brigades; those at Prospect Hill and Medford each supported one brigade.

Charles Miller, who had earlier served as deputy to John Pigeon in provisioning the Massachusetts troops, headed the main issuing store at Cambridge and employed the largest number of clerks. Trumbull established purchasing agents known as deputies who were paid a commission. He employed purchasing agents in Newburyport, New York City, Connecticut, Providence, and elsewhere as needed. The army's primary shortages were for gunpowder, cannons, and clothing—items that had to be imported.

Because there was no advance supply of money provided by Congress for the army's needs, the army's purchasing agents had to acquire goods using their own credit. If the agent had not built up a good business reputation prior to the war, he had difficulty obtaining supplies. The purchasing agents were paid a percentage of the value of the merchandise they bought. The more the goods cost, the more money the agent made. There was no incentive to hold down prices.

The Americans, encircling Boston, had taken up position on a hill in Cambridge Heights. This made the British possession of Boston untenable. The British, with 2,600 soldiers under command of Major General William Howe, twice attacked the 1,500 Americans on the Charlestown Peninsula under a withering fire. They regrouped and made a third charge up the hill. The Americans had run out of ammunition and had no choice but to retreat.

They fought off the third advance with rocks, sticks, and gunstocks, exiting their fortified earthworks as the British entered them. It was a Pyrrhic victory for the British with 226 killed and 828 wounded. They could not sustain that loss rate in their quest to regain control of the colonies.

Because of the heavy loses suffered by the British in the Battle of Bunker Hill, many in American political circles believed it would be a short war. Therefore, a big stockpile of supplies for the army was considered an unnecessary waste of money and there was no effort to build a military war chest of supplies.

In order to remove the British threat of a descent down Lake Champlain from Canada to isolate New England from the other colonies, Congress instructed lumber baron Major General Philip Schuyler of upstate New York to take possession of Canada. Schuyler managed to assemble a force of about 2,000 men from New York and Connecticut, thus forming the nucleus of what became known as the Northern Army. A deputy quartermaster for the Northern Division was created, which increased the demand for goods. Since this army was to fight battles on ice and snow, different types of clothing and equipment were needed. When the invasion of Canada eventually failed, and large quantities of military supplies were left behind as the army retreated.

After the British evacuation of Boston in March 1776, the Continental Army fell back to New York where an attack by the British was expected. Mifflin and Trumbull now having to provide for an American army on the move, set up shop in New York, while securing the supplies still at Boston. Things just kept getting more complicated as supplies were needed in more places.

When Trumbull arrived in New York, he found that Congress had given money to various people to procure different items for the troops. This practice blurred Trumbull's lines of authority. The commissary department was in a state of confusion. It had to compete for much-needed supplies. For example on December 9, 1775, Congress had advanced $3,000 to Carpenter Wharton to supply the Pennsylvania troops with rations. When the Pennsylvania troops relocated to New York, he continued to fulfill his contract as instructed by Congress.[12]

When General Washington arrived in New York, he found that the New York Provincial Congress, at the request of the Continental Congress, had appointed thirty-five-year-old Walter Livingston a commissary to furnish provisions for the Continental troops stationed in this city. He guessed this was done because there was no Continental Army commissary there. He advised Congress that "Mr. Livingston still claims a right of furnishing all the troops, but those lately arrived from Cambridge."[13] It took a month to get the situation resolved. Washington then announced in general orders that Trumbull had taken over supplying the troops previously supplied by Mr. Livingston.[14]

Quartermaster General Thomas Mifflin realized he needed a person known to the local merchants if he was going to be successful at expediting matters in New York. He had Washington appoint Hugh Hughes as assistant quartermaster general. Hughes was a former schoolteacher, who was then serving as commissary of military stores for the state of New York. Mifflin was promoted to brigadier general and resigned his post as quartermaster general as, by law, it was fixed at the rank of a colonel.

On June 5, Washington went back to his aides-de-camp to choose a replacement for Mifflin. He selected Stephen Moylan who was born in Cork, Ireland, in 1737, and educated in Paris. Moylan was experienced in the shipping business, first in Lisbon and then in Philadelphia, where he had moved in 1768. He served as quartermaster general during the evacuations of Long Island and New York City.

In the evacuation of Long Island, the army lost all of the carts and wagons it had taken to Long Island. When New York City had to be abandoned, a large supply of military stores was left behind because of the lack of carts and wagons to move them. Some of the military supplies fell into the hands of the British while others were destroyed in the great fire that burned 20 percent of the city.

On September 20, 1776, Congress resolved that a committee of three be appointed to go to headquarters near New York to inquire "into the state of the army and the best means of supplying their wants." The committee members were thirty–two-year-old Massachusetts delegate Elbridge Gerry, sixty-three-year-old retired New York merchant Francis Lewis, and fifty–five-year-old Connecticut delegate Roger Sherman.[15] While at headquarters at Harlem, they talked Colonel Moylan into resigning in favor of General Mifflin, which he did on September 28. Moylan returned to Washington's staff.

More supplies were lost when Fort Washington on northern Manhattan Island surrendered on November 16 and when Fort Lee on the New Jersey

Palisades was abandoned to the British on November 20.[16] Like a boxer struggling to stand on his wobbly legs, the Continental Army was reeling from one disastrous blow after another.

Mifflin was sent to Philadelphia to take charge of the military stores as Washington was leading the remnants of the Continental Army across New Jersey to Pennsylvania. After the Continental Army crossed into Pennsylvania, the New Jersey side of the Delaware was open to Philadelphia and the magazine was at risk of being captured by the British. Mifflin spent his time raising troops in the counties that surrounded Philadelphia to slow the British advance on the city.

Trumbull went to Hartford, Connecticut, to supervise the procurement and packing of salt provisions in New England for the next year's campaigning. He left Carpenter Wharton in charge of keeping Washington's army supplied. Wharton was not equal to the task. After the American victory at the Battle of Trenton, Washington had moved the Hessian prisoners and the captured stores to Pennsylvania. Because of Wharton's failure to procure supplies, Washington was held up for two days before he could cross back into New Jersey. Washington was forced to permit the troops to find food wherever they could. To get around Wharton's incompetence, Washington appointed Colonel Thomas Lowrey of the New Jersey Militia as deputy commissary general.[17]

The constant loss of supplies did not stop until after the American victories at Trenton and Princeton and with the Continental Army encamped for the winter at Morristown, New Jersey. In the space of little more than a week, Washington recovered most of New Jersey and destroyed the Hessian aura of invincibility. Morale among the American troops was generally restored. However, vast stores of military goods would have to be replaced. At the same time, Mifflin was having major problems getting the army resupplied because of a lack of money.[18]

To resolve the transportation problems of an army on the move, Thomas Mifflin wanted separate forage and wagon departments established before the spring campaigning began. Both Washington and Congress approved. On May 14, Congress gave Mifflin the authority, with Washington's concurrence, to appoint whatever assistants he needed to conduct the business of his department. Along with this authority, Congress called for a monthly return to be furnished by the general to be forwarded to the Board of War. However, not until July 1 would an assistant, Colonel Henry Emanuel Lutterloh, be appointed as deputy quartermaster general.

Lutterloh had excellent credentials. He had been in the Quartermaster Department of the army of the Duke of Brunswick. He began his service in 1750 and rose from an ensign to a major. Lutterloh was sent to London after the Seven Years War (1756–63).[19] There he met Benjamin Franklin. Franklin provided Lutterloh with a letter of recommendation and funds for his trip. He joined the American Army in May 1777.[20]

The summer of 1777 was a tumultuous time for the Commissary and Quartermaster Departments. Carpenter Wharton, who earlier had failed to keep Washington's Army supplied, was charged with purchasing large quantities of flour, pork, and rum far above market price, thereby increasing his commissions. Specifically, the charges against him were

> That during the last campaign, he neglected his duty in not seasonably supplying the army with provisions, and put the general under the necessity of appointing a commissary in his stead.

> That in the fall of the last year, he brought to Fort Lee, such a large number of cattle [by his own acknowledgment, not fewer than 700; others say more] at a time that they suffered greatly for want of proper keeping, and became unfit for beef. Many of them were in such state when delivered, and from the largeness of their numbers many were lost. Upon the retreat of our army across Delaware river, droves of cattle by his direction were brought in, out of one of which droves, 254 cattle were taken as unfit for killing and sent to his farm to winter, which he acknowledged were afterwards sold, the loss upon which, it was supposed, the public was charged with.

> That he purchased large quantities of flour to supply the magazines and army, at extravagant prices, much beyond what the same might have been procured for, employing persons to purchase, either wholly unacquainted with business, or such as designedly raised the prices with a view to increase their profits, under the idea of receiving commissions.

> That he raised the price of pork by bidding either by himself or agents, much greater prices than people he purchased from had agreed to sell the same for, to other commissaries; that he also purchased rum at prices higher than the same might have been obtained for.

> That so far from endeavoring to serve the public faithfully, he refused to confer with other commissaries for concerting a mode for preventing the extravagant rise of provisions, by their bidding upon each other, said he would take his own method of purchasing, and others might do the same.

That he neglected his duty in not purchasing larger quantities of pork, in the proper season, when the same might have been had on reasonable terms.[21]

Wharton was removed from office and ordered to close his accounts. The auditors were furnished with all information against him so that any frauds might be detected. Wharton fled to the British during their occupation of Philadelphia. In June 1778, when the British Army left Philadelphia, he went with them.[22] His case did nothing to allay congressional concerns that commissaries and quartermasters were responsible for the massive depreciation of the Continental currency. It was far easier to blame them than for Congress to solve the complex problem of restoring the credit of the country's currency.

Meanwhile other assignments would distract Mifflin from his efforts to keep the army supplied. During the summer of 1777, Washington directed Mifflin to obtain information about the roads and places of possible encampments on both sides of the Delaware River.[23] As the British Army was marching on Philadelphia, Congress fled across the Susquehanna River to York, Pennsylvania, in September 1777. Congress was busy on matters dealing with the British occupation of Philadelphia and did not concern itself with supplies for the Continental Army now encamped at Valley Forge.

On October 8, Mifflin submitted his resignation from the military due to ill health. Congress refused to accept his resignation as major general but accepted his resignation as quartermaster general. Congress wanted him to continue in the job of quartermaster general until a successor was found. At the same time, they elected him to the Board of War.[24] However, Mifflin left his deputy Henry Lutterloh to run the Quartermaster Department for the next four months before a successor was in place.

At Christmastime, Washington realized how bad the situation was at Valley Forge and blamed it on the Commissary Department, as he was getting no help from the directionless Quartermaster's Department.

I was in my representation of matters in the Commissary's Department yesterday, fresh, and more powerful reasons oblige me to add, that I am now convinced, beyond a doubt that unless some great and capital change suddenly takes place in that line, this army must inevitably be reduced to one or other of these three things. Starve, dissolve, or disperse, in order to obtain subsistence in the best manner they can; rest assured Sir this is not an exaggerated picture. . . . I have abundant reason to support what I say.

Washington went on to say that the only purchasing agent of the Commissary Department who was at Valley Forge informed him that he did not have a single animal to butcher and had fewer than twenty-five barrels of flour for the entire army. When Washington asked how soon supplies were expected, he was told by the agent that he did not know. Washington further reported, "Since the month of July, we have had no assistance from the Quartermaster General and to want of assistance from this department, the Commissary General charges great part of his deficiency."[25] Just the day before, a surgeon at Valley Forge had written in his diary, "I am tempted to steal fowls if I could find them, or even a whole hog, for I feel as if I could eat one."

The troops had a standing order to have two days worth of provisions with them so that they could move quickly into action. Washington told the Congress that they had been greatly impeded or totally obstructed from taking advantage of the enemy because they had not been able to comply with this order. "Soap, vinegar and other articles allowed by Congress we have seen none . . . since the battle of Brandywine." He pointed out that they had little use for the soap as the men only had one shirt and some none at all. "We have by a field return this day made no less than 2,898 men now in camp unfit for duty because they are bare foot and otherwise naked. There are 2,000 men who sit up all night by fires because of a lack of blankets. No man, in my opinion, ever had his measures more impeded that I have by every department of the army." Washington also related how a number of soldiers were in the hospital and farmer's houses due to not having shoes. "Military arrangements and movements in consequence, like the mechanism of a clock, will be imperfect, and disordered, by the want of a part."[26]

Congressman Francis Dana, who was at Valley Forge in February 1778, described the army's situation: "A great proportion of the soldiers were in a very suffering condition for want of necessary clothing and totally unfit for duty. A greater evil was the want of provisions. Congress will wonder, that the army, or any part of it, have wanted bread, since but a short time before we assured them that there was no probability of a deficiency in that article and that there was a sufficiency already purchased and engaged." This assertion had been made on information provided by Colonel Ephraim Blane. Several brigades complained they had been destitute of flour two, three, and four days. "We reexamined Colonel Blane on February 7, who assured us that if such a want took place, it must be owing to neglect in the issuing commissaries or quartermasters, as flour was deposited in the magazines."

On February 15, Dana rode on his horse into camp and passed through several brigades. He enquired separately of all the officers he knew, of various ranks, and was satisfied that by comparing their accounts he learned the real state of these brigades. They had not suffered for flour but upon an average, every regiment had been destitute of fish or flesh for four days.

On Saturday evening, some received three-quarters and others half a pound of salted pork per man—not one day's allowance. No one had any assurance of regular supplies of meat in the future. Dana predicted the want of meat would infallibly bring on a mutiny in the army.

Sunday morning, Colonel Brewer's regiment rose in a body and proceeded to General Patterson's quarters. They told him their complaints and threatened to quit the army. Patterson quieted the mutineers, but was obliged to permit them to leave camp to purchase meat if they had the money to do so. Otherwise he would pay for it.

The same spirit of rebellion was rising in other regiments, but had been suppressed for the present by the prudence of some of their officers.

> But no prudence or management, without meat, can satisfy the hungry man. In plain terms, 'tis probable this army will disperse if the commissary department is so damnably managed. Good God! how absurd to attempt an expedition into Canada, when you cannot feed this reduced army! All the meat you have in magazines or can purchase in any part and transport here, will not be more than sufficient to satisfy the daily wants of this army for months to come. The passes on the North River must be secured, or without question this and the neighboring states of New Jersey, Delaware and Maryland must be evacuated by our army. They cannot be fed with meat but from New England.

Dana believed that if the quartermaster general was with the troops, the failure to supply the army could have been avoided. The quartermaster general would know what was needed and could get the issues resolved. According to Dana, a quartermaster general's "orders must be obeyed through every branch of the department upon the peril of life, and until some villains are hanged or quartered, great will be the obstructions in it."[27]

The army needed a quartermaster general who understood military logistics and who would be most sympathetic to the proper supply of soldiers. Major

General Nathanael Greene wanted to stay a field commander but, upon the urging of a committee from Congress and the personal plea from George Washington, in March 1778, Greene agreed to become the new quartermaster general. The committee recommended John Cox, a Philadelphia merchant, and Charles Pettit, a New Jersey lawyer and accountant, as Greene's two assistant quartermaster generals. Both men were related to Joseph Reed, one of the committee members who recommended them.

Cox was to make the purchases and examine the merchandise while Pettit kept the accounts and the petty cash. The three men, Cox, Greene, and Pettit were to equally share a 1 percent commission

Major General Nathanael Greene in an illlustration based on the painting by Charles Wilson Peale. (*William L. Clements Library*)

on the items purchased. Greene had assumed his duties on March 23, which left little time to restock the military magazines for the year's campaigning.

Greene stayed in the field with the army. He and his staff performed to the satisfaction of Washington and Congress. However, prices rose dramatically and Congress formed a committee to oversee both the Commissary and Quartermaster Departments.[28] Eventually, the supervisory function was turned over to the Board of War. Under Greene, the Quartermaster Department improved but it increased in staff to almost 3,000 by 1780.

In the spring of 1779, Greene was having problems getting money from the Treasury Department. He informed the committee that his department was "considerably in debt, and that the orders he has received from the Commander in Chief cannot possibly be complied with in the tune specified for that purpose, unless he can receive very considerable supplies of money." He also told them about his problem with obtaining wagoners and that "unless an answer can be had to his former requests touching the assistant and deputies in his Department, they will not continue in the service."[29]

Ephraim Blaine, deputy commissary general wrote a few days later to Joseph Reed, president of the Pennsylvania Supreme Executive, about the "great difficulty procuring provisions due to poor crops, unstable money. . . . The late frost has almost destroyed all the rye and early wheat. This great misfortune with melancholy depreciation of our money makes it almost impossible to obtain any supplies from farmers."[30]

MEDDLING BY CONGRESS AND the states in the operation of the Quartermaster's Department caused its own problems. On July 9, 1779, Congress resolved that the governor or executive authority of each state should examine the conduct of every person within that state employed in either the Commissary or Quartermaster's Departments where there was a strong suspicion of official misconduct.[31] Employees of these departments now had two or more supervisors to whom they were responsible, a situation that could not possibly work. They could be prosecuted in several states at once depending on the number of states in which they worked. To add to the problem, Congress directed that no subordinate could resign without permission and that permission should not be granted in the midst of a campaign.[32]

New Jersey needed to raise money and, in 1779, passed a wage tax law on the assistant quartermaster and deputy quartermaster generals in the state. They were to be taxed not less than 1,000 pounds but not more than 10,000 pounds. Deputy Quartermaster General Moore Furman resigned immediately. Assistant Quartermaster General John Cox and Charles Pettit petitioned Congress for relief. Congress left them to pay the bill.

Greene had successfully supplied Washington's army through the campaigns of 1778 and 1779. He had grown tired of Congress's unresponsiveness to his requests. On December 12, 1779, a fed up Greene wrote to the president of Congress offering his resignation.[33] He cited the depreciation of the Continental dollar as the main cause of all of the Quartermaster Department's problems. Congress neither responded to his request nor to the supply problem.

That same month, in an economizing effort, Congress decided to shift responsibility to the states for supplying their troops in the field. Unfortunately, the states were not up to the task. George Washington once commented that Congress "thinks it is but to say presto begone, and everything is done."[34] Congress never addressed how the supplies were going to be transported beyond a state's border where it was purchased or who was going to pay for the shipping. Congress assumed that the Quartermaster Department would be reorganized in time to handle the transportation. The reorganization took longer than expected and supplies rotted in state warehouses while the men starved.

Congress did not become aware of the problem until five months later. Their response was to pass the problem on to the state governors.[35]

The supply situation continued to worsened. After Christmas, some of the Massachusetts troops at West Point mutinied. Two days after the mutineers from Brigadier General John Glover's Brigade had finally been "overtaken and secured" and were on their way back to camp, General Greene sent a follow up letter informing Washington that the soldiers and his department were operating hand to mouth. He advised that the department could not be "long supported on credit."[36]

Congress's answer to the problem was to form a three-person committee to determine how to cut expenses by means of downsizing. One of the committee members had to also be a member of Congress and in January 1780 they chose Major General Philip Schuyler while he was absent. He was a good choice for the job as he had been chief commissary for the British army in upstate New York in 1756. The other two committee members were Timothy Pickering, a member of the Board of War, and General Mifflin.[37] Roger Sherman of Connecticut and Allen Jones of North Carolina were selected as advisors to the committee. When Schuyler returned to Congress, he refused the committee appointment and refused to be an advisor as he felt that Mifflin and Pickering were unfriendly to General Washington.[38] General Schuyler's opinion of the committee's voluminous report was that "it will starve the army in ten days" and was "replete with absurdity." The plan would remove four thousand officers from duty.[39]

Congress was not able to reach a decision on the report so it formed another committee. This time the committee was composed of General Schuyler, John Mathews of South Carolina, and Nathaniel Peabody of New Hampshire.[40] In June, Schuyler presented the reorganization plan to Congress, which revised the report and approved it on June 15, 1780. Congress removed the redundancy, which it had previously created. It had required uniformity in the organizational structure of the Quartermaster's Department regardless of the workload. There was a perception that unscrupulous agents were submitting inflated costs to procure goods thereby increasing their commissions and getting rich at the public expense. There definitely were cases where numbers were padded by unethical staff. But the

real villain for the increased operational expenditures was the wartime inflationary demand spiral on goods and the massive depreciation in the
Continental currency. Congress did away with paying commissions based on
the cost of the items purchased. Pay was now going to be based on a fixed
salary. Entitlements to rations and forage were eliminated.

Greene finally received a copy of the reorganization plan on July 26, 1780
and immediately resigned. He did not believe that the changes could be successfully implemented in the middle of a campaign. Because the department
would be inadequately staffed, he believed that it would lead to "a physical
impossibility of performing the duties that would be required of him."[41]

Congress accepted General Nathanael Greene's resignation as quartermaster general on August 5, 1780. Greene was given command of the
Southern army and left for South Carolina to once again lead troops in the
field. Congress appointed Timothy Pickering as his successor. They made him
a colonel but gave him the pay and rations of a general. At Washington's
request, Greene continued to perform the duties of the quartermaster general
until Pickering arrived at camp on September 22. Pickering spent the next
several months reorganizing the department. Luckily, he was able to talk
Charles Pettit into accepting a reappointment. Having Pettit's experience in
obtaining fund from the treasury was a major benefit to Pickering. After ten
months under the new system, Pettit quit. Congress saw a chance to save
$166 per month and did away with the job. Pickering now had to be both the
director and chief financial officer of the Quartermaster Department.

It was five months before the reorganization was completed in January
1781, but by that time a storm was already on the horizon.

4

A Perfect Storm

NO FOOD, NO MONEY, NO SOLDIERS, NO OFFICERS

*W*afting through the air at British General Sir Henry Clinton's Christmas Ball in New York City was the sound of music from a cello, flute, and violin. The small orchestra played selections from the general's large collection of sheet music. Clinton loved music. He had James Rivington, the king's printer in New York, bind his sheet music into volumes.

During the winter recess from campaigning, attendance at balls and plays was the order of the day for British army officers. They were diligent in fulfilling winter social obligations. Anyone with political aspirations who managed to get on Sir Henry's invitation list would be sure to attend and compliment him on his ability to play a violin. Nonattendance was political suicide.

During the musical interludes, the conversation always turned to the lack of firewood through the long cold winter months and the price gouging by the woodcutters. The demands of the British army and loyalists for dimensional lumber for construction and split wood for cooking and heating had caused the cutting of every tree and sapling over four feet high on York Island. It was during one of these interludes that Frederick Smyth, the former chief justice of New Jersey, informed William Smith, the royal chief justice of New York that British spies had set out that night to deliver their proclamation. Their committee had toiled an entire month to perfect the document.

The very next day, Saturday, December 30, 1780, James Rivington, published their proclamation in his newspaper, the *Royal Gazette*. Copies of the *Royal Gazette* would be exchanged for copies of American newspapers at Elizabethtown, New Jersey, by the next flag of truce, which would help spread the word of Sir Henry's offer of clemency for anyone who wished to return to the Royal Standard.

The proclamation was also to be translated into German for circulation to the Pennsylvania German-speaking population. The translation and distribution of this proclamation was given to Daniel Coxe. William Smith believed that 10,000 to 12,000 copies were going to be printed for a general distribution.[1]

The thirty-nine-year-old Daniel Coxe had been a lawyer with an elegant house on Second Street in Trenton, New Jersey. He was one of the largest land owners in the state with properties in Burlington, Cape May, Hunterdon, Salem, Somerset, and Sussex Counties in New Jersey. During the British occupation of Philadelphia, he served as a magistrate without pay. Coxe had planned to go to England on the *Solebay* in October 1779.[2] However, Sir Henry Clinton thought so highly of Coxe that he asked him to stay and help the British war effort.[3]

Though the British army and civilians in New York had a sufficiency, but not an abundance, of food and clothes, there was a constant shortage of fuel. On the other hand, the main body of the American army, encamped in the hills around Morristown, New Jersey, suffered from a severe shortage of clothing, food, and money just as they had every winter since the start of the war. Even when supplies became available, transporting the goods through the snow or the mud was difficult if not impossible.

On November 28, 1780, George Washington moved his headquarters to William Ellison's house at New Windsor, New York. Here he would stay until March. It was not a happy time for him; he once referred to his New Windsor headquarters as his dreary quarters.[4] He wrote to Benjamin Lincoln on December 11, 1780 that

> some states have been largely deficient in their specific supplies; otherwise we should not at this alarming period of the year be totally destitute of flour. . . . To add to our other difficulties, the situation of the Army, in respect to clothing, is really distressing. By collecting all our remnants, and those of a thousand colors and kinds, we shall scarcely make them comfortable. Uniformity, one of the essentials of discipline and every thing in the appearance of a soldier, must be dispensed with; and what makes the matter more mortifying is, that we have, I am positively assured, ten thousand complete suits ready in France, and laying there because our public agents cannot agree whose business it is to ship them. A quantity has also lain in the West Indies for more than eighteen months owing probably to some such cause.[5]

The army's situation was so dreadful and deteriorating so rapidly that, two days later Washington wrote to General Nathanael Greene, the former quartermaster general of the Continental Army, "I have been driven, by necessity, to discharge the levies. Want of clothing rendered them unfit for duty, and want of flour would have disbanded the whole army if I had not adopted this expedient for the relief of the soldier(s) for the war."[6] However, it did not produce the desired results.

> I am extremely unhappy that our want of magazines [stores of supplies], and precarious mode of supply, subject us, to such repeated inconveniencies and distresses; but hope the flour from Ringwood or Red Hook will arrive soon, to give at least a temporary relief. By the general Return of the Issues, I observe the number of rations to be much greater than I apprehended and that they do not diminish in the proportion, I expected from discharging the Levies: I wish you (William Heath) therefore to have a critical examination made into this matter; that from comparative view of the number of men, and rations, should there be any abuses, they might be corrected.[7]

The shortage of flour had caused the army to be reduced to "half and quarter allowances." As in previous winters, the army's horses had been moved to where forage was available so they would be ready for the spring campaigns. Only a very few would be kept in the winter camp for the use of officers, staff, and express riders.

The previous January, the conditions at Morristown were so bad that at times the army were "five or six days without bread, at other times as many days without meat, and once or twice two or three days without either. . . . At one time the soldiers eat every kind of horse food but hay." The prospects for this year looked just as bleak. General Anthony Wayne, writing to President Reed of Pennsylvania on December 16, stated,

> We are reduced to dry bread and beef for our food, and to cold water for our drink. Neither officers or soldiers have received a single drop of spirituous liquors from the public magazines since the 10th of October last, except one gill per man some time in November, this, together with the old worn out coats and tattered linen overalls, and what was once a poor substitute for a blanket (now divided among three soldiers), is but very wretched living and shelter against the winter's piercing cold, drifting snows and chilling sleets. Our soldiery are not devoid of reasoning facul-

ties, nor are they callous to the first feelings of nature, they have now served their country with fidelity for near five years, poorly clothed, badly fed and worse paid; of the last article, trifling as it is, they have not seen a paper dollar in the way of pay for near twelve months.[8]

John Marshall said "the soldiers were perpetually on the point of starvation and were often entirely without food, were exposed without proper clothing to the rigors of winter and had now served almost twelve months without pay." Lafayette described the conditions under which the men of the Pennsylvania Line served as "to be in want of food and clothes to be more than a year without pay, some even having been forced to serve a year beyond their engagements, these are extremities which would not be born in any army."[9]

IN ADDITION TO COMPLAINTS about the scarcity of supplies, there was increasing resentment over the payment of enlistment bounty money. Pennsylvania soldiers who had enlisted before February 1778 received $20. Those enlisting after, were given $100. Other states had increased their bounties to keep up with inflation. New Jersey was paying $250 and Virginia $750.

On February 1, 1777, Washington admonished the Massachusetts General Court, "Although your inducements for granting an additional bounty to the troops to be furnished by your state, were certainly meant to serve the cause; that you will find them most prejudicial in the end. One reason will be, that by your departing from the bounty prescribed by Congress, the troops in the other states will be discontented, upon hearing of this; unless they receive the same; and another and a more forcible one." Washington was warning them that an ever-increasing inflationary spiral had begun and if they persisted, each additional bounty payment would, of necessity, have to be higher.

On January 23, 1779, to help resolve recruiting and retention problems for the army, Congress voted "that the Commander in Chief be authorized . . . to re-enlist for the continuance of the war, all such of the continental troops as are not expressly engaged for that period . . . to complete the battalions to their proper complement; and for those purposes, besides the bounties of clothing, and at the expiration of the war, of money and land heretofore provided by Congress, for encouraging the recruiting service, to grant to each able bodied soldier now in the service, and who shall voluntarily reenlist during the war, a bounty according to the circumstances of his present engagement, but not to exceed in any case 200 dollars."[10] The bounty of two hun-

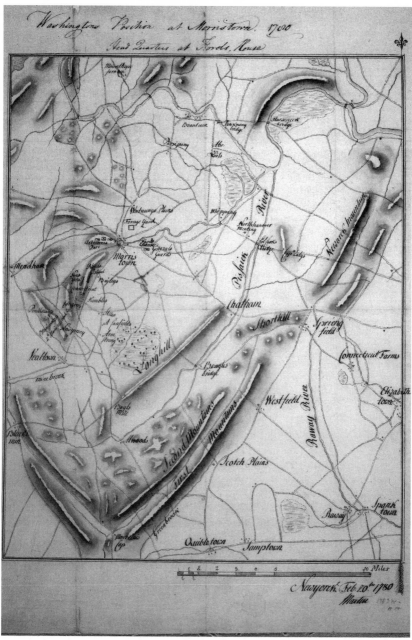

British headquarters map of the American army encampment at Morristown, New Jersey, made at New York on February 20, 1780. (*William L. Clements Library*)

dred dollars was worth around twenty-five dollars in silver coin. This action infuriated the Pennsylvanians who were told that they were already enlisted for the duration of the war and did not qualify for the money.

Aware of the discontent among the soldiers of the Pennsylvania Line, Washington wrote on June 9 to the War Board of the Continental Congress. "In consideration of the services of the soldiers who engaged at an early period, to serve during the War, and the great disproportion between the bounties they received, and those given to others for the service of a few Months, or perhaps not more than a year at most, I have sometimes thought it might not be improper to give them, by way of gratuity and as an acknowledgement 100 Dollars, which, besides operating as a reward, might have a good effect and quiet their discontents."

Washington thought there should be "an explicit declaration that the money given was entirely as a gratuity, and to place them upon a more equal footing with respect to other parts of the army who had received greater bounties for shorter service, they who stand engaged during the War, might compose the soldiery in the Pennsylvania line and those from Maryland."[11]

In response to Washington's request, Congress resolved,

> [to] entertain a grateful sense of the virtue and services of those faithful and zealous soldiers who, at an early period, engaged in the armies of these states during the war; and to encourage a continuance of their exertions, and as far as circumstances admit, to put them on a footing in pecuniary matters with other soldiers, General Washington be empowered to order a gratuity of one hundred dollars each, to be paid to the men so enlisted during the war; this gratuity to be paid only to such soldiers as enlisted before the 23rd day of January, 1779.[12]

In July, Washington paid the Pennsylvania Line troops and the situation was defused for the time being. At the end of the 1779 campaigning season, the Pennsylvania Line went into cantonment at Morristown.[13] Their camp was about four miles away from the town at a place called Mount Kemble. Initially, they pitched tents while they repaired the huts occupied the previous year by the Connecticut Line.[14]

There, the army suffered through the coldest winter (1779–80) of the eighteenth century, which was accompanied by ice and deep snow. Upper New York Harbor and the Arthur Kill were covered with ice. It was reported that sleighs were to be able to pass from Paulus Hook (Jersey City) across the

Hudson River to New York City and one could walk from Elizabethtown, New Jersey, to Staten Island. The East River was also frozen. It was possible to walk from New Jersey to Long Island and not get your feet wet. On Long Island, they were telling tall tales of ducks being found frozen solid. When the ducks were brought indoors, they would come to life and fly around the kitchen. Dr. Thacher described the January storm in his journal.

> On the 3d instant, we experienced one of the most tremendous snow storms ever remembered; no man could endure its violence many minutes without danger of his life. Several marquees were torn asunder and blown down over the officers' heads in the night, and some of the soldiers were actually covered while in their tents, and buried like sheep under the snow. . . . My comrades and myself were roused from sleep by the calls of some officers for assistance; their marquee had blown down, and they were almost smothered in the storm, before they could reach our marquee, only a few yards, and their blankets and baggage were nearly buried in the snow. We are greatly favored in having a supply of straw for bedding, over this we spread all our blankets, and with our clothes together, preserve ourselves from freezing. But, the sufferings of the poor soldiers can scarcely be described. While on duty they are unavoidably exposed to all the inclemency of storms and severe cold; at night they now have a bed of straw on the ground, and a single blanket to each man; they are badly clad, and some are destitute of shoes.

The deep snow compounded the difficulties in getting supplies to the army as the roads became impassible for man or beast.

General Washington told Governor Trumbull of Connecticut of the dreadful situation of an army on the verge of starving to death.

> The army has been near three months on a short allowance of bread; within a fortnight past almost perishing. They have been sometimes without bread, sometimes without meat, at no time with much of either, and often without both. They have borne their distress in which the officers have shared a common lot with the men, with as much fortitude as human nature is capable of; but they have been at last brought to such a dreadful extremity, that no authority or influence of the officers no virtue or patience in the men themselves could any longer restrain them from obeying the dictates of their sufferings.[15]

The soldiers had started to take the situation into their own hands, plundering the "neighboring inhabitants even of their necessary subsistence."[16]

Washington knew that if he did not find an immediate solution to the problem, he would have to disband the army or the army would dissolve on its own.

In January 1780, Washington had no choice but to procure the supplies,
cattle, and grain, through the local magistrates. In a circular letter of January
8, he told them of the desperate situation of the troops at Morristown. "Both
officers and men have been almost perishing for want. They have been alter-
nately without bread or meat . . . with a very scanty allowance of either and
frequently destitute of both." He called upon the merchants to act. If they did
not, the military would impress the needed supplies. The local officials, realizing that the supplies where going to go to the army one way or the other,
chose to comply with Washington's request.[17]

By 1781, many soldiers in the Pennsylvania Line had served for three years
or more and had only received from the state twenty dollars upon enlistment
and one hundred dollars as a gratuity in 1779. The real value of the soldiers'
bounty pay had depreciated significantly. New recruits were getting more
money at current rates.

The inequity of this practice was amplified when soldiers of the
Pennsylvania Line, believing their enlistments had expired or would soon
expire, were informed that they were considered enlisted for the duration of
the war. They were told they would not get any additional reenlisting bonuses.

The men's enlistments, which had been extended from two years to "three
years or the duration of the war," resulted in a battle of interpretation. The
men of the Pennsylvania Line interpreted the phrase "three years or the duration of the war" to mean whichever came sooner. Therefore, their three-year
enlistment would expire on January 1. Congress, naturally, believed the men
were committed for "the duration of the war" and they would have to stay with
no additional bounty money. If the men got the discharges to which they
thought they were entitled, they could reenlist and get bounty money for
doing so.

Inflation was rampant and had been so since Valley Forge. In order for
Congress to pay its bills, it received secret subsidies from France and Spain.
In 1777, the United States secured a loan of 2 million livres, worth about
381,000 Spanish silver dollars from the Farmers General. The Farmers
General had a monopoly on collecting taxes for the French government; the
organization kept a percentage of the revenue collected. The money was to be

Row of reconstructed enlisted men's huts at Jockey Hollow, Morristown National Historical Park, New Jersey. (*Lisa Nagy*)

repaid with future deliveries of tobacco. Two shipments of tobacco with a value of 150,000 livres were sent to repay the 1 million livres that were actually drawn down. Congress also borrowed money from the general public and issued bonds.[18]

But even these arrangements were not enough to meet all the fledgling country's fiscal commitments. So the Continental Congress just printed more paper money. Between May 1775 and May 1780, Congress issued $241,550,000.00 of Continental currency. To say that something was "not worth a Continental" meant it was worthless.

Money was not the only problem plaguing the army in 1780. American spy reports "from New York are so complicated and contradictory that very little credit is to be given to anything we hear." So wrote the American Brigadier General Anthony Wayne on Christmas Day, 1780. General Wayne believed the British expedition, led by the turncoat traitor Benedict Arnold that had departed New York four days earlier, was a deception "that they only wish to amuse us by some trifling manner in order to mask the grand operation."

Wayne remembered that horrible night in September 1777 and how his troops had been attacked and defeated by British General Charles Grey at Paoli, Pennsylvania. The nighttime battle was so exceptionally brutal that it became known as the Paoli Massacre. He was not about to let his army's defenses lapse. He kept his troops busy during the day working on the defenses of Fort Hill. The men received their usual miserable meal due to the lack of bread and meat. At nightfall, the exhausted men retired to their dirty bunks in cold huts. They had no blankets, no clothes, and no pay, and they felt they had been forced to stay after the expiration of their agreed-upon tour of duty. The situation resembled a bomb waiting to explode.

On December 29, Brigadier General James Potter of the Pennsylvania Militia and member of the Pennsylvania Council had arrived in camp to pay bounties. Bounty money was paid to new recruits or to men whose terms were expiring and who would reenlist. However, he did not have enough funds to pay everyone. The soldiers knew that when the officers were displeased with their rations and pay they sent a memorial petition to Congress for redress. The memorial was read in Congress on November 18, 1779. If a petition to Congress was an acceptable procedure for the officers then it might also help the enlisted men get their desperate situation resolved.

Congress had instructed that a reduction of the army was to take place on January 1, 1781. On November 1, Washington had informed the men through a general order that the regular army would "consist of 4 regiments of cavalry, or light dragoons; . . . 4 regiments of artillery; 49 regiments of infantry, exclusive of colonel Hazen's regiment; 1 regiment of artificers. . . . That the officers who shall continue in the service to the end of the war, shall also be entitled to half pay during life, to commence from the time of their reduction." It was also announced that new recruits

> who shall join the Army and that a sum not exceeding fifty dollars be allowed to every such Recruit. That the clothing be furnished and regularly served out to the troops as it becomes due and that a full compensation be made for any arrearages of clothing. The General directs that the officers of the several lines will meet accordingly and agree upon an arrangement as speedily as may be, of the officers who remain in service and of those who retire, reporting the same to Head Quarters. It is of course to be understood, that none can retire with the benefit of the provision here made, except such a number as exceeds that which is required in the establishment of the regiments.[19]

This reorganization plan did not sit well with the soldiers, as new recruits were going to receive fifty dollars and they had not received their pay in months. They were supposed to be issued new clothes, but after two months, they had not received anything to shield them against the cold winter winds. This, despite there being 564 coats, 408 shirts, 62 vests, and 367 pairs of shoes in the Philadelphia magazine, according to James Wilkinson in his December 9 clothing report.[20]

Interior of a Morristown National Historical Park hut showing the bunks and fireplace. (*Lisa Nagy*)

Mrs. Susan Blair, wife of Samuel Blair of Philadelphia, had succeeded Mrs. Reed as treasurer of the Ladies Donations of Pennsylvania. They had taken donations of money from throughout Pennsylvania for material that the ladies of Philadelphia had made into 2,005 shirts. On December 8, 1780, Mrs. Blair had notified Washington that the shirts were ready to be turned over to the army and they had used up all funds they had collected except for some trifling amount.[21] Washington wrote her a personal thank you and asked that the shirts be turned over to Colonel Samuel Miles, who was the deputy quartermaster general in Philadelphia.[22]

On the 23rd, Washington sent Miles instructions that he was to have the shirts loaded into tight casks. Eight hundred were to be sent to General Wayne of the Pennsylvania Line near Morristown; two hundred to go to Colonel Israel Shreve of the New Jersey line near Pompton; and the remainder to the deputy clothier general at Newburgh, New York. "You will inform each of the above, at the time of forwarding, from whence the shirts came."[23] Washington notified Shreve and Wayne that shirts were on their way to them from Philadelphia. Once the shirts arrived, they were to be distributed among the soldiers who were most in need or by lot.[24]

The soldiers who had experienced Valley Forge and the previous horrendous winter at Morristown knew what lay ahead—cold days and nights. They would have no money to buy food even food could be found. They would be reduced to eating firecake or horse feed if they could get it.[25] There would be days without any food at all. There would only be the snow to satisfy their hunger.

All the threatening clouds over the Continental Army were moving fast together. There was no food and no rum. And the terms of many soldiers were set to expire (or so they thought) on the same day as the reorganization and downsizing of the officers' ranks, January 1, 1781.

5

The Mark of Cain

THE PENNSYLVANIA LINE MUTINY I

*J*anuary 1, 1781, was a quiet day of seasonable temperature. No one foresaw the eruption that would take place among the troops that night. A reorganization of the Continental Army had taken effect on New Year's Day. Everyone knew it meant some officers would be leaving as their jobs had been eliminated. Since it was the last time the officers of the regiment expected to be all together, they had an elegant regimental dinner and entertainment. All the officers were present partaking in the festivities. At West Point, a similar event took place. That afternoon the officers in the Artillery Park dined with General Henry Knox.[1]

The noncommissioned soldiers of the Pennsylvanians believed that this was going to be their last day together, and that was the main topic of conversation. The terms of their enlistments were up and they had not received any reenlistment bounty money nor any clothing. This was going to be the end of being cold, hungry, and nearly naked. Adding to the unrest and discontent were copies of Sir Henry Clinton's proclamation offering free pardons to those who would return to the royal standard. These pardons would have been sneaked into the American camp over the weekend by British spies.

A gill (four ounces) of rum was part of the normal ration supplied to both the American and British troops. The American troops had been on half rations. Rum had been given only once in the last sixty days of 1780.

In his General Order of December 31, Washington had instructed "a jill [gill] of rum to be delivered to each of the soldiers who remain in service upon the occasion" of a "new arrangement of the army pursuant to the resolves of Congress of the 3rd and 21st of October and published in General Orders of the 1st of November following is to take place" on New Year's Day. A ration of rum was certainly not enough to make a grown man riotously drunk. The soldiers were enjoying the high spirit of what they believed was their final day of military service.

The soldiers purchased alcoholic spirits from the locals with whatever money they could scrounge together. Some may have been inebriated but that number would have been very small.

About eight o'clock at night, the men of Colonel Adam Hubley's 11th Pennsylvania Regiment began to "huzza" (an eighteenth-century cheer). The unit, which consisted of mostly Irish- and English-born soldiers, had a reputation for being unruly even when sober.

The 5th Pennsylvania had its own rowdies. For example, Lieutenant Abraham Wood, who had been in the unit at one time, had been tried for "his conduct unbecoming an officer and a gentleman by keeping a tippling house [tavern] and shuffle board and entertaining Soldiers."[2] He was found guilty. His commission was revoked and he was discharged.[3]

A few of the soldiers were well fortified with alcohol, and it took a several officers to quiet the men and get them into their huts by nine o'clock. Within an hour, Lieutenant Enos Reeves heard a disturbance.

> We were disturbed by the huzzas of the soldiers upon the Right Division, answered by those on the Left. I went on the Parade and found numbers in small groups whispering and busily running up and down the line. In a short time a gun was fired upon the right and answered by one on the right of the Second Brigade, and a skyrocket thrown from the center of the first, which was accompanied by a general huzza throughout the line, and the soldiers running out with their arms, accoutrements and knapsacks.[4]

The firing of the muskets and a skyrocket was a signal. Soldiers with their weapons and knapsacks came pouring out of their huts like a tidal wave onto the parade ground.

Lieutenant Enos Reeves stated that "the officers in general exerted themselves to keep the men quiet, and keep them from turning out. We each applied himself to his own company, endeavored to keep them in their huts and lay by their arms, which they would do while we were present, but the moment we left one hut to go to another, they would be out again. Their excuse was they thought it was an alarm and the enemy coming on."[5]

Charles Thomson, secretary of Congress, said the instigators of the mutiny were some British deserters who had enlisted in the Pennsylvania Line.[6]

The mutineers had formed groups near the Fort Hill Road and began to move off. While trying to stop the groups of mutineers, Captain Samuel Tolbert of Company G of the 2nd Pennsylvania Regiment was killed by Absalom Evans. Lieutenant Francis White of the 10th was shot through the thigh, and forty-eight-year-old Captain Adam Bitting was killed.[7]

The soldiers had become a mob. The night was lit up by the random firing of muskets. The smell of sulfur and the sound of musket fire were everywhere. The officers were forced to back off.

Using the disturbance near Fort Hill Road as a distraction, a group of mutineers broke open the magazine and took possession of four cannons facing east toward the enemy and spiked two fieldpieces.[8] "In taking possession of the cannon they forced the sentinel from his post and placed one of their own men. One of the mutineers coming officiously up to force him away (thinking him to be one of our sentinels), received a ball through the head and died instantly."[9]

The men argued among themselves over whether to fire the cannon or not; they feared it might arouse the locals against them. During the yelling and just before fistfights broke out, the gunner put a match to the cannon, discharging the ordnance. The scene in camp deteriorated quickly. Soldiers who were participating in the mutiny and those who were not both were wounded and killed that evening.

General Anthony Wayne, the hero of the Battle of Stony Point, and several mounted officers arrived. Wayne and Colonel Richard Butler pleaded with the mutineers to end their escapade and return to their huts. The mutineers "rejoined, it was out of his power; their business was not with the officers, but with Congress and the Governor and the Council of the State; 'twas they had wronged and they must right. With that, several platoons fired over the General's head. The General called out, 'If you mean to kill me, shoot me at once—here is my breast!' opening his coat."[10] They replied that it was not their intention to hurt or disturb an officer of the line (two or three individuals excepted); they had nothing against their officers; and they would oppose any person who attempted anything of the kind.

Meanwhile,

a part of the Fourth Regiment was paraded and led on by Captain Thomas Campbell, to recapture the cannon; they were ordered to charge and rush on. They charged but would not advance, then dispersed and left the officer alone. Soon after a soldier from the mob made a charge upon Lieutenant Colonel William Butler, who was obliged to retreat between the huts to save his life. He went around one hut and the soldier around another to head him, met Captain [Adam] Bettin who was coming down the alley, who, seeing a man coming towards him on a charge, charged his spontoon to oppose him, when the fellow fired his piece and shot the captain through the body and he died two hours later.[11]

"About twelve o'clock they sent parties to relieve or seize the old camp guard, and posted sentinels all round the camp."[12] At one o'clock, the cannons of the 4th Continental Artillery had been moved to the center of the parade ground and here they fired a shot. Some of the mutineers then moved down the parade ground, rousting soldiers who stayed in their huts and disbursing the soldiers of the 4th, 5th and 9th.

Pennsylvania Regiments who had not mutinied formed in an attempt to recapture the fieldpieces. The mutineers fired several shots over the heads of the 5th and 9th Regiments. They threatened to turn the artillery on them if they didn't move off.

Other mutineers were busy securing ammunition, horses, wagons, tents, cattle, and provisions. They took some of General Wayne's horses out of his stable and had them pull the fieldpieces.[13] "The mutineers continued huzzaing and a disorderly firing till they went off, about two o'clock, with drums and fifes playing, under command of the sergeants, in regular platoons, with a front and rear guard."

It was reported to British intelligence staff that only five or six mutineers were wounded in the night's escapade.[14] Some of the men "returned that night" and "collected more men."[15]

The mutineers, now totaling around 1,500 men, moved off the parade ground and down the road. One-half of the Pennsylvania Line was in open revolt. General Wayne stood blocking the road that led to Chatham and Elizabethtown and, therefore, the British. Wayne feared this insurrection was the work of British secret agents and that a British army might have already landed at Elizabethtown Point.

General Wayne endeavored to persuade them back, but to no purpose; he then inquired which way they were going, and they replied either to Trenton or Philadelphia. He begged them not to attempt to go to the enemy. They declared it was not their intention, and that they would hang any man who would attempt it, and for that, if the enemy should come out in consequence of this revolt, they would turn back and fight them. "If that is your sentiments," said the General, "I'll not leave you, and if you won't allow me to march in your front, I'll follow in your rear."[16]

The mutineers in columns, under the command of sergeants, marched off very civilly in the direction of Princeton and Philadelphia. They were going there to demand of Congress and the Pennsylvania legislature what was owed to them. This was not a mob now but an army on the move.

Before dawn, on January 2, 1781, Wayne wrote a request to the mutineers "to appoint one man from each regiment to represent their grievances to the General, who on the sacred honor of a gentleman and a soldier does hereby solemnly promise to exert power to obtain immediate redress of those grievances and the future plights that honor that no man shall receive the least injury on account of the part they have taken on the occasion. And that the persons of those who may be appointed to settle the affair shall be held sacred and inviolate."[17]

Wayne had lost half his command and was trying to get them back. His tone was conciliatory when he wrote, "The General hopes soon to return to camp with all his brother soldiers who took a little tour last evening."[18]

New Jersey militiamen, hearing the firing of cannons and muskets at the American camp, thought it was under attack. They fired their signal guns and lit the pyramid-shaped signal beacons on hilltops leading to the shore. That was the signal for the militia to assemble. Wayne, seeing the signal fire in the night sky, thought the British had landed in New Jersey. He sent an order to the Continentals at Pompton to hasten to Chatham and form up with the militia to repel the advancing British troops. Wayne took off after his mutinous troops hoping to get them back.

French and Indian War veterans General James Potter and Colonel Francis Johnston of the 5th Pennsylvania Regiment, who had witnessed the mutiny, left camp for Philadelphia to inform Congress of what they had seen.

Wayne wrote to General Washington about nine o'clock on Tuesday, "I am this moment with Colonels Butler and Stewart, taking horse to try to halt them on their march to Princetown [Princeton]. As a last resort, I am advised to collect them and move slowly towards Pennsylvania. . . . Their general cry is to be discharged, and they will again enlist and fight for America, a few excepted."

Richard Butler was a native Irishman whose brother was commandant of the 4th Regiment with three younger brothers in the Pennsylvania Line of the Continental Army. Walter Stewart was a Pennsylvanian of Irish descent and one of the youngest colonels in the 11th Pennsylvania Regiment. Thirty-six percent of the sergeants and 22 percent of the rank and file of the regiment had been born in Ireland. Wayne hoped that the Irish soldiers would look favorably on proposals from Irish officers.

The American camp was left in turmoil, which lasted through most of Tuesday. Some of the mutineers sneaked back to camp during the day in small groups; they hoped to coax or force other men to join the revolt. New Jersey Congressman Elias Boudinot, writing from Basking Ridge, about two miles east of the mutineers, confirms that the mutineers made contact with those of the Line who stayed in camp and they were successful in getting others to join them.[19] "The men have continued going off in small parties all day. . . . When we came to draw provisions and State stores this day, we found that near half of the men of our regiment had remained."[20]

After an orderly four-mile march the main body of mutineers stopped at Vealtown (Bernardsville). There was a large supply of wood that the troops had cut for huts the previous year; the huts had never been completed. Here the mutineers waited for the stragglers to catch up with them. At about one in the morning, a hundred head of cattle arrived from the east. The mutineers intercepted this shipment and drove the herd "to their main body, which lay in a wood near Vealtown, leaving a few behind for the use of the officers."

On Tuesday morning, the mutineers' army pushed off from Vealtown toward Pluckemin about eight miles away. Cornelius Tyger, a loyalist who was at Pluckemin, watched them all march past. "They were in very high spirits. They marched in the most perfect order and seemed as if under military discipline."[21] This army of enlisted men now included camp followers, as well as nearly one hundred head of cattle.

They continued their march and came to a halt at Middlebrook, New Jersey. They were now near Bound Brook and out of the Watchung Mountains. This was familiar ground to them as the American army had wintered here in

A drawing of the Pennsylvania Line Mutiny from the *Life and Service of General Anthony Wayne* (1845), the earliest known depiction of the event. Note that the actual huts were one story, not two, and General Wayne confronted the mutineers on the road heading out of camp, not inside the camp grounds. (*Willliam L. Clements Library*)

1778–79. If the mutineers wanted to join the British, they were just twenty miles from Perth Amboy by an easy journey over flat land. The British stronghold of Staten Island lay just across the Arthur Kill from Perth Amboy. The question on everybody's mind was, what were the mutineers going to do?

Wayne sent a message to the mutineers' army asking for a sergeant or man from each regiment to come to his quarters to present their complaints. Wayne, Butler, and Stewart are believed to have quartered at Derrick Van Veghten's house. The sergeants came and presented their grievances, and told how they wanted them resolved. The sergeants returned to the troops but left a sergeant and twelve men with Wayne, Butler, and Stewart. The trio wasn't sure if the guards were their protectors or their jailers.

That same day, Elias Boudinot, while at Basking Ridge, wrote to New Jersey governor William Livingston to inform him of the mutiny of the Pennsylvania Line. Boudinot gave his letter to John Breese who rode his horse at high speed all the way to Trenton to deliver the letter to the Governor. Breese was paid six dollars by Governor Livingston for his effort.[22]

Boudinot was the former colonel commissary general of prisoners and then New Jersey delegate to the Continental Congress. The fifty-year-old lawyer reported to the governor that the Pennsylvania Line had turned out at nine o'clock after being remarkably still until that time. They seized the ammunition and the artillery, spiked two fieldpieces, and marched off with four others. Boudinot says that "the whole neighborhood was alarmed by their noises and depredations." His report stating that they abused many of the inhabitants and took what they pleased does not appear to be totally accurate. Although some random acts of violence probably occurred from individual soldiers, no one else reported such abuses. All the other reports tell of the orderly military conduct of the mutineers.

Boudinot confirmed that the mutineers did make contact with those of the Pennsylvania Line who stayed in camp. They were successful in convincing others to join the revolt. He stated that "I just now followed the rear of the whole" and had conversations with some of the mutineers. They told me they wanted to go to Congress to insist on their pay, clothing and discharge for all above three years enlistment." He confirmed the mutineers encamped at Vealtown.[23]

Brigadier General James Potter and Colonel Francis Johnston notified Brigadier General Nathaniel Heard of the mutiny before they left early on Tuesday for Philadelphia. By noon on Wednesday, General Heard had sent instructions to deploy the New Jersey Militia between the mutineers and the enemy. There was a post at Elizabethtown so he positioned Colonel John Webster and the 1st Regiment of Middlesex County Militia to guard between Rahway and Perth Amboy, Colonel John Taylor, his state troops to South Amboy, and Colonel Frederick Frelinghuysen and the 1st Battalion of Somerset County Militia to Quibbletown (New Market). He also sent Colonel Hendrick (Henry) Vandike (Van Dyke) and his state troops to Raritan Landing (on the north shore of the Raritan River west of New Brunswick), and Colonel Nathaniel Scudder and the 1st Regiment of Monmouth County Militia to New Brunswick. Heard would command from New Brunswick "to give the necessary orders that the regiments may support each other in case of necessity."[24]

By Saturday, these units would be supplemented by Colonel Courtland's Regiment, which was called into the field.[25] Heard's concerns were that the British would reestablish the floating bridge across the Arthur Kill near Elizabethtown Point, which would allow them to quickly move an army from Staten Island into New Jersey. The British dominated the coastal water along the New Jersey coast. The Americans were rightly concerned that they could land troops anywhere they wanted.

On Wednesday, January 3, news of the mutiny had reached Joseph Reed, president of Pennsylvania. In July 1775, Reed had traveled with General Washington from Philadelphia to Cambridge, Massachusetts, and served as Washington's secretary during the siege of Boston. In 1776, he was the adjutant general of the Continental Army. He understood the potential consequences of the mutiny and that the Continental Army was on the brink of a total collapse. Now president of Pennsylvania and residing in Philadelphia, Reed knew anarchy would rule the city if the mutineers reached it and took out their frustrations on unarmed civilians. Reed had always seen himself as a moderate and the great mediator of Pennsylvania's fractionalized political parties. Now he would put this skill to work resolving another problem.

Reed sent a message to Captain Samuel Morris of the First Troop Philadelphia City Cavalry (also known as the Philadelphia Light Horse) that, by last account, the mutineers "were in full march for the city, but I hope this will not be the case. It is our duty to be prepared for all events, and I have, therefore, to request you would attach three of the light horse to accompany General St. Clair and the Marquis de la Fayette . . . in the meantime the whole troop to be in readiness, as directed today."[26]

General Arthur St. Clair, the ranking officer of the Pennsylvania Line, was a Scottish-born physician in his late forties. He had served in the British army in the 60th Regiment of Foot under Generals Amherst and Wolfe at Louisburg and Quebec. He continued his service in Boston until he resigned in 1762 and moved to Bedford, Pennsylvania. His business enterprises prospered after he moved to the Ligonier Valley. He became the largest landholder in Western Pennsylvania and a justice of the court.

The Marquis de Lafayette and Lieutenant Colonel John Laurens, aide to Washington, were on another assignment and had planned to pass through Trenton and Princeton on their way to Washington's headquarters. At daybreak the next morning, an assemblage set out from Connolly's Tavern on Race Street in Philadelphia accompanied by three members of the Philadelphia Light Horse. The assemblage was composed of Generals Lafayette and St. Clair; twenty-six–year-old Lieutenant Colonel John Laurens, the son of Henry Laurens former president of the Continental Congress; and forty-one-year-old Irish-born Colonel Thomas Proctor, a Philadelphia carpenter, of the 4th Continental Artillery, previously a major of the Pennsylvania Artillery.[27]

After Congress learned of the mutiny of the Pennsylvania Line on Wednesday, they did what they did best: On the evening of January 3, they appointed a three-person committee to confer with Joseph Reed and the Pennsylvania Council. The committee consisted of John Mathews, a thirty-one-year-old lawyer in Charles Town, South Carolina; John Sullivan, a forty-year-old New Hampshire lawyer and former major general in the Continental Army; and John Witherspoon a fifty-seven-year-old Scottish-born Presbyterian minister and president of the College of New Jersey, which later became Princeton University.

Witherspoon, who had graduated from the University of Edinburgh and arrived at Princeton in 1768, was the only minister to sign the Declaration of Independence. He maintained traces of his Scottish brogue until his death.

On the 5th, two more people, Dr. Theodorick Bland and Samuel J. Atlee, were added to the committee. Bland, a thirty-eight-year-old Virginia-born graduate of the University of Edinburgh where he studied medicine, was from Prince George County, Virginia and had been a colonel in the 1st Continental Regiment of Light Dragoons. Atlee, a forty-one-year-old from Lancaster, Pennsylvania, had been a captain in the French and Indian War and colonel of the Pennsylvania Musketry Battalion in 1776. He was one of the heroes of the Battle of Long Island on October 27, 1776. He had stayed and fought from the Old Stone House until his Pennsylvania Musketry Battalion was forced from the residence.[28]

General William Alexander, also known as Lord Stirling, came to Atlee's support and twice they recaptured the house. They battled three British Regiments under the command of General Charles Cornwallis. Atlee's unit fought at the Old Stone House until noon, thus allowing most of the Continental Army in Brooklyn to withdraw to Brooklyn Heights. That afternoon, General Alexander surrendered with his troops when the Hessians were able to cutoff their link with the other American troops. Colonel Atlee was wounded in the battle, taken prisoner, and held by the British until he was exchanged in October 1778.

Since some of the mutineers had enlisted in 1776, they had most likely made their escape at the Battle of Long Island due to the heroic stand made by Colonel Atlee and his men. It was hoped that he, along with the other committee members who were in the Continental Army, would be able to wield their influence with the men. The committee was given the authority

"to take such measures as may appear necessary to quiet the disturbance in the
Pennsylvania line."[29]

On Wednesday morning, the mutineers'
army left the Middlebrook encampment and
continued in a southerly direction. Small
parties of men continued to leave
Morristown intending to catch up with the
mutineers on the march. Dissension arose in
the ranks of the mutineers as some wanted
to push on to Philadelphia and Congress
while others wanted to halt at Princeton.

French print of Major General
John Sullivan from a painting by
Alexander Campbell of Williams-
burg, Virginia.
(*William L. Clements Library*)

The residents of Princeton, who had gotten word that the mutineers were going to
pass through their little town on their march
to Philadelphia, had the Reverend Samuel
Smith write a plea to Governor Livingston.
Smith was a professor of moral philosophy at the College of New Jersey. The
residents were fearful that they were about to be plundered of provisions and
firewood. They wanted permission to use the public stores to supply the mutineers. They were aware that officers of the regular army had gone to the
Delaware River to remove all the boats so that the mutineers could not cross
to Pennsylvania. They feared the wrath of the mutineers when they discovered
this.

Smith, the handsome blue-eyed well-dressed Princeton resident, said
these were Pennsylvania soldiers and "their own state ought to be exposed to
the inconveniences which they may occasion rather than the Jerseys . . . .
With the [Delaware River] betwixt them and the enemy and in the heart of
the country, the Congress will be able to treat them upon a better footing."[30]

After arriving at Princeton on the 4th, a committee of sergeants met with
Wayne, Butler, and Stewart and again aired their grievances. It was agreed
that a committee would continue the journey to Philadelphia and present
their grievances to Congress. The mutineers' army would come to a halt as
they encamped on Colonel George Morgan's farm to the southeast of the college town between the road to Trenton and the Millstone River.[31]

The Board of Sergeants occupied Nassau Hall for their quarters. Built in

1756, it housed the College of New Jersey, and was named for King William III, Prince of Orange–Nassau. It was planned by Robert Smith and Dr. William Shippen of Philadelphia. The design called for a building 177 feet by 54 feet. It contained a dining room, lecture rooms, library, prayer hall, and living quarters for the faculty as well as rooms for the students. It was to house 147 students with 3 to a room. The college provided a bed, mattress, table, and chair, while the students brought their own blankets, linens, and rug. The stone building was in poor condition after having been used by the British in December 1776 as a barracks and a stable. Wayne, Butler, and Stewart most likely were housed in one of several taverns across the street.

In compliance with Wayne's request, a sergeant from each regiment met with Butler, Stewart and Wayne and stated their complaints.

> Many men continued in the service, after the expiration of the enlistment.
>
> The arrearages of pay, and the depreciation not yet made up; and the soldiers suffering every privation for want of money and clothing.
>
> That it is very hurtful to the feelings of the soldiery to be prevented from disposing of their depreciation certificates as they please, without consulting any person on the occasion.
>
> It is agreed on the part of the General and Colonels that one disinterested sergeant or private from each regiment shall, with the commanding officer of the corps, when an enlistment is disputed, determine in the case.[32]

A sergeant from each regiment was to be appointed to carry an address to Congress, backed by the general and field officers.

WASHINGTON WAS AT HIS HEADQUARTERS at New Windsor, New York, when Major Benjamin Fishbourne, aide to General Wayne since April 1779, arrived about noon with Wayne's letter and the news of the mutiny of the Pennsylvanians. Washington immediately feared for the safety of West Point and sent to inquire of the situation of the New England troops stationed there.

The reorganization ordered by Congress had been accomplished at West Point on January 2, as well as the dispensing of a gill of rum to the soldiers. New clothes were promised to the men but they were told that they would be sent in a day or two. On the 5th, the soldiers received clothes but no coats. The coats never came, and the men made overcoats and waistcoats out of blankets.[33]

The previous year, a large number of Massachusetts soldiers at West Point left camp intending to go home as they considered their enlistments were up. They had to be forcibly brought back to camp. Washington had reported that situation to Congress two days later.

It is with infinite pain I inform Congress, that we are reduced again to a situation of extremity for want of meat. On several days of late, the troops have been entirely destitute of any, and for a considerable time past they have been at best, at half, a quarter, an eighth allowance of this essential article of provision. The men have borne their distress in general with a firmness and patience never exceeded, and every commendation is due the officers for encouraging them to it, by exhortation and example. They have suffered equally with the men, and, their relative situations considered, rather more. But such reiterated, constant instances of want are too much for the soldiery, and cannot but lead to alarming consequences. Accordingly two regiments of the Connecticut Line mutinied and got under arms on Thursday night, and but for the timely exertions of some of their officers who got notice of it, it might have been the case with the whole, with a determination to return home, or at best to gain subsistence at the point of the bayonet. After a good deal of expostulation by their officers and some of the Pennsylvania line who had come to their assistance, after parading their Regiments upon the occasion, the Men were prevailed on to go to their huts; but a few nevertheless turned out again with their packs, who are now confined. Colonel Meigs who acted with great propriety in endeavoring to suppress the mutiny, was struck by one of the soldiers. I wish our situation was better with respect to provision in other quarters; but it is not. They are in as great distress at West Point to the full, and by a Letter of the 19th from Colonel Van Schaick at Albany, he informs me, that the Garrison of Fort Schuyler had then only a month's supply on hand, and that there was no more provision to send them. From this detail Congress will see how distressing our situation is.[34]

Philip Schuyler wrote to New York Governor George Clinton, "It is for the present quelled, but we have too much reason to apprehend that it will show itself soon and more seriously unless provisions arrive. The Officers live chiefly on bread & water to give the men all they can, and the latter have for ten days past much oftener been without than with any and at no time when that period have they had more than half allowance. Our greatest distress is in the article of meat."[35]

Washington had planned to get to Philadelphia ahead of the Pennsylvania mutineers' army and use his influence to turn the tide. He gave orders for a small escort on horseback to be prepared to leave the next morning for Philadelphia. Now that the Pennsylvania Line had mutinied, he feared the New Englanders would follow suit leading to a general mutiny of the entire army.

Washington surely wondered if Sir Henry Clinton was behind this mutiny. Had Clinton sent letters of inducement to the Pennsylvania soldiers as he had the Connecticut troops? The situation could spiral out of control.

Because most of the levies were in truly miserable condition including the lack of clothing to protect them from the winter storms, Washington had been obliged to discharge many men. The rest of the state levies terms of service had expired the last day of December. This had reduced the garrison of West Point to the bare minimum. The troops around West Point were in deplorable condition. General Samuel Holden Parsons described the status of the Connecticut troops as "being wholly destitute of bread within a week and no rum has found its way to camp for a long time past. . . . We have six hundred men unfit for duty for want of proper clothing; most of them have no coat of any kind; they have received no money for near twelve months, and some are fifteen months in arrears of pay."

Because of the lack of pay, the men needed money and were forced to sell their State of Connecticut Pay Table notes. Since the notes were depreciating rapidly, they had to sell them for whatever cash they could get. Speculators and depreciation caused prices to rise and whatever money the soldiers could acquire did not go far.

Parsons provided an idea of the amount of cash in camp. "I believe I have as much money as any officer in camp, and to clearly show you our condition, I have counted every farthing of cash I possess in the world, and it amounts to eight Continental dollars and two-thirds of a dollar and where or when shall I add another, I know no more than a child yet unborn." His $8.66 in January 1781 had the same purchasing power as 9 cents did in January 1777.[36]

Washington had pleaded with Governor George Clinton of New York for supplies for the army along the Hudson River.

> It is with the utmost regret I am compelled to represent to you, the distressed situation of the troops on this river for want of bread, and the disagreeable prospects before us. The army has been served for several days

past, with but a small pittance of their rations, there is no flour in the magazines, and I cannot learn from whence the next supply is to be derived. Under these circumstances, it is impossible for me to be responsible for the important posts on this river, or even to assure myself the troops can be kept together from one day to another.

I have therefore to entreat your Excellency that the most vigorous and effectual measures may be instantly adopted for procuring relief . . . unless some spirited exertions, or coercive means are immediately made use of, for obtaining a supply; I can see nothing but ruin stare us in the face.[37]

Managing the supplies on hand at the posts around West Point became a concern for Washington. A supply of salted beef arrived from the east and he ordered one hundred barrels to be sent to Albany for the use of the Fort Schuyler garrison and "the remainder should be kept in reserve, and not issued on any account whatever."[38]

Two days later, Washington changed his mind and stopped the shipment of one hundred barrels of salted beef that was to have gone to Albany. Officers were allowed an additional ration and the policy had been to allow the extra rations to accumulate for future use. Washington wanted this practice stopped, foreseeing a situation where the officers would demand their banked extra rations when supplies were in short supply. This would have reduced the rations available for the enlisted men who were already on short supply. Washington advised Major General William Heath that the officers were to draw their extra rations regularly and not be allowed to accumulate more than a week's supply of additional rations.[39]

Washington had written to General Benjamin Lincoln concerning the army's situation in respect to clothing, which was "really distressing."

By collecting all our remnants, and those of a thousand colors and kinds, we shall scarcely make them comfortable. Uniformity, one of the essentials of discipline and every thing in the appearance of a soldier, must be dispensed with; and what makes the matter more mortifying is, that we have, I am positively assured, ten thousand complete suits ready in France, and laying there because our public agents cannot agree whose business it is to ship them. . . . You tell me there is clothing enough lately arrived in private bottoms (privately owned ships) to supply the army. This, my dear sir, is only tantalizing the naked; such is the miserable state of continental credit, that we cannot command a yard of it[40]

The West Point garrison needed flour, clothing, and in short everything.

Washington realized that he was needed in New York and that he had to use his influence to keep the New Englanders from following the lead of the Pennsylvanians. He also needed to stay put to ensure that a second Benedict Arnold did not turn West Point over to the British for gold sovereigns.

After the Arnold incident, a campaign to find other turncoats commenced. None were found but a British Headquarters' record recently discovered indicated that they were in contact in 1780 with someone who they believed was another high-ranking American officer in the area of West Point. The negotiations ended when Benedict Arnold fled and John André was arrested. Washington stated that part of the reason he chose to stay was due to the "advice of the general officers at this post [West Point] against the measure strengthened by the advice of [New York] Governor Clinton's opinion, restrained my setting out for the revolted troops upon first notice I had of them."[41]

Washington had definite opinions about dealing with mutineers. In a letter to Artemus Ward on April 4, 1776, he said, "All attempts to mutiny, or disobedience of orders should be severely punished."[42]

Writing from Valley Forge on February 16, 1778, to Governor George Clinton of New York, Washington warned him, "A part of the army has been a week, without any kind of flesh, and the rest three or four days. Naked and starving as they are, we cannot enough admire the incomparable patience and fidelity of the soldiery, that they have not been ere this excited by their sufferings, to a general mutiny and dispersion. Strong symptoms, however, of discontent have appeared in particular instances; and nothing but the most active efforts every where can long avert so shocking a catastrophe."[43] Washington was well aware that mutinies would develop because of how poorly his troops were being supplied with necessities.

Washington knew he could not leave. Therefore, he sent Major Fishbourne back to General Wayne to tell him that he had to manage the Pennsylvania Line mutineers himself. Washington told Wayne to stay with the mutineers and "if you can bring them to a negotiation matters may afterwards be accommodated; but that an attempt to reduce them by force will either drive them to the enemy or dissipate them in such a manner that they will never be recovered."[44]

Wayne was already putting into action this plan. But they differed on how to deal with Congress. Wayne had sent a warning to Congress "to go out of the way to avoid the first burst of the storm."[45] He told Congress to get out of Philadelphia before the mutineers arrived.

Washington, always mindful of the army being subservient to Congress, would never tell Congress what to do. In addition, he was afraid of what might happen if the mutineers found that Congress was not present to hear their complaints. "The mutineers, finding the body before whom they were determined to lay their grievances fled, might take a new turn and wreak their vengeance upon persons and properties of the citizens and in a town the size of Philadelphia there are numbers who would join them in such a business. I would therefore wish you, if you have time, to recall that advice and rather recommend it to them to stay and hear what propositions the soldiers have to make."[46]

General Wayne had sent orders to the officers at Morristown to get their arms and horses and proceed to Rocky Hill just north of Princeton. The officers received the order about 8:00 p.m.; by 9:00 p.m., they left for Bound Brook on the Middlebush Road as a mounted unit under the command of Colonel Craig. About 11:00 p.m., Major Moore and Hamilton were detached, as it was thought that they could safely get past the mutineers and make contact with General Wayne and inform him of what the officers were going to do.

Hamilton and Moore arrived at the outskirts of Princeton at noon on Thursday and were stopped by a guard. The guard treated them with a great deal of insolence and turned them back. They went to Pennytown (Pennington) where they met up with two companies under the command of Colonel Harmar.[47]

On Thursday morning, the Corps of Mounted Officers continued their journey, traveling to Cranberry (Cranbury). Here they waited until evening, at which time they continued their journey to Allentown arriving about seven o'clock. They had taken a position to the southeast of the mutineers' army.

Sometime during Thursday, the committee of sergeants delivered the following proposals to General Wayne.

ARTICLE 1. That all and such men as were enlisted in the year '76 or '77 and received the bounty of 20 dollars, shall be without any delay discharged; and all arrears of pay and depreciation of pay be paid to the said men, without any fraud, clothing included.

ARTICLE 2. Such men as were enlisted since the year '77 and received the $120 dollars bounty, or any more additions, shall be entitled to their discharge at the expiration of three years from the said enlistment, and their full depreciation of pay, and all arrears of clothing.

ARTICLE 3. That all such men as belong to the different regiments as are enlisted of late for the war, that they receive the remainder of their bounty and pay and all arrears of clothing. That they shall return to their respective corps and do their duty as formerly, and no aspersion be cast and no grievances to be repeated to the said men.

ARTICLE 4. Those soldiers that are enlisted and receive their discharge and all arrearages of pay and clothing, shall not be compelled to stay by any former officers commanding any longer time than what is agreeable to their own pleasure and disposition. Of those that do remain for a small time as volunteers, that they shall be at their own disposal and pleasure.

ARTICLE 5. As we now depend and rely upon you, Gen. Wayne, for to represent and repeat our grievances, we do agree, in conjunction, from this date, January 4, in six days for to complete and settle every such demand as the above five articles mention.

ARTICLE 6. That the whole line are actually agreed and determined to support these above articles in every particular.[48]

General Wayne reviewed the mutineers' proposal. Knowing that any resolution had to come from the state of Pennsylvania, he sent the following reply:

That all such non-commissioned officers and soldiers as are justly entitled to their discharges shall be immediately settled with, their accounts properly adjusted, and certificates for their pay and arrearages of pay and clothing given them, agreeable to the resolution of Congress, and the late act of the Honorable Assembly of Pennsylvania, for making up the depreciation, and be discharged from the service of the United States.

That all such non-commissioned officers and privates belonging to the respective regiments, artillery or infantry, as are not entitled to their discharge, shall also be settled with, and certificates given them for their pay, depreciation, and clothing, in like manner as those before mentioned, which certificates are to be redeemable at as short period, as the nature of the case admits; to be paid in hard cash, or an equivalent in continental money of these states, and be immediately furnished with comfortable warm clothing, they returning to their duty as worthy faithful soldiers.

These propositions are founded on principles of justice and honor, between the United States and the soldiery, which is all that reasonable men can expect, or that a general can promise consistent with his station and duty, and the mutual benefit of their country and the line which he has so long the honor of commanding. If the soldiers are determined not to leave reason and justice govern on this occasion, he has only to lament the total and unfortunate situation to which they will reduce themselves and their country.[49]

When the committee of sergeants received Wayne's response, they were concerned as to its true meaning. They had appointed William Bowzar their secretary and had him write to Wayne asking for clarification as to who specifically would get a discharge.

Wayne knew Washington's position regarding Congress and the military, and he also knew that the politicians would probably send the matter to a committee for discussion prior to making any decision. It was anyone's guess what would come out of the committee. He replied to the mutineers, "I cannot think myself fully empowered to decide upon the occasion, but will immediately send off an express to the Governor and Council of the State of Pennsylvania, and desire a committee of that body to meet the Line at Trenton, or elsewhere, who with myself and Colonels Butler and Stewart, will give you a full and explicit answer."[50]

The committee of sergeants was not happy with Wayne's response. They told him that they could receive "any gentleman of rank" right where they were. They threatened that if they were not satisfied "we must take some measures that will procure our own happiness."

A joint letter from Colonels Richard Butler and Walter Stewart and General Anthony Wayne was carried by Major Charles Stewart to Joseph Reed. The letter enclosed the correspondence from the committee of sergeants and their replies. Butler, Stewart, and Wayne asked for an agent with full authority to negotiate a settlement and "what prospects you have of furnishing an immediate supply of clothing and cash, which will be indispensably necessary to ensure success."[51]

About three o'clock on Thursday, Generals Lafayette and St. Clair, Lieutenant Colonel John Laurens, and Colonel Thomas Proctor of the Pennsylvania Artillery arrived at Trenton. They were accompanied by a three-person detail consisting of Privates David H. Conyngham, Isaac Cox, and Thomas Irwin of the First Troop Philadelphia City Cavalry.

St. Clair discovered the mutineers at Princeton were only willing to talk to Colonels Butler and Stewart and General Wayne and would allow only those three to "pass their lines." They had refused a chief justice and some legislators that day. Their post was "well chosen, and the guards regularly mounted."

According to St. Clair some of the mutineers began to talk about New York "which makes it justly feared that there are among them some emissaries of the enemy." This situation "induces Governor Livingston to think it would be prudent, in case they persist, to suffer them to pass the Delaware, as it then would be out of their power to go to the enemy." St. Clair said that he and the marquis were "planning to get to Maidenhead tonight, to be able to get them early tomorrow, before they have opportunity to intoxicate themselves." In a postscript he related that the mutineers "had refused General Wayne's terms and propose to march tomorrow."[52]

Sometime on Thursday, the forty-three-year-old Colonel Stephen Moylan of the 4th Continental Dragoons arrived at Princeton. The mutineers allowed him to join General Wayne's staff. Moylan, born in Cork, Ireland, to wealthy parents, had been educated in Paris. He had engaged in shipping first at Lisbon, Portugal, before immigrating to Philadelphia in 1768. He joined the army at Cambridge and was made muster master. In March 1776, he became a secretary to General Washington and in June, Congress appointed him quartermaster general of the army. he resigned the end of September. In January 1777, he was made a colonel of the 4th Continental Dragoons.

General Wayne now had a staff of three Irish colonels with him at Princeton to negotiate with the Pennsylvania Line Mutineers who were predominately English and Irish.

6

A Sleeping Giant Awakes

THE PENNSYLVANIA LINE MUTINY II

*H*idden by the swamp grass that rises from the marsh to the height of a horse's eye, a solitary figure moves through the darkness. The swamp maze that was the New Jersey shore near Elizabethtown was well traveled by those who wanted to keep their activities away from the prying eyes of the American army and their outpost at Elizabethtown Point. On those nights when the moon shone brightly, the soldiers at the post might catch a glimpse of a solitary figure in the swamp. They knew it was most likely just one of the locals participating in the "London trade" as smuggling was called in New Jersey.

This was an extremely lucrative profession with relatively low risk, as the American army's constant manpower shortages kept them focused on their primary mission, which was detecting the movements of the British army and raids of the loyalist militia. If the soldiers from the outpost went chasing shadows in the swamp and took one misstep in the maze, they would be stuck knee deep in the muck. New Jersey Governor William Livingston said that some participants in the "London trade" had opened stores stocked with smuggled goods. On January 3, Major John Adam, deputy commissary of prisoners, stationed at Elizabethtown, wrote to Livingston that he was aware of the improper conduct of the inhabitants of Elizabethtown on the arrival of emissaries from the enemy that had come under a flag of truce.[1]

Our solitary traveler this night was Joseph Gould, a British spy and a pretend patriot, or so the British thought. John André, adjutant-general of the British Army in America, had called him "my good friend. Joseph Gould." But Gould had been working as a spy for American Colonel Elias Dayton of the

3rd New Jersey Regiment since at least May 1, 1780.[2] Loyalist Brigadier General Cortland Skinner on March 15, 1781, suspected that Gould was no longer in their employment and reported the same to Sir Henry Clinton, but the damage was done.[3]

Joseph Gould had made this journey on many occasions through the salt marsh and then across the Arthur Kill to the swamps on British-held Staten Island. He would be exposed to view only for a very short time while traversing the waters of the Arthur Kill. It was here at Elizabethtown Point that the Arthur Kill was its narrowest. The name Arthur Kill comes from the Dutch and means water channel. It is about ten miles long and has now been widened to six hundred feet across at its narrowest point. At the time of the American Revolution it was lined on both sides by salt marsh for its whole length except for its southern end at the high ground at Perth Amboy. The area made great cover for anyone participating in the "London trade" as well as spies on both sides. There was very little effort on either side to stop an individual who wanted to cross the Arthur Kill.

On two occasions Staten Island had been connected by a dry path to New Jersey. In the winter of 1779–1780, the Arthur Kill froze solid. One could walk across the ice to get to the other side. The other time was when a floating bridge was constructed by the British to connect Staten Island to New Jersey for the quick movement of troops.

After Gould had reached the safety of the Staten Island salt marsh around 10:00 p.m., he heard the boom from the American alarm guns from both Morristown and Newark. When he looked back to New Jersey, he could see in the distance the signal beacon, a very large fire etched against the sky. At Hobart Mountain in Springfield stood a wooden pyramid filled with dry brush, 20 feet high and about 18 feet square at its base. Next to it sat a huge squat mortar, affectionately known as "the Old Sow."

In New Jersey, a chain of signal beacons had been erected at the highest points and when he heard alarm guns call out local militia to warn of a British attack, Gould knew something was amiss—something more important than the information he was bringing. A person by the name of Fegany who came after him told of a mutiny by the Pennsylvania Line of the Continental Army. Gould now had something important to tell at British Headquarters and he would surely be amply rewarded in hard currency.

It was hard currency, gold and silver, that drove men and women to be spies and risk death if caught. If a British spy was caught by the Americans, he would not be given the honor of a firing squad for that was reserved for gentlemen. Being a spy was not conduct befitting a gentleman. Spies were hanged. Beheading the corpse of a spy, sticking the head on a spike, and marching all the troops past the head had not been uncommon early in the war. Washington had discontinued the practice, but this was cold comfort. There had been a long-standing tradition of displaying spiked heads of murderers and traitors on the gate of London Bridge. The practice dates back to at least 1305 when Edward I had William Wallace drawn on a sledge to Smithfield, hanged, emboweled, beheaded, quartered, and his head set on a pole on London Bridge. Simon Fraser's head was at the gate at the north (London) end of the bridge in 1306.[4] In London, the head would be parboiled and covered with tar to keep the birds from picking at the flesh.

An American spy caught by the British under General Clinton's command would get to visit with the notoriously cruel and sadistic William Cunningham, the provost general at the Sugar House. It was said that he would give a starving man poisoned food or tell him the food he was being given was poisoned. If the British thought that there were coconspirators involved, Cunningham was known to have provided daily beatings. The rations he provided consisted of fouled water and maggot-filled biscuits.

A favorite ploy of Cunningham's was to march the spy to the courtyard for an execution to try to get them to talk. He would begin the execution then stop at the last possible moment and hustle the spy back to jail. When Cunningham got tired of his cat and mouse games, he would have the charge transferred to one of the prison ships in Wallabout Bay along the northwestern shore of Brooklyn.[5] The American general Jeremiah Johnson described the British technique for keeping these prison ships from becoming overcrowded: "death made room for all."

Gould was frustrated because he was unable to secure transportation to York Island until the morning of the 3rd. If he got to headquarters first with the news of the mutiny, he would surely get a pouch of silver guineas. British Headquarters in New York was aware that the American alarm guns had been fired and the signal fire lit but had no knowledge of what caused this action. They knew these signals would bring out the New Jersey Militia in droves, but for what purpose? Was this a signal for an attack on a British outpost? If so, where and when? Were the Americans staging another nighttime attack on Paulus Hook as they had on August 19, 1779?

British case agents, the people in charge of spies, knew that Major Oliver De Lancey Jr. would be looking for intelligence related to the signals. De Lancey Jr. was the thirty-one-year-old deputy adjutant general and head of the British army's secret service in New York.

One such case agent was Isaac Ogden, a refugee from Newark. He had been a lawyer in New Jersey and a former member of the New Jersey Provincial Congress in 1775. Prior to his coming into New York, he worked in Brigadier Cortland Skinner's spy network. On the morning of January 3, Isaac Ogden sent a note to Oliver De Lancey that three men had just arrived in New York from Newark. They said there had been a mutiny among the Pennsylvania troops and three officers had been killed. The alarm guns were fired on the occasion and all was confusion. "Mr. Ogden," he said, speaking of himself in third person, "hopes to give more particulars when Gould gets in who is on his way here from Staten Island."[6]

THAT MORNING THE TEMPERATURE WAS MILD but the boat ride across the great expanse of Upper New York Bay was agonizingly slow. Upon landing, Gould had only a short walk to British Headquarters at 1 Broadway at the lower end of the island opposite Bowling Green. It was the very impressive former residence of Captain Archibald Kennedy, formerly of the Royal Navy, one of the largest landowners in New York City, and a British spy.

Kennedy had been on parole in New Jersey until his recent departure for England. The British Army paid rent to Kennedy, the future 11th Earl of Cassillis, for the use of the building. When the large brick building built by Captain Kennedy's father came into view and Gould saw all the couriers just hanging around waiting to be sent back to their respective units, he knew he had made it. He would be first with the news of why the American army's alarm guns were fired and why the signal fire blazed. As he passed through the front door of the British Headquarters, the clink of silver guineas raced through his head.[7]

On this same day, January 3, 1781, the British army had already settled into their winter recess. The business of war was to wait until the spring campaign. The army's main duties were gathering firewood to stay warm, procuring provisions, and recuperate.

Gould's contact at British Headquarters was Major Oliver De Lancey. When Gould delivered his news, it struck like a thunder clap that reverberated throughout British Headquarters. General Sir Henry Clinton, commander of all His Majesty's forces in North America, dispatched the couriers. He sent them to the British Grenadiers, British Light Infantry, 37th and 42nd Regiments, and the Hessian Grenadiers and Jaegers on Long Island with instructions to be ready to march at a moment's notice dressed and with two days' provisions.[8] The couriers galloped away as fast as they could.

The sleeping giant was now awake. Hessian General Carl Wilhelm von Hachenberg states that despite all the activity "at headquarters everything is very secret" and that the soldiers got their information from Rivington's newspaper.[9]

Sir Henry Clinton's plan was that troops could be brought over to Staten Island and from there they could be landed at the British posts of Paulus Hook and Fort De Lancey on Bergen Neck or anywhere from the British post at Sandy Hook to Perth and South Amboy to Elizabethtown. These troops, once in New Jersey, could be used to provide cover to any mutineers wishing to join the British Royal Standard.

In order to formulate a plan, Clinton needed information on the mutineers' intentions. He was good at formulating plans and implementing military actions, such as his successful siege of Charles Town, South Carolina, the previous fall. But quick decisive strokes were not Clinton's forte.

Clinton sent Joseph Gould back to Elizabethtown to contact Andrew Gautier Jr., a resident British spy operating there. Gautier was the son of a noted cabinetmaker and an educated man. He had attended for a year King's College now known as Columbia University. His wife was the daughter of Captain Thomas Brown, a slave trader. The Browns lived in a stone house near Paulus Hook on the New Jersey side of the North, or Hudson, River.

The British received daily intelligence from spies, deserters, and market people who came to town to sell their produce for hard cash. They gathered information on what was happening behind the American lines. One such report came from Hugh Haggerty who had come into New York from Wantage, Sussex County, New Jersey. He brought the information that the "Pennsylvania troops [are] in the old huts at Mt. Kemble near Morristown [and are] much in want of clothing." He reported that "there are a lot of soldiers whose time has expired. There are the three-year men and the six-month men are also expired. The rebels have long been trying to recruit in Sussex but without success."[10]

Abraham and Thomas Ward had left Newark at daybreak. Thomas Ward was an American army deserter who had been a sergeant in Malcolm's Additional Continental Regiment. He went over to the British in June 1777. His property of 100 acres in New Jersey and 600 acres in the Clove in Orange County, New York, were confiscated. He supported himself in New York by conducting a wood-cutting operation for the British military and anyone else with cash. He was often employed by Colonel Edmund Fanning, of the King's American Regiment to go to rebel-controlled areas bordering New York City to enlist men. By 1779, Ward had graduated to intelligence-gathering missions. He was appointed a captain in the Loyal Refugee Volunteers when they were formed in 1779, and in January 1781, he was the commander at Bergen Point.

Abraham and Thomas Ward brought information they picked up from people who had come from Morristown. Their secondhand intelligence was that "the Militia are all in arms about Morristown and that the Alarm Gun was firing about the Mountain and alarm guns fired in Newark."[11]

A deposition was taken from Riverius Lee who had left Morristown on December 26 and Newark on December 30. The New Englander reported on the situation in the American camp: "They do not discharge the men [whose] times have expired nor do they pay them which causes much discontent."[12] Captain Stewart Ross of the armed sloop *Neptune* reported that he had seen the beacon the previous night and Mr. Loyd told him there was a mutiny in the Jerseys.[13]

On Wednesday the 3rd, Andrew Gautier Jr. sent a report in cipher from his sickbed in Elizabethtown which was received at British Headquarters on Thursday the 4th. His correspondence, which was addressed to Daniel Gautier, his brother, told of a mutiny by 1,500 men of the Pennsylvania troops, commanded by General Anthony Wayne.

Gautier reported the troops complained of a lack of clothing, no pay, a shortage of provisions, and that a large number of them were being detained despite their enlistments having expired. He also reported that the troops had marched some seven miles to Vealtown.[14]

Gould returned with an estimate of 1,200 mutineers and reported that an officer had been killed and four wounded, whereas the mutineers had five or six wounded. He reported that the mutineers had elected a sergeant major who was a British deserter with the rank of major general. He said the mutineers' army had marched to Middlebrook on Tuesday and the previous day to

New Brunswick. Both Gautier and
Gould told De Lancey two companies of
rifleman who were near the village of
Bottle Hill now Madison, New Jersey,
had marched off unopposed by the militia to join the mutineers.[15]

Sir Henry Clinton published for
Watson and Dickinson, London,
October 8, 1780. (*William L.
Clements Library*)

Clinton was in a better military position than Washington. He knew he could
depend on his troops. New York City,
Long Island, and Staten Island were safe
from an attack by the American army,
which was in no position to take offensive action. He was unsure of the extent
of the mutiny or of the intentions of the
mutineers. He had heard Benedict
Arnold's promises that he could fill up his
legion with American deserters, yet after
weeks of extensive recruiting, the number of men in Arnold's corps was small.

Clinton wanted to be sure that the mutineers were coming before he sent
his troops into New Jersey in the winter and put them at risk. He did not want
to fight the mutineers; rather, he wanted to protect them if they were
responding to his proposals. Were the mutineers taking advantage of the
proclamation he had sent out the week before? In his proclamation he stated
to "the inhabitants of the British colonies on the Continent of North America
now in rebellion, of every rank, order and denomination (excepting always
such persons who, under the usurped forms of trial, have tyrannically and
inhumanly been instrumental in executing and putting to death any of his
Majesty's loyal subjects). . . . The door is . . . again thrown open (if happily
you are disposed to avail yourself of the opportunity it affords) for commenc-
ing negotiations which may instantly terminate the miseries of your country."
He offered "pardon for all past treasons and the full benefits of the king's
clemency." He had opened the door of reconciliation. Were they now planning to come through it?

Clinton was told the Vermonters were ready to declare for England.
Bringing in the Pennsylvania Line might push Ethan Allen and the other
Vermonters over the line of neutrality and into the British camp. Major

Frederick Mackenzie noted in his diary, "the loyalists in Maryland and the other Southern provinces on hearing of the mutiny of the Pennsylvania troops will immediately rise and declare themselves."[16]

Clinton needed facts not just opinions, hearsay, and gossip. To get those facts he would send ambassadors to the mutineers. Then he could decide what course of action to take. He had a number of options with regard to sending his ambassadors into New Jersey. They could go to Staten Island and cross over the short distance of the Arthur Kill to the swamps at Elizabethtown or to any point of the almost unguarded coast southward to Perth Amboy. They could go to the forts at Paulus Hook, De Lancey, and Sandy Hook in New Jersey. The navy could put the spies ashore on the northern Monmouth County coast at Cheesequake or at South Amboy, Black Point, or Squan where secret service operations maintained contacts.[17]

On Thursday the 4th at 5:00 a.m., at the American post in Elizabethtown, hard-drinking Lieutenant Colonel Jacob Crane of the New Jersey Militia took a deposition from a spy who had just returned from New York. Crane referred to the spy by his initials "AB" most likely Abraham Bancker. When Bancker turned in his own reports, he used the code name Amicus Republicae.

Bancker had stayed on Staten Island when the British troops landed in 1776. In 1780, he left Staten Island and took a job in Manhattan with a merchant. This was excellent cover for his new career as an American spy. Although he may have previously assisted the Mersereaus on Staten Island with their intelligence gathering operations, he had moved up to the front lines in the spy game. The Mersereaus were America's first spy ring operating on Staten Island and then into New York City. It is believed that Joshua Mersereau, a graduate of King's College, was recruited by Washington to set up the operation. He used family members, John, John LaGrange, Joshua, and possibly Paul and friends, Abraham Bancker and Abraham Egbert, to provide intelligence. They started their operation in 1776 and in 1780 were reporting to General Lafayette. Bancker now reported directly to his control agent, John Mersereau. The first of a number of his surviving reports was dated May 17, 1780.

Bancker told Colonel Crane that Major Fishbourne had approved of his trip to New York. This was extremely unlikely as Fishbourne was busy racing between Generals Washington and Wayne. Since Crane was not Bancker's normal contact, he had to make up a story about why he was coming from

New York. He certainly would not want to reveal his true status as a spy stationed in New York City to Crane who was known to be "disguised with liquor while the commanding officer at Elizabethtown." In December 1781, Colonel Crane would be convicted by a court martial for being intoxicated while on duty.

Bancker, in his deposition, said the British had gotten word of the mutiny at noon on the 3rd.

> Nothing could possibly have given them so much pleasure. Every preparation is making among them to come out to make a descent on Jersey; I think South Amboy is their object. They expect those in mutiny will immediately join them. A person, on whom I can rely, told me that Captain Lord was ordered to have all the Flat-bottomed boats ready upon the shortest notice. If they come out, it will be with considerable force, and may be expected within twenty-four hours from this time.[18]

Lieutenant Colonel Jacob Crane added a postscript that the militia has turned out at Elizabethtown and the size was "tolerable for the time they received orders at this place."[19]

Later that day, another report out of Crane's headquarters reported that the British had started to assemble ships at the mouth of the Raritan River off Perth Amboy and Billopp's Point on Staten Island.[20] It included a sixteen- or twenty-gun sloop of war, a sloop, which was her tender, a Virginia schooner, a galley, and about twelve or fifteen flat-bottom boats. A schooner and a brigantine were also heading for a rendezvous with this fleet. "You may depend on it, that Perth Amboy will be their route, and not South Amboy, as is conjectured. The country is open that way, and South Amboy is woody, and the embarkation difficult on account of the [mud] flats. They cannot embark here but at particular times of tide, when they can at Perth Amboy at any time. I saw the agent yesterday, and from his discourse I think they have no other object than the revolters, and from the situation of the vessels, I think Amboy to be the place."[21]

ON A RAINY THURSDAY EVENING AT British Headquarters three copies of a proposal to the mutineers were prepared by candlelight. The fireplaces would have provided additional illumination and taken the damp chill out of the air while the raindrops ran down the windowpanes. Each proposal was carefully encased in a sheet of lead, the kind used to preserve tea. It served the dual purpose of being weatherproof and not drawing undue attention to itself. The proposals promised the mutineers everything but the throne of England if they would come to the British.

General Clinton asked the mutineers to send a representative to Amboy where a conference would be held. The mutineers were also instructed to move east of South River where they would be protected by the British Army. As soon as the proposals were completed, Andrew Gautier Jr. was sent two copies to be forwarded to the mutineers. To ensure their arrival to Gautier, one package containing the proposal was sent by way of Elizabethtown and the other by way of Newark.[22] The third would be sent directly to the mutineers. The armed schooner *Neptune* was to carry all three couriers.

Gould, being an old pro in traveling across the lines and not needing to make any preparations for the journey, made his way to the *Neptune* that night. Captain Stewart Ross of the *Neptune*, taking full advantage of the morning's fog, put Gould ashore at Elizabethtown Point at daybreak.[23] However, Gould did not keep his scheduled pickup time for his return with the *Neptune*.[24]

Uzal Woodruff of Elizabethtown was most likely the other courier to Gautier. Woodruff was set ashore by a boat from the *Neptune* at Newark and returned the same day. Woodruff was a thirty-four-year-old Elizabethtown native descended from an old Elizabethtown family. David Woodruff, his father, was born there in 1688.

Woodruff had served as a dispatch rider in Captain Crane's company of the 1st Regiment of Essex County Militia. He had married Elizabeth Ogden in 1767 when he was twenty years old. They had two children, Eunice born the following year and Elias two years later. Woodruff was a double agent working for Colonel Elias Dayton, the forty-four-year-old commander of the New Jersey Line of the Continental Army. Dayton controlled numerous spies working out of his hometown of Elizabethtown where he had been a merchant before the war.

The third proposal was given to John Mason, who was being released from a British jail to take a copy of Sir Henry Clinton's proposal to the Pennsylvania Line Mutineers. Mason's crime was, according to him, "inadvertently plundering." Mason told General Sir Henry Clinton that he was "plundered of all his substance by the rebels, and suffered everything but death for his loyalty, being confined in two of their Provosts; and consequently would [have] suffered death" if he had "not made his escape from the Morristown jail; the bloody Governor Livingston" having indictments against him "for high treason."

Mason was a resident of Orange County, New York. In November 1778, he was part of a gang led by Claudius Smith. The gang captured Colonel Joseph Ward of Massachusetts who was the commissary general of musters and Lieutenant Colonel William Bradford Jr. of Pennsylvania who was the deputy commissary general of musters. Smith's gang was rewarded with a hundred guineas for their work.

Smith was wanted for horse stealing and the murder of American Major Nathaniel Strong as he was surrendering after being promised quarter, while in his own house on October 6, 1778. In January 1779, the forty-two-year-old Smith was captured by the Americans and hanged at the Goshen jail. Upon Smith's death Mason became the leader of the gang. In retaliation for Smith's hanging they vowed to hang six Whigs for every Tory that was hanged.

On March 27, 1779, Mason's gang took John Clark from his house, killed him and pinned a warning to his coat. It said in part

> You are hereby warned at your peril to desist from executing more friends to Government as you served the unfortunate Claudius Smith and numbers of Loyalists that fell into your merciless hands for the blood of those innocent men, cries aloud for vengeance. You are likewise warned to use the prisoners well and ease them of their irons; that is confined in the goals of Poughkeepsie, Goshen, Sussex and Morristown. If you continue in your murders and cruelties, as you have begun, and it is still determined to give the refugees no quarters, we Loyalists do solemnly declare that we will hang six for one, which shall be inflicted on your headmen and leaders and wherever we loyal refugees find militiamen under arms against us or against any of His Majesty's loyal subjects. We are fully determined to massacre them on the spot.[25]

Late in 1779, John Mason was arrested on Long Island and confined to the Provost in New York City. Two months later his wife was also incarcerated.

In December, Captain John Stapleton, assistant adjutant general of the British Army in America, was looking to recruit spies for his boss Major Oliver De Lancey. He inquired if Mason, who was still in the Provost, could get someone to vouch for him. If he could, he might be "employed from Headquarters."

On December 21, Mason wrote to Stapleton, "should his Excellency most graciously please to receive me into mercy and extricate me from my confinement. I am willing to serve his Excellency in the capacity of a spy." When De Lancey and Stapleton needed someone to undertake the extremely risky mission of contacting the mutineers, Mason was chosen.

William Smith, in his memoirs, gives credit to Isaac Ogden for finding the messenger who went with the third proposal, but does not provide any more information. He had to be referring to Mason as the other two proposals were given to two agents who were well known at headquarters.[26] Mason would be a strongly motivated courier as a successful mission would most likely secure not only his freedom but also his wife's.

Mason, after being released from the Provost, had to be provided with civilian clothes instead of his ratty prison attire. He was familiar with the northern part of New Jersey but needed a guide to make his way undetected across central New Jersey. He would have to circumvent the villages of Cranbury, Old Bridge, and Spotswood to get to Princeton. He and his guide would need to find places to ford the streams as the bridges would most certainly be guarded by the local militia. He had to be informed of his contacts and prepared for a journey that would last several days.

Once the three proposals were dispatched, orders were immediately sent from British Headquarters to two battalions of Light Infantry, the British Grenadiers, three Battalions of Hessian Grenadiers and Jaegers to march immediately to Denyce's Ferry at the Narrows.

The next day would start with Mason being late in reaching his transportation. Captain Ross stated that the other person (almost certainly Mason) had not reached the *Neptune* by 8:00 a.m. When he finally arrived, Captain Ross needed to get Mason on his way as quickly as possible. Not wanting to wait until nightfall, Ross secured two horses and took Mason to the armed galley *Philadelphia*. Ross gave the commanding officer De Lancey's letter along with instructions that Mason was to be landed up the Raritan River that afternoon. Mason would be set on shore early in the evening of the 5th.[27] Mason picked the spot on the south side of the Raritan where he was put ashore.

At 11:00 p.m. on the 5th, at British Headquarters, 1 Broadway in New York, John Stapleton wrote Oliver De Lancey, then on Staten Island, that Captain Ross had arrived there at 4:00 p.m. and confirmed that Gould had left that morning. The second person could not be landed in the Raritan soon-

er than that evening by the Galley.[28] British Agent "Mercury" was to be
Mason's first contact in New Jersey. Mercury, in mythology, was the messenger of the Roman gods and the god of commercial success. This Mercury was
John Rattoon (also spelled Rattoone) who owned a tavern in South Amboy
and a stage. Rattoon had been one of the trusted couriers between New York
and Philadelphia in the Benedict Arnold conspiracy.

Rattoon's tavern was located at the end of the old road to Bordentown in
South Amboy.[29] The building was laid out in an east-west direction nearly parallel with the shoreline. The west side of the building was the original portion
of the tavern; it was two stories high, forty feet long, and thirty feet deep. On
the east side was a story and a half addition that was fifty feet wide and twenty-five feet deep. The tavern had a dock located about a half mile away across
the salt marsh. The marsh provided ample coverage for anyone who wanted
to travel unseen from the bay to the tavern or vice versa. "It was related of
John Rattoon that he was a man of infinite tact, and was able to entertain
British and American officers in the house, at the same time, locating them
in the opposite ends without allowing either to know of the presence of the
other, and was 'hail fellow well met' with all."[30]

Rattoon provided Mason with a guide, Fegany, for the first leg of the journey. Fegany had met Gould on Staten Island and informed him of the
Pennsylvania Line mutiny. Fegany is one of those shadowy people of history,
a name in the records that shows up a few times and disappears.

Traveling by daylight, Fegany and Mason quickly traversed the six miles to
South River. Here, Mason was passed to James Ogden of South River who
would take him the rest of the way to the mutineers at Princeton. James
Ogden was the son of Nathaniel Ogden of Brunswick who had died intestate.
James had just taken Catherine Pitt as his bride on November 6. The need
for money has always been a dilemma for most newlyweds, including James
Ogden. This may have been what motivated him to take on such a dangerous
job. Mason and Ogden began their twenty-two mile journey to Princeton
when darkness fell.[31]

FRIDAY THE 5TH OF JANUARY SAW PLENTY of action at British Headquarters.
Express riders had been sent out the previous night to the troops alerting
them to put their units in order to move out. On the 4th, the Jaeger Corps, in
their winter quarters at Herricks, Jericho, and Westbury, Long Island,

received orders to be prepared to march.[32] At 7:00 a.m., on the 5th, they received orders to march at daybreak that morning. Sunrise on central Long Island on January 5, 1781, was at 7:20 a.m. The Jaeger Corps finally got under way at 9:00 a.m. and marched to the west side of Jamaica. They camped there overnight lodging in barns.[33]

On the morning of the 4th, the 42nd Regiment received its orders to be prepared for a march. At 4:00 a.m. on Friday the 5th, they were told to begin their march immediately. The Battalion assembled at Rapalje's Tavern at the crossroads in Bushwick Village and marched at daylight. They reached Flatbush about ten o'clock in the morning. They stayed there until 9:00 p.m. when they got under way again. They marched to Denyce's Ferry at the Narrows. They had to wait until the British Light Infantry crossed to Staten Island before they were able to embark. When the Jaegers arrived, they were billeted on the road to Decker's Ferry where some were able to get under cover but others slept in the fields all night.[34]

Also on Friday, the British Grenadiers, 37th Regiment, and the Hessian Grenadiers arrived from Kings County. They were billeted on the road to Richmond Town in the center of Staten Island.

Joseph Clark, of Warwick, Orange County, New York, had been working as a British spy and guide for Colonel Beverly Robinson of the Loyal American Regiment. He collected intelligence in his hometown and brought loyalists from Kakiat (now New Hempstead, Rockland County) to New York by way of Ramapo and Fort Lee, New Jersey. He left Ramapo on the evening of the 3rd and arrived in New York on the 4th. Clark reported hearing a cannonade to the south as he traveled.[35] He was sent back out on the 5th to Morristown to collect intelligence.

Isaac Siscoe, a free black landowner in Bergen County, New Jersey, was also sent out on his first intelligence-gathering mission on the 5th. He was sent up the "Clove" toward West Point to determine if the mutiny had spread to the troops there. He would continue working for the British secret service through at least March. The Clove comes from the Dutch word for pass. It was the site of the old Albany post road and the main route of travel through the western Hudson Highlands. It was heavily traveled in winter when the Hudson River froze. The south end of the Clove is in present day Suffern, New York.[36] On his way to West Point, Siscoe would have been able to see if the American army was moving south through the Clove. If he encountered them, he would abort the rest of his mission and report back to British Headquarters.

Also, on Friday the 5th, Oliver De Lancey sent an unidentified courier with a verbal message to the mutineers.[37] Since Sir Henry Clinton believed in covering his bases, perhaps even to excess, three more proposals were to be sent to the mutineers. From the second batch of proposals, one was sent to Cornelius Hatfield Jr. at Staten Island to be sent to the mutineers. Cornelius was part of a large clan of Hatfields, also spelt Hetfield, from Elizabethtown, New Jersey. Cornelius had worked both as a guide and a spy since 1776. Cavalier Jouet, also from Elizabethtown, described him as being a very zealous Loyalist, much employed at Headquarters, but a loose and drinking man.

In Elizabethtown, Joseph Gautier Jr. had received both copies of the first batch of proposals to the mutineers. He sent them by a faithful friend to Princeton and prepared a report to British headquarters on the information he was able to gather. Admiral Marriot Arbuthnot forwarded copies of Sir Henry Clinton's Proclamation to Connecticut that was drafted by William Smith at the end of December in the hope of instigating more soldiers to mutiny.[38]

ON THURSDAY MORNING, JANUARY 4, Philadelphia was enveloped with fog. The first news of the Pennsylvania Line mutiny reached the city as the fog was beginning to lift.[39] Residents feared the mutineers were coming. Rumors went flying about the city: the soldiers of the Pennsylvania Line had mutinied, left their post, killed some of their officers, and were on their way to Philadelphia. The unseasonably warm temperatures encouraged people to get out into the streets, despite the threat of rain. Who knew what horrible events would transpire once the mutineers got there? The residents of Philadelphia "seemed terrified at the thought of their coming to plunder the city."[40]

The rain finally made an appearance in the evening and sent the populous scurrying back into their homes, to the local taverns, or to the city's coffeehouses to discuss the news.

The information of the mutiny had been circulating in the city but not one word had been published. This served only to fan the flames and create more rumors. One such rumor had the mutineers leaving Princeton and arriving at Trenton that evening on their way to Philadelphia. It was false as most rumors tend to be.

On Friday the 5th, General Anthony Wayne's letter of January 2, together with several other letters, was read at the Supreme Executive Council at the Pennsylvania State House.[41] In response to the latest news of the Pennsylvania Line mutiny, a meeting was held between a committee of Congress and the Pennsylvania Supreme Council. Both the topic and the weather were hot. The city was as unpleasant as in summer, causing men to have to wipe their faces several times to remove the perspiration.[42] The Congress's committee was composed of Samuel J. Atlee, Dr. Theodorick Bland, John Mathews, John Sullivan, and John Witherspoon.

It was agreed that Joseph Reed, President, and Councilman General James Potter, of the Pennsylvania Supreme Council would leave immediately for New Jersey and that the committee would follow the next morning with the exception of Mathews who would remain in Philadelphia.[43]

Before leaving town, Joseph Reed sent a letter to General Wayne and Colonels Butler and Stewart informing them their letters had been received and that he and General Potter were to go to the mutineers. Reed told Wayne he should expect to see them shortly after receiving his letter. He asked Wayne to try to persuade the mutineers to move to Trenton where Reed said he would have more hope for a conclusion. Reed believed that "the enemy will certainly avail themselves of the circumstances and in doubt and desperation which men in their honor and virtue may not be proof against temptations of a wicked and artful enemy."[44]

Timothy Matlack, a fifty-year-old Free Quaker who penned the Declaration of Independence, was assistant to the secretary of Congress. Samuel Huntington, a self-taught Connecticut lawyer and president of Congress, directed Matlack to send a request to Captain Samuel Morris of the First Troop Philadelphia City Cavalry. Morris was to immediately order twenty men to be at Huntington's house in Market Street at 4:00 p.m. and be prepared to march to New Jersey. The balance of the Light Horse was directed to follow in the morning.[45]

Huntington also sent an order to Colonel S. Miles, deputy quarter master general, to furnish General James Potter with a very good horse by 4:00 p.m. If Miles did not have one then he was to obtain one by borrowing or impressing one immediately.[46]

Reed, General Potter, and twenty men of the Philadelphia Light Horse left the city of Philadelphia on Friday evening to investigate the affairs of the

Pennsylvania Line. News of their departure and mission were common knowledge in the city.[47]

At 3:00 p.m. on Friday the 5th,
General Wayne gave John Donaldson,
third sergeant of the Philadelphia Light
Horse, an order to "proceed with all possible dispatch to Philadelphia to send up
the auditors of accounts immediately to
settle pay and depreciation of the
Line."[48] Wayne also instructed
Donaldson to advise Reed and members
of the Pennsylvania Council to come to
Princeton.

Donaldson was able to leave
Princeton at 4:00 p.m. On his way
through Trenton, he received a letter

Joseph Reed, member of the
Continental Congress, 1777–78,
president of the Supreme Exectuive
Council of Pennsylvania, 1778–81.
(*William L. Clements Library*)

from Major Charles Stewart to Joseph Reed informing him that the mutineers
were not coming to Trenton but wanted to stay together in Princeton.
Lafayette and St. Clair were going to New Brunswick "on hearing the British
are landed at Elizabethtown. I fear this is true, yet am not certain." Stewart
realized that the hundred head of cattle the mutineers took would not last
long. And hungry troops plundering the countryside for food would soon be
out of control. He wrote to Reed, "We shall soon want beef. Your militia, and
those of Jersey, must be fed and so must those tumultuous troops. I beg, if in
your power, you would order on some cattle."[49]

Joseph Reed had gotten as far as Bristol, Pennsylvania, when he met
Donaldson on Friday evening. Donaldson turned over to Reed his written
order from Wayne. Before returning it to Donaldson, Reed penned a note to
Mr. Robert Morris that he agreed with Wayne that "the auditors should come
forward. It will have a good conciliatory effect."[50]

Donaldson told Reed how Lafayette and St. Clair were allowed to come
into the mutineers' camp but quickly ordered them out. Reed advised William
Moore, vice president of Pennsylvania's Supreme Executive Council (i.e.,
lieutenant governor of Pennsylvania), that the sixty-three-year-old Colonel
Lewis Nicola, of the Invalid Regiment, should be on the lookout for some

mutineers that Reed saw heading to the city. He was "to have an eye on these fellows as they come into town, lest they infest the invalids and spread bad reports among the militia; but by no means to use them ill, lest it have a bad effect on their fellows in Jersey."[51] Reed also stated he wanted clothing forwarded and money prepared. "I fear we must make some douceurs [bribe or gratuity] in some way or another."[52]

If the British did turn out, then Reed was going to try to get the mutineers to come toward Bristol rather then take the chance of the mutineers going up against the enemy. He also advised that the mutineers wanted to stay together as a group at Princeton. Reed hoped that, because the Board of Sergeants was so large, they would begin to squabble among themselves and the mutiny would fall apart. He was convinced that "there will be a variety of sentiments."[53]

Reed and Potter spent the night at Bristol.

At 6:00 p.m., Colonel Moses Jacques of Westfield, New Jersey, who was commanding the New Jersey Militia at Elizabethtown, received intelligence from someone whom he considered a dependable source. His informant, who had apparently been on Staten Island, told him that the British had by 2:00 p.m. that day moved their flat bottom boats from New York to Princess Bay off the southeastern end of Staten Island. The British were also in the process of bringing an armed ship to Princess Bay. The troops on Staten Island had been given orders to be ready to march. They were to have two pair of stockings, two shirts, blanket and three days provisions ready. Lieutenant Colonel Joseph Barton's Company of the 1st Battalion of New Jersey Volunteers and some Hessians were to remain to protect the island. Jacques's informant said the troops were to land at South Amboy, but some thought the landing would be farther down the New Jersey coast.

The intelligencer reported that the enemy had received information about the Pennsylvania Line mutiny from a man who went over in the morning to Staten Island from Woodbridge. The man reported that "the new commandant of the Pennsylvania Line would join them if he could have an opportunity" and, because of the Pennsylvania Line affair, "the British have delayed a fleet from proceeding."[54]

Having British vessels at Princess Bay off the southeastern end of Staten Island made the likelihood of their landing troops at Perth Amboy, South Amboy, the northern coast of Monmouth County, and Sandy Hook a very high probability as they could be reached quickly without the time-consuming maneuvers of traversing the shoals to get out of the bay to the ocean.

Continental Congressman Dr. William Burnet, a lifelong resident of the Newark area, wrote to New Jersey Governor William Livingston advising him that he was unable to locate Colonel Dayton, commander of the New Jersey Line, but he was enclosing some significant intelligence that had just been received. He was turning the information over to Livingston so that appropriate orders could be issued. Burnet did not identify the name of the individual but, from his comments, the person was likely Moses Hatfield. Burnet mentioned that the informant was male and had been used for a long time as a spy. He was specifically used the previous summer (1780) to go into Elizabethtown while it was occupied by the British. Moses Hatfield was sent on such a mission and brought out some useful intelligence.

George Washington, at New Windsor, wrote a circular letter to the New England governors advising them of the situation with the Pennsylvania Line and the other divisions of the Continental Army.

> Sir: It is with extreme anxiety, and pain of mind, I find myself constrained to inform your Excellency that the event I have long apprehended would be the consequence of the complicated distresses of the army, has at length taken place. On the night of the 1st instant a mutiny was excited by the noncommissioned officers and privates of the Pennsylvania Line, which soon became so universal as to defy all opposition; in attempting to quell this tumult, in the first instance, some officers were killed, others wounded, and the lives of several common soldiers lost. Deaf to the arguments, entreaties, and utmost efforts of all their officers to stop them, the men moved off from Morris Town, the place of their cantonment, with their arms, and six pieces of artillery. And from accounts just received by General Wayne's Aid De Camp, they were still in a body, on their march to Philadelphia, to demand a redress of their grievances. At what point this defection will stop, or how extensive it may prove, God only knows; at present, the troops at the important Posts in this vicinity remain quiet, not being acquainted with this unhappy and alarming affair; but how long they will continue so cannot be ascertained, as they labor under some of the pressing hardships, with the Troops who have revolted.
>
> The aggravated calamities and distresses that have resulted, from the total want of pay for nearly twelve Months, for want of clothing, at a severe season, and not infrequently the want of provisions; are beyond description.

The circumstances will now point out much more forcibly what ought to be done, than any thing that can possibly be said by me, on the subject.

It is not within the sphere of my duty to make requisitions, without the authority of Congress, from individual states: but at such a crisis, and circumstanced as we are, my own heart will acquit me; and Congress, and the states (eastward of this) whom for the sake of dispatch, I address, I am persuaded will excuse me, when once for all I give it decidedly as my opinion, that it is in vain to think an army can be kept together much longer, under such a variety of sufferings as ours has experienced: and that unless some immediate and spirited measures are adopted to furnish at least three months pay to the troops, in money that will be of some value to them; and at the same time ways and means are devised to clothe and feed them better (more regularly I mean) than they have been, the worst that can befall us may be expected.

I have transmitted Congress a Copy of this Letter, and have in the most pressing manner requested them to adopt the measure which I have above recommended, or something similar to it, and as I will not doubt of their compliance, I have thought proper to give you this previous notice, that you may be prepared to answer the requisition. As I have used every endeavor in my power to avert the evil that has come upon us, so will I continue to exert every means I am possessed of to prevent an extension of the mischief, but I can neither foretell, or be answerable for the issue. That you may have every information that an officer of rank and abilities can give of the true situation of our affairs, and the condition and temper of the troops I have prevailed upon Brigadier General Knox to be the bearer of this letter, to him I beg leave to refer your Excellency for many matters which would be too tedious for a letter.[55]

General Knox left camp on Sunday the 7th to make a personal appeal to the New England governors for help.[56]

7

Spies at the College of New Jersey

THE PENNSYLVANIA LINE MUTINY III

*T*he sun had not yet appeared above the horizon on Saturday, January 6, 1781, when the English Grenadiers, two Hessian Regiments, and several other units assembled at the docks on lower York Island. The weather was uncommonly moderate as the temperature stayed above freezing even at night.[1] The nearly full moon had had set at 3:38 a.m. ushering in total darkness.

The soldiers were called out to be the bodyguard for General Sir Henry Clinton for his trip across Upper New York Bay to Staten Island.[2] The large bodyguard was needed because of fear of another attempted kidnapping of the general.

Lieutenant Colonel David Humphreys, aide-de-camp to George Washington, had first submitted a plan on December 23 to capture General Knyphausen at Morris's House at the north end of York Island. He projected that he would need one hundred men to be transported in ten whale boats to accomplish this venture. The mission was proposed for sometime after the full moon.

He suggested Christmas or New Year's for the raid when the enemy's guard would be lowered. He wanted a dark or stormy night to elude the guards; his plan was to go down the river with the ebb tide on the west side of the Hudson River. When they got near Morris House they would land on York Island and leave a guard with the boats. The troops, along with the prisoners they captured, were to be debarked at Fort Lee while the boats would proceed upriver. Humphreys explained that even if they did not succeed there were no great consequences for the failure.[3]

George Washington loved the idea and modified the plan to include General Clinton as a target. Washington immediately gave instructions to Lieutenant Colonel David Humphreys,

> Sir: You will take command of such of the detachments of water guards, now on the river, as you may think necessary, and with them attempt to surprise and bring off, General Knyphausen from Morris House on York Island, or Sir Henry Clinton from Kennedy's House [1 Broadway] in the City; if from the tide, weather, and other circumstances you shall judge the enterprise to be practicable. In the execution of it, you will be guided by your own discretion, and I have only to suggest, that secrecy rapidity, and prudence in making good your retreat will be indispensably necessary to insure the success.[4]

Lieutenant Colonel Humphreys wrote himself the following instructions to cover his actions: "Colonel Humphreys is directed to visit the post at Dobbs's Ferry, to reconnoiter and report the state of matters below. He will take such of the guard boats with him as he thinks necessary."[5]

On the night of December 25, Humphreys's troops had left King's Ferry with forty men in three whale boats. Private Cornelius Haskins of the 2nd Massachusetts Regiment said the detachment was composed of one colonel, three captains, one lieutenant, one ensign, thirty-five continental soldiers, and two guides. One of the guides was a Captain McCannon who commanded a sloop at West Point. Zacheus Holmes, a deserter from the 3rd Massachusetts Regiment who participated in the escapade, said the another guide was Captain McGuin who also commanded a small vessel.[6] Captain Buckhannon was reported to have also been a guide.

The boat commanders were Colonel Humphreys, Captain Weles, and Lieutenant Harte.[7] In Humphreys's boat were three axes and two crow bars. The plan was that "four men from each boat were to have landed under the command of Captain Wells under the burnt church; another party was landed lower down under the command of Lieutenant Harte. They had orders not to fire on any account." If they were fired upon, they were to retreat to the boats.

Cornelius Haskins was not told any more of the plan but believed they intended on taking General Clinton.[8] If they succeeded, the general would have been put in the lieutenant's boat and taken upriver. One of the other boats was to go to the Jersey shore and make a light as a distraction.[9]

The other soldiers in the adventure were selected from those stationed at Nyack at the time. They set off at dusk and traveled to Dobbs's Ferry about an hour later. They stayed there a short while then started rowing down the river; there was very little wind at that time. They traveled to Fort Lee when the wind picked up.

They attempted to cross over from New Jersey to New York but the wind that night was so strong and contrary that the boats were driven on shore at two o'clock in the morning under the battery by the brew house. They broke one of the oars and had a hard time getting the boats back in the water. The boats were driven below the city and one of them, commanded by Captain Weles, was forced down below the Sandy Hook lighthouse. The effort was aborted.[10]

All three boats passed through Upper New York Bay despite its being lined with British ships and then passed through the Narrows. They then went down the east side and around the south side of Staten Island and landed all three vessels at Perth Amboy, New Jersey, bringing everyone off safe.[11]

It was generally believed at British Headquarters that the American plan was to capture General Clinton from his own quarters in New York. Mother Nature had intervened and saved the day for the British. On January 15, 1781, Andrew Gautier's intelligence report from New Jersey advised British Headquarters that Sir Henry Clinton was indeed the target. The American officers said the plan failed because of the high winds.[12]

JUST BEFORE DAWN ON JANUARY 6, General Sir Henry Clinton visited with William Smith, a member of the Royal Governor's Council and the Royal Chief Justice of New York for half an hour. They discussed the Pennsylvania Line mutiny. Clinton wanted the mutineers to move to Monmouth County where they could be easily embarked before he could send the troops in to New Jersey. He was afraid that if he approached them with an army, they would run away. If he negotiated a bargain first, then he could approach them in force.

While the meeting was under way General Clinton's staff had assembled outside of Smith's house, which was just three doors down from British Headquarters. Clinton, upon seeing his staff outside, ordered Captain Smith to deliver two boxes of intercepted letters to William Smith for his perusal.

The letters had been captured by Captain Gilbert Livingston of Benedict Arnold's American Legion. Clinton returned to Staten Island where he planned to stay for four or five days while he considered how to bring the mutineers to the Crown.

Clinton informed Smith that if the mutineers came to Monmouth County, he was to be prepared to move two to three thousand troops into New Jersey for their protection. Smith believed Sir Henry was unsure if the mutineers were intending to come over to the British or just trying to extract concessions from the Continental Congress. Smith wrote in his memoirs that Clinton did not believe that Congress could comply with the mutineers' demands.[13]

As British troops went aboard their vessels at 6:00 a.m. on Saturday the 6th the weather was mild.[14] It was a full fifty minutes before twilight when General Clinton and his entourage set sail under the cover of darkness across Upper New York Bay.[15]

Clinton had left Major Frederick Mackenzie, the son of a Dublin merchant, and Captain John Stapleton in charge of British Headquarters in lower Manhattan. They were there to process any intelligence that was brought into the city and forward anything of significance to him on Staten Island. One such document arrived that day. Undated and addressed only from KM to OD, it was from Knox McCoy, a British spy operating from western Connecticut to the Hudson River, to Oliver De Lancey. McCoy reported that "there was great grumbling for want of pay as they have not received a shilling of pay in twelve months past. . . . We see the officers going home to visit families and friends borrowing or begging money to bear their expenses."[16]

John Eaton and Jaspher Hart, both of Hackensack who came into New York City with wares to sell, were interrogated, as were Cesar and Tom (two free blacks) who came with them.[17]

Once Clinton landed on Staten Island, he lodged near Decker's Ferry on the north shore opposite Bergen Neck, New Jersey.[18] Should positive reports come from the Pennsylvania malcontents, he wanted to be readily available to lead the British and Hessian troops into New Jersey. Once there, he would provide protection for those Pennsylvanians who were going to take the Royal standard. This would be a chance to grab newspaper headlines in England and gain the favor of King George, which could result in military, political, and financial gain for him.

With Sir Henry Clinton and Oliver De Lancey on Staten Island, a flurry of military activity commenced there. About noon, the 42nd Regiment marched into temporary quarters. To the west of Richmond Town, the British Light Infantry camped. Richmond Town is at the center of the fifty-nine-square-mile island and is the headwaters for the freshwater Richmond Creek that flows into Fresh Kills. The British and Hessian Grenadiers were placed between Richmond Town and Cole's Ferry at the Watering Place (modern Tompkinsville) at the northern end of Staten Island.[19]

Staten Island was originally part of the New Netherlands colony and under the Dutch was called Staaten Eylandt. In 1667, it passed to the British, and in order to encourage European settlements, the English, in 1671, resurveyed Oude Dorp (which became known as Old Town) and expanded the lots along the shore to the south. These lots, settled primarily by the Dutch, became known as Nieuwe Dorp (meaning "New Village"), which later became anglicized to New Dorp.

In 1683, the colony of New York was divided into ten counties and Staten Island was designated as Richmond County. The name derives from the title of an illegitimate son of King Charles II. By 1708, the entire island had been divided into 166 small farms and two large manorial estates—the Dongan estate and a 1,600-acre property on the southwestern tip of the island belonging to Christopher Billopp.[20]

In 1729, the county seat was established at the village of Richmond Town in the center of the island. It was near the 410-foot-high Todt Hill. When the British military arrived in New York in 1776, they debarked onto Staten Island with General Howe who established his headquarters at the Rose and Crown Tavern in New Dorp.

After a month's preparation, in August 1776, the British forces crossed the Narrows to Brooklyn. In the Battle of Long Island they routed the American forces under General George Washington who fled with his troops to New York. After several other engagements, New York City, including Staten Island, was abandonded to the British.

At 7:00 a.m. on January 6, just after dawn, the Jaeger Corps departed from Jamaica, Queens, which is twelve miles east of New York City on Long Island. They marched through the farm lands of Long Island and the predominately Dutch town of Flatbush.[21] Their journey would take them across Long Island to Denyce's Ferry at the southwestern part of King's County at the Narrows.[22] The Narrows is the body of water that separates Long Island from Staten Island and forms the entrance to Upper New York Bay.

The Narrows was first visited by Europeans in 1524 by Italian explorer Giovanni da Verrazzano. He had been sent by King Francis I of France to explore the area between Florida and Newfoundland looking for a route to the Pacific Ocean. It was here at Denyce's Ferry's stone building that the Jaeger Corps embarked on schooners for their ride to Staten Island. This same stone building had been the target of the guns of the *Rainbow* during the British landing on Long Island in 1776.

Not until dusk, about 5:00 p.m., did the schooners complete their journey across Upper New York Bay and into the Kill van Kull, which connects Newark Bay and Upper New York Bay.[23]

The Jaeger Corps landed at Decker's Ferry.[24] Decker's burned stone house at the ferry had been converted into a fort by the British in 1779. It had an abatis, a barricade of trees with bent or sharpened branches directed outward. Upon their arrival, the Jaegers found that the Hessian Grenadiers and the British Light Infantry had arrived ahead of them and had naturally taken the best spots for their quarters. The Jaegers were given two unheated barns as quarters for their entire corps.[25]

In New York City the scuttlebutt was that Sir Henry now had amassed some 5,000 men on Staten Island.[26] Rumors abound in any army. On this day, the tale circulated among the Hessians that the mutineers had "spiked the cannons at Morristown and burned the magazines there. They have built defenses with four cannons on the heights near [Perth] Amboy, in the Jerseys."[27]

The signal fires from the direction of Morristown would explain the story of the American magazines being torched. Concerning the cannons on the heights at Perth Amboy, they had been placed at Saint Peter's churchyard on the heights prior to the mutiny. The American troops stationed there had excelled in the practice of mooning, showing their uncovered posteriors, to the Hessians stationed across the Arthur Kill at the Billopp's House on Staten Island.

Sometime during the day, Captain Stewart Ross of the *Neptune* reported to Oliver De Lancey that he was successful in picking up Uzal Woodruff of

Billopp's House on Staten Island, New York, is a U.S. National Historic Landmark and the only pre-Revolutionary War manor house still surviving in New York City. It is also known as the Conference House because it was the site of an unsuccessful peace conference between Benjamin Franklin, John Adams, and Edward Rutledge and Lord Howe and General Sir William Howe on September 11, 1776.

Elizabethtown and that Joseph Gould had failed to make his scheduled appearance.[28] Woodruff most likely was the courier who brought Andrew Gautier's Friday letter from New Jersey. The coded letter reached Oliver De Lancey on Saturday; it was quickly deciphered.[29]

Gautier advised that the two the proposals sent to him had arrived safely. He dispatched them "by a faithful friend express to Prince Town [Princeton] where the Pennsylvania troops make a stand." He also advised that the Americans were expecting the British to land at Amboy and "all the rebel militia of New Jersey are ordered out."

The New Jersey troops had been moved from Pompton to Morristown. Gautier's intelligence was right on target. The only information that Gautier got partially wrong was that Washington was on his way from West Point and was to meet with General Wayne on Saturday. Gautier reported Washington's original plan but Washington had decided to stay with the New England troops at West Point and use his influence to keep them from following the example of the Pennsylvanians.

Some time during the day, two more proposals encased in tea lead were delivered to British couriers. One was given to Caleb Bruen who was an American double agent. Many years after the war, Bruen would tell how he had volunteered to carry the treacherous correspondence to the mutineers hoping to find a way to serve the American cause. Bruen, a former captain in the Essex County New Jersey Militia ordnance company, had been captured and taken prisoner by the British in April 1777 and released on parole later that year.[30] The British intended him to work as a spy for them, but after an unsuccessful stint as a double agent for the Americans, he dropped out service, possibly being confined to the Provost for passing on misinformation to the British.[31] He eventually regained the trust of the British and, by May 1780, Bruen had resurfaced and was under the direction of Colonel Elias Dayton as part of his American spy ring operating out of Elizabethtown, New Jersey. Bruen's cover was that he was carrying on an illegal trade but was not believed to have much money.[32] In other words he was a small insignificant player in the "London trade."

After leaving the British lines with a copy of General Sir Henry Clinton's proposal to the mutineers, Bruen went directly to Colonel Dayton upon arriving in New Jersey. He told him everything he knew about the situation.[33]

The other proposal that went out on Saturday was given to Thomas Ward who had deserted from the American army on June 16, 1777. The British sent him on recruiting and intelligence gathering missions. Ward's cover was that he was selling cloth to the rebels.[34] Ward received his mail at the Sign of the Ship, which was at the corner of Fair Street and Broadway in New York City.[35] Ward's mission this day was to get a copy of the proposal to Samuel McFarlan, who would take it the rest of the way.[36] It would not be Samuel McFarlan's first spy mission; he had been on an undercover assignment to Albany in 1779. He was discovered and incarcerated. John McDole, a resident of Albany, had assisted him in making his escape from the American confinement.[37]

At 1:00 p.m., at New Brunswick, New Jersey, Brigadier General Nathaniel Heard of the New Jersey Militia received an intelligence report from the post at Elizabethtown, which he summarized and forwarded to New Jersey Governor William Livingston. His information said the British had brought a number of flat boats and some armed vessels to Princess Bay on the southeastern side of Staten Island. The troops on Staten Island were under marching orders to prepare three days' worth of provisions.

Heard advised that the troops he had previously ordered out were at their respective posts; he also called Colonel Courtland's Regiment into the field. He advised that should the enemy invade the state then he would send an express with the news. He added a postscript that if the enemy did not make any additional movements then he thought it prudent to start discharging some of the militia that had been placed in active service.[38]

Joseph Reed had arrived around noon at Trenton, New Jersey, from Bristol and moved into Colonel John Cox's house, which was known as Bloomsbury. It was a homecoming for Reed. He was born on August 27, 1741, in Trenton, which had

General Anthony Wayne, published by E. Savage in 1796. (*Library of Congress*)

about one hundred houses at the time. It was the Hunterdon County seat with a courthouse and jail on King Street. Reed's father had been part owner of the Bordentown Iron Forge in 1743, which he sold before moving to Philadelphia. In 1752, his father bought a part interest in the Mount Holly, New Jersey, Iron Works. When Reed's mother died in 1753, he was sent back to Trenton. He had practiced law at Trenton, he passed the bar between 1762 to 1770, then moved to Philadelphia. His homecoming was not a joyful affair.

Reed immediately sent a letter requesting Wayne to meet him. The mutineers allowed the letter to be delivered to General Wayne. They decided after the delivery that they wanted to see it. Wayne turned the letter over to them. An agreement was reached that Wayne would read the letter to the troops at morning roll call. The letter mentioned that the mutineers had refused to negotiate with General St. Clair the day before, which convinced him that he could not go safely into their camp for fear of violence against him. He also invited Wayne to meet with him. He wrote to the Committee of Congress asking that he, on behalf of the state of Pennsylvania, be permitted to take the first position in negotiations with the mutineers. The committee, going second, could then make any additional concessions it felt necessary.

Reed decided to go to from Trenton to Maidenhead (now Lawrenceville), which was only four miles southwest of Princeton. Maidenhead was named for a Thames River village that was later incorporated into the City of London.

The mutineers allowed General Anthony Wayne to send a letter to Reed. It was dated at Princeton at 6:00 p.m. and acknowledged Reed's noon letter from Trenton. Wayne wrote that he had communicated the contents of the letter to the sergeants at his quarters. He was telling Reed that his mail was not secure and that he had guards posted at his room. He told Reed that Blair McClenachan and Alexander Nesbitt of the Philadelphia Light Horse would give him further details. Wayne was hopeful that "tomorrow morning will probably produce a change of sentiment." He said that Reed would be safe that night.[39]

It was getting late in the day and Reed decided to go back to Trenton for the night. Reed had sent a letter addressed to General Wayne, Colonels Stewart, and Butler saying that "as the anxiety of suspense is very great in town you will continue the intelligence directed to William Morris."[40] Reed, General Porter, and the Philadelphia Light Horse stayed the night in Trenton.

William Bowzar sent a short note to General Wayne saying, "It is the request of the Board of Committee of Sergeants for to send or inform by the bearer the order you issued at Mount Kemble, if you can inform us where we can procure them."[41]

The sun had dropped below the trees on the Pennsylvania side of the Delaware River on Saturday evening when the Committee of Congress arrived at Trenton. They immediately met with Reed by candlelight and fixed upon a course of action in dealing with the mutineers.

They agreed that the soldiers of the Pennsylvania Line would get everything to which they were rightfully entitled. The soldiers who had enlisted for three years or for the duration of the war would be discharged. However, if a soldier had voluntarily reenlisted for the duration of the war, he would continue in the service. They also affirmed General Wayne's offer of January 2 to the mutineers of a general amnesty and added that there would be only two or three exceptions to the general amnesty.

They were pleased at the very good behavior by the soldiers during their march from Morristown to Princeton and their conduct since their arrival at Princeton. General Wayne and Colonels Butler and Stewart were with the soldiers. They were not prisoners as first supposed, but were definitely not in

"View of Nassau Hall. Princeton." by Connecticut engraver Amos Doolittle (1790). Built in 1756, Nassau Hall housed the College of New Jersey, and was named for King William III, Prince of Orange–Nassau. It was planned by Robert Smith and Dr. William Shippen of Philadelphia. The design called for a building 177 feet by 54 feet. It contained a dining room, lecture rooms, library, prayer hall, and living quarters for the faculty as well as for 147 students, 3 to a room. In December 1776, the British used the hall as a barracks and a stable. (*Princeton University*)

command. However, there was a very great concern that the soldiers were close enough to the British that they could easily go to the enemy if the negotiations fell apart. The mutineers were holding this as a bargaining chip to strengthen their case.

The soldiers gave assurances that should the enemy enter New Jersey they would join up with the militia and fight. A major concern was that if the enemy arrived their words might turn into action.[42] Not all the mutineers agreed with Sergeant George Gosnall, a British deserter, who wanted to march the men in the Pennsylvania Line to the British.[43]

John Mason, carrying one of the lead-encased proposals from General Sir Henry Clinton and guided by James Ogden, successfully avoided detection and reached Princeton. When Mason and Ogden arrived in Princeton, they went straight to the college. Upon his arrival at Nassau Hall, Mason asked the sentry for the commanding officer of the mutineers and was sent up to John Williams's room.[44]

John Williams was from Pennsylvania and owned some property, according to Samuel McFarlan, who had been sent by Sir Henry Clinton to the mutineers, and had now returned. Williams had been captured at Princeton by the British on January 1, 1777. Williams then enlisted in the 2nd Battalion of DeLancey's Loyalist Brigade. He deserted on July 24, 1778.[45] Williams had spent almost nineteen months in the British service.

On July 12, 1780, Brigadier General Anthony Wayne had ordered the Brigade General Court Martial to hear John Williams's case. He was tried for deserting to the enemy and bearing arms in their service. Colonel Walter Stewart was the president of the court martial that heard Williams's guilty plea. Williams, a soldier in the 2nd Pennsylvania Regiment, was found guilty by more than two-thirds majority and sentenced to death. Because of Williams's young age and former good character, the court martial board recommended a pardon. Washington approved the sentence of death, then, because of the court's recommendation, he pardoned Williams.[46] A decision in hindsight Washington most assuredly regretted.

Mason told John Williams he had an express for him. Williams asked from whence. Mason said from Elizabethtown. During Williams's interrogation of Mason, he asked if the British were coming and he was told no. When asked who sent him, Mason replied that British General Sir Henry Clinton sent him and at that point handed over the proposal still in its lead covering. After opening and reading the unsigned letter, Williams inquired who wrote it. When he was informed that it came from Sir Henry, Williams had Mason and Ogden placed under arrest. Williams, with the duo in tow, went to the Committee of Sergeants who quickly agreed that they should turn over Mason and Ogden to General Wayne.

Sometime during the night, another courier arrived at Princeton. This courier was possibly the one sent by Gautier. The unknown courier either got cold feet or heard about the arrest of Mason and Ogden and decided not to risk discovery. The courier dropped the copy of Sir Henry Clinton's proposal wrapped in sheet lead in front of the door of the house where the Board of Sergeants had met and vanished into the night. The dropped letter was found and delivered to General Wayne the following morning.[47]

General Anthony Wayne wrote General Washington that he was awakened about 4:00 a.m. "by two sergeants, who produced a letter from the enemy enclosed in a small piece of tea lead. They also brought under guard two caitiffs who undertook to deliver it to the leaders of the malcontents. One of these culprits said he was a sergeant in Odell's new-raised corps and was promised a considerable reward on bringing back an answer. The soldiery, in general, affected to spurn at the idea of turning Arnolds (as they express it). We have used every address to inflame them against wretches who would insult them by imaging them traitors, for had they thought them virtuous, they would not have carried these overtures."[48]

Wayne wanted to get the two spies out of Princeton as quickly as possible and away from the mutineers. This would remove from the mutineers the temptation of accepting Sir Henry Clinton's offer. Wayne persuaded the sergeants to hand Mason and Ogden over to Joseph Reed.

8

Mutiny in Independence Hall

THE PENNSYLVANIA LINE MUTINY IV

*S*aturday, January 6, 1781, in Philadelphia had started out as a clear morning, but storm clouds built up during the course of the day, and toward night rain began to fall. George Nelson wrote about the events of the day with the Pennsylvania Militia Artillery.

> [We] met the officers of the artillery in the [Pennsylvania] State House [now known as Independence Hall] to consult about what should be done in our present unhappy situation. Captain Laing, Mr. Daniel Benezet and I were appointed a committee to draw up some resolves which were agreed to and Captain Laing appointed a deputy from one battalion to confer with the officers of the musquetry on the propriety of sending a committee to enquire into the cause or causes of the troops present uneasiness and with the consent of his Excellency President of the state and committee of Congress to act as mediators in the present unhappy affair and also to call the several companies together to meet in the state house yard tomorrow at two o'clock.[1]

During the evening as the rain was beating against the twelve-over-twelve windows, they formulated a series of resolves.

> State House Philadelphia January 6, 1781
>
> At a meeting of the officers of the Pennsylvania Militia Artillery, on motion resolved:
>
> First, that the officers of the Pennsylvania Militia Artillery lament the Pennsylvania Line of the Continental Troops and will exert themselves to the utmost to procure them justice and by no means whatever will use

force against them unless they attempt to form a junction with the enemy or manifest a disposition inimical or destructive to the common cause of America. That the said officers are fully convinced of the necessity of complying with his Excellency the President's request for holding the battalion in readiness to march against the common enemy on the shortest notice.

Resolved that the field officers of the artillery confer with the field officers of the several battalions of musquetry respecting the propriety of appointing a deputy from each battalion to form a committee to proceed immediately to his Excellency the President of the state and the committee of congress and with their concurrence to act as mediators between them and the Pennsylvania troops and to return certified extracts to be communicated to their respective battalions as soon as possible.

On Sunday morning, Nelson notified his artillery company to meet at the State House at two o'clock. They showed up and unanimously agreed to the resolves of the previous evening except by young Dr, Rush, son of William Rush, Esq.[2]

Sometime after sunrise on Sunday morning in Princeton, Mason and Ogden were rousted from their confinement, turned over to General Wayne, and marched under guard toward Trenton. They had come and gone from Princeton before most of the mutineers even knew that ambassadors carrying a proposal from Sir Henry Clinton had been in camp.

Also traveling early on this Sunday morning were Joseph Reed, General James Porter, and the Philadelphia Light Horse. They left Trenton headed north toward Maidenhead to be closer to the mutineers.

Reed and his party encountered Mason and Ogden and their guards on the road. Reed immediately sent a Dr. Hugh Shiell to inform the Committee of Congress, back at Trenton, about the spies and that the mutineers were not in cahoots with the British. The spies, Mason and Ogden, were handed over to Alexander Nesbitt and Blair McClenachan of the Philadelphia Light Horse and became custody of Reed's party.

The Irish-born Blair McClenachan had immigrated to the United States at an early age. He settled in Philadelphia where he engaged in mercantile pursuits, banking, and shipping. He was the owner of the ship *Hancock & Adams,* which had been contracted to the Secret Committee of Congress. He was also one of the founders of the First Troop Philadelphia City Cavalry. In 1780, McClenachan subscribed a large sum of money to help the American forces and aided the Continental Congress with money and credit.

Alexander Nesbitt was from Loughbrickland, County Down, Ireland. He and his brother John Maxwell Nesbitt established themselves as merchants after immigrating to Philadelphia. Alexander later went into business with Walter Stewart in the dry goods house of Stewart and Nesbitt.

Reed, upon reaching Maidenhead, made his quarters with Judge Daniel Hunt and proceeded to interrogate the spies.

General Wayne, Colonels Butler, Moylan, and Stewart left Princeton and arrived before noon at Maidenhead to confer with Reed. Just as Washington had always held the army subservient to the civil authority, Wayne would do no less. Now that President Reed of Pennsylvania had arrived to deal with the situation, General Wayne took a back seat in the events that were about to transpire. He would be there to be a stabilizing effect on the mutineers. He would also be there to take command once the civil authorities resolved the mess they had created. They informed him that he would be safe with the mutineers. The mutineers needed to be reassured by someone with authority that their complaints would be addressed.

At one o'clock, Reed wrote to the Committee of Congress that the mutineers were afraid that no one in authority was coming to meet with them. Reed believed it was their plan "to protract and forebear giving answers, they begged to be informed if I proposed coming that they might show me every mark of respect. . . . In such cases some risk is to be run. My personal safety is a small consideration. . . . The consequences of their defection to the enemy are so great and alarming that I think nothing ought to be left unattempted to improve a good disposition. I have but one life, and my country has the first claim for it."[3] Like the consummate politician he was already taking credit for his actions and he hadn't accomplished anything but traveling from Philadelphia to Maidenhead.

Once it was agreed that President Reed would make the trip to Princeton, General Wayne sent a message to the mutineers that Reed would be there that afternoon. As they were preparing to depart for Princeton, they were stopped by two sergeants who had just come from Princeton. They brought a letter from William Bowzar, who was the secretary to the mutineers' Board of Sergeants. The letter was addressed to Blair McClenachan and Alexander Nesbitt of the Philadelphia Light Horse. It stated, "It is the request of the Board, on account of the rumor of the Line, that you will send them two strangers who brought that letter from New York, by the bearers, to sergeants of the committee, as you may depend they shall be brought forth at the request of Governor Reed or any other gentleman when called on as we shall lodge them in security at our quarters."[4]

The mutineers' rumor mill was working overtime. Everyone was talking about what had transpired during the night. As with most rumors, it was a mix of the accurate and inaccurate.

Lieutenant Enos Reeves of the Pennsylvania Line wrote in his letterbook that "three spies who had come from General Clinton were arrested by the revolters, and after being drummed along the line were delivered to General Wayne to be tried."[5]

When William Bernard Gifford, an American officer working as a British spy, finally was able to get to New York, he reported to British intelligence that Governor Reed had offered the mutineers one hundred guineas to deliver the spies up to him. The Committee of Sergeant's refused the money and voted instead for the return of the spies.[6]

The request for the return of the spies caused much confusion among Reed and his entourage. There were several possibilities that could have pre-cipitated this request. The mutineers may have changed their minds and were now considering the British proposal. They may not have believed that Reed was near or that he was really coming to meet with them. This would explain why the letter was addressed to McClenachan and Nesbitt instead of Reed.

It may be that the Board of Sergeants believed that by holding the spies they would have a stronger bargaining position. Reed really had no choice but to return the spies, as General Wayne had given his word that the spies would be returned to the mutineers upon their request. Was this a test to see if Reed and Wayne could be trusted to keep their word? If they couldn't be trusted in the matter of the spies, Mason and Ogden, how could they be trusted in the more important matter of the men's enlistments?

Since General Wayne had sent word to the mutineers that Reed would be at Princeton that afternoon, Reed could not afford to disappoint them. To do so, might send them marching straight to the British.

Reed arrived in Princeton around three in the afternoon. He was saluted and received by the soldiers with great respect under arms. Some of the ser-geants, being suspicious, came up to Reed to check him out. They were only satisfied when some of the sergeants who knew Joseph Reed personally did a close inspection and assured the rest of them that it really was President

Reed. Mason and Ogden arrived later as they most likely walked the five miles from Maidenhead to Princeton. Upon their arrival, Mason and Ogden were "paraded through the lines."

General Wayne wanted the Board of Sergeants to put Mason and Ogden to death. Their execution would remove them from the bargaining table. Wayne stated that their execution would be a "peace offering to the country." The Board knew that keeping the spies alive strengthened their bargaining position.

During the ensuing conference, Reed met with twelve sergeants who represented the group. The sergeants informed Reed that they primarily were upset with some of their own officers and they complained of the very deceptive practices used to obtain their enlistments. The mutineers had reduced their demands. Their position was that "all men enlisted in the years 1776 and 1777 and [who] received the bounty of twenty dollars, shall be without any delay discharged and all the arrears of pay and clothing to be paid unto them immediately when discharged; with respect to depreciation of pay, the State to give them sufficient certificates and security for such sums as they shall be due."

When Reed balked, the men told of how some of them had been physically coerced into reenlisting while others had been arbitrarily detained beyond the expiration of their term of enlistment. The men also told how, in 1779, they had been required to sign documents that were "framed so as to convey an acknowledgement of being enlisted for the war." Reed realized that some very unscrupulous methods had been employed by Pennsylvania recruiters to secure the men's enlistments.

That evening, Reed prepared a proposed settlement that he signed and that was cosigned by General James Potter, councilman of the Executive Council of the State of Pennsylvania. It stated that no soldier should be detained beyond the time "for which he freely and voluntarily engaged." Also, if it appeared that a soldier had been "in any respect compelled to enter or sign" then the enlistment would be "deemed void, and the soldier discharged." Any disputes would be resolved by a three-person committee.

Since this was wartime with its resulting chaos, the original records of some of the mutineers would surely not be located or expeditiously brought to the committee, as they were scattered among the regiments and across Pennsylvania. To resolve this lack of original documentation of their enlistment, the soldier need only take an oath as to the "time and terms of enlist-

ment" to prove that he was entitled to be discharged. This was a major con-
cession to the mutineers. The proposal also stated that "Pursuant to General
Wayne's order of the second instant, no man to be brought to any trial or cen-
sure for what has happened on or since New Year's Day, but all matters to be
buried in oblivion."

The meeting finally adjourned near midnight. The sergeants agreed to
submit the proposal to the mutineers at morning roll call. When Reed left the
meeting, he returned to Maidenhead to await their decision.

THE AMERICANS DEFINITELY KNEW THAT additional couriers had been sent by
Sir Henry Clinton to approach the mutineers. Caleb Bruen had told Dayton
that upon his arrival in New Jersey.

Jonathan Witherspoon, writing for the Committee of Congress now at
Trenton, wanted to warn the commander at New Brunswick or Elizabethtown
that they "have received authentic information that Commissioners (2) are
sent to Amboy from New York to treat with the Pennsylvania troops (we suppose this South Amboy that is meant but it would be prudent to have both
the Amboys in view). The Committee are of opinion you should take such
measures as appear most prudent and practicable, to get possession of those
Commissioners."[7]

The balance of the Philadelphia Light Horse arrived at Trenton on Sunday
the 7th. They continued on to Princeton and went into the mutineers' camp
and to the mutineers' headquarters in Nassau Hall but were not allowed to
remain there. The mutineers, insisting that the officers were their guests and
nothing was going to happen to them, had the Light Horse taken to the
Provost Guard to await orders from General Arthur St. Clair.[8]

General Arthur St. Clair then went on to Morristown, New Jersey, where
he sent a letter by a Mr. Donaldson to Joseph Reed of the failure of his and
Lafayette's mission to the Pennsylvania Line.

Generals St. Clair and Lafayette had been advised to leave Princeton
immediately by the mutineers. The two generals had heard that Colonel's
Butler and Stewart and General Wayne were being held as prisoners. The
mutineers were not allowing them any outside contact. Since it was possible
that they could be held as pawns in the bargaining of resolution, Generals St.
Clair and Lafayette decided to get out of there as fast they could.

General St. Clair's analysis of the situation was that "I have no hopes of
any thing but force reducing them to reason" and "it is certain that British

emissary's have set this matter a going, and many of them have confessed to us that it was proposed to them to lead them all there. This, however, they nobly refused."[9] General Lafayette and Lieutenant Colonel Laurens who had accompanied General St. Clair to Morristown continued their journey to Washington's Headquarters at New Windsor, New York.

Sunday evening, Major Fishbourne arrived from New Windsor, New York, carrying George Washington's letter of instructions to Wayne. Washington had written telling Wayne to stay with the mutineers, try to get them beyond the Delaware River, and not to use force. He told Wayne to represent the army's positions in the negotiations with the mutineers.

During the day, the commissary general of stores at Trenton informed New Jersey Governor William Livingston that there was no beef in the Trenton repository. Livingston realized that the Pennsylvania Line was going to quickly use up the beef cattle they had brought with them from Morristown and a hungry horde would pillage the countryside for food. He prepared an urgent plea to John Butler, the contractor for Burlington County for a supply of meat. He implored him "to use your utmost endeavors to send on as speedily as possible a supply of beef and pork to this post"[10]. Charles Stewart, commissary general of issues added the following post script to the letter. "The troops are to be here to day and we shall have no meat for them unless you send it. Please let me know what may be expected."[11]

In New York and Staten Island, the warm rain that had started the previous night, the 6th, continued until the afternoon of the 7th.[12] The British in New York were waiting for information on what was happening with the Pennsylvanians. As soon as their spies returned they sent them back out again. Uzal Woodruff set out on Saturday morning, the 6th, for Kingston near Princeton.[13]

Frederick Mackenzie wrote at 10:00 a.m. to Oliver De Lancey that he had not received De Lancey's correspondence of the previous night until that morning. No additional intelligence had been received beyond what Stapleton had reported the previous night. "Captain Forshner [Andrew Füstner] who is going down takes the proclamations."

Mackenzie advised that another spy recommended by Colonel Robinson would be sent that evening towards Pompton and up to New Windsor.[14]

On the 7th, John Stapleton sent out Ezekiel Yeomans who was from Kakiat, Orange, now Rockland County, New York. Yeomans returned on the

8th.[15] Because of the quick turnaround, he must have been dropped off and picked up by a boat. Mackenzie followed up at 5:00 p.m. and advised that "we have sent two trusty men into the neighborhood of Washington's army."[16]

Clinton, who was skilled at planning for prolonged events such as a siege where every step was carefully examined, remained cautious and was weighing his options. He called a meeting with General William Phillips, a trusted friend in whom Clinton had carried on a secret correspondence in masked letters to hide their comments from prying eyes. British secret service operated within the British post office department and routinely intercepted and examined mail. They also met with General James Robertson.

There was no expectation of privacy of the mail in the eighteenth century. Beginning in 1765, warrants were issued by each secretary of state ordering the opening of all diplomatic mail going though London. A Mr. Bode, who came from Hanover, was brought over specifically to run the secret service office, which he did from 1732 to 1784. Mr. Bode's assistant was Anthony Todd, who was employed from about 1751 to 1792. At the time of the American Revolution, the most secret intercepts were restricted to the King, Lord North, and the two secretaries of state.

At the January 7 meeting between Sir Henry Clinton and Generals Phillips and Robertson, they all agreed that a landing in New Jersey should not be made unless circumstances made it necessary. There was not enough information to determine what the Pennsylvanians were going to do.[17]

Loyalist Brigadier General Cortland Skinner's spies in New Jersey probably were having a difficult time getting to Staten Island where his headquarters was located. The New Jersey Militia was out in force guarding bridges between the mutineers and Raritan Bay. They were at New Brunswick and from Elizabethtown down Arthur Kill to South Amboy. The New Jersey Militia was determined to intercept anyone attempting to pass. The Continental Line troops were positioned at Chatham, Morristown, and Pompton.

Brigadier General Cortland Skinner, on Staten Island, turned in a report on Sunday the 7th to Oliver De Lancey saying that the mutineers had marched toward New Brunswick and that Wayne was held prisoner among them. His spies told him the mutineers' army had already passed New Brunswick and was at Princeton.

Wayne was with the mutineers, but he was not a prisoner. General Skinner also heard that a man sent with proposals was observed within a mile of the mutineers on Friday evening.[18] This could have been Gould's courier or Mason and his guide.

Fifty-three-year-old Cortland Skinner, one of the political bosses of New Jersey under the Royal Government, was an attorney of significant ability and inflexible integrity. He was appointed the King's attorney general for the Province of New Jersey and, in 1761, was elected to the Provincial Assembly from Perth Amboy. He held these positions until the end of English authority in New Jersey. William Tryon stated that this was "the only instance in America of the same man holding the confidence of King and people."[19] He recruited the New Jersey Volunteers, and, from his base of operations on Staten Island, he ran a very effective spy operation in New Jersey.

On Staten Island, the 42nd Regiment was expecting to parade despite the rain. They traveled from their quarters at Hillyer's to Richmond Town, a distance of about a mile.[20] Upon their arrival, they discovered there would be no parade.[21] Meanwhile the Hessian soldiers were anxiously awaiting orders to leave Staten Island and cross over into New Jersey.[22]

9

Negotiations

THE PENNSYLVANIA LINE MUTINY V

*T*he soldiers awoke to water frozen solid in buckets. At eight on Monday morning January 8, the army of mutineers, keeping to military order, assembled for roll call. The men stood in the clear cold weather and listened attentively as Potter and Reed's proposal for the resolution of their grievances was read to them.[1] The committee of sergeants had kept their word. No record of the events that transpired at roll call has ever been found.

Around two-thirty in the afternoon, Reed heard from some passing soldiers that his proposal had been accepted and that the spies, Mason and Ogden, were being kept in close custody but the mutineers had not settled their fate.

Governor Reed sent an account of his proceedings and a copy of the proposal to the Committee of Congress. Earlier in the day, he had sent a letter to General Wayne to keep him informed of what he was doing.

The auditors arrived and set up operations at Trenton to adjust the accounts of the soldiers equable to the state law. Reed told Wayne that he wanted to hear from him "this evening at all events."[2] Colonel William Butler, commander of the 4th Pennsylvania Regiment who was attacked during the initial hour of the mutiny, was at Princeton, and sent a courier, by way of Pennytown to Trenton, who was instructed to bring all the blankets, shoes, shirts, and other stores that he could get.[3]

The New Jersey Militia, under Brigadier General Nathaniel Heard, had assembled on the lines at New Brunswick and elsewhere. They were to oppose the enemy if they should land at Amboy and to quell the mutiny if reasonable terms should be refused.

The inhabitants of Princeton had allowed the soldiers to mix with them and they kept the Committee of Congress fully apprised of the mutineers activities. They found there were a considerable number of British deserters who had been enlisted in the Pennsylvania line. This was contrary to the repeated directions of Congress and the laws of their own state. Two of these British deserters had even been selected for the Board of Sergeants who managed their affairs. The Committee thought that probably these, as well as some of the other English deserters, had their eyes on New York but were never able to make their sentiments known or dared to express them.

Aware that the New Jersey Militia might be called out to protect the citizenry, the mutineers announced that they only wanted justice. They stated that, should the enemy come out, they would fight under General Wayne. They had, at same time, dropped the threat that if the militia came upon them before this affair was resolved they would burn and lay waste to the country.

The Committee of Congress prepared an additional declaration. This, having been sent to President Reed, was by him communicated to the mutineers. That evening, they sent a written declaration commenting on the terms. About this time, the Committee received a copy of General Washington's letter to General Wayne, by which it appeared that he recommended the very measures of leniency and justice that had been adopted by them.

President Reed adhered to his own propositions and those of the Committee. He rejected the idea of choosing an equal number of the commissioners, who would determine the particular claims. He insisted that they should immediately accept or refuse the terms, and if they accepted, that they should march to Trenton to have the plan carried into execution. This was accordingly agreed to.[4]

Thomas Craig, at Pennytown, New Jersey, wrote to General Wayne that he had received his correspondence from the previous day, the 7th. Wayne had heard some disparaging comments about himself and Colonels Butler and Stewart that supposedly had come from the trailing officers. Craig wrote that he had conducted an inquiry and had found no one with negative opinions of their behavior. Most held the opinion that "by your remaining so close with the troops it would make them have more important idea of their consequences."[5] The only concern he found was "almost all have their fears that if they go to the enemy they will make you a prisoner and carry you with them."

He went on to say that the comments "proceeded altogether from their regard for you and not from any disrespect."[6]

At 11:30 a.m., General Wayne and Colonels Butler and Stewart sent a joint letter with attachments to the officers who had followed the mutineers' army from Morristown. The letter was carried by a Mr. Nesbitt. The letter, with its attachments, brought them up to date on everything that had transpired concerning the mutineers. They advised that the previous day "President Reed and a Committee from Council arrived with full power to settle this unhappy disturbance. They were met by twelve sergeants who laid before them the grievances complained of by the troops." The mutineers' "demand of having the 20 dollar men all discharged, seems still to remain unalterable in their minds, and you may rest assured as inadmissible in ours."[7]

General Wayne and the two colonels made them aware they were waiting for an answer from the mutineers which would determine how to proceed. They were happy to report that their being with the mutineers had helped to cool things down among them. Somehow, the officers had gotten information to Wayne that they wanted him and Colonels Butler and Stewart to be with them. They believed the mutineers might turn on their guests and make them prisoners.

Wayne advised that he had planned to give the mutineers an ultimatum and if they did not comply, he was going to leave them to their own devices. However, he could not carry the threat to fruition because of contrary instructions from General Washington and the opinion of Governor Reed.

One of the attachments was a copy of the letter from British General Clinton that had been brought by the spies Mason and Ogden. Wayne was very clear that he wanted the spies hung. The letter concluded with a plea for a response, as the only information they could obtain was from people who had been among the officers.[8] Wayne did get a response from Colonel Adam Hubley of the 13th Pennsylvania Regiment and resident of Lancaster County, the next day, which was also Hubley's forty-first birthday.[9]

Around three in the afternoon, General Wayne, at Princeton, received a letter from William Bowzar, secretary to the Committee of Sergeants. The letter informed him that at the morning roll call President Reed's proposal was communicated to the soldiers. They agreed that all the soldiers who were enlisted for the bounty of twenty dollars ought to be discharged immediately with as little delay as possible. Those soldiers who had voluntarily reenlisted were to be excluded.

Reed had proposed a board of three persons to be appointed by the president and Council of Pennsylvania to resolve disputes. The mutineers agreed with Reed's proposal except for the composition of the committee. The Committee of Sergeants wanted the right to appoint an equal number of people to sit on the board. They wanted to be sure they were going to be treated with justice and honor.[10]

Wayne forwarded Bowzar's letter to Reed at Maidenhead. At 4:30 p.m., Wayne sent for the sergeants. Washington had insisted that Wayne stay with the mutineers, not use force, but get them to the Delaware River. Wayne was going to bluff. He insisted that they march to Trenton in the morning where there was a store of supplies. If they refused, Wayne told them that he and the colonels would leave them to act as they pleased and suffer the effects of their actions. The sergeants, realizing that an army needs to be fed, agreed to move out for Trenton in the morning, bringing their bargaining chip, the two spies, with them.[11]

Sometime that evening, Reed received Bowzar's letter and sent a reply back by a Mr. Caldwell.[12] He was displeased with the mutineer's wanting to appoint board members. Reed, in his reply, made it very clear that this condition was unacceptable: "This implies such a distrust of the authority of the state which has ever been attentive to the wants of the army that the impropriety of it must be evident."[13] This was a politician's version of the truth. Clearly the state had not been attentive to the wants of the army. If the state had taken care of the army, then this mutiny would probably never have occurred.

Reed was not about to add soldiers to the board. To do so would mean sharing authority with the soldiers and there would be no way to resolve deadlocks. He did agree to allow soldiers the liberty to bring before the commissioners any person to represent their case. In his reply to the mutineers, Reed advised that the Committee of Congress wanted the spies turned over to them and in exchange "will proclaim a general oblivion of all matters since 31 December" with the proviso that the terms offered in the last letter were accepted and the mutiny was ended. Reed ended the letter with the recommendation that the mutineers "should march in the morning to Trenton where the stores are." He was repeating what he had said in his earlier letter but he wanted to get the mutineers as far away from the British as possible for he was still uncertain what would happen if negotiation failed.[14]

Francis King had come to New York from New Jersey at the Blazing Star on January 8, 1781, and claims to have been with the mutineers.[15] British Brigadier General Cortland Skinner said he thought King's story was true and mentioned that King had been to Staten Island often.[16]

On January 8, Isaac Ogden sent Francis King and Abraham Sanford with their companions to Oliver De Lancey to get a pass to go out of the British lines. Ogden asserted that Sanford and King were people upon whom they could depend. He mentioned that they had previously brought in written intelligence and that if De Lancey needed someone to send "out on business," he would have confidence in Sanford or King.[17] They were sent out on the morning of the 9th.[18]

Not surprisingly, rumors were making the rounds on Staten Island. The Hessians had heard that the ranks of the mutineers had swollen to three thousand.[19]

On the British stronghold of Staten Island, the troops paraded at 11:00 a.m. at Richmond Town in the clear cold weather. General Phillips was busy checking the alarm posts about the fort above Richmond Town. The 37th and 42nd Regiments were kept in readiness for an immediate movement.[20] The 42nd relocated to Egberts, which was northeast of Richmond Town.[21] William Smith wrote in his memoirs that he received a report from Sir Henry Clinton that "two men had been with him from the mutineers at Brunswick and were gone back again." He had visited with the governor but was unable to get additional information on the mutineers from him.[22]

TUESDAY THE 9TH WAS A DAY OF COLD, raw weather in Princeton when the mutineers turned out for roll call at 8:00 a.m.[23] The men lined up; their breath clouded the morning air. The mutineers kept their promise to General Wayne, and by 9:00 a.m., they began an orderly march to Trenton.

A mile and half down the road to Trenton they passed the Princeton Battlefield where, on January 3, 1777, the American army had met and defeated a British army comprising the 17th Foot, the 55th Foot, and a troop of the 16th Light Dragoons, under the command of Lieutenant Colonel Charles Mawhood. Many of these soldiers had fought in that battle four years earlier.

Pennsylvania Governor Reed quickly got word to the Committee of Congress that the mutineers were on their way to Trenton. John Sullivan, the former major general in the Continental Army, writing as a member of the committee, notified New Jersey Governor Livingston that "the troops are paraded and in motion for this place after having received and excepted the terms offered to them." The Committee requested that he give "all the aid in your power to the Quartermaster and Commissary Departments in providing for the troops."[24]

Slowed by the cold, bad roads, and underfed horses pulling wagons, the mutineers' army took five hours to cover ten miles, arriving at Trenton at 2:00 p.m.[25] The Committee of Congress watched as they marched into town and encamped in a field north of the ferry. Because the men were in a good disposition, the committee did not feel any trepidation. However, they thought it would have an improper appearance if they remained in town under the influence of men in arms. Therefore in the afternoon, the committee took up residence across the Delaware River in Colvin's Ferry (Morrisville), Pennsylvania, on a 220-acre farm owned by Thomas Barclay, where they moved into his two-story brick house (Summerseat). Reed and Wayne went to the residence of John Cox, which was called Bloomsbury. The Board of Sergeants took up residence at Jonathan Richmond's tavern in Trenton.[26] Richmond's was located on the east side of South Broad Street south of the Assunpink Creek.

For the first two days of 1777, Jonathan Richmond's tavern had been George Washington's headquarters. It was next door to George Bright's bakery thereby ensuring the Board of Sergeants of good food and drink. That evening, the Committee of Congress had a long conference with the Committee of the Council of Pennsylvania. Without delay, they appointed commissioners for hearing and determining the claims of the soldiers. The commissioners were Colonel Atlee of the Committee of Congress, General Potter of the Committee of Council, and Captain Morris and Mr. Blair McClenachan of the Light Horse. The decision was made to make a peremptory demand the next morning for the two British spies being held by the soldiers.

One of the couriers carrying General Clinton's proposal to the mutineers went to Morristown and showed the proposal to General St. Clair. To be certain of the mutineers' intentions, St. Clair had sent the man with the proposal to General Wayne. The man had assured St. Clair that he would return to him with the mutineers' answer. St. Clair told Wayne that they heard, at Morristown, the mutineers had detained two who came to them with proposals. He asked Wayne if that should happen to this man, to intercede if possible.[27]

THE BRITISH AWAKENED ON JANUARY 9 to a frost covering Staten Island.[28] The weather was turning bad as the British waited for news.[29] The troops on Staten Island were paraded at 11:00 a.m. and given their provisions.[30] At noon, word finally arrived in the form of a ciphered message from Andrew Gautier. Oliver De Lancey reported to Sir Henry Clinton that Andrew Gautier was his most trusted contact in New Jersey. Gautier reported that the person he sent to Princeton had returned. He had left Princeton that morning after delivering the proposal on Saturday night, the very night Mason and Ogden were taken into custody.

The courier estimated the mutineers to number seventeen hundred and they were well behaved. The mutineers did not allow admittance of any officer except by a flag of truce. He said they had met with General Wayne and Governor Reed of Pennsylvania, but had rejected their offers. Gautier said that the proposal was now well known among the mutineers and officers at Elizabethtown, and it was believed that the mutineers would still come over to the British side.[31]

Joseph Clark, who had been sent out on the 5th, had returned from Morristown by way of his home town of Warwick, New York, before getting back to New York City at 3:00 p.m. on the 8th. The next day, Colonel Beverly Robinson recorded Clark's report that the mutineer's were at Princeton. It was feared at Morristown that the New Jersey troops would follow the example of the Pennsylvanians. His other information was of no additional value.[32]

That the mutineers were at Princeton was also confirmed by information received by forty-nine-year-old Major General William Phillips who was commanding the British troops on Staten Island. Phillips wrote to De Lancey that Lieutenant Stuard of the armed sloop *Vulture* had just arrived at 2:00 p.m. on January 8 and reported on a raid on Perth Amboy the previous night. The sloop, under the command of Captain Charles Stirling, which was stationed off Billopp's Point at the southern end of Staten Island, had been requested by Sir Henry Clinton to collect intelligence and send the information to General Phillips.

An armed detachment of thirty men of provincial cavalry under the command of Lieutenant William Stewart from the *Vulture* had landed in the city of Perth Amboy on the morning of the 9th.[33] They surprised a picket of New Jersey Militia under the command of Ensign Asher Fitz-Randolph belonging to Colonel John Webster's 1st Regiment of Middlesex County Militia.[34] The militia was assembled in large bodies to prevent the mutineers from retreating toward the coast. From the twelve men they captured and informants in the city, it was discovered that the mutineers planned to fight should the British enter New Jersey in force and that the two spies, Mason and Ogden, had been taken prisoner and were expected to be hanged that day.[35] He was also forwarding the men they captured in Perth Amboy for his "examination and orders."[36]

Captain Charles Stirling landed at South Amboy and made contact with twenty-six-year-old John Rattoon. Rattoon informed him that the mutineers were not able to cross the Delaware River because the boats had been removed. Two men coming to the British from the mutineers were taken prisoner on Friday night, the 5th at Quibbletown.[37] One man, meaning Ogden, who went out on Thursday evening, had not returned. Within two hours of landing at South Amboy, Captain Charles Stirling was writing his report to General Phillips.[38]

The Hessian Grenadiers had been given orders to depart from Staten Island—not west for New Jersey as they expected, but east for Gravesend on Long Island. They marched to Cole's Ferry at the Narrows and embarked for Long Island in a small craft.[39] They settled into their winter quarters on Long Island the next day.[40]

The Jaegers took over the buidings that the departing Grenadiers had vacated.[41] De Lancey believed the order for the Hessians to move was issued because of the bad weather.[42] There was speculation among the troops that Sir Henry Clinton was not going to risk them on an expedition to New Jersey.

It was on this day that General Clinton made a note about the couriers he had sent. As a precaution he had written their names in his personal shorthand.

> Gould came in to Staten Island with an answer to my letter to [Gautier], acknowledging the receipt of two copies of the proposals sent the 4th. [Gautier had acknowledged the receipt of the two copies three days before.]
>
> [Bruen] sent out the 6th with a proposal.
>
> [Mason] sent out the 4th, landed the 5th in the Raritan, a proposal.
>
> Hatfield a proposal on the 5th to sent out.
>
> Dr. [Dayton] says they are at Trenton, some dispersed. [This was Dr. Jonathan I. Dayton of Elizabethtown, a relative of Colonel Elias Dayton of the American secret service. At some time during the past year, Dr. Dayton had been kidnapped and brought into New York, but afterwards permitted

to go home on parole. There he had "behaved very civilly to all who visited Elizabethtown" from the British and "friends coming in." Now he himself had come in, with unknown motives. Some of the loyalists in New York
distrusted him as much as any of his patriot neighbors could have done.
He had, at first, been a loyalist; then, under pressure from the rebels, had
taken the oath of abjuration and allegiance; after his capture by the British
he had given his word to serve them in secret. He was a double-dealer trying to safeguard his future no matter which side should win the war.]

[Woodruff], twice over, says at Princeton. [Woodruff did not agree with Dr.
Dayton as to where the mutineers had gone from Morristown. On the day
they marched to Trenton the British were still comparing conflicting
reports on the line's whereabouts.]

Mr. A. J. [Andrew Gautier, Jr.], [mutineers] at Princeton, in today. [Gould
may have said that Gautier was coming, but he did not arrive.]

General Skinner, [mutineers] at Princeton and at Trenton. [The information Skinner had received from his New Jersey spies had the mutineers at
Princeton and that the mutineers had also arrived in Trenton.]

[Samuel McFarlan], at Princeton, went out 5th with a proposal given to
[Thomas] Ward. [Since McFarlan had not been heard from since he left,
this presumably means that before going he had said the Pennsylvanians
were at Princeton and he would go to that place.]

[Brink] sent out 5th.[43]

Clinton, in this list, named four of his emissaries—Mason, Bruen,
McFarlan, and Brink—and referred to the proposals given to Gautier and
Cornelius Hatfield that were to be sent out by two more emissaries. Of the
four named, Mason was taken; Bruen and McFarlan had gone to General
Wayne; and Brink had disappeared from sight so far as the records show. He
may have been the double-dealing emissary who went to St. Clair or that may
have been Hatfield's messenger.

The British were under the same handicap as any army of occupation:
they could not rely on the agents they used among the people. The honest loyalists were refugees inside the British lines, while the honest patriots were citizens inside the American lines. The no-man's-land between the two armies
was usually traversed only by people of doubtful character.

Though the British had money to buy spies, the double-dealers had local
attachments to their own country. It might be, in some respects, more prof-
itable to join the British openly but it was almost sure to be, in the long run,

more comfortable to stay among their countrymen. Any spy employed by the British was likely to have taken some kind of pains to stand well also with the Americans.

On one of the later spy reports among the British secret service papers, Clinton wrote an endorsement that gave his conclusions about the matter. "I had sent six spies; the two last were two too many. They [the mutineers] were saved to Americans by good management, not lost to us by bad management. Had the Americans tried force we should have had them. Their chiefs were inclined to lead them to us, but were afraid to sound them out."[44]

Major General William Phillips was at his headquarters in Richmond Town, Staten Island. He wrote down his analysis of the situation for General Clinton. "By comparing your intelligence with what I sent you from Stuard, you will observe how nearly they agree. I am still of the opinion that any movement into the Jerseys would only alarm and might facilitate a reconciliation. If they have your proposals they know we are ready."[45]

Clinton respected Major General Phillips's opinions on military matters. Clinton accepted Phillips's conclusion that the mutineers were not coming.[46] Three days later, Clinton would write back to his close friend Phillips agreeing with Phillips's position and stating it as his own: "I am apprehensive that these people have no intention of joining us unless some violent act of Washington or Congress should force them to it. And as I fear any move of ours might facilitate reconciliation, it is my opinion to wait for events in our present situation."

THE ONLY NEWS THAT REACHED PHILADELPHIA ON JANUARY 9 concerning the mutineers was that two spies had been captured at Princeton. It started snowing in the evening but then changed to rain. It rained hard all night but cleared by morning.[47]

On Wednesday morning the 10th, the mutineers proposed an additional condition, which was they should continue in arms until the whole regiment was settled. They would not disperse as they received their discharges. President Joseph Reed, at Trenton, positively refused the condition; he said it was absurd. He advised them that he would have a final answer to the former propositions within two hours.

During this period, the mutineers declared they were satisfied with the nomination of the commissioners. They withdrew the additional condition submitted that morning. Reed requested as a proof of the sincerity of their professions to the country to turn over custody of the spies. The mutineers, as promised, immediately delivered up the spies. Mason and Ogden were sent to the Committee of Congress.[48]

In the meantime, General Wayne sent a note to the council that in order to resolve this situation of which soldiers were entitled to their discharges, it was necessary that all enlistment documents be collected as quickly as possible. The commanding officers and paymasters for each regiment would also need to attend when the commissioners set up their command to resolve these discrepancies.[49]

Up along the Hudson River at New Windsor, George Washington sent a message to General Heath. "You will be pleased immediately to summon all the general officers and the colonels or officers commanding the regiments of the lines under your command to meet punctuality at ten o'clock to morrow morning at your quarters, I will be down myself by that time."[50]

Five minutes before he got into a boat to head down river to West Point, Washington sent off a quick message to Philip Schuyler at Albany informing him that he had summoned the officer of the corps to meet him and that it was very probable that he would to go to Morristown.[51]

On Staten Island, January 10 broke wet, unseasonably mild, and foggy. Because of the miserable conditions, there was no parading of troops. With the soldiers just trying to stay dry and passing time, the rumor mill got into full production. A story circulated that the mutineers had moved into Monmouth County, which was totally untrue.[52] Oliver De Lancey and General Sir Henry Clinton were waiting for intelligence. There would be no midday influx of secret reports as no agents returned to the British line that day.

-10

Hanging Spies

THE PENNSYLVANIA LINE MUTINY VI

*M*ajor General Lord Stirling, the highest ranking officer at Trenton, called for "a court of inquiry to set this afternoon, Wednesday the 10th, at four o'clock at Summer Seat, State of Pennsylvania to hear and report their opinion whether John Mason, late of New York and James Ogden of South River, State of New Jersey, were found within the lines of the American Army in the character of spies; and if said court find the charge, then to give their determination thereon."

After some pointed discussion, the spies under strong guard were turned over around dusk to Joseph Reed and General Anthony Wayne at Bloomsbury House. Mason and Ogden were then taken to the Committee of Congress who would determine their fate. The court of inquiry scheduled for 4:00 p.m. was finally able to meet at 8:00 p.m.

There is no record of the testimony at the trial. James Ogden mostly likely claimed to have no knowledge of Mason's mission. John Mason did try to strike a bargain by telling of a plot to capture General Washington. The plan was to be executed by Thomas Ward, a turncoat and British spy, along with "thirty more desperadoes." The court of inquiry ruled that they were "decidedly of opinion that the said John Mason and James Ogden came clearly within the description of spies and that, according to the rules and customs of nations at war, they ought to be hung by the neck until they are dead."

General Stirling confirmed the verdict and the sentencing by the court of inquiry. He fixed the time for the hanging at nine the next morning, January 11, "at the cross-roads from the upper ferry from Trenton to Philadelphia at the four lanes' ends" with Major Benjamin Fishbourne in charge.

Private David H. Conyngham of the Philadelphia Light Horse, a thirty-year-old Philadelphia merchant in civilian life, spent the night guarding the two spies. He wrote that Ogden was "much agitated and overcome hearing his sentence." Mason "seemed to feel his situation, but declared . . . that if they hung him, he was in fault, but that he would die a true and loyal subject of George III." During the night Mason and Ogden begged Conyngham to find out if there was any hope for them. Conyngham noted, "I went and spoke to General Wayne, who decidedly told me nothing could save them, unless we let them escape, which would involve us in trouble. I then procured a Bible from Mr. Barclay and passed the night in reading it to them. Mason was devout, but Ogden was in terror and distress. I got them something to eat, and in the morning Mason slept a little."

Mason wanted to see General Wayne before the execution. However, it was not to be.[1] Mason was repeating his tale of the plan for capturing General Washington. He insisted that the "intelligence he mentioned the previous evening was literally true."

Early Thursday morning the 11th at Trenton, the Philadelphia Light Horse broke camp. It was a fine pleasant morning.[2] They crossed to the opposite side of the Delaware River to where four roads merged by Patrick Colvin's Ferry.[3] The village of Colvin's Ferry (Morrisville), Pennsylvania, was named for Colvin who had purchased a large plot of land there in 1772. Mason and Ogden, with their hands bound, were brought out from their confinement. They stood as their sentences of death by hanging were read to them.

The Philadelphia Light Horse then took Mason and Ogden behind Colvin's one-story stone ferry house where a tree was selected for the hanging. No one had thought to bring a rope—a clear case of everyone thinking it's someone else's job. First Lieutenant James Budden, a Philadelphia merchant and six year veteran of the Light Horse, came to the rescue. He saw that the servant of Private Conyngham had "just arrived with clothes from Philadelphia" and had a rope collar on a his horse. Mason and Ogden would cheat death for a few more minutes while the horse collar was transformed into a pair of executioner's nooses.

Once the rope situation was resolved, the execution of Mason and Ogden could begin. Colvin's black slave was commandeered to be the hangman.[4] The newly made nooses were placed around their necks and Mason and Ogden were quickly dispatched back to their Creator. The entire business was concluded by noon.[5] Later General Lafayette wrote that he was surprised that the mutineers would turn over General Clinton's envoys to be hanged. They gave up their strongest bargaining chip.[6]

The Light Horse, having received orders to return to Philadelphia, departed quickly and left the two spies hanging from the tree. They were still swaying in the wind on Saturday the 13th and were not taken down until Tuesday the 16th.[7]

Samuel Wallis was a Quaker shipper and speculator in Philadelphia and a British secret agent. He sent a message to forty-year-old Daniel Coxe, a lawyer formerly from Trenton and now in New York City. Wallis stated Mason "behaved with great bravery. He told them he had but one favor to ask which was that General Clinton might be informed that he had done everything in his power to execute his trust, that he had been unfortunate, and died like a brave man."[8] The message to Clinton was most likely an attempt by Mason to get his wife released from jail.

AFTER THE SPIES WERE EXECUTED, the Committee of Congress directed the commissioners to settle the claims of the soldiers in the different regiments. One or two regiments were settled with before the committee left Trenton. By the report of General Wayne, there appeared a very general disposition in those who were discharged to reenlist, to which nothing was wanting but money to pay the bounty in advance.

Some of the recruits who had enlisted the previous summer claimed they had not received the balance of their bounty money since they got to camp. Reed asked Colonel Lewis Nicola about the situation. Nicola responded that he had sent in three shipments on August 16 by Lieutenant Bigham, September 9 by Captain McSheton, and November 29 by Lieutenant Wigton, for a total of £13,518. He asked Wayne to determine if the money had been distributed. The day before, Reed had sent to Philadelphia for £5,000 in state of Pennsylvania money. In the meantime, he got what money he could in Trenton and sent it up that afternoon.[9]

One circumstance ought not to be omitted because it does the mutineers much honor. When they delivered up the British spies, Governor Reed offered them one hundred guineas, which they refused. They said what they did was only a duty they owed their country and they neither desired nor would receive any reward but the approbation of that country, for which they had so often fought and bled.[10]

Summerseat, a Georgian manor house, was built in the 1770s for Thomas Barclay in the town of Colvin's Ferry (Morrisville), Pennsylvania. On January 10, 1781, it was the site for the trial of British spies, John Mason and James Ogden. Summerseat is a U.S. National Historic Landmark. (*Library of Congress*)

James Burnside was in a street side room of Jonathan Richmond's tavern in Trenton and described it as being a very noisy place.[11] Understandable, since he had to share space in the same building with the Board of Sergeant's who set up their headquarters in the same tavern on the 9th. He sent a letter from the Richmond's tavern to William Livingston, governor of New Jersey, who was still in Trenton on the morning of the 11th.

Although the mutineers had conducted matters with the greatest decorum, the residents of Trenton would be happy when they were gone. Livingston packed up some time after the 14th and moved to Bordentown by the 18th. He was afraid the mutineers might get out of hand and "make a holyday with my public documents."[12]

John Witherspoon wrote up the Committee of Congress's report. It stated, "That this disturbance however unhappy and threatening at first, has now afforded an undeniable and pleasing proof of the firm attachment of the soldiery as well as the country in general to the American cause. . . . There was not the least appearance of any previous concert with the enemy, nor any disposition to hearken to overtures when made by them. It ought not to be forgotten that the seizing of the spies was previous to any steps being taken for accommodating the difference."[13]

The committee also recommended that British deserters should not be enlisted in the army and that perhaps those who were in the army should be discharged. The report also stated that every state should be asked to pay the strictest attention to supplying the needs of the army.[14]

ON JANUARY 12, BRITISH GENERAL SIR HENRY CLINTON was still unsure of what was transpiring with the mutineers in New Jersey. Uzal Woodruff returned from his latest journey behind the American lines where he had obtained some information. On January 11, he reported that the Pennsylvanians were as before and the guards of militia were so thick that no one could pass. British headquarters sent a message to Andrew Gautier that day: "Pray let me know by the bearer the name of the person who commands the Pennsylvanians. How the militia are distributed and if you can send any body to Princeton tell them they will be supported if they come to South Amboy. They should send an officer to us."[15]

South Amboy was selected because of it was the closest navigable point on the New Jersey seacoast to the mutineers and in close proximity to the British ships collected at Princess Bay. British secret agent John Rattoon ran a tavern a short distance from the Raritan Bay at the end of the road in South Amboy and would quickly know of any strangers in the area.

The day of fine mild weather was perfect for conducting military adventures. The British Light Infantry took along two three-pounders and marched to Billopp's Point at the southern end of Staten Island opposite to Perth Amboy. They spent the day observing the Americans in Perth Amboy and returned to their encampment by evening.[16] A scouting party that was sent into the country was fired upon in three or four locations. The commanding officer was informed by a friend that a person had come from Princeton that morning and said everything was the same as before. The mutineers were still refusing all the offers presented to them.[17]

Uzal Woodruff indicated that he was going back out on the morning of the 12th.[18] He was landed on Friday from the *Neptune*'s boat, and was to be picked up at noon on Sunday the 14th. Captain Stewart Ross of the *Neptune* indicated that in the meantime, he would patrol in the Raritan "Bay and along the meadows all night and tomorrow to cover any person wanting to come over."[19]

Later that night, a gentleman whom De Lancey thought was reliable, came in. He reported that some of the Pennsylvanians who had not mutinied but were now of the same mind as the mutineers and were going to join the revolt. The gentleman was told that a sergeant major of the 4th Battalion was in command.

While the British were attempting to assess the state of the mutiny, on January 12, word reached Philadelphia that the situation with the mutineers had been resolved. Some of the people who had gone on the mission to meet with the mutineers had returned and were spreading the word about the hanging of Mason and Ogden.[20] It was the news of the day in the city.

Wayne wrote to Washington that he had sent some correspondence the previous morning, the 11th, through Mr. Craig. Since then he had received Washington's letter of the 8th. Wayne had told Washington about the executions and about Mason's story concerning the plot to kidnap Washington. Wayne cautioned him to "request that you would be well guarded and not commit yourself (as much as you need to do) to the machinations of assassins and to the attempt of Partisans."[21]

Information that British General Clinton had sent ambassadors to the mutineers offering to make good on their back pay reached the troops at West Point on the 11th.[22] Washington held a meeting with the officers. It was almost the universal opinion that their men were dependable. Washington gave instructions for a detachment of one thousand men to be prepared and held in readiness to march. Since General Wayne indicated that "things are in a train of negotiation," he thought it would send the wrong signal to the mutineers if he sent the troops between Trenton and the enemy "and make them fly to the enemy for safety.[23]

Washington, at New Windsor, sent instructions on the 12th to General St. Clair and acknowledged his message of the 9th, which had enclosed one from General Wayne. Washington was getting confused as to what was happening to the spies.

> I had heard from General Sullivan and Lord Stirling that the mutineers had delivered up the British emissaries immediately upon their arrival in Princetown. From this, I was in hopes that they had precluded themselves from all assistance from that quarter, and that the reduction of them by force, should matters come to extremities, would not be difficult. But now their conduct appears to me in this light: they have made known the

propositions offered by Sir H[enry] Clinton, only by way of threat, and seem to say, if you do not grant our terms we can obtain them elsewhere.

He was unaware that after having given up the spies, the mutineers had demanded them back, and then had given them up for good.

Washington continued,

I do not think it prudent to write to the Committee of Congress; to Governor Reed, or to General Wayne, lest my letters should be stopped. I think therefore from a consideration of the subject in every light, that it will be best for you to go down to the Pennsylvania side opposite Trenton and send for some of the gentlemen [to come] over. There enquire minutely into the situation of affairs, and if there are no hopes of a reasonable compromise, get from them an opinion of what ought ultimately to be done. If force should be determined upon, the Governors of Pennsylvania and [New] Jersey should instantly make arrangements for bringing out as many of their militia as can be collected.[24]

Up in the New York Highlands, a detachment commanded by Rhode Islander Lieutenant Colonel Ebenezer Stevens of the 2nd Continental Artillery with six fieldpieces were ordered to be ready to march at 11:00 a.m. The New Jersey and Pennsylvania militia would meet the one thousand men Washington would be sending from New York.[25] Though the command was never issued, they were told to be ready to go at a moment's notice.[26]

11

The End of the Line

THE PENNSYLVANIA LINE MUTINY VI

*O*liver De Lancey, head of British intelligence, knew that time was now running out if they were going to have any chance of getting the Pennsylvania Line to come to them. He told John Stapleton "to send down to him as soon as possible Colonel Taylor and Captain Crowell with as many people as they can bring who will undertake to go into the country by Sandy Hook and then the lower parts of Jerses. Those that will go among the Pennsylvanians and bring us good intelligence of their situation and intentions. I will reward most amply." He was willing to provide a very handsome reward if they were able to find out the mutineers' intentions.[1]

Stapleton who was at British headquarters on York Island wrote him back that he had nothing to report and was not able to procure anyone to go to the Pennsylvanians.[2] Soon, however, Stapleton was able to report to Oliver De Lancey, "I send you Mr. Thomas Oakerson recommended to me by Captain Crowell as a very trusty man. . . . Mr. Oakerson's character may be found out by applying to Colonel Lawrence."[3] De Lancey contacted Lawrence but Lawrence replied that he knew three men by the name of Oakerson, specifically John, Samuel, and Thomas, but did not know of which one De Lancey was inquiring. Lawrence said all three were loyal and could be depended upon.[4]

Thomas Oakerson was a thirty-one-year-old native of Upper Freehold Township in southwestern Monmouth County, New Jersey. He spent time in 1776 at both the Burlington county jail and Trenton jail for being a Tory.[5] On December 15, 1776, he was appointed a lieutenant in the 1st New Jersey Loyalist Volunteers.[6] On April 7, 1778, he was the pilot on the British raid on

Squan Inlet to destroy the saltworks.[7] On June 9, 1779, he led a group of fifty New Jersey and New York loyalists on a raid from Sandy Hook to Tinton Falls and Shrewsbury, New Jersey, on June 11. They captured five rebel officers.

On January 15, 1781, Oliver De Lancey sent Oakerson on a mission to obtain information about the Pennsylvania Line Mutineers.[8] Lieutenant Oakerson returned to the British lines at 4:00 a.m. on February 1, 1781. His report indicated that De Lancey had sent him out on the 15th and that he landed at Shrewsbury, Monmouth County, New Jersey on the 17th, arrived at Monmouth Courthouse on the 18th and at Crosswicks the 19th.[9] He stayed at Crosswicks on the 20th and 21st. On the evening of the 22nd, he went to a friend's house near Whitehorse (four miles east of Trenton). He stayed there until the evening of the 23rd when he began his return journey. He reported that the 2nd, 3rd, and 4th, along with Proctor's Regiment of Artillery, were discharged on the 22nd. Half of the 5th and two thirds of the 6th were discharged and two regiments were furloughed for two months. Oakerson says they received eight weeks pay. The remaining five regiments were offered a choice of two months furlough or returning immediately to the army. About two-thirds went right back to the service. Oakerson believes that between three and four hundred men were still at Trenton at the time. His report was generally accurate, but by the time De Lancey received it, it was too late.

On the 14th, the early morning snow in Philadelphia gradually changed to rain.[10] Word was circulating there that Joseph Reed and his party had returned to the city. The word spread that the mutineers were to get their pay and clothes due them. Those whose period of enlistment were expired were to be discharged, and these men would be traveling through the city on their way home.[11] And it was true. Two days earlier, on Friday, the 12th, Joseph Dean was sent by Joseph Reed at Pennytown, New Jersey, with £500 for the use of the officers.[12] By act of the Pennsylvania Assembly two auditors were appointed to adjust the accounts of the soldiers. Dean arrived at Trenton first; Jonathan B. Smith, the other auditor arrived on the 13th. Governor Reed instructed Dean to bring Smith up to speed concerning the situation. The two auditors were anxious to begin and advised Reed of the same.[13] Some officers would find excuses for not appearing when the auditors did their work. Colonel Francis Johnston of the 5th Pennsylvania had several excuses. He claimed not to know anything about enlistments of his men. All the paperwork necessary to settle with the regiment had been sent to Lieutenant

Colonel Francis Mentges. He claimed that he had been treated very cavalier-ly by the men of the 9th Pennsylvania Regiment and even prohibited from coming among them. He also said that Colonel Adam Hubley of the 11th Pennsylvania Regiment would inform General Wayne of this situation. He advised that he had no plans to go to Trenton and was leaving for Philadelphia in the morning, but was staying with Colonel John Cadwalader that evening. Colonel Adam Hubley and Colonel Francis Johnston retired on January 17.[14]

General Wayne was in Trenton trying to deal with another problem. The commissioners determined that they needed Wayne to get large wooden boxes made as quickly as possible. Weapons and equipment were always in short supply. Therefore, as part of the discharge and furlough process, each soldier had to produce a receipt that they had delivered their arms and other army gear to their regimental quartermaster before they could receive their discharge or furlough papers. Because few men left without getting their doc-uments, there had been little loss of army property. The wooden boxes were needed to store and transport these items. If boxes could not be obtained quickly, the items would have to be shipped down the Delaware River to Philadelphia in bulk.[15]

Joseph Borden of Bordentown, New Jersey, had received a note from Governor Joseph Reed on January 14 advising him that the Pennsylvania troops that would be retained in service were going to be sent to Bordentown. Early Sunday morning a fearful Borden wrote to General Wayne asking him to reconsider the decision. He explained that Bordentown was a small place and it would be very inconvenient to have so many soldiers in town. He com-plained that it would be unfair to have the men housed at Bordentown while there was a perfectly good unused barracks and an issuing commissary at Burlington. Borden asked for Wayne's help.[16]

Meanwhile Wayne continued to fight fires. The soldiers were willing enough to reenlist for the current bounty money but Wayne did not have enough cash on hand. He heard rumors that New Jersey recruiting officers were on their way to Trenton with money to sign up the discharged men which would be a disaster for the Continental Army as it might result in a bid-ding war for recruits among the states.[17]

The British were still busy sending spies back across the river to find out what was happening. Ezekiel Yeomans, who had returned to the British lines on the 11th, was sent back out for intelligence on Monday, January 15.[18]

Andrew Gautier's report of January 15, written in code from New Jersey to Dan Gauthier in New York City, said that Washington did not go to Congress as he had said in an earlier report. He also advised that the Pennsylvania Line Mutineers were not paying attention to General Clinton's offer. He mentioned that locally (that is, in Elizabethtown, New Jersey) there was a concern that the mutineers still might choose to go to the British if Congress did not give them what they wanted. Because of these concerns, the New Jersey Militia was being kept in the field.

Andrew Gautier's report was apparently brought in by Uzal Woodruff who returned that day. Woodruff had been in on Thursday the 11th and went out either that day or on Friday the 12th. Gautier's courier to the mutineers was at Kingston just north of Princeton on Saturday morning. Here, he met a sergeant of the Pennsylvania Line who was going home toward New Windsor. The sergeant said the troops had left Princeton on Thursday morning. They stopped two miles from Trenton where they spent the night before going to Bordentown. This part of his story matched very closely with the story he told on January 9, when he said he met a picket instead of a sergeant and he was going home to New Windsor.

Woodruff most likely retold the story with a few embellishments. He stated that Congress's committee, of which Sullivan was a member, was demanding the mutineers move down toward the river. The New Jersey Militia was ordered out. The man sent returned by way of "the back road by Chatham which is the only road that can be traveled with safety. The guards on the other roads stop all people without passes." The sergeant said the militia was so thick that he could not get to New Brunswick. The sergeant reported that the militia had intercepted two Pennsylvania soldiers carrying letters who were coming to Sir Henry Clinton and sent them to Pennsylvania.[19]

On Tuesday, January 16, General Clinton, realized the game was up. He and some of his staff left Staten Island and sailed back across Upper New York Bay to British Headquarters in lower New York City. Major General William Phillips was left in charge of the troops on Staten Island.[20]

By the 17th, word was circulating in New York City that the mutineers had left Princeton and were heading toward Bordentown while the New Jersey Militia watched the shore.[21]

General Washington was pleased with the news he was getting.

It gives me great satisfaction to learn a final and cordial accommodation was like to take immediate effect. The decided and unequivocal step the

Pennsylvanians have taken, by delivering up the emissaries from Sir Henry Clinton, is a strong mark of their attachment to the cause of their country, and detestation of the insidious conduct of the enemy. In addition to this, their respectful and orderly behavior in the whole course of the affair (except in the first instance) gives us reason to expect that they will return to their duty like faithful and good soldiers.

Washington even cast off the somber tone so prevalent in his letters, and said to John Sullivan,

I have the pleasure to inform you that the army in this quarter, amidst all their complicated sufferings and distresses for the want of money, clothes, and frequent provisions, continues still quiet. Congress will probably have advised you before this time of the mode I have recommended for furnishing three months pay immediately to the army. I cannot but flatter myself the united efforts of Congress and the states will be exerted to prevent by redressing the real grievances, a repetition of similar or even more dangerous disturbances than those which have happened in the Pennsylvania Line.[22]

On Thursday the 18th Philadelphians awoke to a sprinkling of snow. But it melted by early afternoon and was replaced by a dark, cloudy day.[23]

It was certainly a dark day for Joseph Reed, president of Pennsylvania, who was having problems with the political second-guessers. Originally happy with his handling of the Pennsylvania Line mutiny, now they thought he had given away too much to the mutineers in reaching a solution. Some insisted that he had assumed powers beyond his office as president of the Commonwealth. In a letter addressed to the merchants and citizens of Philadelphia, Reed, speaking of himself in the third person, said, "he has done nothing which is not consistent with the laws of government of the state and is ready to answer public conduct when properly required. But to remove farther complaints he now wholly withdraws his requests of pecuniary assistance and will endeavor to excuse the non performance of his engagements as well as he can being conscious of having done every thing in his power to settle this unhappy affair to the best public advantage under all circumstances."[24]

A number of the soldiers from the Pennsylvania Line who had been given their release were arriving in Philadelphia.[25] Their presence in the city made the citizens nervous.

Richard Peters at the War Office was made aware that a lot of the discharged soldiers and noncommissioned officers were going to Philadelphia even when it was out of their way. They were coming to Philadelphia looking for provisions and had no orders for them. Peters asked Wayne that provisions "be furnished by the different commissaries on their route to their respective places of habitation with one ratio of provisions for every twenty miles to support themselves on the way and that the quantity ordered furnished be endorsed on their respective discharge." Peters wanted this accomplished before the men were discharged from the army.[26]

Another unforeseen problem arose. Because of the large number of discharges from the Pennsylvania Line, the recruiters were trying to get the men to reenlist. They quickly found they were in competition with the merchants of Philadelphia who wanted these men to fill out the crews of their merchant vessels. General Wayne wrote an open letter asking the merchants of Philadelphia to cease and desist from employing these men. He asked for a temporary embargo. He acknowledged it was a hardship but one that was needed.[27] A week later, General Irvine advised Wayne that the Philadelphia merchants said they would not let any of the discharged men enroll on their ships.[28]

RUMORS ARE AN INTEGRAL PART OF WAR AND the Pennsylvania Line mutiny would prove to be no exception. The Chevalier de Luzerne informed General Greene that he heard that a spirit of revolt had spread to the Hessians who "declare aloud that the time of their services is expired that they are neither clothed or paid conformably to the promises which have been made to them and they add that the ferment hath appeared such that they have been obliged to break a part of there corps and to mix them with the English to make themselves secure of their fidelity. The German officers equally complain of the little punctuality with which they have performed the promises made to them."[29]

James Potter and Joseph Reed submitted an article to the *Pennsylvania Gazette* that was printed on Wednesday the 24th. Their report to the public took major liberties with the actual events. When Wayne sent a copy of the paper to Washington, it was a circumstantial account "of the defection of the Pennsylvania Line in which you'll find some gentlemen have taken full credit for the part they have had in this affair."[30] Wayne's implication was that he was significantly absent from the story.

Potter and Reed acknowledged that "uncertain enlistments, deficiencies in clothing, arrearages in pay and depreciation of currency" had occurred, but they put the primary blame for the Pennsylvania Line eruption on the exaggerations of too many British deserters in that corps. There were a number of British deserters in the Pennsylvania Line. Potter and Reed claimed that a series of extenuating circumstances that caused the fracture.

They also mentioned New Year's Day being a day of festivities. However, the only festivity recorded at Morristown was the dinner of the commissioned officers. Further, they said an "extra portion of rum was served." It was not an "extra" portion of rum as no regular portion had been given for a very long time. And it was only half a portion of the regular ration that was distributed. They said the men purchased alcoholic beverages locally. Not much of anything could have been purchased as the men of the Pennsylvania Line had no money since they had not been paid.

Potter and Reed claimed the alcohol inflamed the minds of the men to both real and imaginary injustices, which caused the outbreak of disorder. They stated, "the line left their camp, in a most tumultuous and disorderly manner." This was another untruth. The men of the Pennsylvania Line marched off in a very disciplined military fashion.

James Potter and Joseph Reed stated the news reached the enemy in New York who, despite heavy rains, assembled an army at Staten Island that was to land at South Amboy to assist the mutineers. The British believed that the mutineers were only waiting for an opportunity to come to them. Potter and Reed said the British were informed of this intelligence by a person from Woodbridge who went over to Staten Island. In this case, they had to lie about the hometown of the informant who was now a double agent. If they told the truth and his identify were discovered, he would certainly be jailed or hung. They also knew there was more than one person traversing the Arthur Kill that separated New Jersey and Staten Island.

They said that when the news of the event reached Philadelphia they (president of the state and a committee of Congress attended by the Philadelphia Light Horse) sprang into action and raced off to Trenton to meet with the mutineers.

In the meantime, General Wayne was meeting with a board of sergeants but was "yet in doubt as to the real designs of the mutineers." They did leave Philadelphia quickly, but Wayne had a good understanding of the wants of the mutineers. He was simply unsure what would happen if their demands were not met. The mutineers insisted that they would fight if the enemy entered the state, but Wayne feared that Pennsylvania Line would march to the waiting arms of the British if negotiations went sour. When the mutineers turned over the two British spies, they gave up their biggest bargaining chip.

Reed tells how he went to the mutineers, despite fearing for his own safety, notwithstanding assurances from the mutineers. At that time the mutineers demanded the return of the spies. The article also relates how Reed wrote to the vice president of Pennsylvania at Philadelphia, saying, "I have but one life, and my country has the first claim to it. I therefore go with cheerfulness, which attends performing a necessary, though not a pleasant duty." The article goes on to tell how when he arrived at "Princeton the whole line was drawn up for his reception and every mark of military honor and respect shown him." That was not strictly true as there was no military rifle or cannon salute and the mutineers were trying to see who it was that had come to meet with them.

After several days of negotiations between tenacious malcontents, with unwavering firmness on the part of President Reed, an agreement was reached. This ends the portion of the article about James Potter and Joseph Reed. Overall, the article is reminiscent of a political campaign speech.[31]

So as to resolve the terms of enlistments of the noncommissioned officers and privates of the Pennsylvania Line, the commissioners had set up their operations in the town of Nottingham, the northernmost town of Burlington County on the east bank of the Delaware River between Bordentown and Trenton. The first regiment to be settled was that of Colonel James Chambers, 1st Pennsylvania.[32] McFarlan said that Williams said he would not enlist again. Colonels Craig and James Chambers were particularly dissatisfied.[33] Colonel Craig was most likely Captain Samuel Craig of the 1st Pennsylvania Regiment who retired on January 17.[34] Colonel James Chambers also retired on January 17.[35]

By Sunday January 28, the commissioners of Congress had basically completed the settlement of the enlistments of the Pennsylvania Line except for the notoriously rowdy 11th Regiment. This regiment consisted of mostly Irish- and English-born soldiers. They were the soldiers who had started the mutiny with their huzzas back at Morristown. That same day, General Wayne reported from Trenton to General Washington that the commissioners had so far determined that 1,220 men were to be discharged. Another 1,180 men had been given furloughs until March or April.[36] He also sent copies of the printed forms for discharges and furloughs. Wayne had been busy signing discharges and furloughs, which he described as his "distressing duty."[37]

On Monday the 29th, the commissioners of Congress had completed the settlement of the enlistments of the Pennsylvania Line with just a few stragglers left to be resolved. General Wayne sent in what would be the final numbers to General Washington: 1,250 infantry and 67 artillery men were to be discharged and another 1,150 men had been given furloughs. Recruiting sergeants and musicians were not given the option of a furlough because of the needs of the army.

Wayne's work was almost done at Trenton. He still had to forward to Philadelphia the remaining weapons and accoutrements that were still in Trenton. He then found out there were cases of clothing left at Pennytown that had to be sent forward.[38] On the 28th Wayne had ordered John Hughes Jr., the division quartermaster, to forward the public stores to Morristown. On the 29th, Wayne was still shuffling arms and accoutrements belonging to the Pennsylvania Line from Morristown and Princeton to Philadelphia.[39] The month and the nightmare were coming to an end when Wayne left New Jersey for Philadelphia on Tuesday morning.

Washington had been forced to hold the troops together in New York and had to be a bystander in the affair. He thought that the Pennsylvania Line mutiny had "been singularly mortifying and disagreeable in all its progress. Its influence threatens the whole army."[40]

Washington sent a letter that expressed his thoughts on Wayne's performance. "I am satisfied, that every thing was done on your part to produce the least possible evil from the unfortunate disturbance in your line, and that your influence has had a great share in preventing worse extremities. I felt for your situation. Your anxieties and fatigues of mind, amidst such a scene, I can easily conceive. I thank you sincerely for your exertions."[41]

There was one more card to be played in the Pennsylvania Line mutiny. A court martial, ordered by Brigadier General Nathaniel Heard of the New Jersey Militia, was held on March 15, 1781 at the five-bay house of Jacob Hyer in Princeton.[42] Ensign Lewis Baremore had refused to march with Major Robert Nixon's regiment when it was called out to deal with the

Pennsylvania Line mutiny. He was found guilty of unofficer-like behavior and was cashiered.[43]

Intelligence arrived in New York about another mutiny and the attention of British Headquarters shifted to this new incident. The weather in Long Island was moderate and the rumor among the troops was that the New Jersey Line had come to Elizabethtown.[44]

The Domino Effect

THE NEW JERSEY LINE MUTINY

*G*eorge Washington had dispatched General Henry Knox with his circular letter of January 5, 1781, to the New England politicos. He was once again begging for money and supplies. As to be expected, they were short on funds. Knox's job was to stress to the elected officials how desperate the army's situation was.

The Massachusetts assembly voted to provide the gratuity Washington asked and also coats for its soldiers who were noncommissioned officers and below. The New Hampshire assembly agreed to make a similar gesture to its troops. The Rhode Island assembly was called into session to consider Washington's plea. They also agreed to provide a gratuity to the men.

The Connecticut legislature was not in session and Governor Jonathan Trumbull chose not to call an emergency session. He had heard the desperate pleas for assistance before. Trumbull did not want to alarm the whole state. The emergency had subsided by the time Connecticut voted to provide clothing to men enlisted for three years of the war. Each man was to receive two pairs of white stockings, two pairs of shoes, two pairs of overalls, two linen shirts, and one coat.

General Arthur St. Clair at Morristown sent a letter to Joseph Reed on January 7. Problems were already developing with the New Jersey Line of the Continental Army as they were favorably disposed to the Pennsylvania Line mutineers. This "induced Colonel Francis Barber who commands them, to move them to Chatham; so that we are here in a very awkward situation."[1]

While the state legislatures were responding to the Pennsylvania Line mutiny and Washington's latest plea for assistance, on January 17, twenty-two sergeants from Massachusetts submitted a list of their grievances to

Lieutenant Ebenezer Sprout of the 2nd Massachusetts Regiment. It was the beginning of a domino effect. The Massachusetts men were certainly motivated to speak up now that the Pennsylvania Line had their grievances redressed. The Pennsylvania Line mutiny had opened the door to the possibility that other units might react in kind. The Massachusetts sergeants' complaints were:

FIRST: Our State bounty we have not as yet received, though been lawfully required and demanded;

SECONDLY: Our wages we have been kept out of beyond all reason;

THIRDLY: Our clothing has certainly been kept from us (which is our due) either by disaffected men, or neglect of others. Be it as it will, we suffer for the same;

FOURTHLY; Our provision is certainly extremely short, by what means we are unable to say; but this we know, it is inconsistent with human reason to think men can live on such allowances.[2]

It was signed by the following soldiers: Jonathan Farnam, Sergeant Major, and the Sergeants Israel Gillitt, Nathaniel Frost, Silvanus Bardham, Moses Bolland, Elisha Bates, Thomas Doty, Jacob Mitchell, Reuben Mitchell, Ithamar Johnson, Daniel Lawrence, Ebenezer Richardson, Ephraim Pratt, Theodore Sprague, Moses Buck, John Dewey, James Bailey, Simeon Hayward, and George Eliot.

There was no immediate threat included in their petition. However, New England troops had mutinied in the past and no one knew when the breaking point might come. There had been serious trouble with the Pennsylvanians; a hint of a problem was evident with the men from Massachusetts; and then the New Jersey Line erupted.

About the middle of January, some five hundred of the New Jersey Line were bivouacked for the winter at Pompton. Another group was at Suffern protecting the route to West Point. The composition of the New Jersey troops included a high percentage of foreign-born individuals, as had the Pennsylvania troops. Many men from New Jersey preferred to join the militia to protect their homes from the constant skirmishes with the enemy who was just across the waters in New York City and Staten Island or in the posts already in New Jersey on the Hudson Peninsula or Sandy Hook.

Not surprisingly, lack of food and clothing at Pompton was just as severe as at Morristown. The ladies of Trenton were busy making stockings for their soldiers. Mary Dagworthy wrote George Washington just after Christmas of 1780 that 380 pairs of stockings would soon be sent to the troops. They arrived as promised but too late to ease the pent-up grievances of the troops.

The complaints of the New Jersey Line were similar to those of the Pennsylvanians. There were grumblings about the lack of pay, and when they received some money, the value had depreciated to the point where it was almost worthless. There were also problems with enlistments. Had the men enlisted for three years or the duration of the war? Enlistment documents were so poorly kept that many times they contradicted each other concerning the same soldier.

The officers were unhappy over the situation. With the Pennsylvanians revolting at Morristown, Princeton, and Trenton the metaphorical storm winds were blowing through Pompton.

Colonel Israel Shreve commanded at Pompton. Shreve was seriously overweight, out of money, depressed over the length of the war, but still loyal to the cause. Washington believed he had been promoted beyond his ability. In December, Washington had stated, "Here I drop the curtain," meaning there was no way he would allow Shreve to be promoted. Colonel Elias Dayton commanded the 3rd New Jersey at Chatham. Washington thought highly of Dayton and wanted to promote him to brigadier general. Those Pennsylvanians who had not mutinied at Mount Kemble, were moved to Chatham where they were to serve under the very capable Colonel Dayton.

In late December and early January, the New Jersey legislature had rejected an act for the "more speedy and effectual procurement of supplies for the Army of the United States." However, with the Pennsylvanians already in revolt and just eight miles away, the New Jersey legislature decided to pass the legislation.

On January 6, they passed "An Act for Making Compensation to the Troops in the Service of the United States for the Depreciation of Their Pay." Three commissioners were appointed to settle the discrepancies in pay based on a scale from one to sixty, with January 1777 equal to one and July 1780 set at sixty. The commissioners were to deduct all articles of clothing and state stores that had been supplied. The resulting subtotal was to be divided by one-fourth, which would provide the amount due each soldier in state money. The other three-quarters was to be provided in bonds due in three years at 6 percent interest retroactive to August 1780. The bonds were bearer certificates and could be transferred or used in payment of debt. Two days later, the

New Jersey legislature passed another act to raise by loan a sum of money for "discharging the bounty to be paid to the troops."[3] This would allow the state to pay troops their bounty upon enlistment.

The assembly ordered two commissioners to draw £2,250 from the state treasury in order to advance money to the New Jersey Brigade. Each officer was to get twenty dollars; each noncommissioned officer and each private was to receive five dollars. These advances were to be deducted from the 25 percent cash payment due under the act of January 6, 1781.[4] The advances were paid between January 15 and 20.

The New Jersey Line camp followers were notorious for selling the soldiers moonshine. A goodly number were reported to have spent their newfound wealth on alcoholic beverages. It was a quick way to forget the boredom.

As early as January 7, there were signs that the New Jersey Line was going to be a problem. Some members of the New Jersey troops posted handbills on their officer quarters that they were going to follow the Pennsylvanians and mutiny for a redress of their grievances.[5] The handbills, which were also hung on fences, stated: "To the officers and soldiers of the Continental Army, Shake off the Congress and despise them with their France and Spain allies. Their paper money trust no more. We have all been cheated enough before fight for great George. Make no more delay for Briton's sons will gain the day."[6]

Colonel Francis Barber, who commanded the New Jersey Line at Morristown, was aware that the New Jersey Line looked favorably on the Pennsylvania Line mutineers and that problems such as the handbills were beginning to happen. Because of this situation, Colonel Barber moved the men to Chatham.[7] The discontent in the New Jersey Line was growing.

Uzal Woodruff reported back to British Headquarters after one of his many trips to New Jersey that, in January, he had been to the American camp at Chatham. He reported that the New Jersey men were barefoot and naked. He reported that Colonel Elias Dayton had promised his troops forty pounds in new emission of New Jersey money to make up for their depreciation loses. He ordered the men to shoulder their arms; very few responded. Woodruff said Dayton "was very much disconcerted and did not know what to do."[8]

Cornelius Hatfield Jr. of Elizabethtown, another active spy, also brought in his report on the events at Chatham. "Colonel Dayton had spread a report that the Pennsylvanians had made up matters on which his own people of the Jersey brigade made the same demands. He was obliged to contradict the report to quiet them."[9]

American Captain William Bernard
Gifford, who was working as a British spy
at the time, wrote on January 18, "The
detachment at Chatham is much dissatisfied, also the rest of them at Pompton.
Parson [James] Caldwell is now paying
twenty dollars of this new trash [paper
money] to each officer and five to each
private. This is a present from the
state."[10] Reverend James Caldwell "the
fighting parson" once gave the order, "give
them Watts," being the pages of his Watts
hymnals, which he distributed as wad-
dling to the American riflemen during the
Battle of Springfield, New Jersey.

Colonel Francis Barber, an engrav-
ing based on a soldier's sketch.
(*William L. Clements Library*)

Caldwell, a Presbyterian minister
from Connecticut Farms, New Jersey, had been serving as a deputy quartermaster general since 1778. The New Jersey legislature had selected him to
distribute the depreciation gift money to the New Jersey troops.
Twenty–seven-year-old attorney and former Continental Congressman
Colonel Frederick Frelinghuysen of the New Jersey Militia also had gone to
Pompton as a commissioner for the state.

A female camp follower reported to Colonel Israel Shreve late in the afternoon of Saturday the 20th that the New Jersey troops were going to mutiny
and leave their huts. Colonel Shreve "immediately ordered all the men off
duty to be paraded, with the design to detach them in different parties for the
night; but found very few that would turn out."[11] This time there was no great
eruption. No one was hurt. The men marched out of camp at eight that night.
Shreve thought the mutineers were heading straight for the New Jersey legislature at Trenton. He was concerned that the New Jersey troops at Chatham
would join the revolt.

Colonel Elias Dayton in command at Chatham received word that the
New Jersey Line at Pompton had mutinied and were on their way to Chatham
to get more New Jersey soldiers to join their march. Dayton acted quickly,
placing some New Jersey men on a short-term furlough. He also sent others
out on details. He was trying to get the men out of Chatham and prevent
them from joining the mutiny.

Colonel Shreve wrote to General Washington on January 20 at 10:00 p.m. from Pompton, New Jersey,

> It is with pain that I inform your Excellency that the troops at this place revolted this evening, and have marched towards Trenton: their behavior and demands are similar to those of the Pennsylvania Line; though no blood has been spilt. I was informed by a woman of their intentions, late this afternoon, and immediately ordered all the men off duty to be paraded; with an intention to detach them in different parties for the night; but found but very few that would turn out. I was amongst them for some time but could not prevail upon them to desist. They have lately received a part of the depreciation of their pay, and most of them are much disguised with liquor. Col. Frelinghuysen, one of the commissioners of the state is now here. We mean to follow them in the morning and endeavor to bring them to reason. I apprehend the detachment at Chatham will join them.[12]

If the other detachments left their posts, Shreve planned on having Major Benjamin Throop of the 5th Connecticut Regiment cover Dobbs's Ferry and protect the military stores at Kingwood and at Pompton. He expected Dayton to have an influence on the men at Chatham.[13]

On Sunday the 21st, two hundred mutineers under the leadership of the sergeants, followed by Colonel Shreve, arrived at Chatham.[14] The men had selected Sergeant Major George Grant to be their leader. Before the January 1 reorganization, he was in the 3rd New Jersey Regiment. He was said to have been a British deserter. He had spent the last four years in the New Jersey Line. Grant had served in General Sullivan's expedition of retaliation against the Iroquois in New York State. The second in charge of the mutineers was Sergeant Jonathan Nichols and third was Sergeant Major John Minthorn, both of the 1st New Jersey Regiment.

On Tuesday January 23, Colonels Dayton and Shreve along with the commissioners who had given out the advances met with the mutineers.[15] Dayton advised them of what had already been done for them by the New Jersey legislature. He promised that as soon as their mutinous behavior ceased, their grievances would be resolved. The mutineers insisted that their sworn oaths should be taken as evidence of their expired terms of service as had been done for the Pennsylvanians. Dayton refused and the mutineers finally conceded the issue.

The sergeants wrote a petition for a general pardon similar to the one that had been granted to the Pennsylvanians. Dayton and the commissioners presented the men with an alternate pardon as the only version that they would approve. It offered a pardon on the condition that immediately all hostilities ceased, the soldiers returned to duty, and they conducted themselves in a soldierly manner. If they did not comply then they "must expect the reward due to such obstinate villainy." They voiced their approval with three huzzas, the eighteenth-century cheer. The next morning, the 24th, they marched backed to Pompton under the command of Colonel Shreve.

News of the New Jersey Line mutiny reached George Washington about ten Sunday evening. He was adamant that an immediate stop must be made or the rest of the Continental Line was going to follow the Pennsylvanians and the New Jersey Line. He immediately sprang into action. He was not going to be a bystander this time. He was going to determine the outcome. The candles burned late into the night at his headquarters in New Windsor.

Washington had David Humphreys write to General William Heath at West Point informing him of the New Jersey Line mutiny and that he was determined "at all hazards to put a stop to such proceedings, which must otherwise prove the inevitable dissolution of the Army." Heath was to put together a detachment of five or six hundred of the most robust and best clothed men, properly officered to accomplish this task. The detachment was to be immediately assembled and prepared to go. Heath was told to be ready for a visit from Washington in the morning.[16]

At 11:00 p.m., Humphreys was busy dashing off a letter to Major Benjamin Throop, who was at Ringwood, New Jersey, with one hundred Connecticut men, that a change in plans had occurred. Earlier that day he had been ordered through Colonel Francis Barber of the New Jersey troops to return to West Point. His orders were now being countermanded. Washington, in light of the New Jersey Line mutiny, wanted him to stay in place and be ready to march wherever he was needed. Washington, trying to bolster the men's morale, stated that he "relies most confidently on the New England troops, of this you may let them know, and as he doubts not you will find the best disposition in your detachment, he wishes you to cultivate it, and inform him if any thing extraordinary should happen."[17] Washington wanted to know if the Connecticut troops would join the New Jersey troops.

Washington had Alexander Hamilton draft a letter to former Provincial and Continental Congressman Colonel Frederick Frelinghuysen of the Somerset County, New Jersey, militia. Frelinghuysen was at Pompton as a state official, in his role as commissioner, and as a military officer, a colonel of the Somerset

County Militia. Washington addressed his a as colonel rather than as commissioner, his civilian title. His request thus became a military order.

Washington stated that he was

extremely chagrined at the disagreeable intelligence you communicate in your letter of the 20th. This dangerous spirit will subvert the whole army, if not quelled by a decisive effort of authority. I have ordered a large detachment to march from West Point to compel the mutineers to submission and I must entreat you to employ all your influence to inspire the militia with a disposition to cooperate with us, by representing the fatal consequences of the present temper of the soldiery not only to military subordination, but to civil liberty. In reality both are fundamentally struck at by their undertaking in arms to dictate terms to their country.[18]

Washington also wrote to Colonel Shreve,

With not less pain than you communicate it, I receive the information contained in your letter of yesterday. This affair, if possible, must be brought to an issue favorable to subordination, or the army is ruined. I shall therefore immediately march a detachment from these posts to quell the mutineers. Colonel Frelinghuysen will impart to you what I have written to him. In addition to that, I am to desire you will endeavor to collect all those of your regiments who have had virtue enough to resist the pernicious example of their associates. If the revolt has not become general, and if you have force enough to do it, I wish you to compel the mutineers to unconditional submission. The more decisively you are able to act the better.[19]

Alexander Hamilton also drafted a letter for Washington to John Sullivan, chairman of the Committee of Congress of Arrangement, saying that Washington had just received the disagreeable intelligence of the New Jersey Line having followed the example of the Pennsylvanians. "This spirit will spread itself through the remainder of the army, if not extinguished by some decisive measure. I shall as quick as possible, at all events, march a detachment to compel the mutineers to submission, and I beg leave strongly to recommend that no terms may be made with them."[20] This spirit of mutiny had to be exterminated here and now. Washington was going to make an example of the New Jersey troops.

The next day Washington went to West Point. He had Alexander Hamilton write out the orders for Major General Robert Howe, which he then corrected before he issued them. Howe was to take the detachment that was assembled at West Point and proceed against the New Jersey Line mutineers. Washington was very specific that he wanted no quarter to be given. "The object of your detachment is to compel the mutineers to unconditional submission, and I am to desire you will grant no terms while they are with arms in their hands in a state of resistance. The manner of executing this I leave to your discretion according to circumstances. If you succeed in compelling the revolted troops to a surrender you will instantly execute a few of the most active and most incendiary leaders."

Howe was to gather to him the New Jersey Line troops that did not revolt and any militia that he could locate. He was to emphasize "to them how dangerous to civil liberty the precedent is of armed soldiers dictating terms to their country." He was also to make contact with Colonels Dayton, Frelinghuysen, and Shreve.[21]

David Humphreys was busy writing a draft letter to fifty-seven-year-old Governor William Livingston of New Jersey, which Washington edited. Humphreys told Livingston that Colonel Shreve had informed him of the defection of the New Jersey Line. Washington stressed that because of the dangerous consequences that might ensue unless an immediate stop should be put to such horrid proceedings, he was taking vigorous coercive measures. He wanted Livingston to know what he was doing in order to prevent any compromise being made with the mutineers.

Washington also requested that Governor Livingston have the state militia held in readiness to assist Major General Howe in quelling the insurrection. Washington emphasized that having a redress of grievances demanded with arms was both an affront to the state as well as the military authority. He said it was "unreasonable conduct of the Jersey troops in revolting at a time when the state was exerting itself to redress all their real grievances." Washington asked Livingston "to take your measures with secrecy and advise the commanding officer [General Howe] of the detachment of them who will march (if the heavy fall of snow last night does not prevent it) by the route of Ringwood, Pompton, etc."[22]

Washington also sent a circular letter to the Governors of Connecticut, Massachusetts, New Hampshire, New York, and Rhode Island notifying them of the New Jersey Line mutiny:

> Sir: I have received the disagreeable intelligence that a part of the Jersey Line had followed the example of that of Pennsylvania; and when the advices came away it was expected the revolt would be general. The pre-

cise intention of the mutineers was not known, but their complaints and demands were similar to those, of the Pennsylvanians.

Persuaded that without some decisive effort, at all hazards to suppress this dangerous spirit it would speedily infect the whole army. I have ordered as large a detachment as we could spare from these posts to march under Major General Howe with orders to compel the mutineers to unconditional submission; to listen to no terms while they were in a state of resistance, and on their reduction to execute instantly a few of the most active, and most incendiary leaders. I am not certain what part the troops detached for this purpose will act, but I flatter myself they will do their duty. I prefer any extremity to which the Jersey Troops may be driven, to a compromise.

The weakness of the garrison but still more its embarrassing distress for want of provisions made it impossible to prosecute such measures with the Pennsylvanians, as the nature of the case demanded, and while we were making arrangements, as far as practicable to supply these defects, an accommodation took place, which will not only subvert the Pennsylvania Line, but have a very pernicious influence on the whole army. I mean however by these remarks only to give an idea of the miserable situation we are in, not to blame a measure which perhaps in our circumstances was the best that could have been adopted. The same embarrassments operate against coercion at this moment, but not in so great a degree; the Jersey troops not being from their numbers so formidable as were the Pennsylvanians.

I dare not detail the risks we run from the present scantiness of supplies.[23] We have received few or no cattle for some time past, nor do we know of any shortly to be expected. The salted meat we ought to have reserved in the garrison is now nearly exhausted. I cannot but renew my solicitations with your state, to exert every expedient for contributing to our immediate relief.[24]

A letter was also sent to Congress, summarizing the events that had transpired and what Washington was doing in a response. Washington complained that a permanent way of funding the war needed to be found. "The events that have recently taken place are an alarming comment upon the insufficiency of past systems. We continue under the most distressing embarrassments in the articles of provision and forage."[25] Washington placed all the blame for the mutinies on the want of clothing, pay, and provisions. "It creates evils from which we scarcely know how we shall be able to extricate ourselves."[26]

Humphreys was busy getting assignments of troops dispatched. He had sent an order the previous day to the detachment of artillery from the artillery park at Murderers Creek near New Windsor. It was commanded by Captain William Stevens of the Corps of Artillery, with three 3-pounders. That day, he ordered it to parade immediately.[27]

In New York City, British military headquarters at the Kennedy House at One Broadway was always a busy place. People were constantly coming and going. Express riders picked up and dropped off reports. Officers dropped off memorials and citizens their petitions, both hoping for some favor from British General Sir Henry Clinton.

Monday, January 22, would bring in reports from Joseph Gould and Uzal Woodruff, two spies from Elizabethtown who had been to Chatham, the current location of the New Jersey mutineers. Woodruff stated that Jonathan Nichols, second in charge of the New Jersey mutineers, was his cousin. Gould claimed to have talked to some of the mutineers who indicated that the group was coming to Elizabethtown.

Clinton was aware that the New Jersey Line mutineers had the same complaints as the Pennsylvanians who had achieved a peaceful resolution to their grievances. British General Clinton thought there was little chance of the men switching sides since the politicians would acquiesce to the demands. He sent General James Robertson and Oliver De Lancey to Staten Island opposite Elizabethtown, New Jersey, to coordinate the British secret service operations with regard to the mutineers.

Clinton knew there would be little glory in England for getting the two hundred New Jersey mutineers to switch allegiance while the thousands of the Pennsylvania Line, got away. If he went to Staten Island again and was unsuccessful, he would lose face among his own men. However, if De Lancey and Robertson, by some stroke of luck, were able to pull off the miracle, he could quickly make the short trip across Upper New York Bay to Staten Island. Once there he could take charge and receive all the credit without any risk.

Due to the bad weather, Oliver De Lancey probably arrived on Staten Island on the 23rd. He immediately sent a man to the mutineers.[28] The man returned at 9:00 p.m. He confirmed that the New Jersey troops were in a state of mutiny and were still at Chatham. On the morning of the 24th, he sent out at least two men to New Jersey. One of the men reported by 1:00 p.m. on the 25th that the mutineers were still at Chatham and their demands were the same as the Pennsylvanians. He also reported that the mutineers were promised the same terms that had been given to the Pennsylvanians. The accuracy of his report is highly questionable.[29] He might have reported hearsay information he picked up along the way, without ever reaching Chatham, or he could be a double agent providing a false report.

Also on the 25th at about one in the afternoon, De Lancey received a report in cipher from Andrew Gautier whom De Lancey said was his most reliable correspondent in New Jersey. The writer was personally going to Chatham.

General James Robertson said that during his time on Staten Island during the revolt he sent spies to the mutineers offering the money that Congress owed them, to receive them as friends, to confer with anyone they would send, and to provide military protection to anyone who would come to Elizabethtown.[30] These were most likely the same messengers sent out by Oliver De Lancey.

That same day, De Lancey sent out two copies of a proposal to the mutineers and was sending "out some more tho without much hope of success." He had prepared two documents, one addressed to "the person commanding the Jersey troops" and another to "the Jersey brigade." Uzal Woodruff carried the second correspondence and may have also carried the first as his cousin was one of the commanders of the mutineers.

De Lancey sent in his report to Sir Henry Clinton at 7:00 p.m. He was expecting one man to return that evening and two more the next day.

On Wednesday January 24, 1781, Jonas Crane, who had been working as a British spy since July 1, 1780, had left Newark and traveled to Bergen Point. He left Bergen Point at 3:00 p.m. on Thursday but did not get to New York City until midnight, finally arriving at headquarters at 10:00 a.m. on the 26th. He was sent back to Newark on the evening of the 26th with instructions to bring two men to Bergen Point and immediately convey them to Oliver De Lancey on Staten Island.[31]

IN THE AMERICAN CAMP AT WEST POINT, Monday, January 22, was a cold and raw day. A violent storm of wind, rain, and snow arrived that night and continued into Tuesday morning. A considerable amount of snow fell in the West Point area. The wind blew so violently that large trees were uprooted and some houses were unroofed. Four women were killed.[32]

The snow delayed the departure of Captain Stevens and his artillery detachment to the southward. The artillery was to march as soon as the quartermaster general could get them the horses they needed. They would then move to Ringwood, New Jersey, and meet up with Major General Robert Howe. If Howe had already left, they were to join up with him. William S. Pennington wrote in his diary that they left at daylight on the 25th and marched to Smith's Clove and halted for the night. On Friday the 26th, they marched to Ringwood and joined a detachment of infantry under the command of Major General Howe.[33]

A New Hampshire detachment, commanded by Major Amos Morrill, was to go to King's Ferry and cross the Hudson River to Stony Point. They would continue through Suffern to Ringwood. A detachment of Massachusetts men, commanded by Lieutenant Colonel Ebenezer Sprout, would leave West Point traveling by way of the Forrest of Dean and the Clove to Ringwood. Lieutenant Colonel Ebenezer Sprout would be second in command of the mission.[34] The other field officers were Lieutenant Colonel Mellon and Major Oliver.[35]

Dr. James Thacher, who had been transferred from the 16th to the 9th Massachusetts Regiment on January 1, recorded the march of the Massachusetts men to Ringwood.[36]

A body of snow about two feet deep, without any track, rendered the march extremely difficult. Having no horse, I experienced inexpressible fatigue and was obliged several times to sit down on the snow. [On the] 24th, marched over the mountains and reached Carle's tavern in Smith's Clove, halted for two hours, then proceeded thirteen miles and quartered our men in the scattering houses and barns. [On the] 25th, marched nine miles and reached Ringwood. General Howe and all the field officers took lodgings at the house of Mrs. [Robert] Erskine, the amiable widow of the late respectable geographer of our Army [who had died the past October]. We were entertained with an elegant supper and excellent wine. Mrs. Erskine is a sensible and accomplished woman, lives in a style of affluence and fashion; everything indicates wealth, taste, and splendor; and she takes pleasure in entertaining the friends of her late husband with generous hospitality.

Howe's detachment moved out at one in the morning on the 27th. They marched eight miles, which brought the New Jersey mutineers' huts into view.

The detachment waited for an hour as preparations were made. Some of the officers were very anxious about whether the soldiers would follow orders. Then the order was given to load the weapons. "It was obeyed with alacrity."

General Howe went up and down the line telling the men that mutiny was heinous and emphasizing the need for the mutineers to be brought to an unconditional surrender. The detachment was ordered to completely surround the mutineers' huts. Then the order to present the fieldpieces to the mutineers was given. This was accomplished at daylight, around 6:43 a.m.[37]

General Howe then had his aide-de-camp order to the mutineers to parade in front of their huts unarmed within five minutes. When the men were slow in responding, Howe sent Lieutenant Colonel Francis Barber to tell them that if they did not comply within five minutes he would put them all to the sword. They then surrendered.

Following Washington's orders, "you will instantly execute a few of the most active and most incendiary leaders," General Howe ordered a court martial in the field for the ringleaders: Sergeant David Gilmore, Sergeant George Grant, and John Tuttle. Colonel Sprout was the president of the court martial, which was conducted outside in the snow.[38] Gilmore, Grant, and Tuttle were all convicted and sentenced to death. At the request of the officers, Grant was then pardoned.

Twelve of the guiltiest mutineers were selected as the firing squad. "When ordered to load, some of them shed tears."[39] Very quickly, a sergeant was taken a few yards distant and placed on his knees. Six of the firing squad were called upon to fire with three aiming at the head and three at the chest. All six missed. The remaining six members of the firing squad were called upon to complete the task. They fired and hit their target extinguishing the life of the mutineer. The second mutineer was brought up to the place of execution and was quickly dispatched to the hereafter by the first volley.

General Howe ordered the former officers to take their commands. Howe then addressed the men by platoon, telling them to ask pardon of their officers and to devote themselves to the faithful discharge of their duty as soldiers in future.[40] The mutineers went back to their duty and were given a general pardon.

William Pennington said the artillery went back the same day to Ringwood. He believed they had made the right choice in dealing with the New Jersey Line mutiny. To do otherwise might have encouraged other units to mutiny.

On Sunday afternoon, Pennington paid an unofficial visit to the New Jersey Line "and found them very peaceable."[41]

Uzal Woodruff of Elizabethtown decided to turn the British proposals over to the American officers.[42] Could it have been to save his cousin Jonathan Nichols who was said to be second in command the mutineers? General Howe, convinced of his honesty, reprieved Woodruff.[43] He then took on the role of a double agent working for the American Colonel Elias Dayton.

Word of the New Jersey Line mutiny reached Philadelphia on Thursday the 25th.[44] Rumors would surface in Philadelphia that the New Jersey Line mutiny was very violent and that a general had been killed. The mutineers were unruly but not violent. The rumors reignited fears that the soldiers would be coming to lay waste to the city.

British General James Robertson was ready to end his sojourn on Staten Island on the 26th and head back to New York City unless he received some positive reports. De Lancey proposed to do the same unless he received contrary orders from General Clinton.[45]

THE MUTINY OF MAY 20, 1781, AT YORK, Pennsylvania, was small by any measure. However, its occurrence so soon after the deplorable behavior of the Pennsylvania and New Jersey troops amplified its significance. After those mutinies, no rebellion in the ranks, regardless of how small, would be tolerated.

John Fortescue of the 6th Pennsylvania Regiment was tried that day for mutinous actions and sentenced to death.

That evening, Major James Hamilton of the 2nd Pennsylvania Regiment "struck and confined a man for misbehavior." When he passed Corporal Samuel Franklin of the 1st Pennsylvania Regiment, he "heard him say the soldiers ought to be damned for standing still and seeing a soldier beat and treated in such a manner and ought to go to hell for it." At Franklin's court martial on the 22nd, Lieutenant James Frederick McPherson testified that "after Major Hamilton had struck and confined a soldier, he heard the prisoner say that men who would stand by and see a brother soldier beat in such a manner sought to be damned." Franklin was tried for "exciting mutiny."

Also that evening, Captain Joseph McClellan of the 2nd Pennsylvania Regiment was the officer of the day and was doing his rounds. He passed James Wilson of the 3rd Pennsylvania Regiment. Wilson "must have certainly seen him and to know him to be an officer, he heard Wilson say: 'God damn the officers, the buggers.'" McClellan then turned around and ordered James Wilson to the guardhouse. Wilson did not budge and McClellan repeated his order two or three times, finally pulling his sword to enforce the order. On the journey to the guardhouse Wilson "swore repeatedly he would never leave this town without his pay." James Wilson, at his court martial on the 22nd, pleaded "that he was so drunk that he knows nothing relative to the charge against him." The charge was "exciting mutiny as far as in his power."

Philip Smith of the 2nd Pennsylvania Regiment was tried for "mutinous expressions such as asserting that if any officer dared to touch him he would shoot him." Also tried on the 22nd was William Crofts of the artillery for threats of retaliation against Major Benjamin Eustis of the 4th Continental Artillery and "drunkenness on the parade." Thomas Wilson of the 1st Pennsylvania Regiment was also tried for "exciting mutiny."

By a court martial held on May 22, 1781, with Major James Moore presiding, five more men were sentenced to death. To impress on the troops the need for good behavior, the executions were carried out quickly. The entire Pennsylvania Line was drawn up under arms for the executions that day. John Fortescue, of the 6th; Philip Smith, of the 2nd; James Wilson, of the 3rd; and Thomas Wilson of the 1st Pennsylvania Regiments were shot to death. General Anthony Wayne pardoned William Crofts of the artillery matross and Samuel Franklin of the 1st Pennsylvania Regiment.[46] Although no eyewitness account of the pardon has been found, at a mass execution the usual procedure in the Continental Army was for the general's aide to save at least one man from death. After some executions had taken place the aide would halt the proceedings and pardon the remaining prisoner. The person being pardoned would be told in front of the assembled crowd that he owed his life to the generosity of the general. He would be instructed that the best way to repay the general was to become an exemplary soldier.[47]

-13

General Greene's Travails

MUTINY IN THE SOUTH

On May 12, 1780, General Benjamin Lincoln surrendered the city of Charles Town and the bulk of the Southern Army to British General Sir Henry Clinton. This left almost no organized resistance in the state. In June 1780, General Horatio Gates was given command of the Southern Army, which was poorly supplied and poorly trained. English-born Gates was an experienced soldier. He had served in the British Army in the French and Indian War and on an expedition against Martinique. The hero of Saratoga (when the honor should have gone to Benedict Arnold), howver, lost the battle of Camden on August 16, 1780. This was the second major defeat for the Southern Army in little over three months.

In the fall came treason of the blackest dye. Benedict Arnold tried to turn over West Point to the British. The prospect for American independence was looking very shaky. While the British were busy trying to consolidate their control of the Carolinas and Georgia, the Americans lost their best field commander.

Some people expected Gates to be relieved of command after his flight. Greene, who had been campaigning for the command of the Southern Army, decided that was not going to happen. On October 5, Greene told Washington that he was willing to take the post at West Point. It was not an independent command, but the chance for fame was greater than in the quartermaster's job. On the 6th, Washington wrote to Greene, "I commit this important Post [West Point] to your care in full confidence in your prudence vigilance activity and good conduct."[1] The next day Washington advised Congress of his selection of Greene to command at West Point.[2]

Also on the 6th, the president of Congress ordered Washington to hold an inquiry of General Gates's conduct and for him to appoint someone in his place to command the Southern Army.[3] Knowing that the selection of the new commander of the Southern Army was going to be left to Washington, John Mathews, a delegate in Congress from South Carolina, wrote to Washington on the same day. Mathews said: "I am authorized by the delegates of the three southern states to communicate to your Excellency their wish that Major General Greene may be the officer appointed to the command of the Southern department, if it would not be incompatible with the rules of the army."[4]

The thirty-nine-year-old General Nathanael Greene was given the command of the remains of the Southern Army on October 14.[5] His dream of an independent command was fulfilled. It was a command that had destroyed Generals Benjamin Lincoln and Horatio Gates. Would he be next?

Nathanael Greene came from a very politically connected Quaker family in Rhode Island. A successful iron founder, he walked with a pronounced limp. He was an ambitious man who wanted to be remembered. He was sensitive to criticism. He had first served as a private in the local militia known as the Kentish Guard before being made a general of the Rhode Island troops. His political connections certainly did not hinder such a significant leap in rank.

Greene was blessed with foresight, ingenuity, a strong personality, and good organizational skills. It did not take long for him to impress General Washington with his abilities during the siege of Boston. He was with George Washington at Trenton, Brandywine, Germantown, Valley Forge, and Monmouth. Greene has been described as Washington's favorite officer and an heir apparent to the commander in chief. As a personal favor to General George Washington, he put aside his dreams of an independent command and glory to become the quartermaster general but was allowed to hold his field command. Under Greene's organization, the previously ineffective Quartermaster Department was reformed. The department was able to find the supplies that kept the Continental Army provisioned.

Once Nathanael Greene reached what was left of the Southern Army, he realized how difficult it was going to be just to keep the army in the field. He complained about the supply problems to John Mathews. Greene placed the blame on the commissary for not advising him of how truly bad their situation was. There had been instances when the Southern Army had been without any meat for four days at a time. An army needs clothing, pay, and provisions

Greene realized, but "the want of provisions works an immediate discontent on desertions and sometimes mutiny."

Greene had Captains Mills and William Pierce deliver his letter to the governor and instructed them to give a report of the deplorable situation of the army.[6] After the Battle of Eutaw Springs on September 8, 1781, Captain Pierce carried General Greene's dispatches about the victory to Philadelphia and was awarded a sword by Congress for his efforts.[7]

The Southern American Army, under the command of General Nathanael Greene, was at the High Hills of the Santee, South Carolina.[8] The spirit of rebellion was rising in the ranks due to the three perennial problems: bad food, no clothes, and no pay. The Maryland soldiers were getting very restless, as some of their old officers had been sent away. They expressed their desire to return home. They claimed that out of seven regiments only two hundred soldiers remained and that they had never received any pay.

On the evening of October 20, 1781, a number of the Maryland soldiers were seen sneaking out of camp taking their weapons with them. As soon as the officers became aware of the situation, they had a roll call. The soldiers who had tried to sneak out of camp were notified by their fellow soldiers that they would be discovered before they were very far away. They quickly crept back into camp trying not to be seen. Some of the attempted escapees were seen returning but the officers ignored them.

During the quickly ordered roll call, a drunken Timothy Griffin of the South Carolina Line arrived on the parade grounds. While the officers were admonishing some of the men for their behavior, Griffin cried out, "Stand to it boys, D——n my blood, if I would give an inch" and other more colorful words to the same effect. Captain Samuel McPherson, of the 2nd Maryland Regiment, upon hearing Griffin's oaths, immediately knocked him down. Griffin, without delay, was taken to the guardhouse.[9]

At the American Southern Army Headquarters, Colonel John Stewart, of the 1st Maryland Regiment, presided over the court martial of Private Griffin the following day. Stewart was one of the heroes of the assault on Stony Point. His courageous action had resulted in a unanimous vote by Congress to award him a silver medal, designed by Paris-born engraver Nicolas-Marie Gatteaux.[10] Private Timothy Griffin was found guilty of "encouraging mutiny and desertion" and was sentenced to be "shot to death" on that day between five and six in the evening. The sentence was promptly carried out.[11]

At about the same time as the Maryland troop mutiny and soon after Cornwallis surrendered to the combined American and French forces at Yorktown, the remaining Virginia forces were ordered to assemble at Cumberland Old Court House, Virginia, and then march south to support General Greene. One of these units, a newly formed regiment under the command of Colonel Christian Febiger refused to follow orders. On November 17, 1781, the new regiment's officers presented Colonel Febiger with a memorial stating that they would not march until their men were adequately supplied.[12] The men had no clothing for a winter campaign. Even some of the officers were without blankets and they had no money to buy any. They had not been paid for two, even three, years. They stated they would "march upon the shortest notice to any most distant post . . . if supplied in any suitable manner." Otherwise, they would resign. The five highest ranking officers, including Lieutenant Colonel Thomas Posey, signed the memorial. Colonel Febiger sent the memorial to his immediate superior, General Arthur St. Clair. St. Clair cancelled the order for the battalion to march. He forwarded the memorial to Washington, who in turn wrote to Governor Benjamin Harrison of Virginia pointing out the grievances and asking for help.[13] On January 12, 1782, Washington responded to Febiger. "I expect and insist in the most positive manner, that the detachment shall march." He also advised that every exertion to equip the detachment should be made.[14]

Two months later, in January 1782, a wagonload of spoiled beef was brought into the camp at Cumberland Old Court House. The beef stank so badly that it was "dangerous to be near it." However, an attempt was made to serve it. The men had been without meat for twelve days. Some complained so vigorously they were arrested. One hundred fifty of their comrades "rose in arms to rescue them. But by the vigilance of the officers they were dispersed." Shortly thereafter, Febiger was handed an inflammatory circular that had been passed among the soldiers. Febiger wrote to Colonel William Davies on January 21 to say that he was "trying to prevent an open rupture" and thought "the men might attempt something tomorrow."

Problems continued among the troops assembling at Cumberland Old Court House. In mid-February the last regular battalion of the Virginia Line had arrived and when the units were commanded to strike their tents and prepare to march, the men refused to budge unless they got their back pay.

Lieutenant Colonel Posey wrote three different versions of the events that transpired. To Washington, he wrote that it took just a little threatening and the men moved out the next day, marching because of a lack of wagons.[15] To Governor Harrison, he said that the men left reluctantly "for want of money and clothing."[16] To his friend, Adjutant General William Davies, he wrote, "I got rid of the said detachment after hanging one and whipping 73 of them and they are well officered. . . . I dismounted the officers which has been a good effect. Thus with the officers marching on foot, with the memory of at least one comrade executed for mutiny, and with the backs of 73 men still tingling with welts from floggings."[17] Whatever the real reason, the Virginia Line finally marched away from its barracks and began the trek to join General Greene near Charles Town, South Carolina.[18]

At the end of March 1782, General Greene had become seriously concerned about the morale of the troops. The quality of the beef his army had been receiving was so bad that he was expecting a mutiny. He begged Governor Mathews to order pork, if possible, to be shipped to the troops. "A little variety may silence the growing discontent which is fermented from various causes among which the want of pay and clothing are the principal. A day or two provisions of pork or mutton may greatly alter the present temper of the troops." He wanted immediate action as "no time is to be lost."[19]

Greene, in order to buy some time before his troops mutinied, issued a general order on April 2 telling the troops that a large assortment of clothing was on the way from Philadelphia to the Southern Army. He also assured them that when his troop returns were received at Philadelphia, "not less than two or three months pay will be forwarded."

Greene's statements were based more on hope than reality. He was grasping for some way to quell the rising discontent in his troops. He told them he was aware of their unhappiness over the lack of clothing, pay, and provisions. He wanted them to know that everything was being "done for their relief and that their sufferings result from unavoidable difficulties." He went on to praise them for their patience and past good behavior. He also told them that the enemy at Charles Town was making preparations to come out and attack them. Although Greene believed this to be true, the British had no plans to leave the city.[20] Greene's reduced tension in the troops and bought him some additional time.

Greene then got bad news from Governor Mathews. The additional supplies could not be gathered as quickly as he wanted because the regiment that would have been assigned to the task was "in the utmost confusion." In that regiment, Colonel Morton Wilkinson resigned in a controversy over General

John Barnwell's command of the Beaufort militia district.[21] Most of the rest of the officers sided with Wilkinson and also resigned. The mounted militiamen of the regiment had previously been sent to the forks of the Edisto River. In order to fulfill General Greene's request for meat, Governor Mathews asked for six men from the "invalid horses now at the Horseshoe" to help in a cattle round up until the militia troop of horse could be recalled.[22]

After a week, Greene advised General Washington of the situation in the Southern Army. He told him that "the want of clothing, pay and better subsistence; and being altogether without spirits have given a murmuring and discontented tone to the army and the face of mutiny discovers itself in many parts of it." Greene told Washington that he would do whatever he could to hold the army together but pointed out that there was little he could do "in an exhausted county and unsupported."[23]

Greene had been complaining to anyone who would listen about how slowly the stores had been supplied to his troops. With the items that had arrived, he was able to outfit the 4th Regiment of Dragoons and was close to outfitting the 1st Regiment. Both Lieutenant Colonel Anthony Walton White of the 1st and Captain Erasmus Gill of the 4th Continental Dragoons were instructed to tell the men to take care of the clothes they were issued as they would not be issued replacements for at least the next twelve months.[24] Greene had supplied clothes for the cavalry, except for Lee's Legion, on a priority basis. The balance of his army was almost naked.

General Anthony Wayne, sent to assist General Greene and now located at Ebenezer, Georgia, with several battalions of the Pennsylvania Line, had proposed trading rice to the British in Savannah for clothes. General Greene informed Wayne that the governor had already implemented the practice and his Pennsylvania troops would get their fair share when clothes arrived. Greene did not want to open a second channel of obtaining clothes, as the two procurers would be competing with each other, and he still hoped a supply of clothing was on its way from Philadelphia. Unfortunately, the supplies he desperately needed had not left Philadelphia. Greene was aware of the discontent among Wayne's Pennsylvania Line but thought that it had waned since he issued his general order of April 2 that said pay and supplies were on the way.[25]

On April 7, thirty-four-year-old Colonel Edward Carrington, deputy quartermaster for the Southern Department, told Greene the much-needed supplies were still at Philadelphia. They had not budged except for 140 tents, which had been sent five weeks earlier. The politicians in Congress thought that the British would soon evacuate Charles Town, thereby reducing the need for most of Greene's Southern Army. By delaying the supplies, Robert Morris hoped to save money.

Carrington finally convinced Robert Morris that they needed to get Greene's Southern Army ready for the upcoming campaigning season. Carrington was going to be allowed to leave Philadelphia in about a week with Greene's supplies. Also, a separate agent was being sent from Philadelphia to purchase rum and salt locally and have them delivered to a magazine at Camden, South Carolina. The Quartermaster Department would then transport the supplies from Camden to wherever the army needed them. Robert Morris expected that most of the supplies for Greene's army would be purchased at New Bern or Wilmington, North Carolina.[26]

By April 9, General Wayne had received the clothing supplied by Captain Erasmus Gill's people. However, it was of so inferior quality that he did not expect it to last very long. Wayne had tried unsuccessfully to buy clothing and other supplies from Savannah. The first regiment was still in dire need of clothes. Most of his men did not have coats. Wayne was begging for thread to repair the clothing they had in hopes that it would last through the summer. Many of his men also lacked shoes and overalls. These items were needed "to do duty and to be in condition to appear on parade in so decent a manner as not to offend a modest eye."

Wayne had received additional troops in the form of Colonel Thomas Posey's detachment of three hundred Continentals. They were better clothed than all but the Light Horse. However, some of these men only had the shirts and overalls they were wearing. Additionally, a few needed muskets, bayonets, cartridge boxes, and camp kettles.

Wayne wrote that he was sorry for the murmuring tone that pervaded the army and much more so for a second appearance of a mutiny in a Pennsylvania Line that "I had the honor so long to command! A distemper that I thought effectually cured by a liberal dose of Nitre, etc. administered at York in Pennsylvania." He was happy to hear that General Greene believed that the potential mutiny would be squelched relieved once the clothing and pay arrived."[27]

Greene worried that the British would try to exploit the discord among the troops. Fraternization with the enemy could fan the flames of discontent among his men. It had been suspected for some time that a line of communication was being maintained with the enemy by someone in the camp.[28] To prevent this communication between his men and the enemy Greene issued a general order on April 12 requiring the officers at the outpost were to ensure that enemy personnel who came with flags of truce be kept away from the troops. They were not to be permitted to have any conversations with the men.[29]

CREATING THE SOUTHERN ARMY WITH detachments from different states created a constant change in command, as officers were always coming and going. The officers were complaining about their instability of command. In order to remedy the situation as much as possible, Greene formed the Maryland and Pennsylvania lines into two regiments each.[30] The next day, April 13, 1782, Greene wrote to the president of Congress that his troops were very discontented because of a want for clothing, pay, and spirits. He advised that the country was exhausted and the supplies for his troops were arriving too slowly. He also still expected the enemy to come out from Charles Town and attack him.[31]

Greene wrote to General Benjamin Lincoln, secretary of war and the man who had surrendered Charles Town, repeating his trinity of wants for clothes, pay, and provisions for the Southern Army. He went on to tell him that their supply of beef and rice was exceedingly precarious and the beef that he was receiving was of poor quality. The lack of pay and rum were fueling the discontent among the soldiers. At some point, all that pent-up energy would be released. Greene thought the pressure would be relieved if the men received their pay. He suggested that the spirit of discontent might be alleviated with a little money if the troops were comfortably clothed, adequately fed, and supplied with alcohol.[32]

When Captain Walter Finney of the 10th Pennsylvania Regiment was transferred to the Southern Army, he wrote in his diary: "The troops are remarkably healthy, but badly fed, and wretchedly clothed, at least one third of the men are naked as they came to the world, their blanket and hat excepted, which they belted around them to defend from the [in]clemency of the weather, as well as to preserve that decency which custom has introduced in that part of the globe with which they were conversant."[33] William Moultrie also described the army's situation:

> While the American army lay on the south side of the Ashley River, the greater part of the men were so completely ragged, that their clothes would

scarcely cover their nakedness: every little piece of cloth was taken up to tie about their waists; and that was not the worst of their grievances; the want of provisions was severely felt by them. Sometimes they had meat without bread or rice, sometimes bread and rice without meat, and sometimes were without either. In this situation did they continue for several months, and only sixteen miles from Charleston, where the British army was in garrison, with a greatly superior force; fortunately, Ashley River was between them. By their being encamped so long in one place at this season of the year . . . they began to be sickly, discontented and mutinous.[34]

The men were unhappy about such deplorable conditions. The clothing situation was so bad that some soldiers "do duty with nothing but a bad blanket."[35]

Desertions were on the rise and many troops defected to the British. Both the Maryland and Pennsylvania regiments were expressing their discontent. "It was talked pretty freely among the men, that if pay and clothing did not arrive by such a day they would march their officers to Dorchester, and allow them only a few days more, before they would deliver them up to the enemy, unless their grievances were redressed."

General Greene knew that unless conditions improved the men were likely to mutiny. He knew he had to stop the daily murmuring among the troops before it was too late. Greene was unable to identify the ringleader; he feared that the British had some secret agents in the camp. In hopes of identifying the perpetrators, Greene offered in his general orders, on April 20, a ten-guinea reward to any person who discovered the British emissaries.[36] Such a bounty might tempt soldiers who were flat broke to turn over the culprits.

Greene recalled that the instigators of the Pennsylvania Line mutiny of 1781 were sergeants who had deserted from the British. He ordered Lieutenant Colonel Francis Mentges of the 5th Pennsylvania Regiment to provide a list of soldiers who that met this criterion. After an inquiry, Mentges reported that "no more than four who have deserted the British army and entered our service as sergeants." The names he reported were Gosnell, Hustlar, Eaton, and Upton. "The three later are recommended by the officers as men of good conduct and behavior but there are sergeants who are suspected [and are not defectors]."[37]

Greene's offer of a reward quickly produced results. A woman by the name of Becky told Colonel Josiah Harmar of the 3rd Pennsylvania Regiment that Sergeant George Gosnell of the Pennsylvania Line was one of the soldiers talking about mutiny.[38] It was said that she was the wife of one of the sergeants.[39]

Harmar was a twenty-eight-year-old Philadelphia native who had served in the army since 1775. He instructed Lieutenant Colonel Francis Mentges to have Gosnell arrested and turned over to the prison guard. Sergeant George Gosnell was a British deserter and some suspect he was one of the leaders of the January 1781 Pennsylvania Line mutiny at Morristown, New Jersey. Colonel Harmar suggested to General Greene that the guards over the Pennsylvania mutineers be selected from Lee's Legion to prevent communications between the guards and the prisoners.[40] During the night, a dozen soldiers who were suspected of being involved in the mutiny defected to the British at Charles Town.

Captain Nathaniel Pendleton had gone under a flag of truce to Charles Town to negotiate the treatment of his brother, Henry Pendleton, chief judge of South Carolina. On his return from Charles Town, Pendleton's servant stole his horse and rode to the British requesting protection. Pendleton sent Sergeant Richard Peters to get his horse back. While Peters went to the British lines to try and get the horse returned, he was approached by the British. He was offered a considerable sum of money to have General Greene seized and delivered to the British on the Dorchester causeway. The mutinous sergeants were to secure all the officers at a certain hour and fire a gun as a signal. One hundred fifty British cavalry within one mile of the camp would rush in and surround Greene and his staff.[41]

The next day, General Greene ordered Marylander General Mordecai Gist to take a written deposition from Becky. Afterward, Gist was then to convene a meeting of the officers at his marquee. At 2:00 p.m., Greene ordered that the court martial was to be composed of the field officers of the line and a captain from each brigade.[42] While the court martial was proceeding, Greene sent out his cavalry to patrol for the suspected British accomplices in this plot.

On the morning of Sunday, April 21, 1782, Captain Ferdinand O'Neal and between twenty-four and thirty cavalrymen from Lee's Legion proceeded across Bacon's Bridge to the east side of the Ashley River. O'Neal was patrolling between the town of Dorchester and the Quarter House when he spotted three soldiers of a Black Loyalist cavalry unit in the village. This was the Independent Troop of Black Dragoons led by Captain March, a black officer.[43]

Captain Rudolph, who had volunteered for the mission, was in the lead with two of the Legion troopers. During the clash, one of the Black Dragoons was killed; Rudolph captured a second. The third trooper escaped. Rudolph's prisoner told him that a single troop under the command of Captain Dawkins had gone by the way of the Goose Creek bridge and would return by the way of Dorchester. O'Neal pursued the Loyalist troop and discovered Dawkins passing through the village of Dorchester. Both sides charged simultaneously and a desperate fight began. A bugle sounded and dismounted Loyalist cavalry lying in concealment rose up on all sides. They were armed with carbines and fired a volley into O'Neal's flanks.[44]

William Seymour wrote in his journal, "One of our men engaged and killed two of the enemy's negro horse, and a third, which happened to be a Major, thought to make his escape by running into a swamp where he came up with him, and with one blow of his sword severed his head from his body."[45] O'Neal ordered the men to retreat down Gaillard Road, the only road left open for their escape.[46]

The court martial had found Gosnell guilty of attempting to incite a mutiny. Also accused of inciting a riot was Richard Peters. Sergeant Major William Seymour of the Delaware Regiment wrote in his journal that Richard Peters and his wife were "confined in the provost under sentence of death for corresponding with the enemy, some of the letters being found about him, which specified that he was to recruit a number of men in our service for the enemy."[47] Peters was General Nathanael Greene's steward.

At 10:00 p.m., General Gist sent Major Euliston to General Greene with a description the day's court martial against Gosnell and the news that the charges against Peters had not been proved. The court was going to continue with more cases the following day at nine o'clock.[48]

General Greene informed the troops in his general order of April 22 that a general court martial had been held the previous day. General Mordecai Gist was president when Sergeant George Gosnell of the Pennsylvania Line was tried "for having spoken words tending to excite mutiny. The court, after having considered the evidence for and against the prisoner, . . . are of the opinion, that he is guilty of the charge, and that he is punishable by the 3rd article, of the 2nd Section of the Articles of War and do sentence him to suffer death." Two-thirds of the court were in agreement. The section cited states that any "soldier who shall begin, incite, cause or join in any mutiny or sedition . . . on any pretence whatsoever shall suffer death or such other punishment as by a court martial shall be inflicted."

Greene approved the verdict and the death sentence. In order to demon-strate that justice would be swift, he ordered that Gosnell "be shot to death on the field in the rear" at 3:00 p.m. He also ordered one hundred men from each brigade with an officer to attend the execution.[49]

When the time came for Sergeant Gosnell to meet his maker, he "walked with a firm step and composed countenance" to the place of the execution. As he went past the assembled soldiers, he distributed articles of his cloth-ing. He gave away to different soldiers his coat, hat, and sleeve buttons.

The full plot was revealed as more conspirators were discovered. The mutineers were to seize the artillery and fire two fieldpieces, which would set the events into motion. The revolters were then to take prisoners, possibly even General Greene himself. They would move across the Pempan River and issue their demands.[50] If demands were not met in a few days, they would march with their prisoners to the British in Charles Town.[51]

Another of General Greene's domestics who was suspected to be in league with the mutineers was a person by the name of Owens. He was tried but the testimony against him was not conclusive.

On April 24, Lewis Morris Jr., Greene's aide-de-camp, noted that "disso-lution of the army is much to be apprehended. The troops are naked, and dis-contented, and the spirit of mutiny and desertion prevails to a very great degree."[52]

Greene held four of the mutineers in confinement at the camp near Bacon's Bridge, South Carolina. On April 27, the men sent him the following plea: "We the unhappy prisoners of the Pennsylvania Line confined under your guard do most earnestly beseech your honor to take our case into your gracious consideration and if it seemeth good into you to either release us and let us be of service to our country in the laudable business in which we were employed or have a hearing when it may be in our power to justify our selves both to you and to our country. We remain noble general your dutiful sol-diers." It was signed by John Nicholson of the 2nd, Terrance Connell of the 1st, and John Speer and Thomas Hustlar of the 5th Pennsylvania Regiments.

In the meantime, two more mutineers were tried by a court martial. Evan Tumpton was charged with "speaking words tending to promote sedition and excite mutiny in the army." Tumpton was acquitted by the court. The other soldier was William Henry Savage, a Maryland soldier. In addition to the charges brought against Tumpton, Savage was also accused of "concealing an intended mutiny in the army after it came to his knowledge." The court found Savage guilty and sentenced him to one hundred lashes. On the 28th, General Greene approved Savage's sentence. General Mordecai Gist suspected that three of his servants were also involved in the plot.[53]

While the arrests, trials, and execution were occurring, General Greene sent out patrols. Large bodies of enemy horse and foot were in motion and, during the night, approached closer than usual to the American camp. This convinced the American command that it was more than a coincidence and the enemy were there to support the mutiny.

On the morning after the execution of Sergeant Gosnell, Captain Ferdinand O'Neill of the legion cavalry was out on patrol.[54] A body of enemy horse, under command of Major Frazer, had gone as far as Stan's Bridge. On Frazer's return, he and O'Neill met at Dorchester. Since the British had the superior numbers, Captain O'Neill did not engage but was "vigorously pursued by Frazer." During the chase, O'Neill saw a second body of enemy troops and was forced to select an alternate route back to camp. He succeeded in making his escape but lost ten of his dragoons.[55]

The much-desired clothing that was needed to quell the discontent in the troops still had not arrived. Greene told Wayne the troops were in a constant fever of discontent. "I am certain the enemy have been tampering with my steward. He is in confinement."[56]

General Anthony Wayne was disappointed in the conduct of the Pennsylvania troops under Greene in South Carolina but had similar problems with his troops at Ebenezer, Georgia. Wayne believed that the root cause of the discontent in his soldiers was caused by officers voicing their displeasure before their servants about the lack of clothing and pay. It was also insinuated that some units were getting preferential treatment.

Wayne admonished those officers who were the source of his morale problems.[57] The situation could have been perilous as Wayne's troops were opposed by an enemy force twice their size. Henry Lee believed that the mutineers had a communication with the enemy.[58]

Clothing remained a problem for the Southern Army when Greene wrote to John Moylan. "I hope the supplies of clothing are far advanced on the route to this army. . . . Never was there so naked a body of troops in the field as those under my command."[59] This came from a general who had seen the misery at Valley Forge and Morristown.

Several weeks later, Greene believed that sending some of the suspects from camp under guard to the laboratory at Frohock's Mill near Salisbury, North Carolina, to make cartridges had more of a positive effect on morale than the execution. "The soldiers now think, that although suspicions are not sufficient to hang them, they are for sending them from the army and the disgrace attending it is little less than death." Greene believed that his actions had "prevented the dreadful misfortune of a very considerable, if not total mutiny."[60] The discontent among the troops had dissipated but the suffering continued.

Greene was still having problems getting supplies: "Whatever stores passes through Virginia stops in North Carolina." What few supplies did make it to South Carolina were what no one else wanted. Most of the last batch of cartridges that came from the northern laboratories were too small and poorly made.

Greene was frustrated with the situation. He wrote, "The distresses of the army have been too great for the trial of human virtue" and "discontent, excesses and mutiny approaches." He described his situation as a very ragged, very naked army without pay, destitute of rum or spirits of any kind, and facing a superior enemy. Greene added that the "discontent has almost risen to mutiny." He credited the governor and the council of South Carolina with procuring a little clothing from Charles Town for his army. Without this clothing they provided "we could not have kept the field."[61]

Greene sent one of his aides-de-camp, Captain Nathaniel Pendleton, to General Griffith Rutherford at Charlotte, North Carolina, to help procure wagons to expedite supplies moving south. Pendleton was transferred from the 3rd Virginia to Greene's staff in November 1780. He advised Rutherford of the mutinous conduct and that one of the men had been shot. If clothing and supplies were not provided there was the possibility that the army would not be able to protect the civilians from the actions of an enraged enemy.[62]

Having been made aware that Congress and Continental Army officers were of the opinion that the British were planning to evacuate South Carolina, General Greene tried to get supplies released to his army. He contacted Major General Henry Knox who he thought was a staunch believer in the evacuation theory. Knox was a three-hundred-pound former Bostonian bookseller. He had lost the two smallest fingers on his left hand in a 1773 duck hunting accident. Knox learned military tactics by reading the books he sold.

Greene advised Knox that the delay in sending supplies had already result-ed in a mutiny. One sergeant had been executed and five others sent away in a disgraceful manner. These measures had kept the situation from escalat-ing.[63]

Word of the mutiny in Greene's Southern Army was carried in the newspa-pers of the day. The *Virginia Gazette* of May 25, 1782, printed the following report: "Our latest accounts from the Southward, mention a conspiracy against General Greene. The enemy it seems, had bribed one of his servants, and measures were concerted for carrying General Greene off prisoner. The plot, however, was found out and the traitor executed. The particulars are variously told and we are unable as yet to give any authentic relation of the affair."[64]

Colonel Christian Febiger, who was at Cumberland Old Court House, Virginia "read with horror" the account of the mutiny, most likely in the *Virginia Gazette*, the local paper. He was not surprised by the conduct of the Pennsylvania and Maryland sergeants as he recalled the Pennsylvania Line mutiny in January 1781: "their past conduct especially the former little better could be expected from them."[65]

By the end of May 1782, General Nathanael Greene was advising everyone that the spirit of discontent seemed to have entirely subsided since the perpe-trators had been shipped off to the laboratory at Salisbury, North Carolina. Also, there was the promise of some clothing and supplies from Philadelphia. Greene was hopeful that the discontentment would not reappear.[66]

GENERAL NATHANAEL GREENE WAS JUSTIFIABLY upset with the supply con-tractors. He considered Captain Henry Putnam, for example, negligent in ful-filling the contract to supply the army. In June 1782, Greene told Colonel Peter Horry that one of the causes of the late uneasiness in the army was the lack of rum, which Putnam was to have provided. Greene felt that Putnam was guilty of exposing the army to mutiny and "deserved nothing short of hanging." He wanted to seize his cargo and put him in the Provost. Greene indicated that the only thing stopping him was that it would scare the other purveyors of supplies to the army. He said he was told that Putnam had little more than the cargo he was selling, which made suing him for damages use-less. Greene said, "I believe I shall let him go; and wish him to behave with more fidelity in the future."[67]

14

The Newburgh Conspiracy

*A*t the end of 1782, the Continental Army had gone into its winter cantonment at New Windsor and Newburgh, New York. The fighting was over. Now the politicians would hammer out the peace treaty. There were the arguments of where the boundary should be. Was it to be the Allegheny Mountains or the Mississippi River; and then there was the issue of fishing rights.

With the prospect of no spring campaign, many generals were reluctant to spend the winter in camp. Of the nine generals who were to command the troops in the cantonment, seven were either absent or had applied to be on leave. Rumors were flying in camp on the subject of peace.

Washington was still planning a spring campaign. To keep the men busy, he had them build a new public building. A one-story structure built by the labor and materials from different regiments, it was large enough to hold one regiment. On top of the building were a cupola and a flag staff.[1] Originally built as a place for religious services, it was also used as a meeting place for other events. It was called by various names, including the "Temple," the "Public Building," and "the New Building." The 1st New York Regiment was given the assignment of making five benches for "the Temple." When the building was finished, the next project was to build a causeway across a swamp to connect the Massachusetts Brigade with the New Jersey and New York Brigades. The project would require four thousand bundles of sticks and wood. This would keep the men busy until the start of spring training.

As the end of the war approached, many of the officers were apprehensive over not receiving a guarantee of promised veterans' benefits and their back pay.

In September 1782, a delegation of three Massachusetts officers had taken a petition containing their grievances to the state legislature in Boston. They

198

received encouragement from Governor John Hancock but the legislators were unreceptive to their situation. The delegation returned empty-handed.

Dissent was growing among the officers and the Massachusetts regiments' representatives held a meeting on November 16. They decided to approach Congress with their grievances and asked people from other states to join them. Each regiment was to submit their list of concerns, which noted, in addition to earlier grievances, that some officers had to sell their personal belongings to pay their way home.

December 1782 was a period of watching and waiting. The French were at Boston getting ready to embark, waiting to hear the latest news from London and Paris about the treaty.

The officers had finished their memorial of concerns to Congress but there was a delay in having copies made. Major General John Paterson requested Captain Pemberton to transcribe the memorial but the demands of business prevented his getting it accomplished. Paterson then gave it to Colonel Cortlandt to do it. However, despite repeated requests, Paterson still did not get it accomplished. Paterson told General Henry Knox he would send him a copy as soon as he could get someone to transcribe it.

On December 14, Washington wrote to Joseph Jones, the Virginia Congressman,

> In the course of a few days Congress will, I expect, receive an Address from the Army on the subject of their grievances. The dissatisfactions of the army had arisen to a great and alarming height, and combinations among the Officers to resign, at given periods in a body, were beginning to take place when by some address and management their resolutions have been converted into the form in which they will now appear before Congress. . . . No part of the community has undergone equal hardships, and borne them with the same patience and fortitude, that the army has done.
>
> Hitherto the officers have stood between the lower order of the soldiery and the public, and in more instances than one, at the hazard of their lives, have quelled very dangerous mutinies. But if their discontents should be suffered to rise equally high, I know not what the consequences may be.[2]

If the officers mutinied, Washington could not predict the outcome. It was uncertain who the soldiers in the ranks would follow. Would they fire on their own officers if it came to that?

Washington continued:

"The spirit of enthusiasm, which overcame every thing at first, is now done away; it is idle, therefore to expect more from military men, than from those discharging the civil departments of Government. . . . It is an invidious distinction, and one that will not stand the test of reason or policy, the one set should receive all, and the other no part . . . of their pay."[3]

That is, it was unfair for the politicians to make sure they got paid and let the soldiers dangle in the wind. Washington was well aware that the temper of the army had soured and became more irritable than at any time during the war.

On December 23, 1782, General Alexander McDougall, Colonel Matthias Ogden of New Jersey, and Colonel John Brooks of Massachusetts, "a delegation from the whole," had set out from New Windsor to Philadelphia, Pennsylvania, carrying the memorial that had been signed by fourteen officers from the regiments in the Hudson Highlands.[4] It read:

Cantonments on the Hudson River, December 1782. To the United States Congress assembled;

The address and petition of the officers of the Army of the United States Humbly Sheweth

That we, the officers of the army of the United States, in behalf of ourselves and our brethren the soldiers, beg leave, with all proper deference and respect, freely to state to Congress, the supreme power of the United States, the great distress under which we labour.

At this period of the war it is with particular pain we find ourselves constrained to address your august body, on matters of a pecuniary nature. We have struggled with our difficulties, year after year, under the hopes that each would be the last; but we have been disappointed. We find our embarrassments thicken so fast, and have become so complex, that many of us are unable to go further. In this exigence we apply to Congress for relief as our head and sovereign. . . .

Securities given by the states for some of the pay due over the past four years are of little value] and yet, trifling as they are, many have been under the sad necessity of parting with them, to prevent their families from actually starving. . . . The citizens murmur at the greatness of their taxes, and are astonished that no part reaches the army. The numerous demands, which are between the first collectors and the soldiers, swallow up the whole.

Our distresses are now brought to a point. We have borne all that men can bear—our private resources are at an end, and our friends are wearied out and disgusted with our incessant applications. We, therefore, most seriously and earnestly beg that a supply of money may be forwarded to the army as soon as possible. The uneasiness of the soldiers for want of pay, is great and dangerous; and further experiments on their patience may have fatal effects. . . . Whenever there has been a real want of means, any defect in system, or neglect in execution, in the departments of the army, we have invariably been the sufferers. . . .

[The petition urged] . . . an immediate adjustment of all dues [with a certain amount to be paid at once, and a willingness on the officers' part to commute the half-pay for life pledged by Congress] for full pay for a certain number of years, or for a sum in gross, as shall be agreed to by the committee sent with this address. . . .

To the representation now made, the army have not a doubt that Congress will pay that attention which the serious nature of it requires. It would be criminal in the officers to conceal the general dissatisfaction which prevails, and is gaining ground in the army. . . . They therefore entreat, that Congress, to convince the army and the world that the independence of America shall not be placed on the ruin of any particular class of her citizens, will point out a mode for immediate redress.[5]

On January 1, 1783, as on other New Year's Days, there was going to be a reduction of the regiments and a new method of provisioning the officers. Washington lamented to General Benjamin Lincoln, secretary of war, "I am sensible that almost every innovation is in danger of being viewed in a disadvantageous point of light in the present state and temper of the army."[6]

On January 9, General McDougall wrote to General Henry Knox at West Point. He entrusted the letter to Colonel Jean Baptiste Obrey de Gouvion. Due to the weather, the journey to Philadelphia took a week. After getting settled, the committee had thought it prudent to engage in some lobbying. "It was judged expedient to converse with the delegates of the different States on the subject of our business before the Memorial was delivered, in order that their minds might be fully possessed of the nature and importance of the subject of our errand least [lest] any member unfavorable to us should attempt to give the matter less consideration than it deserves."

The result of these information-gathering interviews was not encouraging.

A great majority of Congress are seriously disposed to do every thing in their power, for the fulfillment of all their engagements to the army. And they are

rather pleased than other wise at the address's coming on. But the great difficulty is cash for present wants and permanent funds. . . . The crux of the
matter lay in the reluctance of the states to levy the taxes for debts contracted by Congress. Will New Hampshire, Rhode Island, Connecticut and
New Jersey pass even vague laws to recognize these debts? . . .
Massachusetts and New York may pass such laws without funds, and make
no provision for the payment of the principal or interest. . . . Would it be
advantageous if the army were to join with other public creditors to gain
redress? This mode or that, I wish you and General Huntington to cast your
thoughts on this subject, as we may probably find it necessary to put the
question to you and the officers for our government.[7]

General McDougall concluded with the prediction that their business in
Philadelphia would not be soon completed.

Major Samuel Shaw, aide-de-camp to General Henry Knox, gave his opinion on the situation. "It is happy for the country that the officers have taken
up the business, since nothing else could have kept the soldiers quiet.
Congress will now be made fully acquainted with the sufferings and the disposition of their troops in consequence of them. . . .It is devoutly to be wished
that this application may have the desired effect."[8]

On New Year's Day, Gouverneur Morris wrote to John Jay in Paris that
three officers—General McDougall, Lieutenant Colonel Brooks, and Colonel
Ogden—had brought to Congress the petition from the army requesting their
pay. He said the army had a supply of food and clothing but were owed back
wages. Congress did not have the money to pay to the army. "No provision is
made for the half-pay promised them. Some persons, and indeed some states,
pretend to dispute their claim to it."[9] Gouverneur Morris brought up a very
strong bargaining chip in the soldiers' favor. "The army have swords in their
hands. You know enough of the history of mankind to know much more than
I have said, and possibly much more than they themselves yet think of."[10] The
implication was that if Congress did not find the money to honor their debts
the army might take what was owed to them by force.

Washington's letter of January 10 to John Armstrong Jr., the twenty-four-
year-old aide to General Horatio Gates and son of Major General John
Armstrong, described the army's situation.

The army as usual, are without pay; and a great part of the soldiery without shirts; and tho' the patience of them is equally thread bear, the states

seem perfectly indifferent to their cries. In a word, if one was to hazard for them an opinion, upon this subject, it would be that the Army had contracted such a habit of encountering distress and difficulties, and of living without money, that it would be impolitic and injurious to introduce other customs in it! We have however, but this depended upon ourselves, built the most comfortable barracks in the vicinity of this place that the troops have ever yet been in.[11]

The army's memorial was finally delivered to Congress on Monday, January 6, after which Congress predictably appointed a committee to study the document. This "Grand Committee," composed of one member from each of the states, set up a conference with the three officers for Friday evening the 10th.

General George Washington drawn from life by Alexander Campbell of Williamsburg, Virginia, and published by C. Shepherd, London, in September 1775. (*William L. Clements Library*)

General McDougall, the ranking officer of the group, was the chief spokesman for the memorial. His observations "turned chiefly on the three chief topics of the memorial, namely an immediate advance of pay, adequate provision for the residue and half-pay."[12] The committee made the point that "the irritations of the army had resulted in part from the distinctions made between the civil & military lists, the former regularly receiving their salaries, and the latter as regularly left unpaid."[13]

When asked what would happen if no pay were immediately advanced, the committee of three implied that "a mutiny could ensue" at the cantonment, and the officers "would with less vigor than heretofore struggle against it." Colonel Ogden stated, "he wished not indeed to return to the army if he was to be the messenger of disappointment to them."

The congressmen were impressed by General McDougall's comment that "the most intelligent and considerate part of the army were deeply affected at the debility and defects in the federal government and the unwillingness of the states to cement and invigorate it. . . . They foresaw that it would take more than a comprehension of this impasse to prevent an almost certain confrontation."[14]

Lieutenant Colonel John Brooks described the situation, "With an impotent congress, and unfeeling refractory states, we may well ask in Gods name, what is to become of us?" Colonel Brooks declared, "In this dilemma we are lost as to our line of conduct," and he hinted that one of the committee might return to camp for further consultations.[15] In the meantime, McDougall and Brooks were to meet with financier Robert Morris, who had hopes of raising a little immediate pay for the army.[16]

General McDougall sent a second letter to General Knox which read:

Upon our first interview with some of the members, they expressed great satisfaction at the army's having taken up their complaint in so spirited a manner, but had to lament their utter inability to give them redress—that their powers were totally inadequate to the great purposes of a central government, that they had long since called on the states for monies without effect—that of the eight millions which were to have been in almost a year ago not one sixteenth was yet received . . . and that the impost, upon which they had put great dependence, had finally failed them. In short, the idea is that unless general funds can be provided, confusion, disgrace and ruin are inevitable.[17]

Alexander Hamilton advised that the army's memorial was received by Congress with a note of urgency. "We have now here a deputation from the army, and feel a mortification of a total disability to comply with their just expectations."

Congress, being a collection of politicians, went into seemingly endless debates on the possibility of collecting taxes to cover the money that was owed. If taxation was to be the method, what was to be taxed? Would it be property? The next question was who should collect it? Would it be the state, Congress or a combination of the two? If it was not going to be taxes, would it be a tariff on trade? The debates went on and on with no solution in sight.

On February 7, 1783, David Rittenhouse sent George Washington his new eyeglasses. Washington was happy with his new spectacles from Philadelphia, which worked well. He was having some problems adjusting to the new reading glasses, but when he did get the right distance they "show those objects very distinctly which at first appear like a mist blended together and confused."[18]

On February 27, Joseph Jones, the
Virginia Congressman, sent Washington
an update of what was happening in
Congress. "Reports are freely circulated
here that there are dangerous combina-
tions in the army, and within a few days
past it has been said, they are about to
declare, they will not disband until their
demands are complied with. Jones con-
tention in the army is that "justice is not
intended to be done to them." He cautioned "those acquainted with the deliberations of public bodies, and especially
of so mixed a body as that of Congress,
allowances will be made for slow deliberation."19

John Armstrong, Jr., drawn from life
in the early nineteenth century.
(*William L. Clements Library*)

Washington related his assessment of the status of the army in a letter to
Alexander Hamilton, dated March 4, 1783.

> The predicament, in which I stand as citizen and soldier, is as critical and
> delicate as can well be conceived. It has been the subject of many contem-
> plative hours. The sufferings of a complaining army on one hand, and the
> inability of Congress and tardiness of the states on the other, are the fore-
> bodings of evil, and may be productive of events which are more to be dep-
> recated than prevented; but I am not without hope, if there is such a dis-
> position shown as prudence and policy will dictate, to do justice, that your
> apprehensions, in case of peace, are greater than there is cause for. In this
> however I may be mistaken, if those ideas, which you have been informed
> are propagated in the army should be extensive; the source of which may
> be easily traced as the old leven [General Horatio Gates], it is said, for I
> have no proof of it, is again, beginning to work, under a mask of the most
> perfect dissimulation, and apparent cordiality."20

Washington suspected that General Gates was behind the unrest among
the officers. This was not the first time the two generals had been on opposite sides of an issue. There was the so-called Conway Cabal at Valley Forge
in 1778, when number of politicians critical of Washington's handling of the
war wanted to replace him with General Horatio Gates, the victor of the

Battle of Saratoga.[21] Now once again facing the possibility of an internal revolt, Washington's plan of action was to

> pursue the same steady line of conduct which has governed me hitherto; fully convinced that the sensible, and discerning past of the army, cannot be unacquainted of the services I have rendered it on more occasions than one. . . . The just claims of the army ought, and it is to be hoped will, have their weight with every sensible legislature in the union, if Congress point to their demands; show (if the case is so) the reasonableness of them, and the impracticability of complying with them without their aid. In any other point of view it would, in my opinion, be impolitic to introduce the army on the tapis;[22] lest it should excite jealousy, and bring on its concomitants. The states cannot, surely, be so devoid of common sense, common honesty, and common policy as to refuse their aid on a full, clear, and candid representation of facts from Congress; more especially if these should be enforced by members of their own body; who might demonstrate what the inevitable consequences of failure will lead to.[23]

Colonel Walter Stewart arrived at the Continental Army cantonment from Philadelphia on Saturday March 8. General Gates wrote that "Stewart was a kind of agent from our friends in Congress and in the administration, with no object, however, beyond that of getting the army to co-operate with the civil creditors, as the way most likely for both to obtain justice."[24] Major John Armstrong Jr. wrote that "Stewart was frank, honest, and assiduous; he saw all grades, and communicated freely with all."[25]

After the arrival in camp of Stewart, the mutinous sentiments were immediately and industriously circulated. It was universally expected the army would not disband until they had obtained justice.

Washington's hunch was correct. One of the chief instigators of the Newburgh Conspiracy was General Horatio Gates. The December petition to Congress was written in Gates's quarters. His aide, Major John Armstrong Jr. admitted, at a later date, to having written the anonymous letters that were circulated in camp.[26] At a Sunday meeting at General Gates's quarters, it is believed that the plotters approved a letter written by Armstrong and made plans to hold a meeting of the officers on Tuesday. An anonymous letter was circulated throughout the camp (see Appendix G for the full text):

To the Officers of the army:

Gentleman: A fellow soldier, whose interest and affections bind him strongly to you—whose past sufferings have been as great, and whose past sufferings have been as great and whose future fortunes may be as desperate as yours—would beg leave to address you.[27]

"A Storm very suddenly arose with unfavorable prognostics."[28]

Washington believed that the "Scheme was not only planned, but also digested and matured in Philadelphia; and that some people have been playing a double game; spreading at the camp and in Philadelphia reports and raising jealousies equally void of foundation until called into being by their vile artifices; for as soon as the minds of the army were thought to be prepared for the transaction, anonymous invitations were circulated, requesting a general meeting of the officers next day; at the same instant many copies of the address to the officers of the army was scattered in every state line of it."[29]

General Horatio Gates, published in January 1778 by John Morris, London. (*Library of Congress*)

Washington, having gotten wind of a second anonymous letter that called for a meeting, sent out the following General Order of March 11, 1783:

The Commander-in–Chief, having heard that a general meeting of the officers of the army was proposed to be held this day at the new building in an anonymous paper which was circulated yesterday by some unknown person conceives (altho he is fully persuaded that the good sense of the officers would induce them to pay very little attention to such an irregular invitation) his duty as well as the reputation and true interest of the army requires his disapprobation of such disorderly proceedings, at the same time he requests the general and field officers with one officer from each company and a proper representative of the staff of the Army will assemble at 12 o'clock on Saturday next at the new building to hear the report of the Committee of the Army to Congress.

After mature deliberation they will devise what further measures ought to be adopted as most rational and best calculated to attain the just and important object in view. The senior officer in Rank present will be pleased to preside and report the result of the Deliberations to the Commander in Chief.[30]

According to a letter written at a later date, Colonel John Brooks, who had traveled to Philadelphia to plead the officers' case, was sent back from Philadelphia with orders to break up the mutiny. Brooks revealed plans for the mutiny to General Washington. Armstrong, who wrote the anonymous letters, informed Gates that he learned about Brooks contact with Washington from Colonel Matthais Ogden.[31] It also explains why Washington was convinced that General Horatio Gates was the mastermind behind the whole plot. Washington quieted Gates by putting him in charge of the public meeting.

Philip Van Cortlandt remembered that when the anonymous letter was circulated General Washington came to camp and sent for the officers commanding the brigades. Van Cortlandt commanded the New York Line at the time and attended the meeting; he was happy to find a unanimous determination to support order and agreed with General Washington's plan to suppress every attempt at disorderly conduct.[32]

Washington told Joseph Jones, the Virginia Congressman, of his actions on discovering the anonymous letters.

> So soon as I obtained knowledge of these things, I issued the order of the 11th in order to rescue the foot, that stood wavering on the precipice of despair, from taking those steps which would have lead to the abyss of misery while the passions were inflamed, and the mind tremblingly alive with the recollection of past sufferings, and their present feelings. I did this upon the principle that it is easier to divert from a wrong to a right path, than it is to recall the hasty and fatal steps which have been already taken. It is commonly supposed, if the officers had met agreeable to the anonymous summons, resolutions might have been formed, the consequences of which may be more easily conceived than expressed. Now, they will have leisure to view the matter more calmly and seriously. It is to be hoped they will be induced to adopt more rational measures.[33]

On March 12, Washington sent a report on the anonymous letters to Congress. "Two days ago, anonymous papers were circulated in the army, requesting a general meeting of the officers on the next day. . . . About the same time, another anonymous paper purporting to be an address to the officers of the army, was handed about in a clandestine manner. . . . To prevent any precipitate and dangerous resolutions from being taken at this perilous moment, while the passions were all inflamed; as soon as these things came to my knowledge." He then sent along a copy of his General Order No. 3 of March 11, as well as copies of the anonymous letters.[34]

On March 15, when Washington arrived at the "Public Building," the officers were already assembled. The officers were startled to see Washington, as his general orders implied he would not be present. When he walked through the door, General Gates had no choice but to ask Washington to address the officers. He walked up to the desk and took out his written address from his coat pocket (see Appendix H). He began reading it and then after reading the first paragraph made a short pause. He took out his spectacles from his waistcoat pocket. He then addressed the officers begging their indulgence while he put them on in the following manner, "Gentleman, you will permit me to put on my spectacles, for I have not only grown gray, but almost blind, in the service of my country." When Washington finished reading, he left the hall.[35]

The proceedings continued and a committee was nominated by General Putnam and seconded by General Edward Hand. It consisted of General Knox, Colonel Brooks and Captain Howard. It was to draw up a resolution and report back within a half hour. Their report stated

> That no circumstances of distress or danger shall induce a conduct that may tend to sully the reputation and glory which they [the army] have acquired, at the price of their blood and eight years' faithful service.
>
> That the army continue to have an unshaken confidence in the justice of Congress and their country. . . .
>
> That his Excellency the Commander in Chief be requested to . . . [entreat] the most speedy decision [from Congress] . . . upon the subject of our late address. . . .
>
> That the officers of the American army view with abhorrence, and reject with disdain, the infamous propositions contained in a late anonymous address to the officers of the army; and resent, with indignation, the secret attempts of some unknown persons to collect the officers together, in a manner totally subversive of all discipline and good order.
>
> That the thanks of the officers of the army be given to the committee who presented to Congress the late address of the army, for the wisdom and prudence with which they have conducted that business.[36]

The report was accepted unanimously. The meeting was then adjourned.

These resolutions, which killed the mutiny, were everything Washington could have hoped. On March 18, Washington wrote to Congress urging a quick resolution:

Having seen the proceedings on the part of the army terminate with perfect unanimity, and in a manner entirely consonant to my wishes; being impressed with the liveliest sentiments of affection for those who have so long, so patiently and so cheerfully suffered and fought under my immediate direction; having from motives of justice, duty and gratitude, spontaneously offered myself as an advocate for their rights; and having been requested to write to your Excellency earnestly entreating the most speedy decision of Congress upon the subjects of the late address from the army to that honorable body, it now only remains for me to perform the task I have assumed, and to intercede in their behalf, as I now do, that the sovereign Power will be pleased to verify the predictions I have pronounced of, and the confidence the army have reposed in the justice of their country.[37]

15

Congress Held Hostage

uring 1783, Congress was busy cutting expenses and furloughing staff. Congress also discussed the issue of retirement pay that had been promised to military officers. They had agreed to give "on interest full pay for five years next ensuing after the end of the war, or the time of their discharge, in lieu and in full satisfaction of the half pay for life"[1]

On May 26, 1783, Congress,

> resolved, that the Commander-in-Chief be instructed to grant furloughs to the non-commissioned officers and soldiers in the service of the United States, enlisted to serve during the war, who shall be discharged as soon as the definitive treaty of peace is concluded, together with a proportionable number of commissioned officers of the different grades; and that the Secretary at War and Commander in Chief take the proper measures for conducting those troops to their respective states homes, in such a manner as may be most convenient to themselves, and to the states through which they may pass; and that the men thus furloughed be allowed to take their arms with them the resolution of to the contrary notwithstanding.[2]

Congress had made no provisions for the payment of back wages that were owed to the troops. The men were concerned that if they left they would never get the money that was owed to them.

Two to three hundred soldiers at the barracks in Philadelphia were employed as guards to British prisoners. Some of these troops had been involved in the January 1, 1781, mutiny of the Pennsylvania Line. Soldiers who had been discharged were now passing through Philadelphia on their way home. About two hundred of the Maryland Line on their way home arrived at the barracks on June 12. "The next day a paper was handed to Congress signed by persons styling themselves a board of sergeants making certain demands with which Congress could not possibly comply. Expressly declaring that they would no longer be fed by promises and requiring an answer before night." Congress instructed the secretary of war to take action to stop the mutiny at the barracks.

On the 14th, the Maryland Line resumed their march. "One of their officers before he left town mentioned it to a member of Congress that he had reasons for saying the mutiny did not originate among the privates or sergeants." Congress did not believe this claim.[3]

Congress's May 26 resolution was announced to the soldiers at the post at Lancaster, Pennsylvania. There was no mention of half pay for life. Early on the morning of June 16, a committee of sergeants informed Colonel Richard Butler, commander of the post, they were going to Philadelphia to obtain justice. Butler was informed that the soldiers were getting ready to leave. He immediately went to the parade ground with Colonel Samuel Atlee who was in town. At the parade ground, Butler had the men form a circle and addressed them. His words had little impact as the eighty armed soldiers marched out of camp at 8:30 a.m. Butler quickly called a meeting of the officers. It was agreed that one of the officers would follow the mutineers.

Butler wrote to John Dickinson, president of the Supreme Executive Council at Philadelphia, advising him of the events. William Henry, gunsmith at Lancaster, confirmed Butler's report. He also cautioned that the men intended to rob the bank and the treasury. Henry also said that General Tuffin Charles Armand's Partisan Corps was expected at Lancaster the next day and he guessed some of them would probably go to Philadelphia as well when they heard of Congress's resolution of May 26.[4]

Also on the 16th, John Armstrong Jr., secretary of the Pennsylvania Council, wrote to General Horatio Gates, "The late unqualified resolve of Congress discharging or furloughing as they are pleased to call it, all those men who have been engaged for the war, without even a settlement of accounts, was taken up very spiritedly by the little corps at this place, consisting of but 300 Men. They addressed themselves to Congress upon the occasion in language very intelligible—'We will not accept your furloughs and demand a Settlement.'"[5]

Congress had already received word of a May 22 letter from Baylor's Dragoons, who had been assigned to the Southern Department to Benjamin Harrison, the governor of Virginia, pleading for relief. The news had reached Philadelphia on June 10.[6]

The Continental Congress received from the executive council of Pennsylvania, that eighty soldiers, who would probably be followed by the discharged soldiers of Armand's Partisan Corps, were on the way from Lancaster to Philadelphia, in spite of the expostulations of their officers, declaring that they would proceed to the seat of Congress and demand justice. This information was given to Messrs. Hamilton, Peters, and Ellsworth, for the purpose of conferring with the executive of Pennsylvania, and taking such measures as they should find necessary. The committee, after so conferring, informed Congress that it was the opinion of the executive council, "that the militia of Philadelphia would probably not be willing to take arms before their resentments should be provoked by some actual outrage; that it would hazard the authority of government to make the attempt; and that it would be necessary to let the soldiers come into the city if the officers who had gone out to meet them could not stop them."[7]

At 2:00 p.m. on the 19th, President of the Continental Congress Elias Boudinot sent word to Major Jackson, assistant secretary of war, to send an express to Major General Arthur St. Clair that his presence was immediately requested in the city. Jackson was instructed to keep the request a secret.[8] He sent the message to St. Clair at 2:30 p.m. telling him that troops at Lancaster had mutinied and were on their way to the city.[9]

Major General Arthur St. Clair had been furloughed from the army and returned home to his Ligonier, Pennsylvania, estate in 1782. His property, including the mill that he had opened for communal use, was in ruins. When St. Clair had gone off to war, he had a comfortable fortune and valuable positions. His beloved Phoebe, the mother of his seven children, became mentally ill in 1777. He was now seven years older and his life was a mess. His chestnut hair was turning graying. A tall man with blue eyes, he was considered a well-mannered, well-educated, intelligent man. St. Clair now suffered from recurrences of gout, which had made his right hand useless since March 2.[10] It prevented him from riding too long on a horse and, in later years, would confine him to long hours in his bed.

St. Clair, though still holding the rank of major general, was elected to the Council of Censors, a committee charged with revising the Pennsylvania state constitution. He was also elected vendue-master (auctioneer) of Philadelphia, a lucrative position in city government. With the war winding down, there would be a lot of state property to be sold. As the auctioneer, St.

Clair would receive a portion of the sale. But St. Clair later claimed that he lost money because he spent more money fronting the auction than he received in commissions and his overages were never reimbursed by the financially distressed city.

The soldiers from Lancaster arrived in Philadelphia on the 20th, under the direction of several sergeants. They professed to have no other object than to obtain a settlement of accounts, which they supposed they had a better chance to accomplish at Philadelphia than at Lancaster.[11]

On Saturday June 21, President Boudinot was informed by Alexander Hamilton there was reason to believe the soldiers in the barracks who had mutinied and cast off the command of their officers were planning to rob the bank on Sunday evening. Boudinot issued summonses for the members of Congress to meet in half an hour. When he got to the Pennsylvania State House, six states with several individual members were represented.

It was one of those hot early summer days. Approximately three hundred mutinous soldiers assembled in the street before the statehouse and surrounded it with Congress inside.[12] Captain Carberry and Lieutenant John Sullivan of Moylan's Dragoons were believed to be the ringleaders of the mutineers.[13] The executive council of the state of Pennsylvania was also meeting in the building. President Dickinson came in and explained the difficulty of bringing out the militia for the suppression of the mutiny. Dickinson thought that the militia could not be relied on.

John Armstrong Jr., who had written the anonymous letters at Newburgh, New York, earlier that year, had been appointed as the secretary of the Pennsylvania Council on March 25. He was perfectly located to judge the responses of the government and the soldiers to each other on this issue. It was probably more than coincidence that a key petition from the Philadelphia troops to the Pennsylvania Council of June 21 was another "anonymous paper" presented to John Armstrong Jr.[14] The mutineers' demands were made in very dictatorial terms. "Unless their demands were complied with in twenty minutes, they would let in upon them the injured soldiery, the consequences of which they were to abide."[15]

President Boudinot sent word to General St. Clair, who was still doing his duties as vendue-master, that his presence was immediately requested. General St. Clair rushed to the scene and confronted the mutineers. St. Clair then gave his assessment of the situation to President Boudinot, Congress, and the Pennsylvania state legislators.

Back of the Pennsylvania State House, Philadelphia. Drawn, engraved, and published by William Birch & Son, 1799. The building is the same as it appeared in 1783. (*Independence National Historical Park*)

The president of the Supreme Executive Council of the state of Pennsylvania entered Congress and presented a paper he had received from the sergeants. In it, they requested to be authorized to appoint officers from their own body in place of those who had deserted them. They would wait twenty minutes for Congress's answer. If they had not received an answer within that time frame they would turn "an enraged soldiery on them and they must abide the consequence." St. Clair informed Congress the soldiers at the barracks had cast off all authority of their officers and had marched under the direction of some sergeants to the Pennsylvania State House. St. Clair was given unlimited power in dealing with the mutineers.[16] He was asked to try to persuade the men to march back to their barracks.

Mr. Izard proposed that Congress should adjourn. Alexander Hamilton proposed that "General St. Clair, in concert with the executive council of the state, should take order for terminating the mutiny."[17] Mr. Reed moved that General St. Clair should try to get the troops to withdraw by assuring them of the disposition of Congress to do them justice. Congress agreed to do nothing "in relation to the alleged grievances of the soldiers, or any other business whatever." Congress then adjourned, awaiting word from General St. Clair that it was safe to exit the building.

Soon after, General St. Clair returned and informed Congress that he hoped they would return to their quarters quietly. Before the congressmen left the room they requested Boudinot as the president of Congress to send an express to George Washington the commander in chief asking that he advance a body of troops toward Philadelphia for the purpose of supporting the dignity of the government.

The soldiers held their positions with sporadic invectives from individual soldiers directed to the Congress. They would occasionally point their muskets and rifles in a menacing fashion at the windows of the Pennsylvania State House. Some soldiers were visiting the nearby tippling-houses to refresh themselves.[18] The establishments began liberally providing the soldiers with spirituous drink.

Congress adjourned at the usual hour, about three o'clock, and began filing out of the building. The situation was extremely tense. After offering a mock obstruction to their departure, the soldiers permitted the members to pass through their ranks without being physically assaulted. When Boudinot had got half way home, six or seven of the mutineers followed him with their weapons and requested his return. However, one of the sergeants saw the scene and desired Boudinot not to pay any attention to the men who were acting without orders. The mutineers returned to their barracks with drums beating and fifes playing.

Boudinot summoned Congress to meet at 6:00 p.m. Congress reassembled and passed the resolutions on a journal of events of the day. It authorized a committee to confer anew with the executive of the state of Pennsylvania. If no satisfactory assurances of protection supporting the public authority were forthcoming and adequate exertions for suppressing the mutiny were not put in place, they authorized the president with the advice of the committee to summon the members to meet at Trenton or Princeton in New Jersey.

The committee, with Alexander Hamilton as chairman, called on the State Executive Council of Pennsylvania to get a guarantee of protection for the government of the United States when Congress was ready to reassemble in the morning. None was forthcoming, there being no pledge of protection by the Pennsylvania Militia. The militia was not likely to act unless some actual outrage was offered to persons or property. A repetition of the insult to Congress would probably not be a sufficient provocation.[19] Elias Boudinot adjourned Congress on June 24.

On Sunday morning, Boudinot forwarded Congress's resolutions by express
to George Washington. The rumor of the
day was that the mutineers had a plan to
seize the members of Congress at their
lodgings the next night. President
Boudinot notified the members of
Congress that they would reconvene in
Princeton, New Jersey. Also on Sunday,
General St. Clair reported that the mutineers had placed sentinels at the powder
house and public magazines.

On Monday morning, Boudinot wrote
by express to Governor Livingston and
the Vice President of New Jersey,
informing them that Congress would
relocate to Princeton. That evening,
Colonels Humpton, Porter, and

General Arthur St. Clair based on a
painting by Charles Wilson Peale.
(*William L. Clements Library*)

Robinson, as well as some other officers of the Pennsylvania Line, called on
Boudinot. They informed him they had been appointed by the majority of officers of the Pennsylvania Line to meet with him and assure him of their complete abhorrence of every part of the conduct of the mutineers. They were
ready to follow the direction of Congress. They were instructed to await the
president's orders, which they would strictly obey. They had not offered their
assistance sooner due to the swiftness and confusion of events.

On Tuesday morning June 24, Colonel Robinson reported to President
Boudinot in the presence of Major General St. Clair that on the previous
evening, the sergeants of the mutineers had presented him with a commission that he refused. It was sent a second time but again he refused. The third
time they threatened him with instant death if he did not accept it. Having
no other option, he was forced to accept. That same morning, the mutineers
were getting rip-roaring drunk.

Tuesday at 2:00 p.m., the committee reported to Boudinot. He immediately notified the members of Congress to meet at Princeton on the following
Thursday, as agreed in their resolution. He also issued a proclamation and had
it put in all the papers. He then left Philadelphia for Princeton.

The *London Morning Chronicle* of August 5 and 6, 1783, carried President Elias Boudinot's proclamation of June 24, 1783, announcing the removal of Congress to Princeton following the mutiny of the Continental Soldiers in Philadelphia on June 21. They reported that the soldiers were angered over an attempt to furlough them with only partial back pay. The *Chronicle* believed the tumultuous events would either "entirely . . . overthrow or more firmly . . . establish the authority of Congress."[20]

George Washington at his headquarters at the Hasbrouck House in Newburgh, New York, received Boudinot's letter of the 21st, which was his first notice of the mutiny, at 3:00 p.m. on the 24th. He immediately ordered three complete regiments of infantry and a detachment of artillery to be put in motion. They were to go by way of Ringwood, Pompton, Morristown, Princeton, and Trenton, and then by water to Philadelphia. Washington instructed General Robert Howe, "The object of your command is to suppress a mutiny which has taken place amongst a part of the Pennsylvania Troops, in the accomplishment of which you will be governed by your own discretion until you can receive the orders of Congress; should the tumult have subsided, you will meet directions from His Excellency the President countermanding your march, you will then return by easy movements." Due to the heat, Washington told Howe to march the men early in the morning and late at night and to rest if possible during the day.[21]

General Knox was sending a detachment with two fieldpieces and they were to meet General Howe at the Clove in the morning of the 26th. The detachment of about fifteen hundred men was a large percentage of the entire force that Washington had with him. He indicated that the troops he was sending were loyal and would "perform their duty as brave and faithful Soldiers." Washington's troops, under the command of Major General Howe, reached Philadelphia on June 30.

Washington commented on the situation of the mutineers:

Upon taking all the circumstances into consideration, I cannot sufficiently express my surprise and indignation, at the arrogance, the folly and the wickedness of the mutineers; nor can I sufficiently admire the fidelity, the bravery and the patriotism, which must forever signalize the unsullied character of the other corps of our army; for when we consider that these Pennsylvania Levies who have now mutinied, are recruits and soldiers of a day, who have not born the heat and burden of the war, and who can have in reality very few hardships to complain of, and when we at the same time recollect, that those soldiers who have lately been furloughed from this army, are the veterans who have patiently endured hunger, nakedness and cold, who have suffered and bled without a murmur, and who with perfect good order have retired to their homes, without the settlement of their accounts or a farthing of money in their pockets, we shall be as much astonished at the virtues of the latter, as we are struck with horror and detestation at the proceedings of the former; and every candid mind, without indulging ill-grounded prejudices, will undoubtedly make the proper discrimination.[22]

Boudinot traveled to Trenton and was received on Wednesday, June 25, at noon by the vice president of New Jersey. Elias Boudinot was now back in his home state. He was assured of their support and received a certificate of lodging provided for about sixty persons. Boudinot, now protected by the New Jersey Militia, wasted no time in dealing harshly with the mutineers.

On June 30, the day after Congress's arrival in New Jersey, a resolution was passed ordering General Howe to march fifteen hundred troops to Philadelphia to disarm the mutineers and bring them to trial. Specifically, it said,

that Major General Howe be directed to march such part of the force under his command as he shall judge necessary to the State of Pennsylvania; and that the commanding officer in the said State he be instructed to apprehend and confine all such persons, belonging to the army, as there is reason to believe instigated the late mutiny; to disarm the remainder; to take, in conjunction with the civil authority, the proper measures to discover and secure all such persons as may have been instrumental therein; and in general to make full examination into all parts of the transaction, and when they have taken the proper steps to report to Congress.[23]

On the afternoon of June 26, Benjamin Rush was walking near the barracks where the mutinous soldiers were bivouacked, where by chance he met two or three of the leaders of mutiny. He spoke to them about quitting the mutiny and laying down their arms. They inquired if he thought the government would accept their submission without punishing them. Rush told them he thought it might be arranged.

Rush then went to see John Dickinson, president of the Supreme Council of Pennsylvania, and informed him of his conversation. Dickinson quickly accepted the initiative and promised them a pardon if they would lay down their weapons and return to Lancaster. Dickinson also promised to intercede on their behalf. Rush returned to the leaders of the mutiny and relayed Dickinson's offer. The leaders held a general meeting explaining Dickinson's proposal. They then took Rush as security against a trap by Dickinson and went en masse to Dickinson's house.

It was nighttime when they arrived. Accompanied by a servant holding a candle, Dickinson came out to meet them. He spoke to them and said he would, if possible, procure them a pardon. The men gave three huzzas and left for Lancaster with a field officer in charge.[24]

General St. Clair's right hand was still useless due to the gout. But he managed to get a letter off to George Washington on July 2, giving him some insight into the late mutiny. Captain Carberry, a deranged officer, and Lieutenant John Sullivan of Moylan's Dragoons, who were the principal instigators of the mutiny, had fled. St. Clair believed that they got on board a ship at Chester bound for London.[25] He also believed that Captain Christie should be brought up on charges for helping to incite the mutiny. St. Clair was livid with the newspaper report of the events in Oswald's Paper, claiming it attacked Congress and placed him in a bad light.[26]

General Arthur St. Clair met with Boudinot on July 3 and Boudinot wrote George Washington that "General St. Clair is now here, and this moment suggests an idea which he has desired me to mention to your Excellency, as a matter of importance in his view of the matter in the intended inquiry at Philadelphia. That the judge advocate should be directed to attend the inquiry. By this means the business would be conducted with most regularity. The inquiry might be more critical and as several officers are in arrest, perhaps a person not officially engaged, may Consider himself in an invidious situation."[27] General St. Clair had already sent this suggestion in the previous day's letter to Washington, who upon receiving it, immediately ordered Judge Advocate Thomas Edwards to Philadelphia.

Theodorick Bland, Arthur Lee, and John T. Mercer wrote to Governor Benjamin Harrison of Virginia from Princeton, New Jersey, on August 14–15, 1783, that two of the ringleaders in the late mutiny had been condemned to death by their court martial.[28]

On September 13, Congress granted a pardon to Christian Nagle and John Morrison, late sergeants in the 3rd Pennsylvania Regiment, who had been convicted by sentence of a court martial held at Philadelphia and were now under sentence of death. A pardon was also granted to gunner Lily and drummer Horn of the 4th Pennsylvania Artillery, and to Thomas Flowers and William Carman, soldiers in the 3rd Pennsylvania Regiment. They had been sentenced to be whipped.[29]

-16

Peace is Declared

From the time the men heard that peace was declared, they began to grow restless. Their terms of enlistment were for the duration of the war. With a peace treaty all but signed, many of the men believed their terms of enlistment had expired and they were free to go. They wanted the back pay and half-pay for life that many believed was due them. They also wanted to get back home and start rebuilding their lives.

Congress attempted to reduce military expenditures now that the British were leaving and the size of the American standing military could be shrunk. One measure was the adoption of a resolution on April 17, 1783, directing "immediate measures be taken for the sale of all the dragoon horses belonging to the United States, and of all such articles in the several military departments, as may not be necessary for the use of the army, previous to its reduction, or for the formation of magazines on a peace establishment."[1]

News of Congress's intentions spread quickly among the mounted troops. The horses belonging to the Virginia troops that were in South Carolina were going to be sold in South Carolina, resulting in cavalry men without horses. Some of the mounted troops wanted to retain their horses for their own use.

On May 12, Major Joseph Eggleston Jr. advised that if the men mutinied to keep their horses he did not have sufficient force to prevent it. He suggested that measures be taken quickly as "the shortest delay might be attended with pernicious consequences." He also speculated that the soldiers had great fears of the South Carolina climate. He believed that they would behave until June 1, but after that he expected dire consequences.[2]

Greene was annoyed by Eggleston's letter of the 12th, and responded on the 17th. He gave him the good news that he had issued orders for the men to get a month's pay. Then came the bad news. "I am sorry to find you seem to think the men are less subject to authority than ever they have been. I wish to avoid severity if possible, but there is not the least shadow of pretension for the men's thinking they have a right to their discharge before the order of Congress on the subject. There is a great difference between a cessation of hostilities and a final peace." He referenced General Washington's General Orders of March 28 in which he announced a general peace but stated "all military arrangements shall continue the same as present until further orders that no relaxation in the discipline or police of the army shall be suffered."[3]

Greene told Eggleston to convince his troops that it was their duty to be subject to authority as much as ever. "Avoid by all means impressing the men with an idea that you hold them by courtesy. Under such impressions, it will be impossible to govern them many days. Point out to them the disgraces and ruin that must attend mutiny and desertion and the honor and glory they will go home with if they have but a little patience. In a word, you must try your address and the influence of the officers of the corps and I can not but hope you will have sufficient influence to manage the men until orders arrive for their moving northerly."[4]

Major Eggleston responded on May 22, "I only meant to inform you that they thought themselves so. . . . No power of reason or argument could make them believe they are not freed from their enlistments; an attempt to do so would raise a flame that would not be easily allayed." He relayed the message from the men that if they were not embarked or marched by June 10, they planned to go. "The cavalry are much pleased at the circumstance of being allowed to bid for their horses and the infantry men mortified that they have no such privilege."[5]

Eggleston's statement about the June 10 deadline was backed up by a report from Colonel Francis Mentges sent the same day to Greene. He had a long conversation with the men of Lee's Legion at Georgetown, South Carolina, who are "discontent of the soldiery merely on account of their being detained in the service" since peace had been declared. They were "now willing to remain until the 10th of June." However, he warned, that because of the negligence of John Banks, the contractor for providing food, there were only "9 barrels of pork and some rum" in the commissary stores. There was a lack of flour and rice and no prospect of getting any more. If none was found he feared the men would disband.[6]

There was also some miscommunication between Nathanael Greene and Captain John Watts on the subject of forage. Watts thought that General

Greene had ordered the horses to be fed on grass alone even when other forage was available. What Greene had intended was that if there were no other forage then the animals should be put on grass. Putting their horses on an all grass diet when other forage was available intensified an already bad situation. Now their horses were being treated poorly—the same horses that were going to be taken from them, which would reduce them to an infantry unit. The situation just kept getting worse.

General Nathanael Greene had decided that the dragoon horses were going to be sold as ordered by Congress, but he was going to allow the dragoons to bid on their horses with the amount to be deducted out of their pay. "This will have the men without an excuse." He was approving this policy even though he had no authority to do so but saw this as a measure to keep the dragoons from mutiny.[7] He felt that if he did not allow the men to purchase the horses, they would leave and take the horses with them. The army would then have very few to sell.[8] But he was too late.

On Tuesday, May 13, 1783, about one hundred of the first regiment of cavalry mutinied. The mutineers were from the 1st Legionary Corps, formerly the 1st Continental Regiment of Light Dragoons that was stationed on the Congaree River. During the commotion, they took clothing from those soldiers who would not join them. They also took the very best horses in camp. The next day, they started their journey to Virginia. They were led by Sergeant Major William Dangerfield and four other sergeants: Thomas Barnes, William Jones, William Shoap, and Daniel Warshun.[9]

On May 17, 1783, James Merriwether, one of the officers of the first regiment of cavalry, arrived at headquarters at Charles Town from the Congaree to inform General Nathanael Green that one hundred of the regiment had mutinied. They had departed in a body headed for Virginia. Merriwether said the remainder of that regiment was very dissatisfied and Lee's Legion, which was at George Town, was in the same state of mind. Major Joseph Eggleston Jr. feared that Lee's Legion would also mutiny.[10]

Greene wanted the mutineers apprehended either en route or in Virginia. He sent Captain Nathaniel Pendelton, a Virginian, with a detachment after the mutineers and a letter to Governor Benjamin Harrison of Virginia. Pendelton was to contact the sergeant leading the mutineers, offering a pardon if they would return. General Greene did not think his offer would be accepted. He then wanted the men punished.[11]

General Greene sent a letter to Virginian General Charles Scott advising him of the mutiny of the first regiment of cavalry. He warned him they were on their way to Virginia. "It is of importance to the service that these men be brought to some exemplary punishment at least the ringleaders at the head of whom is Sergeant [William] Dangerfield. Let no time or pains be spared for bringing the insurgents to trial. . . . If these men go unpunished it will be impossible to keep an army from mutiny should we ever have occasion for another. At the time they mutinied they had nothing to complain of having plenty of provisions."[12]

Greene wrote almost the same instructions the next day to Colonel George Baylor about the dragoons mutinying, plundering other soldiers, and taking the best horses. They acted with "the greatest impropriety and insolence." He ordered him to cooperate with the governor of Virginia and General Scott in the matter. Greene believed that the mutineers' "great object is thought to be to get an opportunity to dispose of their horses."[13]

On May 21, Greene wrote to Governor Harrison advising him of the mutiny and that the mutineers had left the Congaree and were headed his way. The rumor was they were coming to demand their pay from the Virginia legislature. He recommended to the governor that Sergeant Dangerfield should be tried and punished quickly. He needed to be made an example. "The mutineers may pretend to complain of the want of provisions and other sufferings, but at the time of the mutiny they had provisions in plenty." He told of the letters to General Charles Scott and Colonel George Baylor of the 1st Continental Dragoons and his instructions to give all aid in apprehending the insurgents, and that he had sent Captain Pendelton with an offer of pardon if they returned immediately.[14]

On May 22, the mutineers sent a letter to the governor of Virginia that outlined their complaints and the reason for their leaving South Carolina. They said they could no longer stay without risking their lives. Provisions had been in short supply since the fall of Charles Town. They had logistic problems, as they were dispatched more than one hundred miles from the main army. They claimed the contractor never provided the supplies. They had previously prepared to leave and head back to Virginia when their officers came and guaranteed provisions and they would get thirteen months back pay "in three weeks." They waited "three months" and still were not paid the money they were promised.

The other big reason the mutineers gave for their action was the onset of warm weather. The previous summer they had lost many men to malaria. "We are afraid the men will begin to get sick very fast if we stay any longer. We are fully persuaded your Excellency will see us justified."[15]

The Virginia assembly did not arrest or punish the insurgents upon receiving the noncommissioned officers' letter. They stated that their "conduct is disorderly and argues an intemperance and disregard for the public interest which marks an unhappy contrast to their former conduct that the Executive treat it as a weakness rather than a vice and entitled rather to pity and pardon than the severity of government provided they conduct themselves agreeable to the orders they receive in the future. That the Governor write them to this effect and instruct them to move on their way to Winchester. And that he further lay the affair before the Assembly."[16]

Due to George Baylor's poor health, General Daniel Morgan was brought out of retirement to lead the mutineers to Winchester. The state provided money and a commissary to support the troops on their way to Winchester. Captain Nathaniel Pendleton at Richmond, Virginia, wrote to General Greene on July 17, two days after his arrival, with the news that the Virginia Assembly did not know what to do with the mutineers. They gave them some pay and moved them out of Richmond to Winchester "where they have been since furloughed by the advice of General [Horatio] Gates and are now going about the country and selling their horses. [Sergeant William] Dangerfield, I am informed is still there. If he remains so upon my arrival, I will have him tried and executed if I can."[17] Sergeant William Dangerfield was never arrested.

GOVERNOR BENJAMIN HARRISON worked actively on the mutineers' behalf. He wrote to the Virginia delegates to Congress on May 31 saying that he had "sharply reprimanded" the mutineers "for their conduct but promised in consideration of their past services to overlook it as far as it relates to me. They are really a band of heroes who have performed great and meritorious services and I am satisfied would not have taken this rash step if their sufferings had not been very great."[18]

The letter of the noncommissioned officers was read at the Continental Congress on June 11 and was referred to the superintendent of finance and the secretary of war for a report.[19] The combined report was given to Congress on the 17th.

Philadelphia, June 16th, 1783.

Sir,

On the letter addressed by the non-commissioned officers of Colonel Baylor's Regiment to the Governor of Virginia, referred to the Superintendent of Finance and Secretary at War, we beg leave to report the following draught of a resolve.

That the Secretary at War be empowered to issue a proclamation offering pardon to those soldiers of the first regiment of Dragoons, who shall deliver up their horses, and surrender themselves on or before the [blank space] day of [blank space] and informing those, who shall disregard the pardon proffered them, that they will be dealt with in such manner as the articles of war prescribe.

We have the honor to be with perfect respect

Your Excellency's most obedient servants

Robert Morris

B. Lincoln[20]

On May 22, Captain John Watts said he would have Lieutenant Merriwether deliver a return of the regiment. Watts said, "nothing in the course of seven years hard service ever gave me half [the] concern [as] the very extraordinary behavior of the soldiers of the 1st Regiment have done, [they have acted in] such a manner as to reflect eternal disgrace on themselves." He was referring to their plundering other members of their own regiment. The men who mutinied were under his command. They were also having a problem with John Banks, the contractor, who was not able to supply the troops. However, he did have some good news for General Greene. The men that remained seemed to be satisfied on being allowed to purchase their horses.[21]

When Lieutenant James Merriwether arrived, General Greene immediately sent him to Colonel George Baylor and to Governor Harrison with copies of his letters. In his letter to Colonel Baylor, Greene complained about the practice in Maryland of forgiving deserters as it had encouraged others to desert who would not have otherwise considered doing it. He advocated bringing the mutineers to justice. Greene, by the 25th, had also begun furloughing the men of Lee's Legion.[22]

General Benjamin Lincoln, at Philadelphia, wrote General Greene that they were having problems with dragoons quartered there who were refusing to give up their horses unless they were allowed to bid on them. He was going to deny the request at Philadelphia.

Robert Morris had hoped to raise badly needed cash from the sale of public property including the dragoon horses. The money was to be used to pay the army's expenses and provide some money to pay the soldiers. General Lincoln was going to urge the Governor of Virginia to arrest all the mutineers. He warned Greene that, because of public opinion, he did not expect Virginia to pursue the matter vigorously.[23]

"Another problem that came to light," Greene said, "was some of the cavalry officers promised the dragoons at the close of the war they would be given their horses. Major Swan and others say they had orders to give the men such assurances. I have never seen any such order of Congress or from the war office nor do I believe there ever was any."[24] Major John Swan from Maryland was in Baylor's Regiment of Dragoons.

Greene said that any such assurance happened before he arrived on the scene. He wondered if it was done to get the men to take good care of their animals. He had not been able to find any such order but the men believed it. Because of the mess, he believed that the public would be best served by indulging the dragoons than not. If he did not he was convinced that "they would have all gone off in a body and afterwards dispersed in such a manner as to have rendered it difficult if not impracticable to have collected any considerable part of the cavalry horses."[25]

The Marylanders created a tumult as they wanted to go home. The Marylanders had been deserting a few each night. Colonel Josiah Harmar had assembled and addressed his orderly sergeants. They held down the desertions for a few days before they commenced again and several men were apprehended trying to leave.[26] Captain Walter Finney of the Pennsylvania Line wrote in his diary that on Sunday May 4, 1783, a plan had been arranged. The Maryland Line, in place of beating a "Troop" which as used in the morning to assemble the men, beat the "General" which was music played for a guard with arms. The majority of the Maryland Line fell in with their arms, packs, and accoutrements and were preparing to move off.

General Greene had been advised of the plan the night before. The Pennsylvania and North Carolina Line quickly fell in to oppose the Marylanders. The Pennsylvanians took a position on the right and the North Carolinians on the left. General Greene rode on his horse up to the

Marylanders and ordered them to dismiss, which they did. Captain Walter Finney of the Pennsylvania Line said that Greene praised them for responding so well to their officers.[27]

General Nathanael Greene had "never been in a more perplexing situation than since the declaration for a cessation of hostilities. The troops for the war have been so strongly impressed with an idea of their having a right to a discharge that it has been exceedingly difficult to hold them subject to authority."

Command and control problems that existed at the formation of the army in 1775 had returned. The purpose for which men had joined the military had ended. Their enlistments said for the duration of the war and the war was now over. They wanted to go home. They considered themselves free men.

ON MAY 26, 1783, CONGRESS RESOLVED TO furlough the army. Once General Greene received a copy of the resolution, he sent letters on June 26 to Governor Benjamin Guerard of South Carolina and Lyman Hall of Georgia. By July 11, General Greene had furloughed the troops of North Carolina and Virginia. He had Major Edmund M. Hyrne furlough the South Carolinians. The men were given a furlough until the peace treaty was signed.[28]

At the dissolution, Greene wrote these parting words to his men. "We have trod the paths of adversity together and have felt the sunshine of better fortune. We have found a people overwhelmed with distress, and a country groaning under oppression. It has been our happiness to relieve them. . . . Your generous confidence, amidst surrounding difficulties; your persevering tempers, against the tide of misfortune, paved the way for success."[29]

17

Walking the Plank

CONTINENTAL NAVAL MUTINIES

*D*uring the Revolutionary War, in American ships, whether, merchant-men, privateers, or naval vessels, mutiny on the high seas generally occurred because the crew (1) was upset with its lack of pay; (2) thought it was not going to get its proper share of prize money from capturing another vessel; or (3) did not want to be part of an American vessel and wanted to go home to England.

Recruiting seamen for the regular American Navy was a very difficult task. Many men during the American Revolution chose to sign up for privateering vessels. Though a risky venture, it offered the possibility of prize money when a captured vessel and its cargo were sold.

In order to fill out crews, the American Navy was forced to enlist British prisoners to serve on Congress and state vessels. The prisoners often accept-ed this means of being released from confinement. The problem was that many American ships had too many impressed British sailors, which led to insubordination and mutiny problems. When the impressed sailors saw a chance to overpower an outnumbered American crew, they took control of the ship and then sailed the vessel with its cargo to the nearest British port.

When the balance of Americans versus non-Americans shifted too far, it became a mutiny just waiting to happen. Such was the case in the ship *Mercer*. The British ship *Earl of Errol* was taken by the Americans in her pas-sage from the West Indies with rum and cotton. Renamed the *Mercer*, she came under the ownership of Philadelphia merchants Mercer and Schenk. The ship, with Captain Nathaniel Dowse in charge, sailed out of Boston bound for Bordeaux, France, with a stop in Virginia, where she took on a cargo of tobacco. Nathaniel Stewart, the chief mate, filled out his crew with a number of men who had been taken prisoner from British ships and were then confined at Newberry on the Merrimac River northeast of Boston. "These included Jonathan Sharp [second mate]; William Brice, William Burn, Daniel Montgomery, Robert Ferguson, Hugh Winks, Edward Pearson & Robert Pearson [mariners]. Before boarding the ship, Jonathan Sharp proposed to the others that they should try to seize the ship in mid-Atlantic and take her to England."

The *Mercer* left Hampton Roads in Virginia on April 15, 1777, with eighteen on board, of whom sixteen were English, Irish, or Scotch.[1] On May 4, at 10:30 p.m., Jonathan Sharp had command of the watch. As the captain and chief mate were in their cabins, he took control of the vessel.[2] He went down into the cabin and seized three pistols (the only firearms they had on board), a cutlass, an iron poker, a shovel, and any other items that could be used as an offensive weapon. He gave one pistol to Robert Ferguson, another to Hugh Winks, and kept the third for himself. They loaded up with powder and four balls each. "They then altered the vessel's course from E. by S. 1/2 S. to N.E. and squared her yards." A boy was sent down to tell the chief mate that a light had been seen.

When Nathaniel Stewart came up on deck he was shown a pistol and given the choice of sharing the reward for capturing the ship or becoming a prisoner. Stewart cooperated but to what extent is uncertain. One source stated he said, "he would assist them to the utmost of his power" while another reported "he said he would help, but not openly."

In the morning, Sharp took Stewart down to Captain Dowse and announced the new course. When Dowse went up on deck and saw for himself the new heading, he said, "I hope you will use me well, my lads."

On May 9, they made land off Tillin Head in Ireland then steered through the North Channel for Whitehaven. The *Mercer* arrived safe at Whitehaven about ten o'clock on Wednesday night, May 21. "The cargo secured, under proper locks and seals, for his Majesty's use, by George Harrington, Esq.; Collector of this port, to whom the crew have applied for protection and assistance, and have been treated with the greatest humanity." Captain Nathaniel Dowse was imprisoned. He escaped and made it to Bordeaux on May 4, 1778, one year to the day after the mutiny.[3]

The *Mercer's* cargo of 506 hogsheads of tobacco, some fustic, and staves was advertised to be sold at auction at Whitehaven on July 21 by commissioners appointed by the Court of Admiralty.[4]

The cargo brought £31,788/1/9.5. The distribution of the prize money was not determined until December when the judge decreed two-thirds of £125 for one-eighth salvage of the ship, and two-thirds of the proceeds of the cargo, totaling £20,393 14s 8d to be allotted and paid to the crew. He determined that Jonathan Sharp, William Brice, William Burn, Daniel Montgomery, Robert Ferguson, Hugh Winks, Edward Pearson, William Verco, Charles Davy Burnell, Robert Hall, and Nathaniel Stewart were the principal salvers and were entitled each to a double share. He also decreed that J. Murphy, C. Verco, G. Langlands, A. Adair, N. Jackson, and N. Demoulpied were entitled each to a single share as assistants after the capture.[5] The British judge was convinced that the American chief mate was involved in the mutiny; thus he accorded Nathaniel Stewart a double share of the prize money as one of the ringleaders.

By May 1777, both sides had begun the practice of giving the enemy's vessels and cargoes to the crews who would mutiny rise up, take the vessel and bring the ship to port.[6]

The British transport *Molly*, while on a passage from Louisburg to New York, was captured by the privateer *Alfred*. James Bachop was placed on the vessel with her cargo of coal as the prize master. The *Molly* was then placed under the convoy of the *Flora*. The only person from the original crew left on board the vessel was Mr. Lusk, the master of the transport. With the aid of the master and the other men put on board, Bachop led a mutiny and brought the vessel to Londonderry, Ireland. She then continued on to Plymouth, England. On May 12, 1777, the British Navy Board awarded James Bachop one hundred guineas as a reward for his actions.[7]

A sailor's insubordination might result in a transfer and be recorded as "mutiny."[8] It was a quick way to get rid of a recalcitrant sailor.

On April 4, 1777, Michael Love served as a private on board the armed boat *Eagle*.[9] He was made a gunner on June 10, 1777. Love was transferred to the armed boat *Congress* in October. The *Congress* had been built in 1775. John Hamilton was its first captain and the lieutenant was Hugh Montgomery.[10] William Jackson, a private on board the armed boat *Terror*, had only been on board twelve days before he was "put on board the *Province* ship, Captain Allen, September 26, 1777, for mutiny."[11]

John Gilfroy (Gillaffroy,) enlisted on April 11, 1776 and served on the ship *Montgomery* as a gunner's mate. He became a boatswain on June 1, 1777, on the *Montgomery*, which was the flagship of the Pennsylvania Navy. She carried fourteen 18-pounders, sixteen cohorns, and eight swivel guns. Gilfroy was court martialed at Trenton, New Jersey, on May 19, 1778, for mutiny and desertion. He was sentenced to death and the reason stated on his record was "for mutiny." He was pardoned by the Council of Safety on July 25. On November 28, 1775, the Continental Congress set the rules for regulating the Navy. Two articles dealt with mutiny: article 28: "No person in or belonging to the ship shall utter any words of sedition and mutiny, nor endeavor to make any mutinous assemblies upon any pretence whatsoever upon such penalty as a court-martial shall inflict;" and article 29: "Any officer, seaman or marine, who shall begin to excite, cause, or join in any mutiny or sedition in the ship to which he belongs on any pretence whatsoever, shall suffer death or such other punishment as a court-martial shall direct."[12] This allowed the naval courts martial plenty of discretion in assigning penalties.

The Virginia State Navy also had problem cases. The *Scorpion*, sloop of war, was part of the Potomac River fleet. Wright Westcott was the commander of the *Scorpion*.

There was disaffection aboard the warship in August 1776. On the 22nd, Westcott advertised in the *Maryland Gazette* for the capture and incarceration of some runaways and offered an eight-dollar reward for each. The deserters were Thomas Davis, John Lowry, James Parks, David Rees, and George Patterson.[13] A court martial was held in Alexandria, Virginia in August 1776, with John Allinson, president. James Marshall was the acting gunner of the *Scorpion*. He was charged with exciting the marines and seamen to mutiny. He was found guilty and sentenced to eighteen lashes on his bare back and to be drummed out of the service.[14]

The Pennsylvania State Navy had a few rowdies in its ranks. William Green was a seaman in the crew of the Pennsylvania state row galley *Congress*.[15] On November 17, 1775, he was in jail by order of the Committee of Safety for mutinous conduct. Green, like many others, was offered the option of serving a jail term or enlisting in the navy. He found the latter course less disagreeable. He was discharged to enter the continental service on December 19.[16] Green was part of the crew of the *Andrew Doria* under Nicholas Biddle.

The *Andrew Doria* was a merchant brigantine. The Continental Congress authorized its purchase on October 13, 1775, and it was purchased in

November by the Marine Committee. The brig was moored at the Wharton and Humphreys's shipyard. The conversion was done by Joshua Humphreys, who was given the job of strengthening her hull while opening gun ports. John Barry was to superintend her rerigging; John Falconer was to oversee matters of ordnance and provisioning the ship. She was fitted out with fourteen 4-pounders.

The Marine committee also purchased three other merchantmen for conversion to warships. They were the *Black Prince,* which was renamed *Alfred,* "after the founder of the greatest navy that ever existed" that is King Alfred; the ship *Sally,* renamed *Columbus* after Christopher Columbus; and the brig *Sally,* renamed *Cabot* in honor of the explorer.[17] The committee gave command of this small fleet to Commodore Esek Hopkins, a Rhode Islander who had commanded privateers during the French and Indian War.[18]

In December, the following captains were recommended for the Congress fleet: Dudley Saltonstall for the *Alfred,* Abraham Whipple for the *Columbus,* Nicholas Biddle for the *Andrew Doria,* and John Burrows Hopkins for the *Cabot.*[19]

At the first opportunity, Green deserted from the navy. While the ship was at Reedy Island, during the evening of February 13, 1776, Green slipped away.[20] The local sheriff discovered Green was a deserter and placed him in jail. Captain Nicholas Biddle tried to reclaim his runaway from the sheriff after paying the jail fees. However, someone had served the sheriff with a writ for debts that Green owed. Therefore, the sheriff refused to release Green. Biddle went to the local court at Lewis Town and appeared before the local judge to plead his case.

Biddle, read the resolve of Congress's concerning the arrest of men in its service. It required that the debt be attested to under oath before a writ could be issued, which had not been done in Green's case. The resolution also "recommended to all creditors, whose demands against any person who is enlisted, or shall enlist, in the continental service, shall not amount to the value of 35 dollars, not to arrest any such debtor till the expiration of the time for which he is enlisted."[21]

Biddle wrote that when he went to get Green, there were four rascals who were blocking his way and he had to break the door down to get his man.[22]

When the Brig *Cabot* completed its first voyage and entered the port of New London, Connecticut, on April 8, 1776, a petition signed by fifty-eight members of the crew demanding their back pay was sent to Esek Hopkins (see Appendix D). They pleaded that they are "much in want of necessaries which they can not proceed on another cruise without. They humbly hope that your honor will pardon this Liberty, and impute it to the real necessity which they now labour under for want of cash, to procure them what's necessary for their health and preservation."[23]

AFTER CONCORD AND LEXINGTON, General George Washington and the American Army had the British bottled up in Boston. With the only land route to Boston at the Boston neck, an assault on the British in the city was not feasible. The British, at the Battle of Bunker Hill (which was really fought on Breed's Hill) realized how expensive a price they would have to pay in dead and wounded to break out of the city. The British, with its superior navy, could continue to hold the city by being supplied with provisions and reinforced from the sea.

In an attempt to get supplies and break the deadlock, Washington created a navy staffed by army officers and soldiers. He appointed captains in the Army of the United Colonies of North America with the instructions to go "commerce cruising."

Nicholas Broughton received his army captain's commission on September 2, 1775 and was given command of the 78-ton schooner *Hannah*.[24] The *Hannah*, originally owned by John Glover of Marblehead, Massachusetts, was the first armed vessel to sail under Continental pay and control, and was taken over on August 24, 1775. The *Hannah* was named after Colonel John Glover's wife. Her crew came from Glover's regiment. The *Hannah* became the first of eleven vessels chartered to aid the revolutionary cause.

"Washington's Navy," over the six months of the American siege of Boston, captured approximately fifty-five prizes. It provided much needed supplies to the troops. Glover would gain notoriety for his effort at the Battles of Long Island and Trenton. The crew of the *Hannah* would share in the treasure they brought back.

The *Hannah* sailed out of Beverly, Massachusetts, on September 5, 1775, with dreams of riches to be had for the taking. Two days later she took a 260-ton ship called the *Unity*. Unfortunately, it was an American vessel owned by John Langdon of Portsmouth, New Hampshire, who was a high son of liberty. Broughton claimed that the *Unity* was deliberately loitering off Boston harbor so that it could be captured.[25]

Washington ordered that the *Unity* be returned to its rightful owner. Captain Nicholas Broughton protested but had no chance of winning the argument, for to keep the vessel would be an act of piracy. His crew was decidedly upset as they saw the gold and silver slip right through their fingers.

Joseph Searle, private in Broughton's company, headed a delegation protesting the return of the *Unity* to her owner. When his protest became violent, he was arrested. A dozen men rushed to his aid trying to get him free from the warrant officers. They were then ordered arrested. Someone distributed arms and the rest of the crew succeeded in freeing Searle.

The Gloucester Committee of Safety requested assistance from Washington. General Washington sent a detachment to arrest the mutineers. They arrested Searle and thirty-five others.

On September 22, 1775, their case was brought up at a court martial.

[The men charged with] mutiny, riot and disobedience of orders, are severally guilty of the crimes, wherewith they are accused, and the court upon due consideration of the evidence, do adjudge that the prisoner Joseph Scales receive thirty-nine lashes upon his bare back and be drummed out of the Army, and that the prisoners, John Gillard, Jacob Smallwood, John Peltro, Samuel Grant, Hugh Renny, James Jeffery, Charles Alerain, Samuel Hannis, Charles Pearce, James Williams, John Kelly, John Bryan and Philip Florence, do each of them receive Twenty Lashes upon his bare back and be drummed out of the army—The prisoners Lawrence Blake, Samuel Bodin, John Besom, Benj. Bartholomew, Francis Ellis, Joseph Lawrence, John Sharp, John Poor, Joseph Fessenden, John Foster, John Lee, Lawrence Bartlet, Philip Greatey, Peter Neivelle, Samuel Parsons, Jeremiah Dailey, Francis Greater, Richard Pendrick, Robert Hooper, Anthony Lewis, Nicholas Ogleby, and Thomas Metyard; be fined twenty shillings lawful money each. Joseph Foster, Joseph Laurence and Joseph Tessenden, being recommended by the court martial, as proper objects of mercy, the Commander in Chief is pleased to remit their fine, and to order the sentence upon all the others, to be put in execution at guard mounting, tomorrow morning—Those upon Prospect Hill to receive their punishment there; the rest at the main Guard.[26]

Only one person was whipped and Joseph Searle alone was executed.[27]

ANOTHER OF THE FIRST SHIPS THAT MADE UP Washington's Navy was the *Harrison,* under the command of William Coit. The *Harrison* was a former fishing schooner built in 1761, and named the *Triton*. She became one of Washington's vessels on October 22, 1775. She was to capture much needed supplies and to aid Washington in the siege of Boston.

On October 26, under Captain William Colt, the ship set sail from Plymouth, where she had been obtained.[28] In the twilight of November 5, 1775, she happened upon two provision ships from Nova Scotia bound for Boston. She captured the sloop *Polly* of seventy-five tons with Sibeline White master and the schooner *Industry* of eighty-five tons with Charles Coffin, master. These vessels, carrying cattle, geese, pigs, sheep, butter, cheese, cordwood, hay, potatoes, turnips, and fish, were brought into Plymouth.

The *Harrison* departed Plymouth on the 13th going after a transport said to be at anchor off Cape Cod. Two days later, she returned to port as her crew refused to continue the cruise.[29]

Another vessel in Washington's navy was the *Washington*. She was a 160-ton schooner named *Endeavor* acquired by General George Washington in early October 1775 from George Erving and Captain Benjamin Wormwell of Plymouth, Massachusetts. The schooner was fitted out at Plymouth and was rerigged as a brigantine.

On November 3, 1775, *Washington's* charter was consummated and she was authorized to operate off the New England coast between Cape Cod and Cape Ann in the hope of disrupting British shipping.[30] On Tuesday morning November 28, she went back out to sea in search of the enemy's vessels. They had not gotten far when the winds changed and it began to snow. They returned to the safety of Plymouth harbor where they spent the night. In the morning it was breezy, as she was trying to get under way for a trip to Cape Ann the crew mutinied. Captain Sion Martindale, of Rhode Island, asked them what it would take to get them to go back to work; the crew offered no answer. That evening, Martindale sent First Lieutenant Moses Turner to inform General Washington of the situation. The following morning, the crew agreed to bring the ship into Plymouth harbor; they refused to sail or vacate the ship.

Turner returned with Washington's order to get the vessel out to sea. William Watson, agent, finally went to see what the problem was. It is a mystery as to why he waited so long to find out. The crew said their only complaint was they did not have proper clothing. The agent quickly got the needed clothing; the ship then went out to sea after prize money.[31]

Washington was frustrated with his navy's behavior, as they were creating way too many problems. He wrote to the Continental Congress, "The plague, trouble and vexation I have had with the crews of all the armed vessels is inexpressible; I do believe there is not on earth a more disorderly set; every time they come into port, we hear of nothing but mutinous complaints."[32]

In 1776, with the British at the north end of Lake Champlain and the Americans at the southern end, a race for the supremacy of the lake required each belligerent to build a Lake Champlain navy. It was the eighteenth-century version of an arms race and it was in full force. Both militaries were engaged in a furious pace race building their fleets.

Benedict Arnold, acting under the authority of the Continental Army, in charge of the American effort, had to build thirteen new ships to add to the three brought to Lake Champlain. On October 11, 1776, his new American fleet met their opponents for a cannon battle that lasted more than five hours. Known as the Battle of Valcour Island, this win for the British saw eleven American ships go down with high numbers of American casualties. The Lake Champlain Navy stalled the British advance down the lake until it was too late in the campaigning season for them to continue. The British returned to the north end of the lake to wait until the following year.

Zelida Hammon, mate, William Pownwell, boatswain, William Trip and Nicholas Colbut, seamen from the Lake Champlain Navy, refused to fight on vessels. They were brought to trial. On November 6, 1776, a court martial was held with Lieutenant Colonel Craig as president. The men were tried and convicted of mutiny. Zelida Hammon, mate, was to be broke and returned to his former regiment as a private. William Pownwell, boatswain, was to receive ninety-eight lashes on his bare back and do duty as a private in his former regiment. Nicholas Colbut and William Trip were to receive seventy-eight lashes on their bare back and be returned to their former duty on board the ship. The general had approved the sentences and ordered that they receive their corporal punishment that afternoon. "The criminals were to be whipped from vessel to vessel in receiving part of their punishment from each."[33]

SOME SHIPS JUST SEEMED TO BE UNLUCKY. The frigate *Randolph,* with thirty-two guns, sailed from Philadelphia on February 3, 1777. Captain Nicholas Biddle, a twenty-seven-year-old Philadelphian, was her commander. He had previously been the captain of the *Andrew Doria.*

Once in deep water, Biddle turned the ship northward hoping to encounter the British frigate *Milford,* which had been preying upon New

England shipping. The Philadelphia-built *Randolph* sprang her foremast. While the crew struggled to fix a spar as a jury mast, the ship's mainmast broke and fell into the sea. With her mast damaged, she went from hunter to prey. Captain Biddle chose to go to Charles Town, South Carolina, for repairs.

As the *Randolph* struggled to get to port fever broke out and many members of the crew were buried at sea. The *Randolph* was manned primarily with a crew of British seamen from the Philadelphia jail.

Prior to her arrival at Charles Town the British sailors on board the vessel mutinied. Captain Nicholas Biddle, who prior to 1773 had served in the British navy, was able to quickly put down the mutiny and restore order. The *Randolph* finally labored into Charles Town on March 11, 1777, for the desperately needed repairs. The *Randolph's* luck did not improve after her repairs had been completed. As she was about to get under way, lightning splintered her mainmast.[34] On September 4, the *Randolph* captured two transports off Charles Town. However, in a battle with HMS *Yarmouth*, off Barbados, on March 6, 1778, the *Randolph* exploded killing all but four of her crew.[35]

THE BRITISH BRIGANTINE *MAY* HAD LEFT Liverpool bound for Dominica and Jamaica. After unloading part of her cargo at Dominica, she was captured by the Americans off the Dutch island of Saint Eustatius. She had 200 barrels of beef and 100 firkins of butter still on board.[36] She was renamed the *George* and sailed out of the busy port of Charles Town, South Carolina, bound for Bordeaux, France. Gregory Cozens was her captain. The cargo was 319 whole and 85 half barrels of rice and 19 tierces of indigo.[37] She was to return with ammunition and weapons.

One of the crew of the *George* was Archibald McLean, a British highlander. McLean had previously sailed on board the British ship *Caledonia,* which was captured by the Americans. He opted to join the American service rather than go to jail.

On Sunday March 16, McLean and the crew took possession of the *George*.[38] They confined Captain Cozens to his cabin and renamed the ship the *True Briton*. They brought the vessel into Clyde, England, on April 21, 1777. Her cargo was estimated to be worth between 3,000 and 5,000 pounds sterling.[39]

Among the items found on board was a large packet of letters for Benjamin Franklin and Mr. Thomas Morris. Benjamin Franklin was the

Continental Congress's representative to France and Morris was the American commercial agent at Nantes, France.

Also shipping out of Charles Town on April 21, 1777, was the Bermuda-built merchantman sloop named the *Active* with John Osborne, master. The vessel had six carriage guns, two 6-pounders, two of 4, two of 3, and four swivels. She had a crew of fifteen men, of which five were Spanish and two were Dutch. The *Active* was bound for Nantes or any other French port. Her cargo consisted of 208 whole and 52 half barrels of rice, 10 hogsheads of tobacco and 15 casks of Indigo.

On May 2, Joseph Ring, the second mate, with three other Englishmen and the two Dutchmen took possession of the *Active*.[40] When they were off the coast of Kinsale, Ireland, John Osborne, master, and Joseph Price, chief mate, were set ashore by a pilot boat. The *Active* arrived in England on May 27. The crew was sent to Mill Prison except for the second mate and those who assisted in taking the vessel.[41]

Seamen incarcerated in England were usually taken to either Forton or Mill Prisons. Forton was located about two miles outside of the town of Portsmouth. Mill was located on a peninsula of land that extended into the sound between the towns of Plymouth and Plymouth Dock, which was renamed Devonport in 1824.

The vessel *Ronals* was originally from Bristol, England. She was carrying 500 hogsheads of sugar when she was captured by an American privateer. She then shipped out of Providence, Rhode Island, with a cargo of beef, fish, flour, onions, pork, potatoes, and staves. She was bound for Curacao pretending to bring back a load of salt but she was really after ammunition and arms. The vessel was manned by a captain and two mates, who were American, and a crew of fourteen British subjects who had enlisted to get out of jail.

After having stopped at Deseada, an island dependency of Guadeloupe east of Grand Terre, the captain gave orders to steer south by east, but the crew demanded the helmsman steer west northwest to Antigua.[42] The captain pleaded with the crew to take the vessel to a French port and he would buy them a sloop. They could go wherever they wanted. Instead, the crew made a counteroffer that the captain and the mates could use the ship's long boat to leave. The February 1777 British newspapers reported that the captain and the mates chose to stay with their ship.[43]

On March 28, 1776, the Marine Committee of the Continental Congress purchased merchantman *Molly* and renamed her *Reprisal*. A brig with a length of one hundred feet and a thirty-foot beam, she carried eighteen 6-pounders. Captain Lambert Wickes was given command of the vessel with its 130-man crew.

In June 1776 the *Reprisal* was sent on a mission to Martinique to bring back munitions for the Continental Army. As she was heading out of the Delaware Bay, she saw the Continental armed brig *Nancy,* of six guns, was being chased by six British men-of-war as she was returning from St. Croix and St. Thomas with 386 barrels of gunpowder for the army. In order to save her, her captain ran her ashore.

On June 28, Captain Wickes, with the crew of the *Reprisal,* aided by Captain John Barry with the crew of the *Lexington,* was able to hold at bay the boats sent from HMS *Kingfisher* under Captain Alexander Graeme.[44] Their action resulted in saving about 200 barrels of gunpowder. Before abandoning the *Nancy,* they laid a train of gunpowder, which, when the *Nancy* was boarded, blew up taking many British sailors with it. While in the Caribbean, the *Reprisal* also took several prizes. She completed her mission, returning to Philadelphia on September 13.

On October 24, 1776, Congress ordered Wickes to proceed to Nantes, France in the *Reprisal,* taking Benjamin Franklin who had been appointed commissioner to France. She reached Nantes on November 29, the first vessel of the Continental Navy to arrive in European waters.

The *Reprisal* set sail again about the middle of January 1777, cruising along the coast of Spain, in the Bay of Biscay and in the mouth of the English Channel. Six prizes were captured on this cruise, which ended February 14. After taking his prizes into Port Louis, Wickes sailed for L'Orient, France. After arriving at L'Orient, the crew of the *Reprisal* refused to go back out to sea until they got their prize money.

On April 27, 1777, the forty-one-year-old Wickes was ordered to leave port by Mr. Gonet, commissary of L'Orient. In response to complaints from the British government, Mr. Gonet ordered Wickes not to cruise or take prizes on the French coast on any pretense. Wickes was requested to sign a receipt for the orders, which he refused to do. He told Gonet that he took orders only from the Continental Congress and he had "never cruised on the coast of France or made prizes on said coast" nor would he. This was a bold-faced lie. Wickes claimed the *Reprisal* had sprung a leak and received permission to make his repairs Through various excuses he was able to remain in the port while he made ready for another cruise.

Wickes had written to the American commissioners at Paris advising them of his predicaments with the crew and Mr. Gonet and asking for their advice. He had gotten the crew to agree to go to Nantes but did not expect to get them to go any farther until they got paid. The crew had enlisted for one year and that time had expired. The crew had agreed to continue in service if they were paid. He requested the commissioners to instruct Mr. Thomas Morris to pay the crew on their arrival at Nantes.[45]

CAPTAIN JOHN MANLEY, COMMANDER of the *Hancock,* charged Leblum Baker, Phillip Bass Jr., Thomas Carren, David Ensigne, Peter Jennis, Joseph Petters, Robert Stoutly, and Nathaniel Winchester with mutiny. The *Hancock* was one of the first thirteen frigates of the Continental Navy authorized by the Continental Congress.

John Manley was given his commission on January 1, 1776.[46] He was such a popular hero that a song was written about him. It was naturally called the "Manly Song." Song sheets printed at Salem, Massachusetts at the time even had his image done in a woodcut on it.[47] The *Hancock* was built at Newburyport, Massachusetts.

On May 7, 1777, Captain Hector McNeill was on the 24-gun frigate *Boston* which had been launched on June 3, 1776, at Newburyport, Massachusetts. The *Boston* had been built by the firm of Jonathan Greenleaf and Stephen and Ralph Cross. McNeill, in Nantasket Road, Massachusetts, ordered Captain John Paul Jones to attend a court martial to be held the next morning at 9:00 a.m. aboard the 44-gun frigate *Hancock* in Congress Road.[48]

The American commissioners in Paris (Benjamin Franklin, Silas Deane, and Arthur Lee) complained to Lord George Germain, British secretary of state for the American Department, about three ships that were the property of the Congress of the United States and had been taken "by an Act of Piracy, in some of her crew." They said the snow *Dickenson* had been brought to Bristol, England, an unnamed vessel carried to Liverpool, and a third into Halifax.[49]

On February 10, 1777, the *Public Advertiser* newspaper reported having received a letter from Plymouth, England, dated the 4th, that five American vessels were brought into port containing rice and tobacco. The vessels were seized by the crews who then confined the captains.[50]

They were not the only ones complaining about their vessels being taken. Anthony Marmajou was the owner of the schooner *St. Louis.* George Ross was the captain and his crew mutinied against him on July 6, 1778. Marmajou was complaining to anyone who would listen and placed notices in both English and French in the Pennsylvania Packet offering a five hundred pound reward for anyone with information about the mutineers or his vessel with its cargo.[51]

On May 5, 1777, the *London Chronicle* reported that, at St. Kitts, a large American vessel was brought into the island. Ten members of the crew had seized the ship. She had sailed from South Carolina with 500 barrels of rice and 70 of indigo and bound for Martinique. The vessel was sold and her cargo brought £700 sterling.[52]

The British transport *Oxford* from Glasgow met up with its convoy of thirty-three vessels with approximately three thousand soldiers at Greenock in Scotland. The *Oxford* carried part of the one hundred soldiers of the 42nd Royal Highlanders and officers.[53] The convoy was bound for Boston and left Greenock on April 29, 1776. They were delayed for two weeks by the failure of supplies to arrive on time.[54]

The crew of the *Oxford* had heard from another vessel while out at sea that the city of Boston was in the possession of the Americans. They quickly changed course for Halifax, Nova Scotia. On May 5 the fleet ran into a storm that scattered the convoy.[55] The transport *Oxford* had been at sea for seven weeks when at four a.m., on May 29, they spotted an American brig. It was the *Andrew Doria*, a Continental Navy Brigantine, under the command of Captain Nicholas Biddle.[56] *Andrew Doria* carried fourteen 4-pounders and was popularly referred to as "the Black Brig."

The *Cranford* and *Oxford* were northward of the *Andrew Doria*.[57] At six o'clock in the morning, Biddle was able to capture the British vessels without firing a shot.[58] The seas turned very heavy and remained that way all day as he tried to secure the vessels. The waves were breaking over the long boats as they were bringing over all the baggage of value. All the weapons (100 broadswords and 160 small arms) from the two transports were brought on board the *Andrew Doria*. Despite the crew's best effort in the rain, they were unable to keep from losing one of their long boats though no lives were lost.

Biddle put all the soldiers on the *Oxford* and left the officers on the *Cranford*. The officers were Captain John Smith and Lieutenant Robert Franklin of the 42nd Regiment and Captain Norman McLeod, Lieutenant Roderick McLeod, and Ensign Colin Campbell of the 71st Regiment. The wives of Captain Norman McLeod and Ensign Colin Campbell were also on board. Four of the army officers, the mates, navigators, and all the crews were transferred to the *Andrew Doria*. Captain Biddle allowed Captain John Smith, Lieutenant Franklin, Lieutenant Morrow, and Ensign Campbell to take their bedding and a few shirts. The *Cranford* and *Oxford* were manned with the crew from Biddle's ship. Captain Biddle gave command of the *Oxford* to Third Lieutenant John McDougal and Lieutenant of Marines John Trevett.

At four o'clock on the morning of June 14, the *Andrew Doria* was just out of Nantasket shoals off of Newfoundland when Captain Biddle observed five ships to windward. One of the five was a very large man-of-war. Biddle ordered his three ships to split up and make their way to Rhode Island. He may have done this to keep the enemy from thinking they were warships that were trying to corral them. Or he have thought they would have a better chance of escaping.

At 8:00 a.m. a squall helped keep the five enemy ships at a distance.[59] This cat and mouse game continued until nine o'clock at night when Biddle finally got away.

One of his captured ships and the five enemy ships had disappeared over the horizon. When he heard cannons he suspected that the British ships had his ship in range. The odds were overwhelmingly against him, so Captain Biddle got away as fast as he could.

On Friday, June 14, 1776, Biddle brought the *Andrew Doria* safely to Newport, Rhode Island.[60] Biddle's forty prisoners were landed that evening.

The *Cranford* was taken by the *Cerebus* and was placed under the convoy of a sloop. The two vessels, *Cranford* and *Cerebus*, were captured by the American armed sloop *Schuyler* on the south side of Long Island bound for Sandy Hook and then New York.

During the squall the *Oxford* was able to slip away. As she was making for port, the British carpenters of the transport banded together and overpowered the crew from the *Andrew Doria* who were running the ship. The new commanders demanded that the course be changed. They wanted to be taken "to Lord Dunmore, or to some other place where they might meet some ship or ships of war belonging to his Majesty."

When they arrived at Hampton Roads about sunset, they found that the forty-four-year-old John Murray, Earl of Dunmore, the royal governor of Virginia since 1771, was making a stand at Gwynn's Island up the Chesapeake Bay. When the news of Concord and Lexington reached Virginia,

Dunmore, who twice before had dissolved the House of Burgesses for its pro-colonist stand, removed the colony's gunpowder stores to a man-of-war. The angry and aroused Virginians made him pay for the powder. Threats against his life forced him to leave Williamsburg, Virginia's colonial capital, taking refuge aboard the man-of-war *Fowey* at Yorktown on June 8, 1775.

Dunmore remained aboard the warship for many months, gathering sup-porters and strengthening the fleet in the hope of giving Virginia back to the crown.

On December 9, 1775 Dunmore's followers suffered a severe defeat at the battle of Great Bridge. Shortly afterward, he burned Norfolk, then the most populous town in Virginia. His fleet was driven by well-placed batteries from one place to another. He moved up the Chesapeake Bay to Gwynn's Island where he was going to make a stand.

The *Oxford* sighted the armed Virginia Navy boats *Liberty* and *Patriot*, which were captained by James Barron and Richard Barron. The *Oxford* sent a boat to Captain James Barron to make an inquiry. The *Oxford*'s vessel was manned by a sergeant, a private, and one of the crew from the *Andrew Doria* who advised Captain Barron of the situation. Captain Barron then boarded the *Oxford* and took possession.

There is an alternate version of the tale. Lieutenant John Trevett's journal has a different story of the retaking of the *Oxford*. According to Trevett, he was one of the officers put on board the *Oxford* from the *Andrew Doria*. He claims to have simply demanded that the transport be turned over to him.[61] Captains James and Richard Barron brought the *Oxford* to Jamestown. The *Oxford* had 217 Highland soldiers on board along with 100 tents, 200 mattresses, three hogsheads of rum, and two barrels of gunpowder. The Virginia Convention decided to offer the seamen the option of serving in a cruiser or galley. If they chose not to serve then they would be kept as prisoners of war.[62]

The *Oxford* was renamed the *Aurora* with John Hutchinson, master. She sailed from Cumberland on the York River, Virginia, bound for Bordeaux or Nantes, France. Her cargo was 412 hogsheads of tobacco and 2,000 staves belonging to the Continental Congress. She was manned by a crew of fifteen; a Mr. Hall was on board as a supercargo and a Mr. Richards as a passenger. A supercargo is a merchant or ship's officer who is responsible for the ship's cargo and its sale. He would also be responsible for acquiring and disposing of cargo for the next leg of the voyage. Eight of the crew were Englishmen who had gotten out of prison by joining the service. The Englishmen had agreed that if the situation presented itself, they would seize the ship.

On Sunday, January 11, 1777 an opportunity presented itself. William Turner, boatswain and three other Englishmen (two from Lancaster and two from Liverpool) were on the vessel's deck with their loaded fusees.[63] They presented their weapons while the American sailors were up in the shrouds. They ordered the Americans to come down singly and secured them under the hatches. Turner secured the captain and the supercargo in the cabin. The ship landed at Liverpool, England, on Tuesday, January 28.[64] The Americans (John Hutchinson, James Richardson, John Hall, Jeff Jenkinson, Joseph Walker, Huges Jonston, Gilbert Welch, and Jesse Topping) were transferred to the Union Tender.[65]

The frigate *South Carolina* would be the scene of several mutinies in her short career. Before France got officially involved in the war with England, she could not openly provide the British colonies in North America with warships from the French navy or build warships in France for them to use against England. Such an action would precipitate war, for which France was not ready.

Proceeding on to Haiti and Martinique, the munitions were received by Americans. The French had been secretly loaning the Americans money and credit to keep the British focused on their colonies in North America while France was busy rebuilding her military for the next war with England.

In 1774, after serving as ambassador at Trier, Constantinople, and Stockholm, Charles Gravier comte de Vergennes was made foreign minister by King Louis XVI of France. The fifty-eight-year-old Vergennes had Pierre Augustin Caron de Beaumarchais set up a proprietary company to trade with America and send military supplies secretly to the colonies.[66] Growing up, Beaumarchais had apprenticed as a watchmaker. His own watchmaking business was so successful that he became watchmaker to King Louis XV. He purchased the title de Beaumarchais and became a secret agent working for Louis XV and Louis XVI.

Beaumarchais created the proprietary company Rodriguez Hortalez & Cie to accomplish his covert mission. It operated out of the Hotel des Ambassadeurs de Hollande, 47 Rue Vieille du Temple in Paris. By March 1776, France and Spain had agreed to furnish Beaumarchais 1 million livres each. Spain's agenda was to conquer Gibraltar, Minorca, and Portugal while keeping its possessions in North America.

Rodrerigue Hortalez and Company shipped munitions to Haiti and Martinique. The munitions were received by American agents who then shipped war materials to the United States. The French Navy took up positions off the French West Indies to ensure that the British did not interfere with these reshipments while they were near French waters.

Beaumarchais had a fleet of upward of fifty ships moving supplies. After Burgoyne's surrender at Saratoga, Beaumarchais went to England undercover, using the name of Dr. Duval, wearing common clothes and a wig. His visit had two purposes. He wanted to engage some English merchants in a partnership with his French proprietary company, which would supply him with goods that he could use to meet his supply contracts for Congress. He also met with Count de Albrodman, the Spanish ambassador. Their meetings took place at Madam Clerge's in Charlotte.[67]

The Americans wanted some warships to clear the British Navy out of American shipping lanes. The British naval superiority, off the coast of the United States, resulted in the British capturing American merchant ships loaded with valuable cargo. American goods, such as indigo and tobacco, were to be exchanged for war supplies such as arms, ammunition, and clothing. Jacques Boux, a French naval officer who was unable to continue his military ascent as he did not come from the right social class, was a technical advisor for the French navy. He agreed to build the American warships but wanted an American naval rank in return.[68]

On February 12, 1777, Benjamin Franklin and Silas Deane, the American commissioners at Paris, agreed that Mr. Boux would have the rank and pay of a commodore in the service of the United States of America. The commissioners also agreed the pay would begin on the day he left Paris in the service of the United States.[69] It was decided that the warships for America would be built in neutral Holland. Boux selected the Staat's shipyard in Amsterdam and quickly went to work.

The mounting expenses had necessitated reducing the number of planned frigates to one but the expenses were still too much for the American commissioners. To build the vessel, outfit it with sails and supplies, and pay for the crew was an expensive proposition. The American commissioners were able to persuade the French government to take over the vessel.

In a war with England, France would need every warship it could get. The French named the new vessel *L'Indien*. The French needed to get her launched quickly in Amsterdam and brought to a French port before fighting with England commenced. It would be much more difficult to bring her safely down the coast if England and France were at war.

The British spy network was reporting on what was stated to be the biggest ship ever built in Amsterdam. Several vessels were being built simultaneously at Staat's shipyard. Sir Joseph Yorke, the British ambassador at The Hague, had built a very good intelligence network. In 1774, Yorke reported that vessels at Amsterdam were being loaded with firearms.[70] The British also received information from a number of Amsterdam and Rotterdam bankers.[71]

Rotterdam, Holland, was the headquarters of the British spy network in Europe. Being located in a country that England had not been to war with for 150 years, it operated in relative safety. It was run out of a bookshop by Mr. Richard Wolters from the 1740s until his death in 1770, and then by his widow Marguerite Wolters until 1785. The Wolters supplied intercepted correspondence and ships' news from agents in every major port in Europe. The British spy operation had spies watching spies in order to verify the accuracy of the information and to determine if any agents had changed sides.

Marguerite Wolters was competent, shrewd, and resourceful. During the American Revolution, she was the network's sole contact to the British Admiralty. During her operation of the spy network, the Admiralty never complained, due to the lack of information, and she was successfully able to get replacement agents when needed.[72] Because Rotterdam was a financial center, she had no problem in obtaining drafts in any currency to pay her spies.

Because *L'Indien*'s draft was nine feet more than the average depth of the channel, she could not be sailed out to open water. She had to be floated on her side for more than sixty miles to Texel, a Frisian island off the Dutch coast with the North Sea on one side and the Wadden Sea on the other.[73] Texel was the deep water port for Amsterdam. In February 1778, *L'Indien* was floated out of the shipyard but the French were unable to get her to open water before war broke out.[74] Therefore, the vessel sat rotting at anchor at Amsterdam through 1780.

Sometime around March 1, 1780, the French government lent the vessel to the Chevalier de Louxembourg. The *L'Indien* was now a private vessel. The Dutch and French governments now had deniability if the ship found its way into American hands. Being in private hands, the governments would not be responsible if she left port.

The *L'Indien* entered into a contract with Alexander Gillon to get the vessel out of Holland and to capture prizes. Gillon also obligated the state of South Carolina as a cosigner to the contract.

Alexander Gillon, of Scottish ancestry, was born in Rotterdam in 1741. He was multilingual, speaking English, Dutch, French, and German. He moved to Charles Town, South Carolina, in 1766 after stays in London and Philadelphia. He was commissioned by the Continental Congress in November 1777 to purchase produce and other items for Congress for the next three years and ship them to Europe. He was to send back arms, ammunition, clothing, and other articles as directed.[75] He accepted a position in the South Carolina Navy and went to France to purchase three frigates for their fledgling fleet.[76]

Gillon was able to move the *L'Indien* from Amsterdam to Texel by boarding up the hatches and floating her on her side. She must have made a most unusual sight as she made her journey to deep water.[77] Lieutenant Luke Matthewman, who had met Gillon in Rotterdam, wrote, "on my arrival on board the ship then laying about halfway between Amsterdam and Texel everything was in confusion, three of the lieutenants were under arrest and the ship like a mere wreck her crew then about 250 men mostly Americans seven months on board some disagreement—left ship to [go to] Amsterdam."[78]

The *L'Indien* arrived at Texel on October 30, 1780.[79] It would not be until August 4, 1781, that the vessel, now named the *South Carolina*, weighed anchor and set out for open water.[80] The crew of the vessel was composed of three hundred of the Chevalier de Louxembourg's marines, a number of French sailors, Americans, Irish, and probably some Dutch. Communication was no doubt a problem on board the ship.

As the *South Carolina* left Texel a mutiny broke out. The French sailors had not been paid and did not want to leave port until they got their money. Some American and Irish sailors joined them. This was not the first mutiny seen in the waters that surrounded Texel during the American Revolution.

In 1779, the crew of the Dutch frigate *Venus* anchored off Texel mutinied. The Dutch Navy had recently introduced enlistment bounties. The crew would only be able to claim the bounty money if they were discharged and then reenlisted. Sixteen petty officers headed by the boatswain's mate along with many seamen and soldiers mutinied. The situation got so out of control that it took an entire month before it was quelled. Although severe sentences were given to the mutineers, they were pardoned for their behavior by William V, Prince of Orange, who was the stadtholder of the Netherlands.[81]

Commodore Alexander Gillon and Captain John Joyner used vigor, arguments, and marines to silence the mutiny on the *South Carolina,* which lasted for six hours. They were able to isolate the ringleaders. Punishment, as usual following a failed mutiny, was swift. It was reported that one of the ringleaders of the mutiny received 125 lashes. Another received 50 stokes on his back from the flat of a cutlass; another had his arm slashed; others received blows to their heads, which resulted in breaking three swords; and one of the mutineers was placed in irons.[82]

This was not Joyner's first experience with a mutiny. He had had command of a vessel that left for Europe in April or May 1778. His crew was composed of one half loyalist or loyalist sympathizers. While the ship passed the English coast, the crew mutinied and took the ship to Plymouth, England. Joyner, who had family in Bristol, England, was released.[83]

From Texel, the *South Carolina* cruised off the east coast of Scotland after prizes. She turned west between the Fair Isle south of Shetland and the Orkneys.

The *South Carolina* started to experience contrary winds. The *Louxembourg's* marines were restless from lack of activity. They became a discipline problem as they insulted officers and commenced fighting among themselves. The ship was now six weeks out and had not made very much progress heading west, as the winds were not favorable. They were also getting critically low on food and water. Gillon decided it was time to resupply the ship and get to America by the southerly route.

He decided the *South Carolina's* next port of call would be Coruña, Spain. It was the home port to part of the Spanish fleet. It had a large dry dock and plenty of naval stores. Everything he needed.

When the *South Carolina* arrived she was almost out of food, and the sailors still had not been paid. There were also a number of sailors with expired terms of service. The situation was unstable at best. If he had gone to a French port, the French sailors and the *Louxembourg's* marines could not have been prevented from leaving the ship.

It did not take long after the arrival in Coruña before the French sailors mutinied again. This time they had gotten possession of muskets and edge weapons. Expecting trouble, Alexander Gillon was prepared and managed to contain the mutiny. However, one of his men was seriously injured.[84] By selling some of the cargo and obtaining some local credit, Alexander Gillon was able to restock the *South Carolina* with food and water. They spent three weeks in port before setting sail for the New World.

Gillon followed Columbus's route across the Atlantic Ocean using the lower latitudes. The *South Carolina* successfully made the crossing and arrived in Havana, Cuba. In need of money and supplies, Gillon joined in a successful Spanish expedition against New Providence in the Bahamas. It surrendered on May 8, 1782.

Gillon then discontinued operations with the Spanish and sailed for Philadelphia. While he was in port, an intercepted letter critical of Gillon's actions in Europe, written by Philadelphian James Searle, was printed in the *Royal Gazette*. A letter of response written by the *South Carolina*'s officers was published in the *Pennsylvania Packet*. It accused Searle and William Jackson, passengers on the *South Carolina* who had left the ship at Coruña, of encouraging the mutiny at Coruña.[85]

Because of financial difficulties and in anticipation of more trouble with the crew, the ship was moved from Pennsylvania to New Jersey. Commodore Gillon turned over command to Captain John Joyner to keep the ship from being encumbered and to get the vessel out to sea as all the financial claims were against him.

In Billingsport, New Jersey, away from the Pennsylvania creditors and courts, a new crew was recruited for the *South Carolina*. She left Billingsport on December 12, 1782, and started on her way to the Atlantic Ocean.

While still in the Delaware Bay, there was a mutiny. As ships moved in the bay, a sailor would toss a lead weight on a line over the side of the ship and read the depth of the water to the bottom in fathoms. The sailor would yell out the readings as they traveled. The reading would tell the pilot if he was still in the shipping channel or if the ship was in danger. The pilot on the *South Carolina* realized that the man giving the soundings was giving false readings in order to have the ship run aground. Captain John Joyner had several disgruntled men placed in irons. In a few moments a part of the crew came on deck with handspikes to secure the release of the men being confined. The officers, backed by the armed Hessians who had been recruited around Reading, Pennsylvania, and some loyal crew members, prevented the loss of the ship.

Captain Joyner met with a delegation of the malcontent sailors. The crew was composed of sailors who did not want to go on an extended cruise because their enlistments were nearly up, men who had never been to sea and were having second thoughts, and men upset with putrid food that had not been replaced with fresh provisions before leaving port. Although the potentially ugly situation was defused, Captain Joyner doubled the watch and warned the officers to be on the lookout for a repeat performance.

The British Navy had three ships cruising off the Delaware Bay waiting to intercept craft trying to get to open water. The *South Carolina* came out with two other ships and all three were quickly captured on December 20, 1782. The British were taking their prizes to New York. During the journey, the *South Carolina* distanced itself from the other ships in the convoy.

The prize crew placed on board the ship got careless as they allowed prisoners to come on deck and return without latching the staircase leading from the deck to the area below. The sailors realized they had separated from the other ships and an opportunity to take back the vessel was available. The British sailors had not checked the cargo, apparently planning to divide up the spoils once they got to New York City.

Prisoners Joshua Mersereau and Abijah Hunt conspired to take over the ship. They knew what was in store once they reached New York. They would be confined in the *Jersey*. It was an old hulk of a ship built in 1736, that once had mounted sixty-four guns.

In 1776, being unfit for active service, the *Jersey* had been sent to New York to be used as a hospital ship. She was docked in the East River nearly opposite the Fly Market. During the winter of 1779–1780, she was converted into a prison-ship. She was stripped of all her spars, except the bowsprit, a derrick for taking in supplies, and the flagstaff at her stern. Her portholes were closed and securely fastened. Air was supplied belowdecks by two rows of small holes, each about twenty inches square with two strong right-angled crossed bars of iron cut through her sides.[86] The *Jersey* was grossly overcrowded.[87] The horrors of putrid air and human filth were amplified by bad food.

There was some money to be made in supplying the prisons with food. The commissaries would buy food stuffs of low quality at cheap prices but claim to have bought better quality items at more expensive prices and pocket the difference. The *Jersey* quickly made room for her next batch of prisoners as the dead were removed every morning. No one was concerned about complaints from enemy prisoners.

If it was not the *Jersey* then it would be one of the other prison ships in Wallabout Bay, and they were not much better. The twenty-three-year-old Joshua Mersereau had been born on Staten Island, New York, and was a member of the Mersereau spy ring that operated as American spies in British-held Staten Island from 1776 through at least 1780.

Mersereau first checked to see if one of the Americans being held prisoner could sail the ship. The other ships were not very far away. Time was going to be a critical factor. They had to secure the ship and make a fast getaway before the other ships could close in on them. The *South Carolina* carried chests packed with weapons in her hold. The men belowdecks acquired muskets with bayonets. Their plan was to kill or seize the closest British officers near the companionway. The sailors, working aloft, were thought to be unarmed.

On December 22, Mersereau went on deck and was to give the signal for the men to rush forward. Something made a British officer suspicious. The officer, with two pistols drawn, rushed past Joshua Mersereau and threatened to shoot him if he made any hostile move or sound. One of the other British sailors on deck raced over, slammed down the hatch that led belowdecks, and latched it. Their plot to take the ship was foiled. The weapons were put back in storage.

The next day, the *South Carolina,* the largest American warship, reached British-held New York. The American officers were sent to Long Island. The Hessians were turned over to the Hessian commanders in New York; the rest of the crew were interned on the *Jersey* and the other prison ships.

THE *GENERAL GREGORY* WAS AN AMERICAN PRIVATEER named after General Isaac Gregory of the North Carolina Militia who had been wounded at the Battle of Camden on August 16, 1780. Near the end of the war, it was being fitted out at Edenton, North Carolina. While it was still lying in port, a mutiny broke out and several of the officers were killed.[88] Two of the mutineers must have been spotted in Henrico County, Virginia. On July 4, 1783, a warrant for the arrest of David Miller and John Wilkinson who were "accused of mutiny and murder while mariners on board the *General Gregory* who had escaped from jail in Edenton" was issued.[89]

If a captain was not capturing enough prizes, he had to start worrying about a disgruntled crew. At nine o'clock on the morning of April 10, 1781,

Captain Joshua Burgess took the privateer *Fortune* and began a cruise out of Newburyport. The schooner *Fortune* was cruising for prizes off the east coast of Nova Scotia. Their journey had taken them near the northeast end of the Nova Scotia peninsula before Cape Breton Island beginnings.

On Saturday, May 19, the crew mutinied. They thought they were in the wrong place to get prizes. Bowers, J. Smith, and Wheaton wanted to put the captain on shore and cruise off Halifax. Instead, the three of them were put on shore. Smith repented and came right back. The other two stayed on shore all night. The following afternoon, they continued cruising north.[90]

-18

The Madman and the Pirate

*O*ne ship that was a mutiny recidivist was the Congress frigate *Alliance*.[1] She was a thirty-six-gun frigate originally named the *Hancock*. She was built on the Merrimack River at Salisbury, Massachusetts, by William and James K. Hackett and launched by their cousins on April 28, 1778. The *Alliance* had twenty-eight 12-pounders on the main deck, and eight 9-pounders on the quarterdeck and the forecastle. She was renamed *Alliance* on May 29, 1778, by resolution of the Continental Congress. Her first commander was Pierre Landais.

Silas Deane, American ambassador to France, had given a Continental commission on March 1, 1777, to Pierre Landais as captain of the ship *L'Heureux*.[2] She was a French frigate of 300 tons and carried twenty-eight guns. Masquerading as a merchant ship of Rodrerigue Hortalez and Company, her name had been changed to *Le Flamand*.

On September 26, 1777, *Le Flamand* sailed from the French port of Marseilles carrying forty-seven-year-old Baron Frederick William von Steuben, who was listed in the ship's log as Mr. Frank; Pierre Etienne Duponceau, Steuben military secretary and interpreter; Carl Vogel, Steuben's servant; and M. de Francy, the nephew and agent of Beaumarchais. In the ship's hold were 1,700 weight of powder, 22 tons of sulfur, 52 brass cannons, 19 mortars, small fieldpieces, pistols, and muskets for the American army. *Le Flamand* was cleared for Martinique supposedly carrying dispatches for the French governor of the island but actually bound for Portsmouth, New Hampshire.

The *Le Flamand* had a rough journey that included two violent gales, fire in the forecastle three times, and a mutiny by the crew. A total of fourteen men—Landais, the ship's passengers and some trusted crew members—

fought with eighty-four mutineers. *Le Flamand* pulled into Portsmouth, New Hampshire, on December 1.[3]

Landais was a French naval lieutenant who had been unable to get a command. He was an experienced sailor, having circumnavigated the globe from 1766 to 1769 under Louis-Antoine de Bougainville.

In light of this expertise and to appease the French, on June 15, 1778, Congress appointed Landais to the command of the *Alliance*.[4] In hindsight, the decision was a mistake. Pierre Landais was brooding on his inability to get a French naval commission. John Paul Jones, whom the British characterized as a pirate, would accuse Landais of deliberately firing on Jones's vessel the *Bonhomme Richard* in its battle with the *Serapis*.

There was a disinclination of Americans to sail under a French captain and, at Boston at this time, a number of privateers were fitting out. This made it very difficult for Landais to put together a crew for the *Alliance*.

The Navy Board of the Eastern Department tried to encourage seamen from other ships at Boston harbor to enroll on the *Alliance* by offering a bounty of ten crowns to be paid them in France. Several seamen accepted the offer, including some who would be the conspirators of a mutiny. Landais applied to the Consul for French seamen and offered the same bounty and a dividend of prize money upon their arrival in France. Not being able to complete his crew, he was forced to raid the jails for sailors. The crew of the *Alliance* when completed was predominately composed of English, Irish, and Scotch who had been captured by privateers.

A few days before the *Alliance* was scheduled to leave Boston, Landais heard of rumor of a mutiny being planned by the former prisoners. After checking into the matter, he believed it had no basis in fact. The *Alliance* sailed from Boston on January 14, 1779, bound for Brest, France, accompanied by the frigate *Deane,* commanded by thirty-five-year-old Chestertown, Maryland, native Captain Samuel Nicholson. After three days at sea, the two ships parted. The *Deane,* which was built in Nantes, France, was headed for a cruise in the West Indies.

The first assignment of the *Alliance* was to carry Lafayette back to France to petition the French court for increased support in fighting the British, France's sworn enemy. The cargo of the *Alliance* was the Marquis de LaFayette and his staff, Captain Chevalier de Remondis, the late commander of the *Caesar* one of the ships belonging to the king of France, and a parcel of letters to be delivered to Benjamin Franklin.

The mutineers had tried to bring into their group an American seaman who had lived many years in Ireland and was taken to be a native of Ireland. On February 2, he revealed to Landais at noon that the crew believed their cover was blown and they were going to mutiny at 4:00 p.m. Landais then armed the officers and those of the crew that he trusted. Lafayette took command of the armed defenders.

The four ringleaders were seized and quickly placed in irons. The defenders made a thorough search in the ship for arms and ammunition, and found in one of the ringleaders chests, some cartridges and balls, and in another a very indecent knife, "fit only for such horrid purposes." Before the day was done, a total of thirty-eight members of the crew were confined as mutineers.

John Savage, master-at-arms and William Murray, sergeant in the marines, along with others, had hatched a plan to seize the *Alliance*. They planned to force one of the lieutenants to take command and take the frigate to a port in England or Ireland. The plan called for them to break up into four groups. The first group was to seize the magazine and kill the boatswain, carpenter, and gunner. The other three groups were to simultaneously take the cabin, quarterdeck, and wardroom. If there was any opposition, they would turn the loaded 9-pounder forecastle guns aft and fire them.

Once they had control of the ship, they were going to put Captain Landais in irons in a small boat without food or water and set it adrift. The lieutenants, if they agreed, were to take charge of the ship and sail her to England. If they did not agree they were to walk the plank. The ship's doctor and marine officers were going to be hanged, quartered, and thrown overboard. The sailing master was to be tied to the mizzen mast, scarified all over, cut to pieces, and finally thrown overboard.[5] Lafayette was to be placed in irons and turned over to the authorities in England. He would surely bring a large reward.

With the mutineers confined and order restored, Landais then held a court of inquiry on board the *Alliance*. The officers and gentlemen passengers formed a jury to hear the defense of the mutineers. They would stand trial when they reached port. The *Alliance* arrived in Brest four days later. The French were not allowing any foreign vessel in the actual harbor at Brest but the ship was allowed to stay in the road and complete any repairs it needed.

There were not enough American naval captains in France to convene a court martial. Franklin recommended that Landais leave those mutineers who were guilty of lesser crimes in France (replacing them with other sailors) and return to America with three or four of the guiltiest as prisoners.[6]

The mutiny was not the only unpleasant experience for the ship. During her twenty-three day voyage she ran into a gale, which carried away the "Main Top Mast, Top Sail Yards, Sails, and Pinnace. . . . [The] iron work was exceeding bad, failing in all parts of the ship, where the rigging had any strain."

Landais wanted Franklin to provide him with one hundred men that were good seamen prior to heading back out to sea.[7] At the end of February, Landais was to take the *Alliance* from Brest to L'Orient for repairs. He complained to Franklin that he still had to get the prisoners from the mutiny off the ship before he could leave.[8] The thirty-eight prisoners were taken off the ship and transferred to a French prison.[9]

In May 1779, John Adams recorded in his diary his impression of Landais.

This gentleman has been disappointed in love and in his ambition—disappointed in the promotion to which he aspired, and in a marriage of which he thought himself sure. He has not so much activity, dispatch and decision as [one] could wish. He seems not to know how to gain or preserve the affections of his officers, nor yet how to keep them in awe. Complaisance, firmness and steadiness are necessary to the command of a ship. Whether it is his imperfect knowledge of the language, or his absence of mind when poring upon his disappointments, or any defect in his temper or judgment, I know not, but this happy mixture seems to be wanting. His lieutenants are smart men, quick and active—not lettered it is true, but good seamen, and brave.[10]

Three days later, Adams expounded on his analysis of Landais as a troubled soul. "L[andais] is jealous of everything, jealous of everybody, of all his officers, all his passengers. He knows not how to treat his officers, nor his passengers, nor any body else. Silence, reserve and a forbidding air will never gain the hearts, neither by affection nor by veneration of our Americans. There is in this man inactivity and an indecision that will ruin him. He is bewildered—an absent bewildered man—an embarrassed mind."[11]

Landais was beginning to see intrigues against him everywhere. He was becoming unhinged. On the morning of May 12, 1779 he told Adams, "You are a great man but you are deceived. The officers deceive you! They never do their duty but when you are on deck. They never obey me, but when you are on deck. The officers were in a plot vs. me at Boston, and the Navy Board promised to remove them all from the ship and yet afterwards let them all come on board."[12]

Landais and the officers on the *Alliance* had quarreled on the voyage from Boston. The misunderstandings between Captain Landais and the other officers of his ship were so severe that Landais once wrote Benjamin Franklin that he would quit the command rather than continue with them. Some of the officers left the *Alliance* when she docked. That seemed to alleviate the tension.

The quarreling on the *Alliance* had become an embarrassment to Franklin. He wrote to Le Ray de Chaumont, "I beg you would not form an opinion of the Americans in general from this accident. Where a number of men of whatever nation are together with little or nothing to do they are apt to be mutinous and quarrelsome. I hope when they are fully employed they will behave with more discretion and more good nature to each other." He said to Chaumont that "Commodore Jones, whose authority exercised with prudence and temper, will I hope be sufficient to compose these dissensions and re-establish good order and harmony."[13]

John Paul Jones, commanding the *Bonhomme Richard,* took out a squadron from France to cruise the British coast. The *Alliance* under Captain Pierre Landais was one of his vessels.

On the morning of September 23, 1779, the *Serapis*, a Royal Navy man-o-war, and her consort, the lightly armed sloop *Countess of Scarborough*, were convoying forty-four merchant ships. The convoy was heading from Scandinavia to the dockyards in the south of England. The merchantmen's cargo was naval stores of canvas, rope, and timber. They had been on their journey for eight days and were now off the Yorkshire coast. Richard Pearson, a veteran of thirty years at sea, was in command of the fleet. He had won fame as a first lieutenant.

During a hurricane Pearson took over for a disabled captain and guided the *Norfolk*, a ship of line, safely through the storm. On this morning he saw a red flag flying from Scarborough Castle. It was a warning that there was an "enemy on our shores." Shortly after 10:00 a.m., a fishing boat brought a message from shore that a "flying squadron" of American ships had been seen off the coast heading south.

John Paul Jones and his squadron had doubled back and were cruising north. The four ships were the *Bonhomme Richard* of forty guns, the *Alliance* of thirty-six guns, the *Pallas* of thirty-two guns, and the *Vengeance* of twelve guns. Their combined fire power could propel more than a thousand pounds of metal in a single broadside.

About 1:00 p.m., the lookouts of the *Serapis* saw the mast of Jones's squadron on the horizon. Pearson immediately ordered the merchant ships to take cover under the guns of Scarborough Castle. The American squadron was going against the current and was making no more than one or two miles per hour. At 5:00 p.m., the drummers "beat to quarters" and the men on the *Bonhomme Richard* raced to their assigned positions. Jones had assigned at least forty men to go up in the rigging with guns, a small mortar, and baskets of grenades. This was an unusually high number; many captains feared that the flash from the muskets would set the sails on fire.

Jones wanted as much firepower as he could get up in the masts. The ship's armory would be unlocked so that the boarding party could get their weapons quickly. At this time, Surgeon Brooke would be setting up his operating room complete with knives, saws, and tubs for the limbs he would have to remove later that day.

At 6:00 p.m., Jones ordered two blue flags run up the masts—one up the foremast, one up the mainmast—and a blue and yellow flag run up the mizzen. This was the signal to "form line of battle." However, nothing happened. The *Alliance*, under the command of Frenchman Pierre Landais, claimed that Jones's signal had not been heard and that Jones did not respond to his hail.

The *Pallas* continued on her previous course and the *Vengeance* hung back. Jones continued on alone against the HMS *Serapis*, which, with its forty-four guns, could deliver a broadside of 285 pounds.[14]

The *Bonhomme Richard* had a broadside of 265 pounds.[15] Captain Pearson nailed his flag to the stern of his ship, thus alerting the crew that no one could surrender his ship by striking the ship's flag.

Jones wanted to get as close as possible to the British warship. The *Bonhomme Richard* was flying a British flag. When asked by Captain Pearson to identify herself, Jones had the sailing master reply, "*Princess Royal.*" The "*Princess Royal*" was an East Indian merchant vessel about the same size as the *Bonhomme Richard*.

After several stalling moves, Jones realized his ruse was not working. He hauled down the British flag and ran up his Continental Navy ensign. A sailor in the tops of the *Bonhomme Richard* fired a shot and then both ships erupted, firing both broadsides at once. At a distance of twenty-five yards, every shot hit its target.

The concussion from forty-two cannons firing at once was tremendous. The sound of wood and bones splintering would not have been heard over the loud roar of the cannons. The shrieks and cries of the wounded and dying would be heard in the gaps of noise between cannon and musket reloading. The ships were enveloped in a foul smelling sulfur cloud making it difficult to see. The second broadside to hit the *Bonhomme Richard* was worse than the first. The first had opened holes in the ship; the second rained devastation inside the ship as the cannon balls no longer had to penetrate an outer hull. Belowdecks one, possibly two, of the ship's ancient cannons burst.

Jones ordered the gunroom cleared as the other cannons were as unreliable. The *Serapis* was able to get behind the *Bonhomme Richard* and rake the stern. With the wind dying, Pearson backed his sails down and was able to get off several broadsides to the unprotected stern of the *Bonhomme Richard*.

The *Bonhomme Richard* was a scene of devastation, the decks covered with the dead and dying, the wounded and the dismembered. Of the twenty-five marines on the poop deck, twenty-two were dead or wounded. The *Serapis* was the faster ship and the *Bonhomme Richard* now had several holes below the water line. The crew were patching them with canvas and large wooden plugs. The *Bonhomme Richard* was taking on water as the pumps were not able to keep up.

Pearson wanted to rake the bow of the *Bonhomme Richard*. After starting the maneuver, she lost her wind. Jones still had some wind and ordered Samuel Stacey, the sailing master, to "lay the enemy's ship on board." He then ordered a boarding party. Stacey was barely able to steer the ship and get the bowsprit into the *Serapis's* mizzenmast. Jones gave the order to board the *Serapis* but the bowsprit was too precarious a gangway and he had to rescind the order. The *Bonhomme Richard* backed her sails and the two ships drifted apart.

The *Serapis* changed her sails and worked to get parallel again. She fired another broadside and now the *Bonhomme Richard* was barely sailing. She was windward of the *Serapis* and was able to steal her wind. Jones was trying to get in position to rake the *Serapis*. However, because of the damage to the ship, she stalled in front of the *Serapis*. The *Serapis* tried to get clear, but her bowsprit got caught in the mizzen rigging.

A forestay from the *Serapis* fell on the poop deck of the *Bonhomme Richard*. Jones had it lashed to his ship and the two vessels were now hopelessly entangled. Jones ordered the men in the rigging to sweep the deck of the *Serapis* clear.

Captain Pearson controlled the battle belowdecks as his cannons made bigger holes in the *Bonhomme Richard* above and below the water line. He was able to reduce the *Bonhomme Richard* down to three working 9-pounders. Both ships were on fire. With the ships ablaze the fighting ceased as the men of both ships tried to put out the fires.

Jones looked for his other three vessels. He saw the *Pallas* firing on the small *Countess of Scarborough*; the *Vengeance* was biding its time. He could not find the *Alliance* captained by Pierre Landais. About 9:15 p.m., the *Alliance*, passing in front of the bow of the *Serapis* and the stern of the *Bonhomme Richard*, fired a broadside of grapeshot killing men on both ships. The *Alliance* went to the opposite side and fired again.

The *Bonhomme Richard* ship's carpenter, John Gunnison, went into the hold and sank up to his neck. He came up on deck and found gunner's mate Henry Gardner, an Englishman, and informed him the ship was sinking. They believed Jones was dead.

Gardner, believing he was the highest ranking officer, went to the main-mast to pull down the American flag and started yelling for "quarter." When Jones heard this he pulled his pistol from his belt and tried to shoot Gardner, but the pistol had already been discharged, so he threw it. When Captain Pearson heard the request for quarter he asked, "Have you struck? Do you call for Quarter?" According to Lieutenant Richard Dale, Jones said the words that have since become immortal, "I have not yet begun to fight."

The fighting on the ships continued hand to hand. The *Alliance* returned and fired another round at the two ships.

About 10:15 p.m., William Hamilton, a Scotsman, who was the rigging master of the *Bonhomme Richard*, was able to work his way over to the rigging of the *Serapis* with a basket of grenades, which he lit and tossed toward a half-open hatch. He succeeded on the third try and the grenade went through the open hatch.

At first, there was one explosion, then a series of explosions as powder cartridges for the cannons exploded. This set a flash fire racing belowdecks of the *Serapis*. Pearson climbed up to the quarterdeck and called, "Sir, I have struck! I ask for quarter!"

When American pennants were flying from both ships, the other vessels came up. It must have been a very tense exchange as Jones was convinced that Landais had fired on him intentionally.[16]

The *Bonhomme Richard* could not be saved and sank. John Paul Jones brought the *Serapis*, now flying a Continental Navy pennant, to the Dutch island of Texel. Jones sent a report of his voyage and battle with the *Serapis* to Benjamin Franklin. He made sure that Franklin knew that Landais had disobeyed a signal and fired grapeshot at his ship. Franklin wrote to Landais and ordered him to resign the command of the *Alliance* and come to Paris.

A British caricature of John Paul Jones. (*William L. Clements Library*)

Pierre Landais, at Texel, challenged Captain Denis de Cottineau de Kerloguen of the *Pallas* to a duel. The captain was a witness against Landais, which gave rise to the duel. Landais was an expert swordsman. He and de Cottineau met with small swords. DeCottineau was badly wounded. Landais, bolstered by his escapade against de Cottineau, wanted to duel Jones. Jones dispatched men to arrest Landais but he got wind of it and left before they could arrive.[17]

On Saturday morning June 10, 1780, Benjamin Franklin received a letter signed by 125 sailors from the *Alliance*. The letter read, "They would not raise the anchor, nor depart from L'Orient, till they had six months wages paid them and the utmost farthing of their prize money, including the ships sent into Norway." Franklin was absolutely convinced that Captain Landais was behind the demands. The cover letter was in Landais's handwriting and the statement in the letter that they wanted "their legal captain P. Landais" was underlined and the word Landais was in his handwriting.

Franklin told Jones that he believed that Landais instigated the mutiny "probably by making them believe that satisfaction has been received for those Norway Prizes delivered up to the English, which God knows is not true; the Court of Denmark not having yet resolved to give us a shilling on that account." Franklin, accompanied by Le Ray de Chaumont, went to Versailles, showed Landais's incriminating letter to the authorities and asked for the assistance of the French. An order was immediately granted "for apprehending and imprisoning him" and sent to the commissary of the port.

Landais was in very serious trouble as the French considered he had emi-grated without the king's permission. Therefore, he would still be subject to French laws for inciting the mutiny.[18]

Samuel Wharton, a Philadelphia merchant, told Franklin that he believed that Arthur Lee was the real orchestrator of the affair.[19] By the 17th, Franklin was convinced that the latest mutiny on board the *Alliance* "has been advised or promoted by the Honorable Arthur Lee." Franklin had previously instruct-ed John Paul Jones to transport Arthur Lee as a passenger to the United States but, under the circumstances, he now revoked that order.[20]

John Paul Jones had been detained at Versailles for forty hours before he could finish his business there. During this time, Edmé Jaques Genet, chief of the Bureau of Interpreters of the Ministry of Foreign Affairs, with whose family Jones became friendly in 1780 informed him that orders had been sent to the king's officers at L'Orient concerning Captain Landais and the *Alliance*. Jones arrived at L'Orient on the morning of the 20th, some fifty-four hours after leaving Versailles. The express carrying the government's orders still had not arrived.

The *Alliance*, the night before, had been towed from the L'Orient to Port Louis on the coast. Vice Admiral Antoine Jean Marie, Comte de Thévenard, the commandant of the port of L'Orient, had made preparations to stop the *Alliance*. "He had even sent his orders in the evening before I was aware to fire on the *Alliance* and sink her to the bottom if they attempted to approach and pass the barrier that had been made across the entrance of the port. Had I even remained silent an hour longer the dreadful work would have been done." Jones told Ben Franklin that he could not let the ship be sunk. He said that it "would have rendered me miserable for the rest of my life."

On the 20th, Jones sent a letter to Captain Matthew Parke of the Marines on the *Alliance*. He wrote him that government had given orders to stop the *Alliance* rather than let her depart with Captain Landais. He told him that Captain Landais was actually under arrest by an order signed by the French king.[21] Jones enclosed Benjamin Franklin's letter of the 16th to Captain Landais, the officers and sailors of the *Alliance,* and an extract of "the agree-able part" of your letter to Jones of the 12th, respecting money matters. Jones added a postscript desiring an answer in person or in writing and assuring them that if they returned to their duty, he would do all in his power to get them a pardon for their actions.

The *Alliance* was towed on the morning of the 21st through the rocks and was anchored in the waters between Port Louis and the island of Groix. At noon, Jones sent Lieutenant Dale with a letter to Captain Landais. Comte de Thévenard sent on board the *Alliance* the deputy of Jean Daniel Schweighauser, a Swiss-Alsatian merchant and United States commercial agent, with letters under his own cover to Captain Landais and to the officers and men of the *Alliance*. One of the letters was delivered to Captain Landais and the other to the Lieutenant James Degge.

Comte de Thévenard also sent on board an officer with the king's order to arrest Captain Landais, who refused to surrender himself. Jones wrote to Franklin that "Mr. Lee and his party pretend to justify their measures because they say you did not put Captain Landais under arrest. According to them, you can not displace him however great in crimes! If this government does not interfere to crush that despicable party, France and America have got much to fear from it. I verily believe them to be *English* at the bottom of their hearts."[22]

On the 23rd, Comte de Thévenard sent a new requisition to Captain Landais for the seamen on board the *Alliance* who had served with him on the *Bonhomme Richard*. Jones believed that money would persuade the sailors of the *Alliance* to do what was asked.[23]

On the issue of the mutineers claim for prize money, Franklin informed Landais that the first two ships they captured were Swedish and the owners were demanding money on the basis of an illegal capture. The third was an Irish vessel, which traveled under a passport, and was also considered an illegal capture. The three prizes Landais "sent into Norway have been delivered up to the English by the Danish Government, and not a farthing received on their account, or even promised." At the time of the American Revolution, Denmark and Norway were a joint kingdom ruled from Copenhagen. The *Alliance* was not going to be receiving any prize money.

Franklin also let Landais know that he was aware of his role in the demands sent from the sailors. He placed the blame for promoting the mutiny squarely on Landais.[24]

Jean Daniel Schweighauser had gotten a request for supplies for the *Alliance* from Captain Landais and contacted Franklin about what he should do. Franklin advised him to give the provisions to the ship as it might be needed by the innocent people on the vessel.[25]

On the 27th, Franklin sent orders to Landais to take on board as many muskets and as much gunpowder "as you can conveniently stow." The supplies would be delivered to him by order of the Prince de Montbarey, minister of war. These goods were to be delivered to the Board of Admiralty at Philadelphia.[26]

On July 7, 1780, Captain Pierre Landais sailed the *Alliance* out of port with Arthur Lee as a passenger but without the clothing that was so desperately needed by the American army.[27]

Jones was most probably happy to be rid of the madman and the disgruntled crew. Franklin was worried that the crew was so infected with the spirit of discontent that it would mutiny on the high seas and take the vessel and her cargo to England.[28]

The *Alliance* was off the Grand Banks when the crew became unruly. They refused to take the vessel to Philadelphia, fearing they would be captured. They wanted to go to Boston. Landais refused to leave his cabin and confront the crew. Lieutenant James Degge assumed command on August 10.[29]

The frigate was taken to Boston, arriving on August 16, 1780. On September 5, the Board of Admiralty ordered the commissioners of the Navy Board of the Eastern Department to hold a court of enquiry into the conduct of Captain Landais from the time the *Alliance* left the port of L'Orient until its arrival in Massachusetts Bay when Lieutenant Degge took command. The board also wanted the court to determine the ringleaders of the mutiny. Those crew members were to be confined. Captain Landais was to be suspended from command of the *Alliance*.

The board gave the command of the *Alliance* to thirty-five-year-old Irish native Captain John Barry and appointed Hoysted Hacker to be the first lieutenant.[30] Barry was courageous and resourceful. He had been the captain of a 1774 Philadelphia-built ship called the *Black Prince*. The 440-ton merchantman was sold to Congress and renamed the *Alfred*. Lieutenant John Paul Jones, serving under Captain John Barry, was the first to hoist the American (Grand Union) flag on the *Alfred*.[31] Captain John Barry presided over the court martial of both Degge and Landais. Because John Paul Jones was unavailable for the court martial, his charges against Landais were not considered.

On January 6, 1781, Captain Landais was sentenced to be broke and rendered incapable of serving in the American Navy for the future. Degge was cashiered. Lee later would state that Captain Landais was insane.[32]

In 1781 the *Alliance* would once
again see a mutiny on her decks. On
March 29, after spending twenty days in
a French port, she left with a cargo of
military items on a return voyage to the
United States in the company of a vessel
named *Marquis de Lafayette*.

Shortly after sailing, an Indian who
worked in the forecastle informed
Captain John Barry that there was a plot
to seize the frigate. Over the course of
the day, he gave the names of three men
who tried to get him to join the mutiny.
The ship's log recorded that on "Sunday
March 31, 1781 at 5 p.m. put in irons for
mutiny. At 11 found out a number more
that was concerned in the mutiny." John
Kessler, mate of the frigate, wrote that

Captain John Barry from an original
painting by Chappel. (*William L.
Clements Library*)

three men were put in irons.[33] That night all the officers and a few trusted
members of the crew were armed and placed on duty on the deck.

The next morning, a general assembly was called. The officers and the
trusted crew who were armed took up positions on the main deck, quarterdeck, and steerage. The rest of the crew were assembled on the booms forecastle and gangways. The three men who had been placed in irons were
brought on the quarterdeck, stripped, and hoisted by their thumbs to the
mizzen stay. They received a very severe whipping and gave up the names of
their accomplices in this planned mutiny. As each man's name was given up,
they were summoned to the quarterdeck. They, in turn, were stripped, tied to
the ridge-rope of the netting, and whipped. This scene, continued over and
over again until a total of twenty-eight men had been strung up and whipped,
ended only when Captain Barry was convinced no more names were forthcoming. The ship's log lists the names of some of those who were punished:
John Chalford(?), Walter Crooker, John Downey, George Green, Hugh
Mallady, John Mc Daniel, William McElhanney, James Martin, P. Shelden,
Thomas Stokes, and William Vanderpole.[34]

The mutineers had originally intended to take over the *Alliance* on her
voyage to France by killing all the officers in the middle night's watch except

Lieutenant P. Fletcher whom they wanted to sail the vessel to Ireland. The mutineers had planned to have a quartermaster take command. Since the opportunity did not present itself on the voyage to France, they planned to do it shortly after departing France. When the *Alliance* departed L'Orient, one of the ringleaders fell overboard. This being a bad omen for their enterprise, the mutineers had scuttled their plans.

Captain Barry held the three ringleaders securely in irons. Captain Barry's assistant cabin steward had each of the other twenty-five mutineers take an oath on a Bible and pledge their good behavior. They were then allowed to return to their positions. The three ringleaders were tried, found guilty, and sentenced to death. However, the sentence was never carried out.[35]

The *Alliance*, while on a cruise under the command of John Barry, had taken the snow *Commerce* as a prize. While operating as a prize ship, a mutiny was contemplated and possibly attempted. Sailors Robert Cane, Francis Courtreal, Denis Dohorty, and Manuel Jack from the *Alliance* had approached Matthew W. Aron, William Tees, and a third person whose name is not legible on an October 3, 1782 document with the idea of taking control of the *Commerce*. Their plan was, once in control of the vessel, they would sail her to Ireland.[36]

JOHN PAUL JONES CAPTAIN OF THE *Bonhomme Richard* had some mutinies on his watch. The *Bonhomme Richard* was built in 1766 under the name *Duc de Duras* for La Compagnie des Indes, France's version of England's East India Company. The merchantman was purchased by Louis XVI from a Monsieur Berard early in 1779. She was placed at the disposal of Captain John Paul Jones by France's minister of marine, Monsieur Gabriel de Sartine, for operations against the British.

In the summer of 1779, on the *Bonhomme Richard*, the British sailors in the crew had plotted a mutiny. Their plan was to seize the ship and carry Jones as a prisoner to England. Jones confined seventeen sailors for the mutiny. The seventeen imprisoned sailors petitioned Captain Jones saying they regretted their behavior and requesting a return to duty.[37] Upon reaching port, Jones replaced the mutineers with American sailors who had recently been released from British prisons and sailors recruited from Portugal.[38]

While Jones was in command of the *Ariel,* a sloop of war, he again experienced a mutiny. The *Ariel,* which carried twenty-six 9-pounders, had been launched on July 7, 1777, by the Perry Shipyard in the Blackwall district of London. While commanded by Captain Thomas MacKenzie, *Ariel* had headed west across the Atlantic for duty along the American coast. While cruising off the coast of South Carolina, she was forced to surrender to the French frigate *Amazone* on September 10, 1779. *Ariel* was brought back to France and put at the dispossal of Benjamin Franklin. After Captain Pierre Landais seized command of the *Alliance* and took her back to America, Franklin gave Jones the command of the *Ariel*.

After the *Ariel* left France and was bound for Philadelphia, a plot by the British sailors was discovered. From that point, a constant guard with fixed bayonets was maintained. Every officer and passenger was constantly under arms and a watch was maintained. Twenty of the mutineers were placed in irons until the *Ariel*'s arrival in Philadelphia on February 18, 1781. When John Paul Jones stepped ashore at Philadelphia, he had been away three years, three months, and eighteen days.[39]

-19

The King's Problems

BRITISH AND HESSIAN MUTINIES ON LAND AND SEA

*M*utiny was not just an American problem. His Majesty's troops also had their periods of discontent on land and sea.

At a cabinet meeting, held on June 21, 1775, at Lord North's house, the decision was made to send the Highlanders to America.[1] When word got out that the British government was going to raise Highland regiments, Lord Barrington, secretary of war, was swamped with requests for approval to raise the needed regiments. He passed these petitions to his clerks. People were eager to secure a field rank for themselves and positions as lieutenants and captains for their sons.

The Scottish Highland regiments were the biggest source of mutinies in the British Army. Seven of the twelve Highland regiments would mutiny at some time during the American Revolutionary War. There were critics of how the British administered the Scottish regiments. As John Clark exclaimed in 1780, the English Army's *Arts of War* was never translated into Gaelic, the language of the Scottish Highland regiments. He also pointed out that the Mutiny Act was read to the Highland regiments every two months with the utmost punctuality and exactness in English, which they did not speak.[2] It was unreasonable to expect people to comply with the rules when they did not know what they were.

There were no Scottish mutinies until 1778, but only three Highland regiments served early in the war. The 42nd Regiment was the only unit left from the Seven Years War, or as it was called in North America, the French and Indian War.

In October 1775, the British government started to raise the 71st Highland Regiment under Simon Fraser of Lovat. It was the first regiment raised in fourteen years. The men of the 71st regiment, known as Fraser's Highlanders, were supplied with firelocks, swords, cartridge boxes, and shot pouches.[3] The 73rd Regiment, known as Lord MacLeod's Highlanders, was raised in 1777. A total of eight regiments would be raised in 1778. Some were marching units designed for foreign service; fencible units were designed for local defense in resisting invasions and keeping the peace.

Lieutenant General Sir James Adolphus Oughton was made the commander in charge of North Britain in June 1778. He was fifty-eight years old, fat, and had a double chin. He had lived and served in the military in Scotland. The officers under him had a practice of hurling obscenities at the men when giving orders; this practice was resented by the Scottish Highlanders, who considered it improper. The officers also used flogging and the black hole for punishments.

Among the Scottish Highland regiments a rumor circulated that a corps was being sold for the use of the East Indian Company in India. When the 76th, 77th, 78th, and 81st Highland Regiments of Foot were ordered aboard ships, they refused to go, thinking the rumor was true.

Lord Seaforth had been busy raising his corps, the 78th Regiment, or Seaforth's Highlanders. General Oughton sent orders in March 1778 that five hundred of the 78th Regiment be ready to sail for America in two weeks. There were problems in meeting this order as men were still coming into camp. Those soldiers that were in camp were not fully equipped and had not received either their bounty money or pay. When their condition became known, the order was cancelled.

As the season passed, compliments on the corps' drilling and appearance were reported. In the reports nothing was addressed about the men's morale.

In August the men were at Edinburgh Castle when an order for the 78th Regiment to be embarked arrived. However, the destination was different. They were now being sent to the Channel Islands to replace Lord MacLeod's 73rd Highland Regiment, which was being sent to the East Indies. It immediately raised the fear of betrayal.

The 73rd Regiment had joined the army for three years or the duration of the war and was expecting to go to North America. Many had hoped to be able to gets lands in America after the war and stay there. Since the 73rd was being sent to the East Indies, the men worried that they would be the next to go to India. The locals from the town of Edinburgh began taunting the soldiers, saying they had been sold to the East India Company. The men feared that they would be mistreated in India or never be allowed to return.

Down at Leith, their place of embarkation, were six black transports, the hospital ship, *The Brothers,* and the warship *Jason.* General Oughton sent orders on September 21. An enemy ship had been sighted off the coast and the *Jason* was sent to check it out, causing a slight delay.

On Tuesday morning, the 22nd, the drummer beat "assembly" for the men to gather on parade. While assembled, one hundred soldiers of the Macrae Company broke ranks. As they ran, they were shaking their fists and waving their muskets. They were also yelling that they would not be sold and demanded their pay. Three hundred more men joined the Macraes. The mutineers fixed bayonets and swarmed around Lord Seaforth. Some officers quickly came to his rescue.

Shoving and fighting ensued between the officers and mutineers. Many of the officers suffered bruises and torn coats. Suddenly, two pikes were raised from which hung pieces of dark green plaid cloth, which was their standard for the revolt. The four hundred mutineers assembled in columns behind the pikes and began marching off.

Five hundred soldiers remained. Seaforth wondered if they would obey orders, now and when confronted by their fellow soldiers. Seaforth gave the command to march and they did. As the mutineers marched, a mob of townfolk assembled behind them. They also brought food and drink to the soldiers. Seaforth caught up with the mutineers. The crowd parted and allowed Lord Seaforth to get to the mutineers. He tried to address them but was shouted down by the Macraes. Seaforth stumbled or was pushed and fell to his knees. He was then hit in the back with a musket. The officers again came to his rescue. A melee began and many men were injured. Muskets were fired and the smell of sulfur was thick in the air. Rocks were thrown by the mob of townfolk.

Suddenly, the mutineers moved off. They went to Cannongate Tollbooth, the local jail, and freed some of their fellow soldiers. A determined Seaforth caught up with the mutineers again and promised them that they were just going to Guernsey and nowhere else. The mutineers told him that they did not think he could be believed.

A crowd had gathered across Constitution Road from the dunes. The mutineers fired a volley over the heads of the civilians. They then marched to

Arthur's Seat, about a mile east of Edinburgh castle, 823 feet above sea level.[4] Two hundred more soldiers of the 78th Regiment joined the mutineers.

Throughout the night, other military units were brought into Edinburgh. The soldiers elected officers, and on Wednesday, Lieutenant General Sir James Adolphus Oughton opened a parley with the mutineers. Major General Robert Skene would head the committee, which included Lord Seaforth, the Duke of Buccleuch, Earl of Dunmore (the former royal governor of Virginia), and Lord Macdonald. They would be accompanied by a Gaelic interpreter.

The mutineers gave a list of the demands that must be met before they would return to service: free pardon, the money that was owed to them, not to be sold, and punishment for the officers who abused them. The committee returned with some ministers who tried to talk the men into returning.

Late Wednesday night, Lieutenant General Oughton agreed to all the mutineers' terms. It would be recorded as a compromise but was really a total surrender. The mutineers were told of the agreement.

Lord Dunmore brought down six hundred soldiers off of Arthur's Seat. They were assembled into a hollow square and were told by General Skene that a court of inquiry would sit on Saturday to hear their complaints against the officers. The court was held and no complaints were made. [5]

When the mutiny was over, forty soldiers were missing. The 78th Regiment spent two and a half years on the Channel Island before it was sent to India.

News of the 78th Regiment mutiny certainly raised concerns among the local citizens. On October 7, 1778, a letter was written to the Earl of Loudon from Newnham indicating his hope that "the mutiny amongst the Highlanders is over."[6]

THERE WOULD BE NO MORE CRISES UNTIL the following spring. It was a busy time of recruiting and provisioning the troops. Because of all the activity, Lieutenant David Barclay, quartermaster at Edinburgh, was having a hard time negotiating contracts with and getting deliveries from the local merchants.

The 76th Regiment of Foot, raised during 1778, was composed of 750 Highlanders and the rest Irish and lowlanders. They were originally scheduled to embark for America in April. When Lord Macdonald asked for more time to get the men ready his request was denied.

The men had been told that they were needed in America right away, but they had spent the last ten months at Fort George. During this time, many of the officers went home on furlough, which was denied to the rank and file. The men resented this special treatment the officers received. In January 1779, General Oughton recalled all the officers who were on furlough and was annoyed by the slow return of officers to duty.

Baron Jeffery Amherst, commander in chief of the British army, instructed Oughton that the 76th, 80th (Royal Edinburgh Volunteers), and 82nd (Francis Macleon's Highlanders) Regiments were to be sent to America in March. Oughton pointed out that this would leave only the 83rd Glasgow Volunteers as a regular force in Scotland to keep the peace.

The 76th Regiment left their quarters at Fort George and marched south through Perth toward the port of Leith. Their commander, Major Alexander Donaldson, was ill and not with them. They had picked up Lord Macdonald on the way and had progressed as far as Burntisland. Lord Macdonald had gone on ahead to Leith. A rumor got started that they were to be sold into the use of the East India Company. The men protested and presented petitions to their officers. The officers decided not to disturb Major Donaldson with the news, as he was confined to bed.

The officers did not give any assurances to the men. At morning parade, the regiment turned out and marched to the top of the Binn. The Binn was a wooded area of mostly elm trees on steep ground 632 feet high on the edge of Burntisland.[7] It was on the opposite side of the Firth of Forth from Edinburgh.[8]

The officers tried both pleas and threats to regain control but they were ignored. The men maintained discipline and set up camp with sentries. They refused to embark for Leith. Armed parties visited the town for supplies and paid cash for all that they took.

Ignoring the doctor's orders, Major Donaldson went with Lieutenant David Barclay to see the mutineers. He gave them his word that they had not been sold. The men believed him. But there was still the problem of the money they were owed for their back pay. He sent word for Lord Macdonald to return. Lord Macdonald climbed the Binn to listen to the men's petitions. To put an end to the mutiny, he paid the monies due and assured them that they were not going to the East Indies.

The three-day mutiny was over. The mutineers broke camp the following morning and marched back down to Burntisland, where they embarked on boats to Leith. No official report was ever made of this mutiny.[9]

THE ARGYLL (WESTERN) FENCIBLES WERE ALSO HAVING supply problems. They were the seventh Highland regiment raised in 1778. Quartermasters were having a very difficult time getting all the units supplied. Contractors were late with deliveries and charging more, as the demand had increased.

In September 1779, the Argyll Fencibles were stationed at Edinburgh. The men were complaining about the quality of the equipment. They were given cartridge boxes discarded by the Glasgow Volunteers. The men considered it an affront to their self-respect. When the boxes were replaced, the new ones presented problems. They were made of the same material but were larger. The wide belt upon which they hung made it uncomfortable to wear beneath their flowing plaid. Some of the men even thought that they would be wearing a powder horn and shot bag. They thought that they had been tricked. The men also hated their goat skin sporran. It was a replacement for the deerskin sporran they wore back home. The final straw was that the cost for all the gear was subtracted from their pay at what they thought were exorbitant rates.

The men refused to wear their sporran and cartridge boxes. At six-thirty one evening, the soldiers in the barracks threw open their windows and with loud yelling, threw out their cartridge boxes and belts.[10] At parade the next morning, the officers and men acted like the cartridge boxes and belts were not there. On the first command, the men tore off their sporran and threw them on the ground. The officers were surrounded by the men yelling and complaining about the equipment. Their complaints were written down and they were promised action. Three days went by and nothing happened.

On October 3, 1779, Lord Frederick was in Glasgow when he received word of the mutiny and came to Edinburgh. The next morning on parade, he witnessed the refusal of the men to wear their cartridge boxes thought they obeyed all other commands.

On Friday morning, the 8th, the men were paraded to Leith for field exercises. They were ordered to ground their firelocks, which they did. Six troops of the ten dragoons came up on the rear and flanks of the Fencibles. They were then ordered to come and pick up their cartridge boxes. There was no movement.

The six men who were suspected of being the ringleaders were given a field court martial. Two were found innocent and four, guilty. The guilty soldiers were flogged. The men went and picked up their gear as they left the field.[11]

The plan was to disperse the men throughout the country. The men in the castle were actually in possession of the largest military magazine in Scotland. Sergeant MacDougal was sent to Edinburgh to collect the baggage of the two most mutinous companies. At the barracks, he told John MacNeil and several others about the floggings. Upon hearing the news, they ran outside yelling that they had been betrayed. MacDougal then ran into John Brown who started giving him a hard time about getting his bags packed and out to the wagon. Lieutenant Gilfillan heard the noise and came into the yard, and MacDougal went to him to get help. Brown raced between them and swore in Gaelic. MacDougal left the yard and Gilfillan and Brown went back inside to their respective buildings. Brown then grabbed a sword and started ordering that the gate be raised. MacDougal tried to stop the gate from being raised but was pulled away. Men high up in the castle started yelling and other soldiers were waving their weapons.

After less than an hour, Major Medford arrived and asked to be let into the castle. He was popular with the men. He rode a little ways into the castle and was given a report by Lieutenant Dugall Campbell, officer of the guard. Brown was shouting to close the bridge. Major Medford got out before the gate closed. As Medford rode to Leith to fetch the dragoons, he passed Sergeant Major Duncan Livingston and asked him to try and get back in the castle. Livingston went to the castle and pleaded with the men. Brown said no one gets in until the soldiers return from Leith. Livingston gave them an ultimatum: if they didn't instantly surrender they would be put to the sword when the dragoons arrived.

Three troops of the 10th Dragoons arrived, dismounted, and approached the castle. It was an impossible siege, with dismounted troops attacking one of the strongest fortifications in England. Some of the Highlanders had had enough and lowered the drawbridge. The dragoons pursued the Highlanders into the hospital. John Brown, John MacLeod, and three others were arrested as ringleaders. Brown and MacLeod were placed in the black hole.

On November 8, a court martial was held in the great hall of the castle. Brown and MacLeod were both found guilty. Brown was to be shot to death and MacLeod was given a sentence of one thousand lashes on his bare back with a cat-o'-nine-tails by the drummers of the regiment.[12] This was the equivalent of a death sentence.

GENERAL JAMES OUGHTON WAS HAVING A HARD time raising men for the troops. In the last week of March 1779, Oughton received orders that the 83rd Regiment (Glasgow Volunteers) were to be sent to the Channel Islands. The 82nd Regiment, known as the Hamilton Regiment had been assembled in Scotland in 1778.

When the thirteen American colonies declared their independence from Great Britain, the Eighth Duke of Hamilton was appointed to form a regiment to reinforce its troops in North America. Potential recruits from the Lanarkshire district were plied with guineas and bottles of port to join the regiment. Additional men were needed to complete these regiments. Oughton told Amherst that the only way to fill these units was to take men from the 31st Regiment of Foot, which had been recruited in the Edinburgh suburbs and the Highland regiments. But to do so would create problems. The Highlanders had a fierce attachment to their dress and language, and they would not be allowed them in these regiments.

On April 16, General Oughton gave the order for the 42nd and 71st Regiments at Stirling Castle to march on April 19 to Leith and remain there for further orders. The order gave no clue as to what was happening. Five companies with baggage wagons left the castle on Monday morning under the command of Captain James Innes. They traveled twenty miles to Linlithgow where they spent the night.

Captain Ninian Imrie of General Skene's staff delivered new orders that he was to draft fifty men from the four companies of the 71st Regiment and fourteen from the 42nd Regiment to be incorporated into the 83rd Regiment (Royal Volunteers).

The following morning, Captain James Innes gave Lieutenant Thomas Stelfox the names of the sixty-four men. Several months earlier, Captain James Innes had sent thirty men of the 71st to Kent where they were told they were going to be transferred to the 25th Regiment. Fourteen of the men mutinied and refused to accept the transfer. They claimed it was a breach of their enlistment and were returned to Stirling castle.[13] In an incredibly stupid move, Captain James Innes included some of the same men who had previously refused to join the 25th Regiment on the list of men to be drafted.

On Tuesday morning, the sixty-four men and a baggage wagon left under the command of seventeen-year veteran Lieutenant Stelfox accompanied by Captain Imrie. There were three men riding on the baggage wagon, which traveled in the rear. They were Archibald MacIver of the 42nd, who claimed to be sick but was believed to be drunk or malingering; Charles MacWilliam or MacWilliamson of the 42nd, who was definitely drunk; and Robert Budge of the 71st who was drunk, sick, or lazy.

On their arrival at Leith, the three men were left with the cart when the rest of the men continued the journey to the docks. There they met Major Malcolm Ramsay and the officers from the 83rd. Major Ramsay addressed the men and welcomed them as members of the 83rd. Captain Innes had recently arrived and advised the men in Gaelic to accept the officers of the 83rd as their own. They marched to the boat stairs.

When they were told to board, only five of the 42nd and two from the 71st moved. The men shouted in anger and raised their muskets over their head. Just then, Archibald MacIver approached with a fixed bayonet. He was followed by a very drunk Charles MacWilliam of the 42nd who was shouting. Robert Budge of the 71st was trying to catch up to the other two while putting his bayonet on his musket as he went. They were encouraging their fellow soldiers not to go on board the boats. They said they would not go into long clothes nor serve under someone who did not speak Gaelic. The mutineers were now all fixing their bayonets. With all the noise, a crowd of onlookers started to form.

Innes took off for General Oughton to inform him of the situation. Oughton sent him back to get his men under control. Oughton also sent Captain Imrie to Edinburgh to ask the Duke of Buccleuch to send two hundred armed men of the South Fencible Regiment under the command of a field officer. They were to come to Leith, seize the mutineers, and march them to the castle. They proceeded under the command of Major Sir James Johnstone.

When they arrived, they found that the mutineers, who had their backs to the buildings, and the South Fencibles, who had their backs to the water, were twelve yards apart. Innes pleaded with the mutineers to stop but they shouted him down. Innes retreated. Johnstone gave the order to the South Fencibles to prime and load. The crowd went quiet. Then the order to make ready was given. Major Johnstone then, with a Gaelic interpreter, advised the mutineers that he had orders to either put them on the boat or take them as prisoners to Edinburgh Castle. Johnstone turned and went back to his line. A shot was fired and then another followed by a volley. No order was given but a random fire commenced. The two lines advanced on each other in hand-to-hand combat. At the first shot, the crowd fled.

Buccleuch's men were shouting, "Recover" and hitting the men to get them to break off the fight. The Highlanders threw down their weapons. Of the fifty-seven mutineers who took a stand, nine were dead and twenty-two were wounded. There were also five dead and six wounded from the South Fencibles.

The following May, Robert Budge, Archibald MacIver, and Charles MacWilliam were put on trial for mutiny and instigating a mutiny. They were found guilty and sentenced to be shot.

After parading before the firing squad and standing beside the empty coffins, they were given a reprieve by the king.[14] The following refrain from a period song sums up their feelings to the lowlanders:

> I'll go to camp with my Highland Laddie.
>
> Speak not to me of your Lowland lads.[15]

THE DUKE OF ATHOLL WAS GIVEN THE AUTHORITY to raise a regiment of one thousand men at Perth, Scotland. The men were enlisted for three years or the duration of the war. In June 1778, they left for service in Ireland under Colonel James Murray.

The 77th Regiment or Atholl Highlanders had been doing service in Ireland. In 1783, they were transported to England. They expected to be sent home as peace was being concluded. To their surprise, they were informed they were being sent to India. The men believed this was a breach of the conditions under which they had enlisted. Lord Gordon sent a letter to Lord Shelburne, the king's first minister, about the problem but sent the 77th Regiment out of England.

The men were marched to Portsmouth. Major General Francis Smith was the deputy commander of the Portsmouth area acting during Lord George Lennox's absence. When he was asked if the men should be sent to India, he replied very quickly that the war was not over.

The locals were telling the soldiers their officers were not going with them. Colonel Lord George Gordon was sent a letter threatening him with death if he came in front of the men. They said they were not to be sold by him or General James Murray. The men expected to be offered terms for reenlistment and a bounty. They found that the embarkation orders did not include any bounty money. They believed the officers had tampered with their deal.

While they waited at Portsmouth in the center of the southern coast of England, confusion and suspicion were rampant. The officers were booed, their authority despised, and mutinous ballads were composed and circulated among the troops. One such ballad was:

> To the East Indies we were sold
>
> By Murray for a bag of gold
>
> But, hold! for we will a tale unfold
>
> And it will rust his glory.

On Monday morning, some of the Atholl Highlanders released three of their men who were being held in a black hole. On being advised of this, the officers raced into the street and found two hundred men carrying the recently freed prisoners on their shoulders. A group of officers went into the crowd of soldiers and took custody of the prisoners. Someone, a soldier or a civilian in the crowd that had gathered, threw bricks at the officers. There was lots of shouting and verbal abuse but no fighting. The soldiers disbursed noisily. It was thought best to delay the embarkation after this episode.

The men were called to assemble by means of the playing of the troop. They assembled in the ranks but there were lots of comments and murmuring among the men. Sheelagreen, who addressed the men, and reprimanded them and told them to be quiet. John Robertson, who stepped forward from the ranks shouting, "By God, I'll shoot you," fired at Sheelagreen. His musket misfired but the incident precipitated an attack on all the officers present.

The officers were pursued through the streets of Portsmouth. Some of them were clubbed and knocked to the ground. Sheelagreen managed to reach the main guard room, closely pursued by the mutineers. The door would have been broken down by the soldiers, but a message was conveyed to them that Sheelagreen was already dying. This was a lie but was enough to send the mutineers away.

James Murray of Strowan wrote in his report of the affair, "The soldiers now grew perfectly outrageous, searching every public house for their officers, to put them to death, and parading by hundreds in the streets, beating to arms and carrying the Colonel's bonnet upon a bayonet as a trophy of their victory."[16]

On Tuesday morning, some junior officers came into town and met with the mutineers. They were told they would parade and accept orders, but they would not embark.

The Atholl Highlanders paraded each day and accepted all orders given to them by their officers. Even those who had been attacked on Monday were now treated with proper deference. But there was no yielding on the cause of the mutiny. The men made it quite plain that they believed that the terms of enlistment now entitled them to be discharged from service. The men thought once they landed in India they were to be treated as slaves, sold to Indian chiefs and tortured. When some of the men had returned to Deeside, they exaggerated the stories to vindicate their actions.

When the men were informed that two or three regiments were on their way to force them to embark, they took their weapons and went to engage the regiments coming to them. When they found out the report was false, they returned to their quarters. The order for embarkation was countermanded, which satisfied the men. The regiment was marched to Berwick where it was disbanded in 1783.[17]

THE ABERDEENSHIRE HIGHLANDERS OR 81st Regiment of Foot, whose terms of engagement were the same as the Atholl Highlanders, had already embarked for India. While still in port they heard of the results of the Atholl Highlanders mutiny and demanded to be put ashore. The captain did as they wished, as he did not want a battle on board his ship. They marched to the barracks and then to Scotland where they disbanded. None of the men involved in the mutiny were ever brought to trial.[18]

THE MEN OF THE 68TH REGIMENT, a British corps known as the Durham Regiment of Foot, were already on board vessels bound for the West Indies. They loaded their muskets and demanded that the ships be taken back to the harbor. A frigate captain fired across the bow of the ships and stopped all but one vessel, which landed the men at South Beach. Lord George Lennox had arrived from London and took command of a squadron of dragoons. By nightfall, they had rounded up all the men of the 68th on shore and held them prisoner at Hilsea Barracks.[19]

JUST LIKE SOLDIERS IN THE ARMY, SAILORS in the British Navy were complaining about the lack of pay. When the arrears got too large, the anger erupted in a mutiny.

In April 1779, the seventy-four-gun *Invincible* experienced a mutiny at Portsmouth. She had been ordered to duty in the West Indies and her crew had not been paid in six months. When Captain Charles Saxton ordered the men to weigh anchor and get under way, the crew refused. The crew was well behaved. Possibly the presence of the seventy-four-gun *Alexander* alongside the *Invincible* had an influence on the men's behavior. However, no threats or promises could induce them to get under way. The ships did not leave port until November. A court martial convicted four of the sailors, with two receiving five hundred lashes.[20]

Another mutiny over pay occurred on the HMS *Egmont* on September 29, 1779. The captain, John Carter Allen, of the vessel had gone ashore, but without approving their pay.[21] They refused an order to muster and stayed belowdecks chanting "Pay . . . Pay . . . Pay . . . Pay." The officer of the watch, George MacKenzie, the third lieutenant, and Henry Pullen, the fourth lieutenant pleaded with the men. MacKenzie told the men the money could not be distributed without Captain Allen's signature and promised to secure it.

Pullen went below decks with a candle to speak to the men. He asked them to be patient and they would be paid as soon as the captain returned. Their pay was only one month past due. They took their frustration out on him by knocking the candle out of his hand and, in the darkness, pelting him with chalk. The other officers on board the ship came to his aid and got him out from belowdecks. The next morning the squadron's flagship *Blenheim* sent over a troop of Royal Marines to restore order.

Seven seamen had demanded their pay. A court martial with Captain Nicolas Vincent presiding gave four of the men William Antrobus, Thomas Lambeth, Robert Nags, Andrew Thompson, a sentence of three hundred lashes each. William Antrobus was given fifty lashes reduction since he had yielded when George MacKenzie and Henry Pullen had pleaded with the mutineers. John Carr, William Cook, and John Singleton were given the death sentence. All three men submitted the following plea for their lives:

> We, the unhappy condemned objects never willing to offend, now prostrate ourselves imploring mercy, strangers to mutiny, or disaffection, always ready to obey, but now led away through error, misguided by insinuating

men, fall a victim to the martial law. Pity our misconduct and be merciful to us. Take not away our lives but spare us from the approaching and gloomy day, being young in service, that we may live to be an honor to our Sovereign and help our country.[22]

In 1781, THE ENGLISH FRIGATE *Santa Monica* was moored in English Harbor, Antigua in the Caribbean. Antigua, an island of 108 square miles, that had an abundance of sugarcane plantations. On the morning of July 16 Captain Linzee went ashore. The crew refused to follow the orders of First Lieutenant Leekey to muster and gathered forward of the main deck near the bow. Leekey sent a message to Captain Linzee who returned with Captain Stanhope of the *Pegasus*. The two captains began pleading with the men. Some of the men were complaining that they wanted a new captain or to be transferred to another ship.[23]

Linzee with a sergeant and three men tried again to quell the mutiny but were rebuked. At 4:00 p.m. Linzee consulted with Captain Stanhope of the *Pegasus*, Captain Sutherland of the *St. Eustatius* and Captain Iggleston of the *Etna*. It was agreed the marines from the Pegasus would join those of the *Santa Monica* to put down the mutiny. Upon their arrival, the crew began cursing and throwing whatever they could find at the marines. At that point, Captain Linzee gave the order to fire on the sailors. The volley across the deck killed a sailor by the name of Donovan. The rest of the mutineers quickly surrendered.[24]

The court martial was held on the *Barfleur* at St. John's on July 20–24, 1781. Evidence was entered during the court martial that Captain Linzee had a practice of issuing orders and then forgiving the men if they did not execute it. "His nervous fussing was carried to an extreme." The crew claimed Captain Linzee kicked and beat them with a speaking trumpet and a rope. During the court martial Captain Linzee never denied the charges and inquired if he had even been seen to have beaten a man "barbarously." The mutineers agreed he was not "barbarous." Captain Linzee was a worrier with feelings of irritation and failed in enforcing his threats of punishment. He claimed his crew was lazy, inexperienced and lacked alacrity and briskness. The mutineers complained about being denied meals and a proper supply of water. It was brought to light that when the situation occurred it was out of necessity and Captain Linzee suffered equally as the men. One man by the name of Hirst was tried separately as he was accused of being the chief ringleader.[25] Lord Robert Manners, on board the *Resolution* in St. John's Road, Antigua, wrote to his brother, the Duke of Rutland, "I have just returned from a court martial which has ended condemning to death sixty-four men for the mutiny on board the *Santa Monica*."[26]

In 1782, the HMS *Narcissus*, a twenty-gun ship with Captain Edward Edwards, experienced a mutiny, which resulted in six men being hanged and fourteen men being flogged. In 1783, a mutiny aboard the warship *Janus* was quelled by the personal intervention of Earl Howe.[27]

In 1780, James Robinson, commander of the continental sloop *Fly*, was dispossessed by a mutiny by the majority of the ship's crew while at sea. He, the ship's doctor and pilot were put on board a British schooner, called the *Daphne*, bound from Providence, Rhode Island to New York. They took possession of the schooner and carried her, with her cargo, to the French fleet, then off Georgia, where the said schooner *Daphne* and cargo was taken from them by the Captain of the French frigate *Chimére*.[28]

On December 1, 1775, the boatswain on the *Roebuck*, under the command of Captain Andrew Snape Hammond, was confined to quarters because of his behavior. Lieutenant John Orde charged the boatswain with disobedience of orders, contempt to his superior officers, and using mutinous expressions. On January 9, Hammond at Halifax sent a letter to Vice Admiral Samuel Graves asking him to order a court martial for the boatswain who was still being confined and suspended from duty.[29]

The British Navy impressed people to fill out the crew on some of her vessels. Impressed American sailors on board the *Union* tender almost succeeding in their attempt to mutiny and escape from the ship. John Goldsworthy, a British sailor on the ship, had conspired with the Americans. On May 3, 1777, Philip Stephens in the Admiralty Office, recommended to Vice Admiral Molyneux Shuldham that Goldsworthy be transferred to one of His Majesty's Ship at Plymouth, as he was a mutinous, seditious, and troublesome fellow.[30]

In 1779 the *Culloden* would be sailing from Halifax, Nova Scotia to England. Captain George Balfour needed men to complete his crew. His crew included a Frenchman by the name of Grennard as quarter gunner. Balfour also acquired Augustus Murphy, an American who spoke fluent French and a little Spanish, as a midshipman. Murphy had been the master of a captured American vessel that had been taken to Halifax. To get out of prison, he had volunteered for service on the *Culloden*. Using prison volunteers was a risqué act as part of the cargo was a number of prisoners of war including all the men from the American privateer *Royal Lewis* which had been captured by the *Culloden*. Murphy planned to take the ship at night, murder Captain Balfour, overpower the guard on the quarterdeck using hand spikes, get weapons with the cooperation of Grennard, and take the vessel to a French port. Murphy claimed to have the support of the French prisoners. The captain and the lieutenant of the privateer *Royal Lewis* refused to cooperate as they did not believe that his plan would work. They feared they would encounter a British man-of-war before they could sail the *Culloden* to France.

Cato, a black man, was a ship's cook. He had learned of the plot and after dinner informed Captain Balfour on the same night the men were to mutiny. Murphy was seized and brought to trial on board the *Formidable* on June 10. The court martial with Admiral Robert Digby presiding found Murphy guilty and sentenced him to death.[31]

The *Jackal* of fourteen guns was at the Downs with Lieutenant John Gibson in command.[32] Most of the officers had gone ashore. Gibson had received orders to sail on convoy duty to the Baltic. He discovered there were no nautical charts for the Baltic on board the *Jackal* and none were available in Dover. He traveled twenty miles from Dover to Ramsgate on the Isle of Thanet in East Kent to obtain a chart. The Jackal had been left in charge of a midshipman and a pilot who was staying over night on the vessel. Many members of the crew were smugglers who had been taken off the Irish coast.

On November 27, 1779, seventeen members of the crew seized the vessel in the middle of the night. The pilot who was in a cabin below decks was awakened by the noise on deck and felt that the ship was underway. When he tried to get up on deck found all three hatchways were locked shut. He shouted to the watch and was told the cutter was being taken to the channel. He quickly went back to his cabin and checked his compass. He found the ship was heading east toward the French coast. He went back to the hatchway and called to the deck saying they were lying to him. One of the mutineers pointed a pistol through the side window of the skylight and told him that he would be shot if he gave them any trouble. The other members of crew who tried to force one of the hatches but were stopped when the men on deck threatened to fire a four-pounder cannon through the hatch. The mutineers threatened to sink the ship with the crew still locked below decks. The mutineers would have been able to leave the vessel in the ship's boat.

As the ship approached the French coast, the pilot was brought above decks and told to steer the cutter into Calais. He refused claiming that he did not know the harbor. The pilot later reported that the mutineers were armed with cutlasses and pistols and used the filthiest language. The mutineers after they touched the bottom of the channel twice were able to successfully bring the Jackal into port.

She was sold at Calais, converted into a privateer, and renamed the *Boulogne*. She then sailed off the Scottish coast. The *Prudente* of thirty-six guns captured the *Boulogne* in 1781. Some of the original mutineers were serving on the vessel and were executed when they were captured. On January 28, 1780 Lieutenant John Gibson's court martial was held on the *Syren* at Sheerness. He was found to have had a valid excuse for his absence from his command. The British cutter *Active* of twelve guns was taken by mutiny in August 1779 in the English Channel.[33]

THE BRITISH NAVY HAD A MAJOR DESERTION problem during the American Revolution. Of the 175,900 men raised for the navy during the war, 42,069 deserted. When the peace treaty was being negotiated, keeping the men under control was especially difficult. They had enlisted for the war. As far as they were concerned it was now over and they wanted to be dismissed from service.

On the *Raisonnable*, Captain Lord Hervey appealed to the crew to behave themselves.[34] As it became apparent that words would not be enough, he and his officers armed themselves. They then went forward, grabbing the ringleaders and forcing the others to obey. When the *Raisonnable* arrived at Sheerness, four members of the crew were court martialed and condemned to death.[35] On August 11, the four men were sent one each to the *Carnatic*, *Dictator*, *Scipio*, and *Thetis*. The men on the first three ships were executed; the man on the *Thetis* was reprieved at the very last second.[36]

In the American Revolution, England was faced with the prospect of having to put down a rebellion that had spread through many of her colonies on the North American continent. British ranks would be spread too thin to squash the malcontents and protect her other territories around the globe. England turned to the European states for assistance.

As in the past, Europe was willing to come to England's aid—for a price. During the American Revolution, England purchased the services of German soldiers from six German states: Anhalt-Zerbst, Ansbach-Bayreuth, Brunswick, Hesse-Cassel, Hesse-Hanau, and Waldeck. Christian Friedich Karl Alexander, margrave of Brandenburg's territory of Ansbach-Bayreuth covered 140 square miles and had a population of four hundred thousand.[37] At the outbreak of the American Revolution, Alexander's principality was impoverished and he was extremely anxious to remedy the situation through the rental of his troops.

England's treaty of February 1, 1777, with Ansbach-Bayreuth initially provided for him to send two infantry regiments, one company of grenadiers, and one Jaeger company.[38] Each grenadier and Jaeger company had 100 men, and each musket company had 123 men. England was to receive the services of 1,285 men and Margrave Alexander would receive thirty crowns per head in cash and a yearly rental of 45,000 crowns.

At 7:00 a.m. on February 28, the Bayreuth Infantry Regiment of Colonel August Valentin von Voit von Salzburg left its barracks. On March 4, about a half mile before they arrived at Ansbach, they were met by the margrave and his entire entourage. They marched into the city past the royal residence and the castle where they were bivouacked. The other corps assembled at Ansbach on the 5th. On the 6th, all the baggage from both infantry regiments (von Eyb and von Voit) and the Jaeger Company, commanded by Captain Christoph von Cramon, was sent on its way.

The troops began the march from Ansbach on the 7th on what would be a fifty-mile journey to Ochsenfurt. There they would board waiting boats to continue their journey to North America. They were accompanied by the margrave and his staff for a short distance on their way out of Ansbach.[39]

On the evening of the 7th, they were bivouacked in different towns for the evening. The regiment of Colonel Friedrich Ludwig Albrecht von Eyb went to Marktbergel; the Voit Regiment, to Burgbernheim; and the Jaegers, to Ottenhofen. On the 8th, the troops marched to Uffenheim were they all spent the night. The two regiments had a total of 1,285 men.[40]

On the 9th, they reached the walled city of Ochsenfurt, which is just south of Würzburg.[41] Johann Conrad Döhla, of the 4th Company of the Bayreuth Regiment, wrote in his diary about Ochsenfurt.[42] He said it was located in a wine-growing region and was a rather large and beautiful city with drawbridges and towers. They marched through the city to get to the docks.

In the afternoon of March 9, 1777, the Ansbach Jaegers were embarked on the ships in the Main River. The rest of the troops were on board by the evening. They spent a cold night in the crowded, stinking ships at anchor. Stephen Popp wrote in his journal that the boats were so crowded that many men of both regiments had to stand all night; the night was passed in singing hymns and praying.[43] Men in such poor conditions naturally started grumbling; they thought this was how they were going to be sailing for England.

At daybreak on the 10th, some of the soldiers of the Ansbach regiment, whose boat lay near the riverbank, laid down a plank and walked over it to shore. The rest of the regiment followed their example. They then hauled the other boats to land. Within an hour's time the Eyb and Voit regiments were on shore. They forced the officers out of the ships and refused the pleas and demands from their two colonels and other officers.[44] There was so much confusion that the diarists who were present at the event differ on which unit started the mutiny. The only consensus was that it was not the Jaegers.

As there was not enough room on board the ships, they had to wait for additional vessels to be brought from Würzburg. Orders were sent for "bread, meat and other victuals" and wood to warm and feed the starving mutineers. It was thought that if the men had eaten and had something to drink, they would willingly return to the ships. The inhabitants of Ochsenfurt brought the food but unfortunately also brought a large quantity of wine as well. The plan for going back on board the ships called for the Jaegers to go first and then the Eyb Regiment. "Toward noon the troops gathered along the embankment and in their rage and drunkenness, took to their heels."[45]

First a few men began wandering away; then there was a mass migration into the nearby vineyard. The grenadiers who balked at returning to the ships were soon joined by others. Since the Jaegers were still obeying orders, they were ordered to take the high ground. Once there, they were ordered to fire over the heads of the mutineers in order to frighten them into submission. Shots rang out; the mutineers panicked and returned the fire. From the Voit regiment, one man was killed and two were wounded.[46] Others were wounded, as the intermittent firing lasted two hours. Döhla stated that some of the troops were wounded in the legs.[47]

Realizing the situation had gotten out of control, the burghers of Ochsenfurt shut the city gates and drew up their drawbridges to keep the town out of harm's way. The bishop of Würzburg sent hussars and dragoons to help quell the mutiny. By evening, the soldiers began to sober up. They were finally brought under control but some of the men had escaped. Forty men from the Bayreuth Regiment were missing.[48]

Lieutenant Heinrich Carl Philipp von Feilitzsch, who was one month short of his twenty-sixth birthday, was in command of a detachment of twenty men who were sent after some of the mutineers who had run away. They caught up with some of them at Tueckelhausen Cloister where they had taken refuge. He was ordered to stay at the Cartusian Order Cloister the rest of the day. At night, he and his men were ordered to take a position at Uffenheim "to allow the musketeers' hatred to cool off."[49]

An express had been sent to alert the margrave at Ansbach of the mutiny and desertions. Margrave Christian Friedich Karl Alexander was surprised. Alexander rode quickly through the night and arrived at Ochsenfurt early on the morning of March 11. His highness had the two regiments drawn up and he passed from man to man. He inquired into their grievances and promised forgiveness to all who would go to America. He announced that any man might then and there leave the service but he would forfeit his home, all his property, and the princely favor. No one moved. The soldiers reembarked and the troops, minus the Jaegers, left Ochsenfurt between 8:30 and 9:00 a.m.[50] Because of the animosity that now existed since the Jaegers had fired on the other men, the Jaegers sailed a few days later.[51] Margrave Alexander made the journey in the staff ship to Dortrecht to see the men off.[52]

On March 25, they stopped at Nijmegen, Netherlands, disembarked, and marched into the city.[53] In the great square of the castle, they took the oath of allegiance to King George of England and had the articles of war read to them. Their mustering officer was Colonel Charles Rainsford, the English commissary of troops.[54] Each regiment received a present of 100 ducats from the margrave and extra rations during the journey.

On March 30, the troops sailed from Dortrecht in seventeen transports, reaching Dover, England, on April 1. They put into harbor at Portsmouth on the 2nd. They left England five days later, entered New York Harbor on June 3, and were landed on Staten Island.

The margrave had arranged for another batch of soldiers to be rented to the British in the fall. They were to leave at the end of October, taking with them uniforms for his regiments. With more money coming in to fill his coffers, he, with his good friend Lady Craven, set out for Paris on October 16.[55]

On May 1, 1777, Benjamin Franklin, who was known to embellish the facts to meet his own purposes, sent a report about the mutiny from Paris to Mr. John Winthrop of Boston:

The conduct of those princes of Germany who have sold the blood of their people, has subjected them to the contempt and odium of all Europe. The Prince of Anspach [Christian Friedich Karl Alexander, Margrave of Brandenburg], whose recruits mutinied and refused to march, was obliged to disarm and fetter them and drive them to the sea side by the help of his guards; himself attending in person. In his return he was publicly hooted by mobs thro' every town he passed in Holland, with all sorts of reproachful epithets. The King of Prussia's humor of obliging those princes to pay him the same toll per head for the men they drive thro' his dominions, as used to be paid him for their cattle, because they were sold as such, is generally spoken of with approbation; as containing a just reproof of those tyrants.[56]

THERE WAS ANOTHER MUTINY OF HESSIANS at Ziegenhayn. Johann Gottfried Seume wrote of his experiences of the American Revolution. In 1781, he was an eighteen-year-old student at the University of Leipsic (modern Leipzig). He dropped out of school to go to Paris. Seume spent the third night of his journey at Bach, where he was arrested. Any stranger was subject to arrest and recruitment into military service. Seume was going to be sent by the landgrave of Cassel to America in the spring to serve in the army. He said they tore up his academic matriculation papers, as those were the only documents that proved his identity.

While at Ziegenhayn, a General von Gohr employed Seume and treated him very kindly. "Here was an indescribable lot of human beings brought together, good and bad, and others that were both by turns. My comrades were a runaway son of the Muses from Jena, a bankrupt tradesman from Vienna, a fringemaker from Hanover, a discharged secretary of the post office from Gotha, a monk from Warzburg, an upper steward from Meinungen, a Prussian sergeant of hussars, a cashiered Hessian major from the fortress itself, and others of like stamp. You can imagine that there was entertainment enough, and a mere sketch of the lives of these gentry would make amusing and instructive reading."

The prisoner-enlistees had planned a mutiny, and Seume claimed he was offered the command, which he refused on the guidance of an old Prussian sergeant. "The mutineers were to rise in the night, surprise the guard and take their weapons, cut down such as opposed them, spike the cannon, lock up the officers at headquarters, and march fifteen hundred strong across the frontier, which was only a few miles away." Seume said the plot was betrayed, the ringleaders were arrested, and he was arrested along with them.

A court martial was held and two were condemned to the gallows. The others were found guilty and sentenced to run the gauntlet anywhere from twelve to thirty-six times. Seume was one of the lucky men who were released. "The candidates for the gallows were pardoned, after suffering the fear of death under that instrument, but had to run the gantlet thirty-six times, and were sent to Cassel to be kept in irons at the mercy of the prince."

The landgrave of Cassel was interested in shipping the men out as he only got paid for the men delivered to the British. Men rotting in his jails were of no financial gain. As they marched off, some of the men who had been in the jails were released to go to America.[57]

In North America, the king's forces experienced mutinies by the militia. At Hunt's Bluff in Marlboro County, South Carolina, loyalists mutinied on July 25, 1780. A detachment of Royal militia under Colonel William Henry Mills was to escort Lord Nairne and about one hundred sick men in boats down the Pee Dee River to Georgetown. Colonel Mills, a physician, had been a delegate to the Provincial Congress in 1776 and decided to switch sides.

Hearing about the coming flotilla that would be coming down the river to the coast, James Gillespie assembled a group of men at Beding's Fields (later called Irby's Mills), which was three miles from Cheraw. They planned to intercept the fleet. As more men arrived, Major Tristram Thomas of the South Carolina Militia took command.

The South Carolina Militia took a position at Hunt's Bluff about twenty-five miles below Cheraw, between Darlington and Marlborough counties. A battery of logs were assembled and made to look like cannons. They were placed on the riverbank at a bend in the river. When the boats arrived, there seemed to be an impressive array of cannons. Thomas demanded unconditional surrender, saying that otherwise he would use his artillery. The militia immediately rose in a mutiny against Colonel Mills.[58] Lord Cornwallis stated that

> Colonel Mills who commanded the militia of the Cheraw district, though a very good man, had not complied with my instructions in forming his Corps; but had placed more faith in oaths and professions, and attended less to the former conduct of those whom he admitted. The instant that this militia found that [Major] McArthur [and the 71st Regiment of Foot]

had left his post, and were assured that [General Horatio] Gates would come there the next day, they seized their own officers, and a hundred sick, and carried them all prisoners into North Carolina; Col. Mills with difficulty made his escape to George town.[59]

ANOTHER NORTH AMERICAN MILITIA MUTINY happened in Mascouche, just north of Montreal, Canada. In March 1778, British Governor General Guy Carlton was expecting an American invasion by way of the Richelieu River, which flows north from Lake Champlain to the St. Lawrence River. Carlton called out the militia and raised a third of it from the area of Montreal and Three Rivers. Thirty-two members of the militia refused to obey the orders from their captain and were imprisoned. The mutineers claimed that the captain was a drunk and did some injustices to his company. The commander at Montreal heard of the problem and sent a detachment of troops to restore order in Mascouche. Once at Mascouche, instead of restoring order, they "plundered almost all the houses and raped several girls and women." Carlton surprisingly did not take any action against the men.[60]

In the Colony of East Florida in September 1783 the British government had plans to relocate the men of the provincial regiments to the Bahamas. A rumor circulated among the men that they would be sent to the East and West Indies without their consent. The men mutinied and demanded their discharge. They were reduced to obedience and the ringleaders were punished. The men were assured that they could go where ever they wanted without restrictions and could live under the rule of America, England, or Spain.[61]

Conclusion

At the end of the American Revolution, the new United States was a union of independent states. As we have seen, the men who enlisted in the state militias did not consider themselves part of the Continental Army; they were fighting for their individual states. Some of these militia units balked and mutinied over being commanded to leave their state. Major General Benjamin Lincoln, for instance, approved a court martial in April 1779 for this offense for a soldier in Colonel Joseph Kershaw's South Carolina Militia. Seven militia officers refused to take the federal oath claiming they were only responsible to state law.[1] The issue of state's rights including the command and control of the militia would continue long after the American Revolution, and ultimately lead the country into a civil war. That war did not decide the issue of a dual state and federal military for defense, and it would not be resolved for many more years. In 1903 Congress passed the Dick Act, which created the "organized militia" of the states as the National Guard and the remainder described as the "reserved militia" later known as the "unorganized militia". In 1916 Congress federalized the National Guard. During World War I, President Woodrow Wilson exercised the power to draft members of the National Guard into the regular army. Since 1933 all persons who have enlisted in a state National Guard unit have simultaneously enlisted in the National Guard of the United States. It ended the concept of a dual state and federal military for defense.

Other issues that led to mutinies during the American Revolution remained similarly unresolved. Control became a problem when the men believed that their enlistments had expired as in the case of the Pennsylvania Line mutiny. It resurfaced again when peace had been declared in 1783. General Nathanael Greene explained that he had, "never been in a more perplexing situation than since the declaration for a cessation of hostilities. The troops for the war have been so strongly impressed with an idea of their having a right to a discharge that it has been exceedingly difficult to hold them subject to authority." Terms of enlistment in the U.S. military have been formalized by Congress, but the period of enlistment has varied across the history of American wars.

As the army's demands on its supply system during the American Revolution expanded from one army at Boston to multiple commands at many far-flung locations, the system failed. The supply problems outpaced the ability of the people in the jobs to procure and transport the needed supplies. The first mutiny at Valley Forge happened only two days after marching into camp due to a lack of provisions. The only time the supply system met the needs of the army was under the command of General Greene. The unmet needs of the men resulted in most of the mutinies. Captain Nathaniel Pendleton described the situation to General Griffith Rutherford, "nothing will be more effectual to keep the soldiers in good humor than comfortable subsistence and clothing, and as this is all they get, they must have it, or they will mutiny."[2] Brigadier General James Varnum of Rhode Island to get his point across quoted Solomon to Washington, "Hunger will break through a stone wall." Since the American Revolution, the supply system of the military failed in other wars, such as the American Civil War, but the problems were dealt with much more quickly and efficiently so that mutinies did not occur at the scale of those during the revolution. Wartime supply was most spectacularly realized during World War II.

Another aspect of mutinies of the American Revolution is the significant role of spies and double agents in some of the mutinies, including the largest, the mutiny of the Pennsylvania Line. Spies were the means to provide British General Henry Clinton with information on the location and intentions of the Pennsylvania Line mutineers upon which he based his military actions. The spy information also helped him to decide not to take the army he had assembled on Staten Island into New Jersey. Their information correctly told him that if Crown forces entered New Jersey, the mutineers would accept the commands of General Wayne and fight against the British troops. Spies even instigated some mutinies, such as when in May 1780 British spies circulated a document in the American camp at Morristown that was partially responsible for the May 1780 mutiny of the Connecticut Line.

We should, in the end, consider General George Washington's opinion on how a mutinous situation should be handled since this forms the foundation of all subsequent American responses to mutinies. Washington was very clear in letters he sent to Generals Israel Putnam and John Sullivan. Washington

instructed General John Sullivan if a mutinous situation should occur to punish the instigators "instantly and severely." Washington believed that the officers should be attentive to the complaints of the soldiers and act with courage
and decisiveness upon the occasion that all clamor will subside and good
order and discipline will again reign.[3] When General Israel Putnam on
January 5, 1779 notified Washington that he wanted to pardon the mutineers
in General Huntington's Brigade, Washington complemented Putnam for his
efforts in quelling the mutiny. He then gave his answer to Putnam's request
for leniency by telling him what he should do in no uncertain terms. "The
conduct which a commanding officer is to observe, in cases of this kind in
general, is to use every means for discovering the authors of the mischief, to
inflict instant punishment on them, and reclaim the rest by clemency. The
impression made on the minds of the multitude by the terror of the example,
and their inability to take any resolution when deprived of their ringleaders,
are a sufficient security against farther attempts."[4] Washington went on to tell
him that in "any future mutiny . . . the severest and most summary example
must be made of the leaders, while a representation is made to the rest, in
firm and at the same time conciliatory language."[5]

Appendix A: Mutinies by Date

AMERICAN ARMY MUTINIES*

1775

After June 18, 1775 Newtown, New York—Lieutenant Abraham Riker, 4th New York Regiment

August 5, 1775 Congaree Store, South Carolina—The 1st South Carolina Rangers

September 10, 1775 Cambridge, Massachusetts—Thompson's Pennsylvania Riflemen

December 1, 1775 Colonel Henry Babcock assists General Israel Putnam in putting down a mutiny.

—— 1775 Albany, New York—Philip Van Cortlandt's new recruits refused to serve.

1776

January 30, 1776 Quebec, Canada—14 men of Captain Ezra Newhall's Company

January 1776 Orangeburg County, South Carolina—South Carolina Rangers

February 1776 Albany, New York—Company F of the 1st Pennsylvania Battalion

February 9, 1776 Fort Ticonderoga, New York—Detachment under Captain Fitch

February 11, 1776 Fort Ticonderoga, New York—Captain John Nelson's Rifle Company (9th Pennsylvania Regiment)

February 11, 1776 Fort Ticonderoga, New York—Massachusetts Militia

March 17, 1776 (Pre) Williamsburg, Virginia—Captain George Gibson's Virginia Riflemen

April 17, 1776 Quebec, Canada—Forty New Yorkers

June 1776 Bladen County, North Carolina—North Carolina Militia

July 1776 Wilmington, North Carolina—North Carolina Continentals

Summer 1776 Philadelphia, Pennsylvania—Colonel Samuel Patterson's Delaware Detachment of the Flying Camp

September 4, 1776 Newport, Rhode Island—Part of Captain Loring Peck's Company of 1st Rhode Island Regiment

1777

January 4, 1777 Princeton, New Jersey—Major Ludowick Weltner refused orders of Colonel Nicholas Haussegger who was deserting to the British.

February 2, 1777 Fairfield, Norwalk, and Stamford, Connecticut—Connecticut Militia under Brigadier General Gold Selleck Silliman

July 12, 1777 Halifax, North Carolina—9th North Carolina Regiment

August 2, 1777 Peekskill, New York—Lieutenant Roger Moore and Ensign David Russel (Resco) of Captain Roger's company in Colonel Roger Enos's Regiment

---

*One person mutinies are not included as they are most likely just cases of insubordination.

August 28, 1777 Peekskill, New York—Colonel Christopher Greene's 1st Rhode Island Regiment.

November 6, 1777 Hudson River, New York—Two hundred New Hampshire troops refused to march

December 21, 1777 Valley Forge, Pennsylvania—Detachment from all brigades unable to assemble

1778

February 15, 1778 Valley Forge, Pennsylvania—12th Massachusetts Regiment

July 1778 Moon Creek, Caswell County, North Carolina—North Carolina Line

December 30, 1778 Redding, Connecticut—General Jedidiah Huntington's Connecticut Brigade

1779

January 1779 Warren, Rhode Island—2nd Rhode Island Regiment

April 23, 1779 (Pre) Purrysburg, South Carolina—400 South Carolina Militia refusing to go to Georgia

April 23, 1779 Warren, Rhode Island—2nd Rhode Island Regiment

May 1779 Colonel William Malcolm's Additional Continental Regiment was merged with Colonel Oliver Spencer's Additional Continental Regiment. Spencer's corps was at one time known as the 5th New Jersey Regiment. Many of the men in Malcolm's New York raised corps had exhibited such a bad attitude over the merger that Washington thought that "it cannot be considered in any other light than that of mutiny."*

June 1779 Albemarle Barracks, Charlottesville, Virginia—The guards of the Saratoga Convention prisoners.

July 19, 1779 Camp Barber's Heights, Rhode Island—2nd Rhode Island Regiment

July 29, 1779 Camp Barber's Heights, Rhode Island—2nd Rhode Island Regiment

1780

January 1, 1780 West Point, New York—One hundred soldiers belonging to the Massachusetts Regiments (returned 3rd)

January 1780 West Point, New York area—Sixty men from Brigadier General John Glover's Brigade (returned 11th)

May 25, 1780 Morristown, New Jersey—Connecticut Regiments (3, 4, and 5)

June 1780 Fort Schuyler, Rome, New York—Thirty-one men of Colonel Goose Van Schaick's 1st New York Regiment

1781

January 1, 1781 Morristown, New Jersey—Pennsylvania Line

---

*If George Washington says it was a mutiny who am I to argue.

January 6, 1781 Philadelphia, Pennsylvania—Pennsylvania Militia Artillery Non Force Resolution

January 21, 1781 Pompton, New Jersey—New Jersey Line

May 20, 1781 York, Pennsylvania—Pennsylvania Line

July 1781 North Carolina Militia under Colonel Guilford Dudley

October 16, 1781 Newtown, Bucks County, Pennsylvania—Philadelphia County Militia demaning liquor

October 20, 1781 High Hills of the Santee, South Carolina—Maryland troops and Griffin of the South Carolina Line

November 17, 1781 Cumberland Old Court House, Virginia—Virginia Line troops

1782

January (Mid) Cumberland Old Court House, Virginia—Virginia Line troops

February 7, 1782 Cumberland Old Court House, Virginia—Virginia Line troops

March (Late)/April 1782 Fort Pitt, Pittsburgh, Pennsylvania—7th Virginia Regiment

April 20, 1782 Bacon's Bridge, South Carolina—Pennsylvania Line

May 3, 1782 Connecticut Huts, Continental Village, Putnam County, New York Connecticut Troops over terms of enlistment.

1783

March 15, 1783 Newburgh, New York—Officers Mutiny

May 4, 1783 James Island, South Carolina—Maryland Line

May 13, 1783 Congaree River, South Carolina—Baylor's Dragoons

June 16, 1783 Lancaster, Pennsylvania—Eighty men of the Pennsylvania Line

June 21, 1783 Philadelphia, Pennsylvania—Three hundred men of the Pennsylvania Line surrounds Congress

AMERICAN NAVAL MUTINIES*

1775

September 1775 Schooner *Hannah* of "Washington's Navy"—Crew mutinied over return of a captured ship.

November 13-15, 1775 Schooner *Harrison* of "Washington's Navy"—departed Plymouth, Massachusetts and her crew refused to continue the cruise.

November (end) 1775 The brigantine *Washington* of "Washington's Navy"—At Plymouth harbor, the crew refused to sail or vacate the ship due to lack of proper clothing.

1776

April 8, 1776 Brig *Cabot* at New London, Connecticut—Fifty eight members of the crew demanding their back pay.

*Individuals who were transferred from one vessel to another for "mutiny" are not included in this list.

Early summer 1776 The *Oxford* had been capture by the *Andrew Doria* and as she was making for port the British carpenters of the transport banded together and over-powered the crew from the *Andrew Doria* who were running the ship.

August 1776 *Scorpion*, sloop of war Virginia State Navy—James Marshall was guilty of exciting the marines and seaman to mutiny.

October 1776 Lake Champlain, New York, the Lake Champlain Navy—Zelida Hammon, mate, William Pownwell, Boatswain, William Trip and Nicholas Culbut, seaman from refused to fight the British on vessels. The court martial found them guilty and "The criminals were to be whipped from vessel to vessel in receiving part of their punishment from each."

1777

January 11, 1777 The *Aurora*, formerly the *Oxford* The crew mutinied and brought the ship to Liverpool, England on January 28.

February 1777 The vessel *Ronals* shipped out of Providence, Rhode Island. The crew mutined after the *Ronals* stopped at Deseada near Guadeloupe.

February/April 1777 at L'Orient, France—Crew of the Congress brig *Reprisal* refused to go back out to sea until they got their prize money.

March 1777 The frigate *Randolph* sailed from Philadelphia on February 3, 1777. The *Randolph* was manned primarily with a crew of British seaman from the Philadelphia jail. Prior to her arrival at Charleston, South Carolina on March 11, 1777 the British sailors on board the vessel mutinied.

April 1777 Brigantine *George* and sailed out of Charleston, South Carolina. The crew mutinied and renamed the ship the *True Briton*. They brought the vessel into Clyde, England on April 21, 1777.

April 1777 Sloop *Active* left Charleston, South Carolina on April 21, 1777. The crew mutinied and brought the vessel into port in England on May 27.

May 4, 1777 The crew of the *Mercer* mutinied and she was taken to Whitehaven, England on May 21.

May 1777 *Molly*—The crew mutinied brought the vessel to Londonderry, Ireland and continued on to Plymouth, England.

1778

May (?) 1778 *Montgomery* of Pennsylvania Navy—John Gilfroy (Gillaffroy,) boatswain tried by a court martial for mutiny and desertion and was sentenced to death.

July 6, 1778 Schooner St. Louis—Crew mutinied against Captain George Ross

1779:

February 2, 1779 Atlantic Ocean –Lafayette on the *Alliance* took command of the armed defenders and seized the four ringleaders who were quickly placed in irons. A total of thirty eight men were confined as mutineers.

Summer of 1779 *Bonhomme Richard*, the British sailors in the crew had plotted a mutiny.

1780

June 10, 1780 L'Orient, France—125 sailors of the *Alliance* want their pay and prize money.

August 10, 1780 Grand Banks—*Alliance*'s crew mutinied over destination.

December 1780 (late) the *Ariel* (26 9-pounders)—After the naval action of December 1780 with the 20-gun British privateer *Triumph* commanded by John Pindar, the whole plot came to light

1781

March 31, 1781 Atlantic Ocean—*Alliance*

May 19, 1781 off the east coast of Nova Scotia—Privateer Schooner *Fortune*. The crew mutinied because they thought they were in the wrong place to get prizes.

August 4, 1781 At Texel, Holland—*South Carolina* French sailors in the crew mutinied over pay.

October 1781 At Coruña, Spain—*South Carolina* French sailors in the crew mutinied over pay.

1782

October 3, 1782 Atlantic Ocean—Snow *Commerce*

December 12, 1782 Delaware Bay—*South Carolina*

1783

1783 Edenton, North Carolina—American privateer *General Gregory*'s crew mutinied and several officers were murdered.

Crown Forces Mutinies

1775

December 1, 1775 *Roebuck*

1776

None

1777

March 10, 1777 Ochsenfurt (south of Würzburg), Hessian troops

1777 (pre May) *Union* tender

1778

March 1778 Mascouche, Canada—Canadian Militia

September 21, 1778 Edinburgh—78th Regiment Lord Seaforth Highlanders

1779

January 1779 Kent—71st Regiment Fraser's Highlanders

March 1779 Burntisland—76th Regiment Lord Macdonald's Highlanders

April 20, 1779 Leith—42nd (Black Watch) and 71st (Fraser's Highlanders) Regiments
April 1779 Portsmouth, England—*Invincible* (74 guns)
June 10, 1779 (pre) *Culloden*
August 1779 English Channel—*Active* (12 guns)
September 29, 1779 *Egmont*
September 30 1779 Edinburgh—Argyll (Western) Fencibles
October 8, 1779 Leith—Argyll (Western) Fencibles
October 8, 1779 Edinburgh—Argyll (Western) Fencibles
November 27, 1779 Downs (near Dover) England—*Jackal* (14 guns) taken to Calais, France

1780
July 25, 1780 Hunt's Bluff, South Carolina—South Carolina Militia under command of Colonel William Henry Mills
1780 Continental Sloop *Fly*
1780 Schooner *Daphne*—Providence to New York

1781
July 16, 1781 Antigua—Frigate *Santa Monica*
1781 Ziegenhayn—Hessian troops

1782
December 12, 1782 Off the New Jersey Coast—The *South Carolina* had been captured by the British and the American crew attempted to retake the ship
1782 *Narcissus* (20 guns)
1782/1783 *Raisonnable* (64 guns)

1783
January 1783 Portsmouth—68th Durham Regiment
January 1783 Portsmouth—77th Regiment Duke of Atholl's Highlanders
January 1783 Portsmouth—81st Regiment Aberdeenshire Highlanders
September 1783 East Florida—Provincial regiments
1783 *Janus* (44 guns)

Appendix B: Continental Army Mutinies by Location and Cause

Location	Number	Percentage
Canada	2	3.6
Connecticut	2	3.6
Massachusetts	1	1.8
New Jersey	4	7.1
New York	14	25.0
North Carolina	5	8.9
Pennsylvania	9	16.1
Rhode Island	5	8.9
South Carolina	7	12.5
Unknown	2	3.6
Virginia	5	8.9
Total	56	100.00

Cause	1775	1776	1777	1778	1779	1780	1781	1782	1783	Total
Clothing	1		1				1			3
Clothing & Pay			1	1						2
Discipline	1	7	2	1	4	1	2	1		19
Expired Service		1				2	2	1	2	8
Food	1		2	1	1	1	1			7
Food & Discipline								1		1
Pay	1	2	1		2			2	3	11
Unknown	1	2					2			5
Total	5	12	7	3	7	4	8	5	5	56

Appendix C: Oliver DeLancey's Journal[*]

On the third of January in the morning received intelligence by an Emissary (Gould) that the Pennsylvanians had Mutinyed in their Camp in Morristown that the alarm Guns had been fired and Beacons lighted. He was immediately dispatched to a Correspondent [Andrew Gautier, Jr.] in New Jersey.

Orders were sent to the British Grenadiers, British Light Infantry, Forty second, Thirty seventh Regiments, Hessian Grenadiers and Hessian Yagers to hold themselves in readiness to march at a moments notice.

On Thursday the fourth of January received the following Intelligence from a Correspondent [Andrew Gautier, Jr.] dated the third of January The Pennsylvania Troops Commanded by General Wayne Mutinyed on Monday last, there was an universal complaint in the Camp that they had received no Pay, Cloathing, and a Scanty allowance of Provision, that a great number of these Troops were detained longer than they enlisted for, their terms being expired above ten Months, these complaints led them to mutiny to a Man, about 1500 seized on the Military Magazines, provision and Artillery which consisted of four Field pieces, and in a body marched from their Huts the same day to Vealtown, distant about seven Miles General Wayne followed, but they will not listen to any proposals and persist in going to Congress for redress, or to disband, yesterday they Marched to Middlebrook and this Morning towards Princeton- Two Companys of Riflemen detached from the Pennsylvanians and posted at Bottle hill Marched off this Morning to join them- Their officers are following them.

The Messenger [Gould] sent out as above returned with the following Intelligence.

The Pennsylvania line have been for some time much dissatisfied, on Monday last they turned out in number abut 1200 declaring they would serve no longer unless their grievances were redressed, as they had not received either Pay, Cloathing, or Provisions a Riot had ensued in which an Officer was killed and four wounded. The Insurgents had five or six wounded. They collected the Artillery Stores, Waggons, Provision &c &c Marched out of Camp & passed by Wayne's Quarters who sent out a Message to them requesting them to desist or the consequences would prove fatal, they refused & proceeded on their March 'till evening when they took Post on an advantageous piece of ground and Elected Officers from among themselves, appointing a Sergeant Major who was a British Deserter to Command them with the Rank of Major General – On Tuesday they marched to Middlebrook and yesterday to Brunswick where they now are.

On Tuesday morning a Message was sent them by the Officers from Camp, desiring to know their intentions, they refused to receive this Message- A Flag of Truce was sent to the same effect-some said they had served their three years against their incli-

[*]CP 144:12, Oliver De Lancey's Journal (10 page copy).

304

nations and would continue no longer on any account, others said they would not return unless their grievances were redressed – The Rebels have removed all their Boats to the other side of the Delawar least the Rioters should cross the River – On their first rising the Artillery refused to join, but, being threatened with the Bayonet they consented – Two Companys of Riflemen posted at Bottle hill near Chatham had marched to join them, the Militia not daring to oppose them.

On Thursday Evening three Copys of the following proposals were sent off to the Revolters, one by the Raritan River [carried by John Mason] the others by Newark and Elizabethtown (sent to Andrew Gautier Jr. to be forwarded).

It being reported at New York that the Pennsylvania Troops and others having been defrauded of their Pay, Cloathing and Provisions are assembled to redress their grievances, and also that notwithstanding the terms of their inlistments are expired they have been forcibly detained in the service where they suffered every kind of misery and oppression,

They are now offered to be taken under the protection of the British Government, to have their Rights restored free pardon for all former offences, and that Pay due them from the Congress faithfully paid to them, without any expectation of Military service (except it may be voluntary) upon laying down their Arms and returning to their allegiance.

For which purpose if they will send Commissioners to Amboy they will there be met by People empowered to treat with them & Faith pledged for their security.

It is recommended to them for their own safety to move behind South River and whenever they request it a Body of British Troops shall protect them.

It is needless to point out the inability as well as want of inclination in the Congress to relieve them, or to tell them the severitys that will be used towards them by the Rebel leaders should they think of returning to their former Servitude.

It will be proved to the Commissioners they may chuse to send that the Authority from whence this comes is sufficient to insure the performance of the above proposals.

To the person appointed by the Pennsylvania Troops to lead them in their present struggle for their Libertys and Rights.

As soon as the above was dispatched, Orders were immediately sent to the two Battallions of Light Infantry, the British Grenadiers, three Battallions Hessian Grenadiers and the Yagers to march immediately to Denyce's Ferry, whence they crossed the 5th to Staten Island and Cantoned on the Road to Richmond except the Yagers who lay on the road to Deckers ferry.

On the 5th I sent out three copies of the proposals [by Brink, Hatfield's messenger, and possibly another] and a Verbal Message to the same import to the Pennsylvanians.

A number of men were sent out towards West point the Clove and Morristown to watch the movements that way

On the 6th received a letter [from Andrew Gautier, Jr.] acknowledging the receipt of the proposals sent by Newark, informing me they were forwarded by a faithful friend to Princeton where the Pennsylvania Troops had halted, that the Rebel Militia were all ordered out and the Jersey Brigade had moved from Pompton to Morristown that General Washington was on his way from West point to see General Wayne.

On the 7th received Information from General Skinner that the Pennsylvanians continued their March towards Brunswick and that Wayne was detained a Prisoner among them.

That Col. Dayton with the Jersey Brigade was at Morristown but, hearing the Riflemen and some Light horse had joined the Insurgents he halted fearing a defection among his own Troops and that he heard a man sent with proposals was seen safe within a Mile of the Revolters on Friday Evening.

Information by New York that they were at Rocky hill near Princetown.

On the 8th a man came over by the Blazing Star [ferry landing locations in New Jersey and Staten Island] who said part of them were gone to Trenton.

On the 9th there being an appearance of bad weather the Hessian Grenadiers went back to Long Island.

About twelve o'Clock this day Received a letter from the Jerseys [from Andrew Gautier, Jr.] of which the following is an Extract dated Monday Night.

The Person I sent to Princetown is just returned which place he left this morning, your address he delivered Saturday evening, the same night two persons arrived with like addresses they were both detained.

The Pennsylvania Troops are still at Princetown their number 1700, they keep up order in the Town, no Officer is permitted to come into them but by a Flag of Truce – General Wayne and Governor Reed of Pennsylvania had an interview Yesterday and made some proposals, but, they were rejected by the Troops, they require their Pay due in hard money and a discharge.

Your offers are now known throughout the Army and will have great influence over the Majority of them, the most sensible people and Officers here think they will yet join you as interest and Policy ought to lead them to it – I am fully satisfied the Congress can not nor will not give them redress, in this case they will come over to you.

The Commander in Chief received Information also this day much to the same purpose as the above letter, dated the 8th at 10 o'clock in the morning.

Received intelligence by New York that came from Morristown [by Joseph Clark] and also from Major General Phillips, all which agree that the Revolters are at Princetown, still insisting on the compliance of the Congress to their Demands.

This day I sent out some people from the Refugee Post at Bergen Point and one from the Armed Vessel.

On the 10th the Reports the same, no person came in that could be confided in.

On the 11th Received intelligence by a man [Cornelius Tyger] who had passed by the Pennsylvanians, that they were at Princetown, still persisting in their demands, the man sent out the 9th returned this day, reports the situation of the Pennsylvanians the same, says the Guards of Militia along the Coast are so numerous as to prevent any persons geting in.

On the 12th a party went into the Country, the officer who Commanded was informed by a friend that a person who had come from Princetown in the morning, said everything remained in the same situation we had before heard, they still refuse all the offers that have been made them; the Party was fired upon in three or four places.

The man sent out [Uzal Woodruff] was met by a person who informed him the Rebel Colonel Barber came to Elizabeth Town Yesterday and reported that eight hundred of the Revolters had absolutely refused to come to any terms; That on Thursday morning they were supplied with three Waggon loads of Arms and Ammunition that the whole body were to march for Trenton and are supposed to be there now – The Militia had received Orders to follow them – That last night and the night before the Officers of the Jersey Brigade were under the necessity of watching their Camp to prevent their people joining the Pennsylvanians.

This night received the following intelligence from a Gentleman who came in and can be depended on. On the 9th some of the Pennsylvanians who had differed in opinion from the Revolters, told him they were now going to join them having changed their intention. – That a Sergeant Major of the 4th Battalion Commanded them, they had not the least apprehension of the Jersey Troops as they were of the same sentiments with themselves. – Their demands were for their arrears of Pay and Cloathing, and those that had inlisted for three Years insisted on having their discharges, that the depreciation should be made good to them, and they be reconciled the Officers they have now appointed from among themselves are to be continued being determined not to serve under their late Officers. – They have also stipulated a pardon particularly for all the principle Revolters. One of them a Deserter from the 7th Regiment said if Congress did not redress their Complaints they knew what course to take – The Militia of the Jerseys say they are only doing themselves Justice. General Wayne is kept among them as an hostage. Numbers declare they will not serve Congress at any rate. They have take two Men one with proposals, the other served as a Guide. They call themselves 2500 but, he thinks from the best accounts they do not exceed 2000 all the Boats are carried to the West Side of the Delawar and kept Guarded. The Militia are ordered out A friend in the Country [William Bernard Gifford] told him that the reports of their going to Trenton was not true. That two Companys of Riflemen had joined them with one Field piece, some of the insurgents were accidentally killed when they fired upon their Officers, who in general denounce Vengeance against them and declare they will not serve unless and exemplary Punishment is inflicted, it seems that general opinion, that the Jersey Brigade are of the same Sentiments.

On the 13th a man came in from Newark who says they are still at Princetown. The people sent out to them are not yet returned.

On Monday the 15th received the following Intelligence.

William Boyce left Philadelphia on Wednesday last, crossed the Delawar on Thursday at Trenton where the Pennsylvanians are, he spoke to their out Posts their numbers are said to be from 1500 to 2000 – They demand their back Pay, Cloathing and the discharges of those whose time of enlistment ha expired.

There was a Committee of Congress at Barclay's Tavern on the West side of the Delawar in order to adjust matters some were for forcing them, others for submitting to all their Demands – on the West side of the River he was told they were not to be paid for ten days; on the East side they told him it was to be done that day, and they were to have their discharges it however was not decided. They had delivered over two Prisoners taken amongst them with proposals, to the Committee of Congress.

General Wayne is among them as a Prisoner Governor Reed was permitted to have an hours Conversation with him and then sent back to the Committee of Congress. They are Commanded by one Williams, who was a Sergeant Major - They left Princetown on Wednesday last, he met small parties of Soldiers all along the road that seemed to have come from other parts of the Army, some with and some without Arms. – At Philadelphia the People seemed much alarmed as it was reported they had no money and were disappointed in the Cloathing expected for the Army as Paul Jones who was to convoy it put back to L'Orient his Ships being dismasted and in distress. He did not hear that General Washington was at Philadelphia, on the contrary about two miles on the other side Brunswick, he met two Men going with an Express from him to General Wayne, and a Gentleman who was with him and had spoke to the Men sayd Mr. Washington's presence was necessary with his Army as they apprehended a Revolt would take place there.

The Opinion of the people in general is that the Troops are only doing themselves justice – They have killed a Captn Talbot, Tatton and another whose name he does not know There was a report at first of their intention to come over to us but from their moving to Trenton he does not think it likely At Elizabeth Town he heard the two Men taken up were hanged on friday There is a report that five hundred of the Militia are at and about that place.

General Skinner informs me that the Jersey Troops were in the same State as to their Demands, but, have been quieted by a promise of being satisfied in ten days, six of which are elapsed.

Mr. H. [Cornelius Hatfield Jr] informed me that Col. Dayton spread a Report that the Pennsylvanians were satisfied, upon which his own people immediately made the same demands, and he was obliged to contradict his own report to quiet them.

On the 15th received a letter from a correspondent [Andrew Gautier Jr.] saying that the Pennsylvanians had not paid that attention to the offers made them by us, which he thought Policy and Interest would have led them to, that he did not imagine

Congress would grant them relief, but, force them to submission – That General Washington was not gone to Congress, as he had mentioned in his last letter.

A Man (Uzal Woodruff) came in who sayd they had left Princetown, but his Intelligence is not to be relied on, he having received it from a Sergeant, who had deserted them and was going home.

The Pennsylvanians moving so far from us, and in no instance shewing a disposition to accept of the offers made them. The Commander in Chief returned to Town.

No account coming in that could be depended on and no appearance of the Pennsylvanians intending any thing in our favour the Troops were ordered to Long Island the 19th.

The same day I was informed from South Amboy [by John Rattoon], that the Men taken up were people I had sent out, & from the description, I know one of them [John Mason] – They were hanged on Friday opposite Trenton where the Pennsylvanians still remained not having determined any thing. The 20th received accounts of their being at Trenton, that they were discharging some of them, they having settled with a Committee of Congress.

Same Day the account of their being still at Trenton confirmed. The Committee of Congress consists of Genl. Sullivan, Mr. Mathews, Mr. Witherspoon and Mr. Atley, they sit at T. Barclay's Tavern on the Pennsylvania side.

Same day a Man (McFarlan) I sent out the 7th [6th] with a Copy of the proposals got to Princetown on Wednesday where he met a Man [Caleb Bruen], he suspected to be on a similar errand; after some conversation, they found out that their business was the same, they went on together to Trenton to which place the Pennsylvanians had Marched. Finding that two Men had been taken up they dropped their Papers, which were carried to Mr. Reed and General Wayne who offered one hundred Guineas reward for the apprehending whoever brought them. One of them being known by a Colonel Hayes and he having intimated to him some suspicions of his designs, they crossed the Delaware and went into Pennsylvania where they saw the execution of the two men, whom he describes exactly.

They are commanded by a Sergeant Williams who is a Pennsylvanian and had some little property, he was taken Prisoner in the Year 1776 at Princetown and enlisted in one of our Provincial Regiments, raised at that time from which he deserted.

There was a Committee of a Sergeant of each regt. to meet the Committee of Congress, the proposals herewith inclos'd were made to them at Princetown the 7th of January & the answer signed by the Secretary of the Committee of Sergeants was given the 8th and their determination respecting the two prisoners January the 10th at Trenton.

This person adds that they do not intend going home until every Man is discharged and tho' they lay down their Arms as they are settled with yet they do not permit them to be taken away but keep a Centry of their own over them.

The Pennsylvanian Officers are very much dissatisfied, as the Soldiers are allowed to Swear to any thing and their words Credited before any vouched account, which they choose to say they were obliged to sign

He confirms the account of their having on the first of January killed a Captain and wounded another, with a Lieutenant and Ensign, one Soldier was also killed.

They have four pieces of Cannon, they left one spiked at Morristown, he expects the other Man in, who was with him, every moment.

21st. This day a Captain [William Bernard Gifford] of the 3d Jersey Regiment, who I had corresponded with came over to us he confirms the information of yesterday.

He says they will not stir till they are paid and ask hard Money.

The man who was expected [Caleb Bruen], returned this day his accounts are the same.

He says they have shown no intention of coming to us, but on the contrary declared that should the British interfere, they would take up arms to oppose them as readily as ever.

From all accounts the Country is much alarmed the Militia on the Roads made the Communication more difficult, than at any other time, they having also destroy'd all the Boats Cannoes &c

Appendix D: Round Robin of the Continental Brig *Cabot*

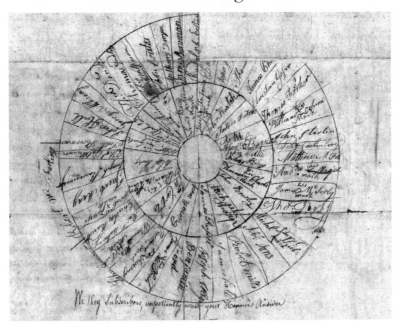

New London, Connecticut, April 8, 1776*

LIST OF SIGNERS

Outer circle, clockwise: Pa[torn]; John J[torn]; Thoma[torn]; James Ch[torn]; Christian Gosner; Thomas Forker; William Osburn (his mark x); John Stirlin; Peter Cashinbury; Mathew M[']Fee; Andrw Magee (his mark x); James McSorly (his mark x); Thos Derby; Michel Shield (his mark x); Abl Jons; Robet Mill[s]; James Hall; Joseph Way[n]; Benjamin Ford; James Black (his mark x); Richard Sweeny (his mark x); Thomas Clark (his mark x); Robt Halladay; Charles Harve[y]; Jacob po[illegible] (his mark x); Jacob Maag; Joseph Ravencroft; Thos Goldthwaite; John Hartman; John Hall; George McKenny; Thos David; Thomas Yad[ley] (his mark x); James Wilkeson (his mark x); John Coates; Anthony Dwyer; James Bowman; Rudolph Edi[na]

Inner circle, clockwise: Joseph Antonio (his mark x); John Roatch; John Patr[ick]; Alexr Baptist (his mark x); John Little; John King; Thomas Charles (his mark x); John Bowles; Michael Thayr; James Russel; John Young; Jno Curtis; William York (his mark x); Mark Alxr Lowry; Willm Small (his mark x); Thos X Clerk Senr (his mark x); Chris Reiney (his mark x); Lewis Reding (his mark x);

Around perimeter of outer circle: John Conner; Robert McFarling

*Rhode Island Historical Society, Hopkins Papers, April 8, 1776

Appendix E: Pennsylvania Line Return of December 11, 1780*

Regiments	Sergeants	Drummers	Rank & File	Total
1	26	10	179	215
2	25	18	294	337
3	21	17	239	277
4	25	12	144	181
5	20	11	203	234
6	18	9	151	178
7	21	11	165	197
8	NA	NA	NA	NA
9	16	13	140	197
10	22	14	241	277
11	24	17	224	265
Artillery	18			143
Grand Total				2473

*Pennsylvania Archives, Vol. 8, p. 647

Appendix F: First Troop Philadelphia City Cavalry

The following is the pay roll list of forty-eight members of the Philadelphia Light Horse that responded to the Pennsylvania Line Mutiny. They would have attended the execution of John Mason and James Ogden on January 11, 1781.

Samuel Morris, Captain
James Budden, First Lieutenant
John Lardner, Cornet
John Patton, Adjutant
Thomas Leiper, First Sergeant
William Hall, Second Sergeant
John Donnaldson, Third Sergeant
William Pollard, Fourth Sergeant
Samuel Penrose, Q.M. Sergeant
James Hunter, First Corporal
John Mease, Second Corporal
William Alricks, Private
John Barclay, Private
Andrew Bunner, Private
James, Caldwell, Private
Samuel Caldwell, Private
George Campbell, Private
David H. Conyngham, Private
Joseph Cowperthwait, Private
Isaac Cox, Private
James Craig, Jr., Private
James Crawford, Private
Benjamin Davis, Jr., Private
David Duncan, Private

Joseph Fisher, Private
George Henry, Private
George Hughes, Private
Matthew Irwin, Private
Thomas Irwin, Private
Thomas Leaming Jr. Private
David Lenox, Private
John Lyttle, Private
Blair McClenachan, Private
Robert McClenachan, Private
Jonathan Mifflin, Private
John Montgomery, Private
Cadwalder Morris, Private
Jacob Morris, Private
Thomas C. Morris, Private
John Murray, Private
Alexander Nesbitt, Private
Francis Nichols, Private
William Nichols, Private
Michael M. O'Brien, Private
Joseph Prowell, Private
John Redman, Private
Robert Roberts, Private
William Turnbull, Private

Appendix G: Officer's Letter at Newburgh*

To the Officers of the Army.

Gentlemen,—A fellow soldier whose interest and affections bind him strongly to you, whose past sufferings have been as great, and whose future fortune may be as desperate, as yours—would beg leave to address you.

Age has its claims, and rank is not without its pretensions to advise; but, though unsupported by both, he flatters himself, that the plain language of sincerity and experience will neither be unheard nor unregarded.

Like many of you he loved private life, and left it with regret. He left it, determined to retire from the field, with the necessity that called him to it, and not till then—not till the enemies of his country, the slaves of power, and the hirelings of injustice, were compelled to abandon their schemes, and acknowledge America as terrible in arms, as she had been humble in remonstrance. With this object in view, he has long shared in your toils and mingled in your dangers.—He has felt the cold hand of poverty without a murmur, and has seen the insolence of wealth without a sigh. But, too much under the direction of his wishes, and sometimes weak enough to mistake desire for opinion, he has till lately—very lately, believed in the justice of his country. He hoped, that as the clouds of adversity scattered, and as the sunshine of peace and better fortune broke in upon us, the coldness and severity of government would relax, and that more than justice, that gratitude would blaze forth on those hands which had upheld her in the darkest stages of her passage from impending servitude to acknowledged Independence. But faith has its limits, as well as temper, and there are points beyond which neither can be stretched, without sinking into cowardice, or plunging into credulity.—This, my friends, I conceive to be your situation,—hurried to the very edge of both, another step would ruin you forever.—To be tame and unprovoked when injuries press hard upon you, is more than weakness; but to look up for kinder usage, without one manly effort of your own, would fix your character, and show the world how richly you deserve those chains you broke. To guard against this evil, let us take a review of the ground on which we now stand, and thence carry our thoughts forward for a moment into the unexplored field of expedients [experiments].

After a pursuit of seven long years, the object for which we set out is at length brought within our reach—yes, my friends, that suffering courage of yours was active once,—it has conducted the United States of America through a doubtful and a bloody war. It has placed her in the chair of independency, and peace returns again to bless—whom? A country willing to redress your wrongs, cherish your worth and reward your services? A country courting your return to private life, with tears of gratitude, and smiles of admiration, longing to divide with you that independency which

*George Washington Papers at the Library of Congress, General Correspondence, Anonymous to Continental Army Officers, March 10, 1783.

your gallantry has given, and those riches which your wounds have preserved? Is this the case? Or is it rather a country that tramples on your rights, disdains your cries, and insults your distresses? Have you not more than once suggested your wishes, and made known your wants to Congress? Wants and wishes which gratitude and policy should have anticipated rather than evaded; and have you not lately in the meek language of entreating memorials, begged from their justice, what you could no longer expect from their favor? How have your been answered? Let the letter which you are called to consider tomorrow reply.

If this then be your treatment, while the swords you wear are necessary for the defence of America, what have you to expect from peace, when your voice shall sink, and your strength dissipate by division? When those very swords, the instruments and companions of your glory, shall be taken from your sides, and no remaining mark of military distinction be left but your wants, infirmities and scars? Can you then consent to be the only sufferers by this revolution, and retiring from the field, grow old in poverty, wretchedness and contempt? Can you consent to wade through the vile mire of dependency, and owe the miserable remnant of that life to charity, which has hitherto been spent in honor? If you can—go—and carry with you the jest of tories and the scorn of whigs—the ridicule, and what is worse, the pity of the world. Go, starve, and be forgotten. But if your spirit should revolt at this; if you have sense enough to discover, and spirit sufficient to oppose, tyranny, under whatever garb it may assume; whether it be the plain coat of republicanism, or the splendid robe of royalty; if you have not yet learned to discriminate between a people and a cause, between men and principles—awake; attend to your situation, and redress yourselves. If the present moment be lost, every future effort is in vain; and your threats then, will be as empty as your entreaties now.

I would advise you, therefore, to come to some final opinion on what you can bear, and what you will suffer. If your determination be in any proportion to your wrongs, carry your appeal from the justice, to the fears of government. Change the milk and water style of your last memorial; assume a bolder tone—decent, but lively, spirited and determined, and suspect the man who would advise to more moderation and longer forbearance. Let two or three men who can feel as well as write, be appointed to draw up your *last remonstrance*; for I would no longer give it the suing, fort, unsuccessful epithet of memorial. Let it represent in language that will neither dishonor you by its rudeness, nor betray you by its fears, what has been promised by Congress, and what has been performed—how long and how patiently you have suffered—how little you have asked, and how much of that little has been denied. Tell them, that, though you were the first, and would wish to be the last to encounter danger, though despair itself can never drive you into dishonor, it may drive you from the field; that the wound often irritated, never healed, may at lenght become incurable and that the slightest mark of indignity from Congress now, must operate like the grave, and part you forever; that in any political event, the army has its alternative. If peace, that nothing shall separate you from your arms but death; if war, that, courting the auspices, and inviting the directions of your illustrious leader, you will retire to some unsettled country, smile in your turn, and 'mock when their fear cometh on.' But let it represent also, that should they comply with the request of your late memorial, it would make you more happy, and them more respectable. That while war should continue, you would follow their standard into the field, and when it came to an end you would withdraw into the shade of private life, and give the world another subject of wonder and applause; an army victorious over its enemies—victorious over itself.

Appendix H: George Washington's Speech at Newburgh*

GENTLEMEN,—By an anonymous summons an attempt has been made to convene you together. How inconsistent with the rules of propriety, how unmilitary, and how subversive of all order and discipline, let the good sense of the army decide.

In the moment of this summons, another anonymous production was sent into circulation, addressed more to the feelings and passions than to the reason and judgment of the army. The author of the piece is entitled to much credit for the goodness of his pen; and I could wish he had as much credit for the rectitude of his heart; for, as men see through different optics, and are induced by the reflecting faculties of the mind, to use different means to attain the same end, the author of the address should have had more charity than to mark for suspicion the man who should recommend moderation and longer forbearance; or, in other words, who should not think as he thinks, and act as he advises. But he had another plan in view, in which candor and liberality of sentiment, regard to justice and love of country, have no part; and he was right to insinuate the darkest suspicion to effect the blackest designs. That the address was drawn with great art, and is designed to answer the most insidious purposes; that it is calculated to impress the mind with an idea of premeditated injustice in the sovereign power of the United States, and rouse all those resentments, which must unavoidably flow from such a belief; that the secret mover of this scheme, whoever he may be, intended to take advantage of the passions, while they were warmed by the recollection of past distresses, without giving time for cool, deliberation of thinking, and that composure of mind which is so necessary to give dignity and stability to measures, is rendered too obvious, by the mode of conducting the business, to need other proof than a reference to the proceedings.

Thus much, gentlemen, I have thought it incumbent on me to observe to you to show on what principles I opposed the irregular and hasty meeting which was proposed to have been held on Tuesday last, and not because I wanted to disposition to give you every opportunity, consistently with your own honor, and the dignity of the army, to make known your grievances. If my conduct heretofore has not evinced to you, that I have been a faithful friend to the army, my declaration of it at this time would be equally unavailing and improper. But as I was among the first who embarked in the cause of our common country; as I have never left your side one moment, but when called from you on public duty; as I have been the constant companion and witness of your distresses, and not among the last to feel and acknowledge your merits; as I have ever considered my own military reputation as inseparably connected with

*George Washington Papers at the Library of Congress, General Correspondence, George Washington to Continental Army Officers, March 15, 1783.

that of the army; as my heart has ever expanded with joy when I have heard its prais-
es, and my indignation has arisen when the mouth of detraction has been opened
against it; it can *scarcely be supposed* at this last stage of the war, that I am indifferent
to its interests. But how are they to be promoted? The way is plain, says the anonymous addresser! 'If war continues, remove into the unsettled country; there establish
yourselves, and leave an ungrateful country to defend itself!' But who are they to
defend? our wives, our children our farms and other property which we leave behind
us? or in this state of hostile separation, are we to take the two first, the latter cannot
be removed, to perish in a wilderness, with hunger, cold and nakedness?

'If peace takes place, never sheath your swords,' says he, 'till you have obtained full
and ample justice.' This dreadful alternative of either deserting our country in the
extremest hour of her distress, or turning our arms against it, which is the apparent
object, unless Congress can be compelled into instant compliance, has something so
shocking in it, that humanity revolts at the idea. My God! What can this writer have
in view, by recommending such measures? Can he be a friend to the army? Can he be
a friend to his country? Rather, is he not an insidious foe; some emissary, perhaps,
from New York, plotting the ruin of both, by sowing the seeds of discord and separation between the civil and military powers of the continent? And what a compliment
does he pay our understandings, when he recommends measures, in either alternative,
impracticable in their nature? But here, gentlemen, I will drop the curtain, because it
would be as imprudent in me to assign my reasons for this opinion, as it would be
insulting to your conception to suppose you stood in need of them. A moment's reflec-
tion will convince every dispassionate mind of the physical impossibility of carrying
either proposal into execution. There might, gentlemen, be an impropriety in my taking notice, in this address to you, of an anonymous production; but the manner in
which this performance has been introduced to the army; the effect it was intended
to have, together with some other circumstances, will amply justify my observations
on the tendency of this writing.

With respect to the advice given by the author, to suspect the man who shall recommend moderate measures and longer forbearance, I spurn it, as every man who
regards that liberty and reveres that justice for which we contend, undoubtedly must;
for if men are to be precluded from offering their sentiments on a matter which may
involve the most serious and alarming consequences that can invite the consideration
of mankind, reason is of no use to us. The freedom of speech may be taken away, and
dumb and silent, we may be led, like sheep to the slaughter. I cannot in justice to my
own belief, and what I have great reason to conceive is the intention of Congress, con-
clude this address, without giving it as my decided opinion, that that honorable body
entertain exalted sentiments of the services of the army, and from a full conviction of
its merits and sufferings, will do it complete justice. That their endeavors to discover
and establish funds for this purpose have been unwearied, and will not cease till they
have succeeded, I have not a doubt.

But like all other large bodies, where there is a variety of different interests to reconcile, their deliberations are slow. Why, then, should we distrust them? and in consequence of this distrust, adopt measures which may cast a shade over that glory which has been so justly acquired, and tarnish the reputation of an army which is celebrated through all Europe for its fortitude and patriotism? And for what is this done? To bring the object we seek nearer? No! most certainly in my opinion, it will cast it at a greater distance. For myself, and I take no merit in giving the assurance, being induced to it from principles of gratitude, veracity, and justice, [and] a grateful sense of the confidence you have ever place in me, a recollection of the cheerful assistance and prompt obedience I have experienced from you, under every vicissitude of fortune, and the sincere affection I feel for an army I have so long had the honor to command, will oblige me to declare in this public and solemn manner, that in the attainment of complete justice for all your toils and dangers, and in the gratification of every wish so far as may be done consistently with the great duty I owe my country, and those powers we are bound to respect, you may freely command my services to the utmost extent of my abilities.

While I give you these assurances, and pledge myself in the most unequivocal manner, to exert whatever ability I am possessed of in your favor, let me entreat you, gentlemen, on your part, not to take any measures, which viewed in the calm light of reason, will lessen the dignity, and sully the glory you have hitherto maintained. Let me request you to rely on the plighted faith of your country, and place a full confidence in the purity of the intentions of Congress; that, previous to your dissolution as an army, they will cause all your accounts to be fairly liquidated as directed in the resolutions which were published to you two days ago; and that they will adopt the most effectual measures in their power to render ample justice to you for your faithful and meritorious services. And let me conjure you in the name of our common country, as you value your own sacred honor; as you respect the rights of humanity; and as you regard the military and national character of America; to express your utmost horror and detestation of the man, who wishes, under any specious pretences, to overturn the liberties of our country; and who wickedly attempts to open the flood gates of civil discord, and deluge our rising empire in blood.

By thus determining, and thus acting, you will pursue the plain and direct road to the attainment of your wishes; you will defeat the insidious designs of our enemies, who are compelled to resort from open force to secret artifice. You will give one more distinguished proof of unexampled patriotism and patient virtue, rising superior to the pressure of the most complicated sufferings; and you will, by the dignity of your conduct, afford occasion for posterity to say, when speaking of the glorious example you have exhibited to mankind—had this day been wanting, the world had never seen the last stage of perfection to which human nature is capable of attaining.

Appendix I: Proclamation by Elias Boudinot

By His EXCELLENCY Elias Boudinot, Esquire,
President of the United States in Congress Assembled,
A PROCLAMATION.
WHEREAS a body of armed Soldiers in the service of the United States, and quartered in the Barracks of this City, having mutinously renounced their obedience to their Officers, did, on Saturday the Twenty-First Day of this instant, proceed, under the direction of their Serjeants, in a hostile and threatning manner, to the Place in which Congress were assembled, and did surround the same with Guards: And whereas Congress in consequence thereof, did on the same Day, resolve, "That the President and Supreme Executive Council of this State should be informed, that the authority of the United States having been, that Day, grosily insulted by the disorderly and menacing appearance of a body of armed Soldiers, about the Place within which Congress were assembled; and that the Peace of this City being endangered by the mutinous Disposition of the said Troops then in the Barracks; it was, in the Opinion of Congress, necessary, that effectual measures should be immediately taken for supporting the public Authority:" And also whereas Congress did at the same Time appoint a Committee to confer with the said President and Supreme Executive Council on the practicability of carrying the said Resolution into due effect: And also whereas the said Committee have reported to me, that they have not received satisfactory Assurances for expecting adequate and prompt exertions of this State for supporting the Dignity of the federal Government: And also whereas the said Soldiers still continue in a state of open Mutiny and Revolt, so that the Dignity and Authorities of the United States be constantly exposed to a repetition of insult, while Congress still continue to fit in this city. I do therefore by and with the Advice of the said Committee, and according to the Powers and Authorities in me vested for this Purpose, hereby summon the honourable the Delegates composing the Congress of the United States, and every of them, to meet in Congress on Thursday the Twenty Sixth Day of June instant, at Princeton, in the state of New Jersey, in order that further and more effectual Measures may be taken for suppressing the present Revolt, and maintaining the Dignity and Authority of the United States, of which all Officers of the United States, civil and military, and all others whom it may concern, are desired to take Notice and govern themselves accordingly.
GIVEN under my Hand and Seal at Philadelphia, in the state of Pennsylvania, this Twenty-Fourth Day of June, in the Year of Our Lord One Thousand Seven Hundred and Eighty-Three, and of our Sovereignty and Independence the seventh.
ELIAS BOUDINOT.
Attest,
SAMUEL STERETT, Private Secretary

Notes

Abbreviations

CP–Sir Henry Clinton Papers at the William L. Clements Library

GP–Nathanael Greene Papers at the William L. Clements Library

GWP–George Washington Papers at the Library of Congress

JCC–Journals of the Continental Congress

Naval–Naval Documents of the American Revolution Series

PBF–Papers of Benjamin Franklin Series

PCC–Papers of the Continental Congress

INTRODUCTION

1 Neagles, *A Survey and Index of Revolutionary War Court Martial*: 34.

2 Putnam, Order Book: 68-71, Sept. 5, 1777.

3 State Records of North Carolina, Vol. XV: 187-188, Petition of Ann Glover, New Bern, Jan. 10, 1780.

4 Fantina, *Desertion and the American Soldier 1776-2006*: 16.

5 *Pennsylvania Archives*, Vol. 9: 437-438, William Crispin to General Lacey, Oct. 17, 1781.

6 *Magazine of American Histories with Notes and Queries*, Vol. 2 (1878): 280-281, Autobiography of Philip Van Cortlandt.

7 Ford, Order Book: 59, Aug. 20, 1777.

8 38 GWP, Varick Transcripts, Letterbook 2:264-266, General Orders, Aug. 19, 1777.

9 Dann, *Revolution Remembered*: 334.

10 Despite a concerted effort no one has been able to locate Bland's report of June 26, 1779, detaining the intended mutiny of his troops caused by "the supply of those necessaries, the want of which seems to have been the principal cause of discontent." Washington believed the punishment meted out to the perpetrators was light. GWP, Varick Transcripts, Letterbook 9: 340-341, George Washington to Theodorick Bland, Aug. 20, 1779. *Papers of Nathanael Greene* 12:639, Josiah Harmar at Camp James Island to Nathanael Greene, May 3, 1783. *State Records of North Carolina*, Vol. 22: 1039-1040 Message to the General Assembly State of North Caroina, July 7, 1781.

11 Garden, *Anecdotes of the Revolutionary War in America*:110-111.

12 *South Carolina Historical Magazine*, Vol. 98 No. 2, Finney Diary: 136.

13 Richards, *Diary of Samuel Richards*: 67-68.

14 New Hampshire Provincial and State Papers Vol. 17: 269, List of the Rank... of the 3rd New Hampshire Regiment, Aug. 1778; Vol. 16: 355, Abigail Badger widow of Zacheriah Beale, Oct. 25, 1784; Paul Allen, *A History of the American Revolution*, Vol. 2 (1822): 123 and GWP, Gen. Correspondence, Israel Putnam to George Washington, Nov. 7, 1777.

CHAPTER I

1 GWP, Letterbook 7:. 88-89.

2 Moses Gill (born Jan. 18, 1734) was a hardware merchant in Worcester County, Massachusetts, and became Lieutenant Governor in 1794 and Acting Governor in 1799. He died in office on May 20, 1800.

3 Massachusetts Archives Collection, Provincial Congress resolve for paying Dr. Church and Gill for escorting Washington, Watertown, July 6, 1775.

4 Adams Family Papers, Abigail Adams to John Adams, July 25, 1775.

5 *Archives of Maryland*, Vol. 435, A History of Printing in Colonial Maryland: 1686-1776: 247 No. 352, Broadside by M. K. Goddard, Baltimore, Aug. 10, 1775.

6 *Pennsylvania Archives Second Series* Vol. X: 8-10.

7 Is it Leamon or Seamon? It is a case of who does the deciphering of a difficult handwriting. Since the Massachusetts Historical Society is the home team in this case and from its sources says it is Leamon. I will defer to their call.

8 Colonel Daniel Hitchcock's 2nd Rhode Island Regiment was recruited from the militia of Providence County.

9 *Pennsylvania Archives Second Series* Vol. X: 8-10.

10 GWP, Varick Transcripts, Letterbook 1: 74-76, General Orders Sept. 11, 1775.

11 Ibid.

12 GWP, Varick Transcripts, Letterbook 1: 76, General Orders Sept. 13, 1775.

13 JCC, 4: 37, Jan. 6, 1776.

14 Peckham, *The Toll of Independence*: 11, Dec. 31, 1775.

15 JCC, 4: 39, Jan. 8, 1776.

16 GWP, Gen. Correspondence, Philip J. Schuyler to George Washington, Jan. 13, 1776.

17 GWP, Letterbook 7: 191-193, George Washington to Philip J. Schuyler, Jan. 18, 1776.

18 GWP, Letterbook 7: 194-195, George Washington to CT, MA, and NH, Jan. 19, 1776.

19 Roberts, *March to Quebec*: 488, Caleb Haskill's Diary.

20 The companies of Dorsey, Jones, Davis Williams, and Jenkins with Lt. Col. Irvine and Major Morris made it to Albany.

21 Philip Schuyler Papers on Microfilm, Court Martial at Albany, New York, Feb. 9, 1776 and Tussell, *The Pennsylvania Line*: 41. Jones, *History of the Campaign for the Conquest of Canada in 1776*: 18–24.

22 Wayne Papers, Anthony Wayne to Colonel Joseph Wood, Mar. 2, 1777.

23 Abatis is a defensive obstacle made by laying felled trees on top of each other with branches, sometimes sharpened, facing the enemy.

24 Wayne Papers, Major Hay to Wayne, Feb. 9, 1777.

25 Berg, *Encyclopedia Continental Army Units*: 78; Captain John Nelson was made a captain in the 9th Pennsylvania Regiment on November 15, 1776.

26 Wayne Papers, Complaint of Josiah Holida at Ticonderoga to Col. Timothy Robinson, Feb. 11, 1777. Holida signs with an "X." Schuyler in a document lists him as Holiday.

27 Wayne Papers, Anthony Wayne to Gen. Schuyler, Feb. 12, 1777.

28 Wayne Papers, Officers' Remonstrance to Col. Timothy Robinson, Feb. 11, 1777.

29 Wayne Papers, Anthony Wayne to Gen. Schuyler, Feb. 12, 1777.

30 Wayne Papers, Gen. Schuyler at Albany to Anthony Wayne, Feb. 16, 1777.

31 Wayne Papers, General Orders, Gen. Schuyler at Albany to Anthony Wayne, Feb. 16, 1777.

32 Wayne Papers, Gen. Schuyler at Albany to Anthony Wayne, Feb. 19, 1777.

33 Wayne Papers, Anthony Wayne to Gen. Schuyler, Feb. 24, 1777.

34 Haussegger is sometimes spelt Hawsaikse, Houseacker, or Houseker.

35 Pennsylvania State Archives, Revolutionary War Military Abstract Card File and LOC, Washington Papers, General Correspondence, George Washington to Congress, Sept. 11, 1776.

36 Coryell's Ferry is New Hope, Pennsylvania, and Lambertville, New Jersey.

37 LOC, Washington Papers, General Correspondence, George Washington General Orders, Dec. 10, 1776.

38 Peckham, *Memoirs of the Life of John Adlum*: 119.

39 Ibid.: 120.

40 Ibid.: 118-124.

41 Wayne Papers, Col. Joseph Wood to Anthony Wayne at Fort Ticonderoga, Feb. 10, 1777.

42 GWP, Varick Transcripts, Letterbook 9: 333, George Washington to John Beatty, Comm. Gen. of Prisoners, Aug. 19, 1779.

43 Bray, *Diary of a Common Soldier*: 133, Dec. 12 to 26, 1778 and Jan. 1779.

44 Ibid.: 135, April 23 and 24, 1779.

45 Barber's Heights is a hill about 200 feet high that is four miles south of Wickford, on the shore north of Saunderstown.

46 Bray, *Diary of a Common Soldier*: 137-138, July 29, 1779.

47 Field, Edward, editor. *Diary of Colonel Israel Angell*: 66-73.

48 Neagles, *Summer Soldiers*: 203

49 *Papers of the Historical Society of Delaware*, Vol. 2 #14 Letters to George Read, 1776.

50 GWP, Varick Transcripts, Letterbook 2: 66-69, George Washington to Continental Congress, Nov. 11, 1776.

51 Collections of the Massachusetts Historical Society, 7th Ser, Vol. 2: 98-101, Gold Selleck Silliman at Fairfield to Gov. Jonathan Trumbull, Feb. 2, 1777.

52 Ibid.

53 Butterfield, *Washington-Irvine Correspondence*: 351, Captain John Finley to William Irvine, Feb. 2, 1782.

54 GWP, Gen. Correspondence, William Irvine to George Washington, Feb. 7, 1782.

55 The 7th Virginia Regiment of 1781 was the former 9th Virginia Regiment of 1778 under Colonel John Gibson. Prior to September 14, 1778, it was known as the 13th Virginia Regiment under Colonel William Russell, and was formed in 1776.

56 There is some truth to this. Colonel Daniel Brodhead had paid "Captain Wilson," an Indian scout, a horse for his service to the United States.

57 The 8th Pennsylvania Regiment jointly occupied Fort Pitt with the Virginia troops.

The depreciation pay was to account for the depreciation in the value of Continental Currency.

58 C. W. Butterfield suggests that this letter was written in late March or April 1782.

59 Butterfield, *Washington-Irvine Correspondence*: 111-112, General Irvine Orderly Book, After Orders April 30, 1782.

60 Playing ball was a forerunner of the game of lacrosse. Lederer, *Colonial American English*: 24

61 GWP, Gen. Correspondence, Col. Heman Swift to George Washington May 6, 1782 morning.

62 Ibid.

63 GWP, Varick Transcripts, 15:101 George Washington to Heman Swift, May 6, 1782.

64 The first name of Gerred Bunce also appears as Jerred on the same document.

65 GWP, Varick Transcripts, 6: 152-154 George Washington General Orders, May 12, 1782.

66 GWP, Varick Transcripts, 6: 240-245 George Washington to Robert Morris, May 17, 1782.

67 There are two Captain Bailey's in the 2nd Massachusetts Regiment. They are Adam and Luther and they served under their father Colonel John Bailey.

68 GWP, General Correspondence, William Heath to George Washington, Jan. 10, 1780.

69 Smith, *William Smith's Historical Memoirs 1778-1783*, provided the weather reports.

70 Heath, *Memoirs of Major General William Heath*: 226-227 and GWP, Gen. Correspondence, William Heath to George Washington, Jan. 10, 1780. The Jan. 11th report of the capture is on the back page of Jan. 10th letter.

71 The modern preferred spelling is Thomson but in the eighteenth century it was spelled both Thomson and Thompson. Thomson would be the hero of the Battle of Breach Inlet in June 1776.

72 The "Dutch" were actually German and Swiss immigrants who settled in the area between the Saluda and the Broad Rivers (called Dutch Fork) in Saxe Gotha Township and in Amelia Township on the Santee River.

73 Gibbes, *Documentary History of the American Revolution*, W. H. Drayton and Rev. William Tennent at Congaree Store (130 miles from Charleston) to the Council of Safety, Aug. 7, 1775: 128- 129 and William Tennent Journal, Aug. 2, 1775 to Sept. 15, 1775: 225-236.

74 Colonel Fletchall lived on Fairforest Creek is in modern Union County, South Carolina.

75 Gibbes, *Documentary History of the American Revolution*, W. H. Drayton and Rev. William Tennent at Congaree Store to the Council of Safety, Aug. 7, 1775: 129-130.

76 Ibid.: 130-131.

77 Captain Kershaw could be either Ely or Joseph who were brothers.

78 Lewis Dutarque's first name also has been given as Louis.

79 Gibbes, *Documentary History of the American Revolution*, W. H. Drayton and Rev. William Tennent at Congaree Store to the Council of Safety, Aug. 7, 1775: 131.

80 Ibid.

81 Purdies, *Virginia Gazette*, p. 3 c. 1, Dec. 15, 1775.

82 *Southern Literary Messenger*, Vol. 4 No. 4 (1838): 215, Biographical Sketch of General Hugh Mercer. The *Virginia Gazette* reported on March 30, 1776, a letter from First Lieutenant William Linn of Gibson's company of regulars. Linn indicated that Captain Gibson was away and he was in charge of the company. He sent and the newspaper printed General Howe's General Orders of March 17 effecting this. His letter stated that Colonel Mercer realized he had exceeded his authority in his treatment of Captain Gibson's Company. Mercer, the article said, had requested the commanding officer to declare in orders that he had no personal intent in his actions and desired to acknowledge that he was wrong and assured the company that he was sorry for what happened. Dixon, *Virginia Gazette*, p. 3 c. 3, Mar. 30, 1776 and Purdies, *Virginia Gazette*, p. 3, col. 3, April 5, 1776.

83 New-York Historical Society Collections, 1872, Lee Papers, Vol. II:. 34-36, Charles Lee at Halifax to Edmund Pendleton, May 24, 1776.

84 Friedman, *A Brief History of the University of Pennsylvania*.

85 New-York Historical Society Collections, 1872, Lee Papers, Vol. II: 50, Edmund Pendleton at Williamsburg to Charles Lee, June 1, 1776.

86 Ibid.: 34-36, Charles Lee at Halifax to Edmund Pendleton, May 24, 1776.

87 Ibid.

88 Ibid.: 38, Charles Lee at Tarborough to Edmund Pendleton, May 25, 1776.

89 Jones, *A Defense of the Revolutionary History of the State of North Carolina*: 265.

90 *State Records of North Carolina*, Vol. XI: 329-330, Council of Safety to Gen. John Ashe, July 25, 1776.

91 Graham says he enrolled in the 6th North Carolina Regiment but he says he was under Colonel Archibald Lytle in Captain Christopher Gooden's Company. According to Heitman, *Historical Register of Officers of the Continental Army*, they were in the 6th North Carolina Regiment.

92 *State Records of North Carolina*, Vol. XIX: 956-964, Pension declaration of Joseph Graham.

93 Purrysburg, South Carolina is gone except for a cemetery.

94 McCrady, *History of South Carolina in the Revolution*: 333-335

CHAPTER 2

1 GWP, Letterbooks, George Washington at Kingsbridge to Joseph Trumbull, Oct. 20, 1776.

2 GWP, Varick Transcripts, Letterbook 3: 135-142, George Washington to Continental Congress Dec. 23, 1777.

3 Ibid.

4 GWP, General Correspondence, James Varnum to George Washington, Dec. 22, 1777.

5 GWP, Varick Transcripts, Letterbook 3: 135-142, George Washington to Continental Congress Dec. 23, 1777.

6 *The Papers of General Nathanael Greene*, Vol. 2: 259-261, Nathanael Greene to Gen. Alexander McDougall, Jan. 25, 1778.

7 GWP, Varick Transcripts, Letterbook 3: 62-64, General Orders, Feb. 15, 1778 and Enoch Poor's Valley Forge Order Book Jan. 28–Feb. 20, 1778

8 Letter of Delegates to Congress, Volume 9: 109-111, Francis Dana to Elbridge Gerry, Feb. 16, 1778.

9 Ibid.

10 GWP, Varick Transcripts, Letterbook 5: 60-61, George Washington to William Smallwood, Feb. 16, 1778.

11 GWP, Varick Transcripts, Letterbook 2: 241-242, George Washington to George Clinton, Feb. 16, 1778.

12 Ibid.

13 GWP, Varick Transcripts, Letterbook 1: 73-75, George Washington to John Cadwalader, Mar. 20, 1778.

14 Anthony Wayne to Richard Peters, May 13, 1778.

15 Wayne, in this letter in reference to "Shakespeare's apothecary" was referring to *Romeo and Juliet*, Act 5, Scene 1 when Romeo is looking for a way to illegally purchase poison. Romeo says:

I do remember an apothecary,—
And hereabouts he dwells,—which late I noted
In tatter'd weeds, with overwhelming brows,
Culling of simples; meagre were his looks,
Sharp misery had worn him to the bones:
And in his needy shop a tortoise hung,
An alligator stuff'd, and other skins
Of ill-shaped fishes; and about his shelves
A beggarly account of empty boxes,
Green earthen pots, bladders and musty seeds,
Remnants of packthread and old cakes of roses,
Were thinly scatter'd, to make up a show.
Noting this penury, to myself I said
'An if a man did need a poison now,
Whose sale is present death in Mantua,
Here lives a caitiff wretch would sell it him.

"Meagre were his looks, / Sharp misery had worn him to the bones" described the condition of Wayne's sick and starving troops.

16 Stillé, *Major General Wayne and the Pennsylvania Line*: 137-139, Anthony Wayne to Richard Peters, May 13, 1778.

17 Richards, *Diary of Samuel Richards*: 53, Feb. 1778.

18 GWP, General Correspondence, Samuel Parsons to George Washington, Dec. 23, 1778.

19 Gruber, *John Peebles' American War*: 238-241.

20 Hall, *Life and Letters of General Samuel Holden Parsons*, General Orders Dec. 27 and 29, 1778 and Parsons to Gen McDougall, Dec. 27, 1778: 205-206.

21 Martin, *Private Yankee Doodle* (1962): 149-150.

22 Collections of the Massachusetts Historical Society, 7th Series Vol. 2: 325-327, Return Jonathan Meigs to Titus Hosmer, Dec. 26, 1778.

23 Ibid.

24 Richards, *Diary of Samuel Richards*: 66.

25 Todd, *History of Redding, Connecticut*: 57-58.

26 The events of the mutiny were recorded by David Humphreys from Derby, Connecticut, who had been appointed Putnam's aide-de-camp on December 18, 1778. He later became aide-de-camp successively to Greene and Washington.

27 GWP, Gen. Correspondence, Israel Putnam to George Washington, Jan. 5, 1779 and Petitioners to Israel Putnam, Jan. 5, 1779.

28 GWP, Varick Transcripts, Letterbook 8: 25-27, George Washington to Israel Putnam, Jan. 18, 1779.

29 GWP, Varick Transcripts, Letterbook 8: 16, George Washington to Jedidiah Huntington, Jan. 8, 1779.

30 GWP, Varick Transcripts, Letterbook 8: 10-14, George Washington to Israel Putnam, Jan. 8, 1779.

31 Hall, *Life and Letters of General Samuel Holden Parsons*, Parsons at Greenwich to Gov. Clinton Jan. 2, 1779 and Parsons to McDougall, Jan. 5, 1779: 207.

32 Martin, *Private Yankee Doodle*: 150

33 Fitzpatrick, *The Writings of George Washington*, George Washington to Continental Congress, May 27, 1780, note 63.

34 Richards, *Diary of Samuel Richards*: 77.

35 Richards, *Diary of Samuel Richards*: 67-68.

36 GWP, Varick Transcripts, Letterbook 4: 345-347, General Orders Mar. 1, 1780.

37 GWP, Varick Transcripts, Letterbook 4: 376-377, General Orders April 5, 1780.

38 GWP, Varick Transcripts, Letterbook 5: 23, General Orders May 9, 1780.

39 GWP, Varick Transcripts, Letterbook 5: 48, General Orders May 1, 1780.

40 GWP, Varick Transcripts, Letterbook 5: 29, General Orders May 18, 1780.

41 GWP, Varick Transcripts, Letterbook 5: 33-34, General Orders May 24, 1780.

42 Richards, *Diary of Samuel Richards*: 67-68 and a modern author says parts of the 4th Connecticut Regiment were also involved.

43 JCC, VIII: 579-580., By resolution of Congress, 25 July 1777, an elegant sword to be presented to Lt. Colonel Return J. Meigs, of Connecticut for his distinguished "prudence, activity, enterprise and valor in the expedition to Long Island." This sword is on display at the Smithsonian Institution, Washington, D.C.

44 Richards, *Diary of Samuel Richards*: 67-68

45 Letters of Delegates to Congress: Volume: 15: 271, John Morin Scott to Ezra L'Hommedieu, June 6, 1780.

46 Lake Canandaigua is the fourth largest of the New York finger lakes and is between Syracuse and Rochester. It is 15.8 miles long and 1.5 miles wide.

47 Thatcher, *Military Journal During the American Revolutionary War* (1823 edition): 233-235, May 26, 1780

48 There are several Stevensons in the Pennsylvania Line but only two at this time. There is George Stevenson who was a surgeon's mate in the Hospital Department who served from 1778 to 1781 and there is Stephen Stevenson who was a Captain Lieutenant

in the 9th Pennsylvania Regiment and most likely the visitor.

49 Richards, *Diary of Samuel Richards*: 67-68

50 GWP, Varick Transcripts, Letterbook 11: 358, George Washington to Henry Champion, May 26, 1780.

51 GWP, Varick Transcripts, Letterbook 3: 283-284, George Washington to Jonathan Trumbull, May 26, 1780.

52 GWP, Varick Transcripts, Letterbook 2: 61-68, George Washington to Joseph Reed, May 28, 1780.

53 GWP, Varick Transcripts, Letterbook 5: 188-192, George Washington to Continental Congress, May 27, 1780.

54 Fort Schuyler is in Rome, New York.

55 GWP, Varick Transcripts, Letterbook 5: 211-215 George Washington to Continental Congress, June 20, 1780.

56 GWP, Varick Transcripts, Letterbook 11: 411-414, George Washington to Robert Howe, June 20, 1780.

57 GWP, Varick Transcripts, Letterbook 3: 309-312, George Washington to George Clinton, June 20, 1780.

58 GWP, Varick Transcripts, Letterbook 11: 417-418, George Washington to Colonel Goose Van Schaick at Albany, June 20, 1780.

CHAPTER 3

1 Sparks, *Writings of George Washington*, Volume III: 507-508, Lord Dartmouth at London to Gen. Thomas Gage at Boston, Jan. 27, 1775.

2 French, *General Gage's Informers*: 164-165.

3 Gage Papers, Vol. 127, Gage to Lt. Col. Smith, April 18, 1775 and for an illustrated listing of the items see John C. Dann, *One Hundred and One Treasures*: 80.

4 French, *General Gage's Informers*: 31

5 Mackenzie, *Diary of Frederick Mackenzie*, I: 18 (April 18, 1775).

6 Belknap, *Journal of my Tour to the Camp*: 77-86.

7 Although there is no absolute proof that she was the source of the intelligence. There is very strong circumstantial evidence and there are no other serious suspects.

8 Hutchinson, *Diary and Letters of His Excellency Thomas Hutchinson, Esq.*, Vol. I: 497-498

9 Fischer, *Paul Revere's Ride*: 386-387 fn 6, 14 and quoted from Charles Steadman, *History of the Origin, Progress, and Termination of the American War*, Vol. I: 119 and Frothingham, *Warren*: 456

10 Hugh, Earl Percy was thus actually born Hugh Smithson in Aug. 1742.

11 JCC, 2: 190, July 19, 1775.

12 JCC, 3: 419, Dec. 9, 1775 and Vol. 4: 210, Mar. 16, 1776.

13 GWP, Letterbook 8: 46-49 to Congress, April 22, 1776.

14 GWP, Varick Transcripts, Letterbook 1: 260-261, May 24, 1776, General Orders

15 JCC, 5: 808, Sept. 20, 1776.

16 In July of 1776, work was begun on this site, which was first named "Fort Constitution." The name was later changed to "Fort Lee," to honor General Charles Lee.

17 GWP, Varick Transcripts, Letterbook 1: 398, George Washington to Robert Ogden, Jan. 24, 1777.

18 PCC: Feb. 6, 1777, Thomas Mifflin to John Hancock.

19 Seven Years War (1756-1763) in America is known as the French and Indian War.

20 BFP, Henry Emanuel Lutterloh to American Commissioner or Commissioners, Jan. 8, 1777.

21 JCC, 8: 499-501, June 26, 1777.

22 *Pennsylvania Packet*, June 17, 1778.

23 PCC, July 28, 1777, George Washington to Thomas Mifflin.

24 JCC, 9: 874, Nov. 7, 1777.

25 GWP, General Correspondence, George Washington to Continental Congress, Dec. 23, 1777.

26 From the Diary of Albigence Waldo, Surgeon at Valley Forge, 1777 America Firsthand. Volume I: 121-124

27 Letters of Delegates to Congress, 9: Feb. 1, 1778 - May 31, 1778, Francis Dana to Elbridge Gerry, Feb. 16, 1778.

28 JCC, 12: 1115, Nov. 10, 1778. The members of the committee were Gouveneur Morris, Nathaniel Scudder, and William Whipple.

29 JCC, 14: 503, April 23, 1779.

30 James S. Schoff Collection, Ephraim Blaine at Carlisle, Pennsylvania, to Joseph Reed, April 29, 1779.

31 JCC, 4: 812-13, July 9, 1779.

32 JCC, 14: 944, Aug. 11, 1779.

33 PCC, RG11 CC Papers Item 173 4:243-254, Dec. 12, 1779.

34 GWP, Varick Transcripts, Letterbook 1: 26-31, George Washington to Robert Moises, Mar. 2, 1777.

35 Carp, *To Starve the Army of Pleasure*: 181-182.

36 PCC. Item 155 1:196 Greene to President of Congress, Jan. 13, 1780.

37 JCC 16: 75-77, 79, Jan. 20, 21, and 22 1780.

38 Risch: 53.

39 GWP, Gen. Correspondence, Greene to George Washington, Mar. 28, 1780.

40 JCC, 16: 357 and 362, April 12 and 13, 1780.

41 PCC, RG11 CC Papers Item 155 1: 399-402 Greene to President of Congress, 26 July 1780.

Chapter 4

1 Smith, *William Smith's Historical Memoirs 1778-1783*: 370.

2 CP 72:13, Daniel Coxe to John Andre, Oct. 21, 1779.

3 CP 90:12, Daniel Coxe at New York to John Andre: 3, Mar. 28, 1780.

4 GWP, Varick Transcripts, Letterbook 2: 190-191, George Washington to William Gordon, Mar. 9, 1781.

5 GWP, Varick Transcripts, Letterbook 12: 399-401, George Washington to Benjamin Lincoln, Dec. 11, 1780.

6 GWP, Varick Transcripts, Letterbook 2: 141-144, George Washington to Nathanael Greene, Dec. 13, 1780.

7 GWP, Varick Transcripts, Letterbook 12: 416-417, George Washington to William Heath, Dec. 20, 1780.

8 Reed, *Life and Correspondence of Joseph Reed*, Vol. 2: 315-317, Anthony Wayne to Joseph Reed, Dec. 16, 1780.

9 Stevens, *Facsimiles*, Vol. 17 No. 1632: 37-38, Lafayette to Comte de Vergennes, Jan, 30, 1781.

10 JCC, Vol. XIII: 108, Jan. 1–April 22, 1779.

11 GWP, Varick Transcripts, Letterbook 4: 274-281.

12 JCC Volume 14: 758, June 22, 1779.

13 During the summer of 1779, two regiments of infantry and one of artillery of the Pennsylvania Line had been sent on Major General John Sullivan's campaign against the Six Nations of Iroquois who had joined forces with the British in attacking towns and settlements in New York and Pennsylvania. They returned to the main army at Totowa, New Jersey in the fall.

14 The huts were laid out using the procedures given in the general orders of December 17, 1777 at the encampment at Valley Forge. Each hut was to be fourteen feet wide and sixteen feet long with six-and-half-foot-high side walls. The log huts would be notched at the ends. The gaps between the logs would be filled with a mix of clay and mud to keep out the weather. The roofs were made of whatever was available. Some were made of shingles, split logs or smaller logs extending down from a ridge pole.

On the street or parade end, a doorway was made with a door composed of split oak slabs, unless boards could be had, and it was hung on a wooden hinges. On the opposite end was a fireplace built of logs covered in clay on the inside eighteen inches thick. (GWP, Varick Transcripts, Letterbook 2: 323, George Washington General Orders, Dec. 18, 1777.)

The chimneys had to be two feet higher than the roof to prevent fires. Windows, if there were any, were holes cut through the side wall and a shutter mounted on wooden hinges used to close the opening. The floor was packed dirt.

Each hut had bunks made of planks where ten or twelve men slept. The parade ground was clear of trees and policed to remove any trash. Attention was paid to draining the camp ground and building of necessaries (latrines).

British spies had been about the American camp just as they had been in the past. British headquarters had a detailed map of the American camp with the positions of the troops in the area of Morristown in 1780 (see map on page 69).

Spies like Joseph Gould reported, on December 18, 1780, that, "the Pennsylvania troops are in the same huts that the New England troops lay in last year in the neighborhood of Kembels."

15 GWP, Varick Transcripts, Letterbook 3: 195-197, George Washington at Morristown to Jonathan Trumbull, Jan. 8, 1780.

16 GWP, Varick Transcripts, Letterbook 3: 195-197, George Washington at Morristown to Jonathan Trumbull, Jan. 8, 1780.

17 GWP, Varick Transcripts, Letterbook 3: 197-200, George Washington at Morristown to New Jersey Magistrates, Jan. 8, 1780.

18 For a look at the certificates that were issued see William G. Anderson's *The Price of Liberty* (University Press of Virginia, 1983).

19 GWP, Varick Transcripts, Letterbook 5: 207-211, George Washington General Orders, Nov. 1, 1780.

20 GWP, General Correspondence, James Wilkinson Philadelphia Clothing Report, Dec. 9, 1780.

21 GWP, General Correspondence, Mrs. Susan Blair to George Washington, Dec. 8, 1780.

22 GWP, Varick Transcripts, Letterbook 4: 48-49, George Washington to Mrs. Susan Blair, Dec. 22, 1780.

23 GWP, Varick Transcripts, Letterbook 12: 419-420, George Washington to Samuel Miles, Dec. 23, 1780.

24 GWP, Varick Transcripts, Letterbook 12: 426-427, George Washington to Anthony Wayne, Dec. 28, 1780 and pp. 430-431, George Washington to Israel Shreve, Dec. 29, 1780.

25 Firecake is a mixture of flour and water. Salt would be added if available. It would be formed into a cake and baked on a rock in the fire or over the fire, usually in the ashes until blackened.

Chapter 5

1 *Proceedings of the New Jersey Historical Society*, 64:34, Diary of William S. Pennington, Jan. 1, 1781.

2 Lieutenant Abraham Wood had been in the 5th Pennsylvania Regiment when he was wounded and taken prisoner at Brandywine in September, 1777. He was exchanged and transferred to the Invalid Regiment in 1778.

3 GWP, Varick Transcripts, Letterbook 5: 248-249, George Washington, Jan. 2, 1781, General Orders.

4 *Pennsylvania Magazine of History and Biography*, Vol. XX and XXI (1896 and 1897), Lieutenant Enos Reeves's letterbook, Jan. 2, 1781.

5 Ibid.

6 New-York Historical Society Collections 1878, The Thomson Papers: 53, Charles Thomson at Philadelphia to John Jay at Madrid, July 11, 1781.

7 Reeves gives the name as Billings. Boudinot gives the name as Captain Adam Bitting. William Livingston Papers Microfilm Edition, Elias Boudinot to William Livingston, Jan. 2, 1781. There is a memorial to Adam Bitten along Jockey Hollow Road near Morristown, New Jersey.

8 William Livingston Papers Microfilm Edition, Elias Boudinot to William Livingston, Jan. 2, 1781.

9 *Pennsylvania Magazine of History and Biography*, Vol. XX and XXI (1896 and 1897), Lieutenant Enos Reeves' letterbook, Jan. 2, 1781.

10 Ibid.

11 Ibid. A spontoon is a shafted weapon having a pointed blade with a crossbar at its base that was used by infantry officers in the 17th and 18th centuries. It is also called a half-pike.

12 Ibid.

13 Heath, *Memoirs of Major General William Heath*: 269.

14 CP 144:12 Oliver De Lancey's Journal.

15 *Pennsylvania Magazine of History and Biography*, Vol. XX and XXI (1896 and 1897), Lieutenant Enos Reeves's letterbook, Jan. 2, 1781.

16 Ibid.

17 *Pennsylvania Archives Second Series*, Volume XI (1890): 660, General Anthony Wayne at Mount Kemble to the Troops, Jan. 2, 1781. Sunrise at Morristown, New Jersey, on Jan. 2, 1781 was at 7:23 a.m.

18. Ibid.

19 William Livingston Papers Microfilm Edition, Elias Boudinot to William Livingston, Jan. 2, 1781.

20 *Pennsylvania Archives Second Series*, Volume XI (1890): 660 Diary of Captain Joseph Mc Clellan of 9th Pennsylvania Regiment, General Anthony Wayne at Mount Kemble to the Troops, Jan. 2, 1781.

21 CP 140.9 Intelligence by Cornelius Tyger, Jan. 11, 1781.

22 Livingston Papers Microfilm Edition, William Livingston to John Breeze, Jan. 9, 1781. Although it is addressed to Breese, it is signed Brees.

23 Livingston Papers Microfilm Edition, Elias Boudinot to William Livingston, Jan. 2, 1781.

24 Livingston Papers Microfilm Edition, Nathaniel Herd to William Livingston, Jan. 3, 1781 at noon. Units determined from Stryker, Official Register of the Officers and Men of New Jersey.

25 Livingston Papers Microfilm Edition, Nathaniel Herd to William Livingston, Jan. 6, 1781. 1:00 p.m.

26 Wilson, *Book of the First Troop*: 37, Joseph Reed to Capt. Samuel Morris, Jan. 3, 1781.

27 Thomas was a member of the Carpenter's Association, the Sons of Saint Tammany of Philadelphia and an active member and Master in 1779 of the Free Masons, Lodge No. 19.

28 The Old Stone House was a large two–story three-bay stone residence with a smaller two–story three-bay addition that sat on high ground.

29 JCC, Volume 19: 20 and 25.

30 Livingston Papers Microfilm Edition, Samuel Smith at Princeton to William Livingston, Jan. 3, 1781. Samuel Smith lived in the five bay College of New Jersey (now Princeton University) President's House (now know as the Maclean House) which was built in 1756 near Nassau Hall. New Jersey was settled as two British Colonies of East and West Jersey. The grants were returned to the crown and reissued as the Colony of New Jersey in 1702.

31 George Morgan (1743-1810) had been agent for Indian Affairs and a colonel. He was appointed Deputy Commissioner-General for Purchases Western District. He retired in 1779. The property was known as "Prospect near Princeton." Continental Congress held a number of its sessions at Prospect in 1783 before establishing itself in Nassau Hall. Morgan's stone farm house was replaced in 1849.

32 *Pennsylvania Archives Second Series,* Volume XI (1890): 660 Diary of Captain Joseph Mc Clellan of 9th Pennsylvania Regiment, Jan. 3, 1781.

33 Nichols, *The Doughboy of 1780:* 462.

34 GWP, Varick Transcripts, Letterbook 5: 188-192, George Washington to the Continental Congress, May 27, 1780

35 Reprinted from Clinton, Papers (Hastings), 5:759-61. RC (N: Clinton Papers). Charred. May 27, 1780.

36 Hall, *Life and Letters of General Samuel Holden Parsons:* 321-322, Samuel Parsons to Jeremiah Wadsworth, Jan. 14, 1781

37 GWP, Varick Transcripts, Letterbook 4: 41, George Washington to George Clinton, Dec. 10, 1780.

38 GWP, Varick Transcripts, Letterbook 12: 387, George Washington to William Heath, Dec. 8, 1780.

39 GWP, Varick Transcripts, Letterbook 12: 395, George Washington to William Heath, Dec. 10, 1780.

40 GWP, Varick Transcripts, Letterbook 12: 399-401, George Washington to Benjamin Lincoln, Dec. 11, 1780.

41 GWP, Varick Transcripts, Letterbook 2: 161-162, George Washington at New Windsor to Philip J. Schuyler, Jan. 10, 1781.

42 GWP, General Correspondence, George Washington at Cambridge to Artemus Ward, April 4, 1776.

43 GWP, Varick Transcripts, Letterbook 2: 241, George Washington to George Clinton, Feb. 16, 1778.

44 GWP, Varick Transcripts, Letterbook 13: 33-35, George Washington at New Windsor to Anthony Wayne, Jan. 3-4, 1781.

45 Ibid.

46 Ibid.

47 Stillé, *Major General Wayne and the Pennsylvania Line:* 254, Major Moore to Gen. Wayne, Jan. 5, 1781 at 3:00 p.m.

48 PCC, Microfilm, m247, r170, i152, v.9: 449, Committee of Sergeants Proposal to Anthony Wayne.

49 PCC, Microfilm, m247, r170, i152, v.9: 479-480, Anthony Wayne's Response to Mutineers, Jan. 4, 1781.

50 PCC, Microfilm, m247, r170, i152, v.9: 485, Anthony Wayne, Jan. 4, 1781.

51 *Pennsylvania Archives Second Series,* Volume XI: 635 Butler, Stewart, and Wayne to Joseph Reed, Jan 4, 1781.

52 *Pennsylvania Archives Second Series,* Volume XI: 636 Gen. St. Clair to Joseph Reed, Jan 4, 1781 and Smith, St. Clair Papers, Vol. I, 532-533.

CHAPTER 6

1 Prince, *Papers of William Livingston*, Vol. 4: 118, John Adam to William Livingston, Jan. 3, 1781.

2 PCC, Microfilm, r53, i42, v1, p.361, Elias Dayton pass for Caleb Bruen, Joseph Gould and Gilbert Smyth to pass to New York and return on public business, May 1, 1780. All three are spies.

3 CP 149:39 Cortland Skinner to Henry Clinton, Mar. 15, 1781.

4 'London Bridge', *Old and New London*: Volume 2 (1878): 9-17. URL: www.british-history.ac.uk/report.asp?compid=45071. Date accessed: 29 Aug. 2006.

5 Wallabout Bay is between the Brooklyn and Manhattan Bridges and became the site of the Brooklyn Navy Yard.

6 CP 138:42 Isaac Ogden to Oliver De Lancey, Jan. 3, 1781.

7 CP 138:35 and 138:36 Gould's Deposition, Jan. 3, 1781.

8 Gruber, *John Peebles' American War*: 423.

9 Burgoyne, *Revolutionary War Letters Written by Hessian Officers*: 59, von Hachenberg to Hereditary Prince Frederick II of Hesse-Cassel, Jan. 23, 1781.

10 CP 138:23 Hugh Haggerty Deposition, Jan. 2, 1781.

11 CP 138:45 Abraham and Thomas Ward's Depositions, Jan. 3, 1781.

12 CP 138:39 Riverius Lee Deposition, Jan. 3, 1781.

13 CP 138:43 Captain Steward Ross's Report, Jan. 3, 1781.

14 CP 138:30 Andrew Gautier to Daniel Gautier, Jan 3, 1781 Annotated as Andrew Gautier at the time in John Stapleton's handwriting. 138:29 AG=Washington, ii=New Jersey, ss=troops, o=Morristown, rr=rebel, miltiac=Wayne, and k=West Point.

15 CP 139:12 Gold (Joseph Gould) Report, Jan. 5, 1781.

16 Mackenzie, *Diary of Frederick Mackenzie*, Volume 2: 447.

17 Black Point is now Rumson, New Jersey. Squan was at the entrance of the Manasquan River and could be either Brielle or Point Pleasant, New Jersey.

18 GWP, General Correspondence, Jacob Crane to Anthony Wayne, Jan. 4, 1781 at 5:00 a.m.

19 Ibid.

20 Billopp's Point is the southern end of Staten Island.

21 *Pennsylvania Archives Second Series*, Volume XI (1890): 665-666. Information at Elizabethtown for General Wayne, Jan. 5, 1781 at 5 a.m. Believed to be from Abraham Bancker.

22 Oliver De Lancey's Journal states that the two proposals went by way of Elizabethtown and Newark.

23 CP 139:15 Capt. Stewart Ross to Oliver De Lancey, Jan. 5, 1781 Gould put ashore at Elizabethtown Point.

24 CP 139:16 and 139:23 Capt. Stewart Ross to Oliver De Lancey, Jan. 6, 1781.

25 CP 54:24, John Mason to Sir Henry Clinton, Mar. 27, 1779 and July 5, 1780.

26 Sabine, *Historical Memoirs of William Smith 1778-1783*: 373, Jan. 5, 1781.

27 CP 139:15 (at 4:00 p.m.) and 139:29 (incorrectly dated 7th should be the 6th),

Stewart Ross to Oliver De Lancey, Jan. 5 and 6, 1781.

28 The person landed on the evening of Jan. 5, 1781 in New Jersey was John Mason. CP 139:17, John Stapleton at New York to Oliver De Lancey, Jan. 5, 1781.

29 Rattoon's tavern is identified as the Railroad House Hotel (A. D. Vanpelt, Proprietor) on the *Map of the County of Middlesex, New Jersey* by Smith Gallop and Co. published in 1861. The Bordentown Road in South Amboy is now known as Main Street.

30 Clayton, *History of Union and Middlesex Counties*: 824.

31 The moon was three-quarters full.

32 Burgoyne, *Journal of the Hesse-Cassel Jaeger Corps*: 131.

33 Ibid: 133.

34 The location of Rapalje's Tavern is found in Armbruster, *Long Island its Early Days and Development*: 27. CP 144: 12 Oliver De Lancey's Journal and Gruber, *John Peebles' American War*: 423.

35 CP 139:3 Joseph Clark's Report, Jan. 4, 1781.

36 The Clove is from Suffern to Monroe, New York. Both New York State Route 17 and the New York Thruway travel through the pass.

37 The only documentation is from De Lancey's Journal and he does not identify the courier.

38 Sabine, *William Smith's Historical Memoirs 1778-1783*: 373, Jan. 5, 1781.

39 *Pennsylvania Magazine of History and Biography*, Vol. XLI No. 4 1917: 399, Journal of Samuel Rowland Fisher and Diary of George Nelson, Jan. 4, 1781.

40 *Pennsylvania Magazine of History and Biography*, Vol. XLI No. 4 1917: 400, Journal of Samuel Rowland Fisher.

41 *Pennsylvania Colonial Records*, Vol. XII: 592-593, Supreme Executive Council, Jan. 5, 1781.

42 *Diary of George Nelson*, Jan. 5, 1781.

43 *Pennsylvania Council Minutes*, 12: 593.

44 Wayne Papers, Joseph Reed to Wayne, Cols Stewart and Butler, Jan. 6, 1781 (Correct date should be Jan. 5, 1781).

45 *Pennsylvania Archives First Series Vol. VIII*: 699, Timothy Matlack to Colonel S. Miles, DQMG, Jan 5, 1781.

46 Ibid.

47 *Pennsylvania Magazine of History and Biography*, Vol. XLI No. 4 (1917): 399, Journal of Samuel Rowland Fisher and Diary of George Nelson, Jan. 5, 1781

48 *Pennsylvania Archives Second Series*, Volume XI (1890): 668, General Wayne at Princeton to John Donaldson, Jan. 5, 1781 at 3:00 p.m.

49 *Pennsylvania Archives Second Series*, Volume XI (1890): 668, Major Charles Stewart at Trenton to Governor Reed, Jan. 5, 1781 at 5:00 p.m.

50 *Pennsylvania Archives Second Series*, Volume XI (1890): 668, General Wayne at Princeton to John Donaldson, Jan. 5, 1781 annotated on back J. Reed to Mr. Morris.

51 *Pennsylvania Archives Second Series*, Volume XI (1890): 667 Joseph Reed at Bristol to unknown recipient, Jan. 5, 1781.

51 Ibid.

53 Ibid.

54 William Livingston Papers Microfilm Edition, Moses Jacques at Elizabethtown to William Livingston, Jan. 5, 1781.

55 GWP, George Washington to Meshech Weare, et al, Circular Letter on Pennsylvania Line mutiny, Jan. 5, 1781.

56 *Proceedings of the New Jersey Historical Society*, 64: 34, Diary of William S. Pennington, Jan. 7, 1781.

CHAPTER 7

1 Sabine, *William Smith's Historical Memoirs 1778-1783*: 374, Jan. 6, 1781

2 Staten Island remained in British possession through out the war and was the final staging ground for the British evacuation of New York in 1783.

3 GWP, General Correspondence, David Humphreys to George Washington, Dec. 23, 1780.

4 GWP, Varick Transcripts, Letterbook 12: 420, George Washington to David Humphreys, Dec. 23, 1780.

5 GWP, General Correspondence, David Humphreys to George Washington, Dec. 23, 1780.

6 CP 142:21 Deposition of Zacheus Holmes deserter from 3rd Massachusetts Regiment, Jan. 24, 1781.

7 Weles could also be Welles or Wells. If one had to guess, the most likely person is Captain Roger Welles of Webb's Additional Continental Regiment. The unit in 1780 became the 9th Connecticut regiment. He was transferred on Jan. 1, 1781 to the 3rd Connecticut Regiment.

8 Holmes, who was in the same boat with Haskins, said the day before the enterprise, Colonel Humphreys and the two guides came from West Point to Nyack.

9 CP 142:21 Deposition of Cornelius Haskins deserter from 2nd Massachusetts Regiment, Jan. 24, 1781.

10 New-York Historical Society Collections 1882, von Kraft's Journal: 128-129 says on the night of the January 2 American troops had attempted to cross over from New Jersey to New York in flat boats. However the raid was on the night of December 25, 1780.

11 *Proceedings of the New Jersey Historical Society*, 64:34, Diary of William S. Pennington, Jan. 1, 1781 William Heath and Haskins say the boats went past Perth Amboy to New Brunswick but that does not seem logical to go so far past a safe landing place. Perth Amboy was in American control. Collections of the Massachusetts Historical Society, 7th Series, Vol. 5:170-171 William Heath at West Point to William Hull, Jan. 2, 1781, and CP 142:21 Deposition of Cornelius Haskins deserter from 2nd Massachusetts Regiment, Jan. 24, 1781.

12 CP 141:5, Andrew Gautier to Daniel Gautier, Jan. 15, 1781.

13 Sabine, *William Smith's Historical Memoirs 1778-1783*: 374, Jan. 6, 1781.

14 Gruber, *John Peebles' American War*: 423.

15 U.S. Naval Observatory, Astronomical Applications Department, Jan. 6, 1781 at

http://aa.usno.navy.mil/cgi-bin/aa_pap.pl

16 CP 139:20 KM [Knox Mc Coy] to OD [Oliver De Lancey], undated but received Jan. 6, 1781.

17 CP 139:47 Deposition of John Eaton, Jaspher Hart both of Hackensack and Cesar and Tom.

18 Bergen Neck is now part of Bayonne, New Jersey.

19 Gruber, *John Peebles' American War*: 423. Cole's Ferry would be east of the present ferries to Manhattan.

20 Dongan estate made up the former town of Castleton which had 3,880 acres on the northeastern part of Staten Island.

21 Flatbush is about 5 miles southeast on New York City.

22 Denyce's Ferry is about where Shore Road and 79th Street are now.

23 The Kill van Kull is a three mile long tidal strait that connects Newark Bay and Upper New York Bay. It separates Staten Island and Bayonne, New Jersey.

24 Decker's ferry is now known as Port Richmond, Staten Island, New York.

25 Burgoyne, *Journal of the Hesse-Cassel Jaeger Corps*: 133-134.

26 Sabine, *William Smith's Historical Memoirs 1778-1783*: 374, Jan. 6, 1781.

27 Burgoyne, *A Hessian Officer's Diary of the American Revolution Translated From An Anonymous Ansbach-Bayreuth Diary and The Prechtel Diary*: 194.

28 CP 139:15 Steward Ross at the Neptune, Jan. 5, 1781 at 6:00 p.m. to Oliver De Lancey and 139:16 and 139:23 Steward Ross to Oliver De Lancey, Jan 6, 1781.

29 Gautier's letter may have been brought from New Jersey to New York by Uzal Woodruff but there is no documentation as to who was the courier.

30 PCC, Microfilm, r53, i42, v1: 367-372, Alexander McWhorter' statement at Newark on Caleb Bruen to Gen. Knox, Mar. 27, 1786.

31 PCC, Microfilm, r53, i42, v1: 367-372, Alexander McWhorter's statement at Newark on Caleb Bruen to Gen. Knox, Mar. 27, 1786.

32 PCC, Microfilm, r53, i42, v1: 372, Alexander McWhorter' statement at Newark on Caleb Bruen to Gen. Knox, Mar. 27, 1786.

33 PCC, Microfilm, r53, i42, v1: 375, Elias Dayton at Elizabethtown statement on Caleb Bruen's secret services, Dec. 31, 1785.

34 CP 146: 3, Cortlandt Skinner to Oliver De Lancey, Feb. 11, 1781.

35 CP 159:39 William A. Kite of the ship *Bedford* to Capt. Edward Mc Michael or Capt. Thomas Ward, June 19, 1781. The name of Fulton Street between Broadway and Pearl Street was Fair Street was until 1816.

36 Van Doren and other historians have guessed that McFarlan was Andrew McFarland who had been captured with Captain William Bernard Gifford. Gifford had become a spy for the British. However General Anthony Wayne gave the first name of McFarlan as "Samuel" when he wrote out a pass for the two British spies, Bruen and McFarlan. PCC, Microfilm, r53, i42, v1: 358, Gen. Wayne, at Trenton, pass for Caleb Bruen and Samuel McFarlin to pass to Newark, Jan. 22, 1781.

37 Paltists, *Minutes of the Commissioners for Detecting and Defeating Conspiracies in the State of New York*, Vol. II: 413.

38 Livingston Papers Microfilm Edition, Nathaniel Heard at (New) Brunswick to William Livingston, Jan. 6, 1781 at 1:00 p.m.

39 Wayne Papers, Anthony Wayne at Princeton to Joseph Reed, Jan. 6, 1781 6:00 p.m.

40 Wayne Papers, Joseph Reed to General Wayne, Colonels Stewart and Butler, Jan. 6, 1781.

41 Wayne Papers, William Bowzar to Anthony Wayne, Jan. 6, 1781.

42 Sabine, *William Smith's Historical Memoirs 1778-1783*: 375. JCC, 1774-1789, Wednesday, Jan. 24, 1781: 79-80.

43 Balch, *Papers Relating Chiefly to the Maryland Line*: 175, Edward Dyer to Gen. Smallwood, April 24, 1782.

44 CP 141:38 McFarlane's [McFarlan] Report. Jan. 20, 1781 states that Mason "went to the college where Williams was."

45 McFarlan's Report clearly states John Williams "enlisted in one of General De Lancey's Battallions, under Capt. Cunningham, from whom he deserted by King's Bridge." Based upon information on De Lancey's Brigade provided by Todd Braisted to my questions, there was no Captain Cunningham in De Lancey's Brigade, but there was a Ralph Cunningham who was a captain lieutenant of the 2nd Battalion, De Lancey's, but he was gone from the unit by 1778. There was an Ensign/Lieutenant/Adjutant Thomas Cunningham in the 1st Battalion, De Lancey's. The 2nd Battalion was at Kingsbridge in 1777 and 1778, so this appears to be the most logical choice.

46 GWP, Varick Transcripts, Letterbook 5: 81, General Orders July 13, 1780.

47 Wayne Papers, General Wayne, Colonels Butler and Stewart, to President of Congress, Jan. 8, 1781.

48 GWP, General Correspondence, Anthony Wayne to George Washington, Jan. 8, 1781.

CHAPTER 8

1 Historical Society of Pennsylvania, Diary of George Nelson: Jan. 6 and 7, 1781.

2 Ibid.

3 Reed, *Life and Correspondence of Joseph Reed*, Volume 2: 326, Joseph Reed at Daniel Hunt four miles from Princeton to Executive Council, Jan. 7, 1781.

4 *Pennsylvania Archives Second Series*, Volume XI (1890): 680, William Bouzar [Bowzar] to McClanagan [McClenachan] and Nesbit [Nesbitt], Jan. 7, 1781.

5 *Pennsylvania Magazine of History and Biography*, Vol. XXI (1897): 78, Lieutenant Enos Reeves's letterbook.

6 CP 141:35, William Bernard Gifford to Oliver De Lancey, Jan. 20, 1781. It is hard to believe that men who were desperate for money would turn the offer down when they going to return the spies.

7 *Pennsylvania Archives Second Series*, Volume XI (1890): 680, Jonathan Witherspoon to Committee of Congress, Jan. 7, 1781.

8 Wilson, *Book of the First Troop*: 38 and JCC, 1774-1789 Wednesday, Jan. 24, 1781: 80-81.

9 *Pennsylvania Archives First Series*, Vol. VIII: 701, General Arthur St. Clair to Joseph Reed, Jan 7, 1781.

10 Prince, *Papers of William Livingston*, Vol. 4: 120, William Livingston to John Butler, Jan. 7, 1781.

11 Livingston Papers Microfilm Edition, William Livingston to John Butler with Charles Stewart post script, Jan. 7, 1781.

12 Sabine, *William Smith's Historical Memoirs 1778-1783*: 375.

13 CP Uzal Woodruff of Elizabethtown Report Jan. 9, 1781.

14 CP 139:26 Frederick Mackenzie to Oliver De Lancey, Jan. 7, 1781 at 10:00 a.m. Since Stapleton's letter Frederick Mackenzie and Stapleton had already sent a spy toward Morristown.

15 CP 140:14, 140:15, and 140:18, John Stapleton at Headquarters to Oliver De Lancey, Jan. 11, 1781 He left the Clove at 2:00 p.m. Kakiat is now New Hempstead, Rockland County, New York.

16 CP 139:27 Frederick Mackenzie to Oliver De Lancey, Jan. 7, 1781 at 5:00 p.m.

17 CP 139:24 Sir Henry Clinton, [Jan. 7, 1781].

18 CP 139:31A Cortland Skinner to Oliver De Lancey, Jan. 7, 1781.

19 *Shelburne Papers*, Vol. 66: 557, William Tryon to Shelburne, July 15, 1782.

20 Gruber, *John Peebles' American War*: 424 says Hilyers but it is believed to be Hillyer's.

21 Ibid.: 424; General Phillips' quarters were located at the tavern in Richmond Town.

22 Burgoyne, *Journal of the Hesse-Cassel Jaeger Corps*: 134.

CHAPTER 9

1 Gruber, *John Peebles' American War*: 424 and Diary of George Nelson, Jan. 8, 1781.

2 Wayne Papers, Joseph Reed to Gen. Wayne, Jan. 8, 1781.

3 Wayne Papers, Col. William Butler at Princeton to courier, Jan. 8, 1781.

4 JCC: 81-82 Wednesday, Jan. 24, 1781.

5 Wayne Papers, Craig at Pennington to Gen. Wayne, Jan. 8, 1781.

6 Ibid.

7 Wayne Papers, General Wayne, Colonels Butler and Stewart, to President of Congress, Jan. 8, 1781 and Stillé, *Major General Wayne and the Pennsylvania Line*: 255-256, Anthony Wayne and Colonels Butler and Stewart at Princeton to Officers, Jan. 8, 1781 at 11:30 p.m.

8 Ibid.

9 Stillé, *Major General Wayne and the Pennsylvania Line*: 257, Colonel Adam Hubley to Anthony Wayne at Trenton. Jan. 9, 1781.

10 Stillé, *Major General Wayne and the Pennsylvania Line*: 259, William Bawser [Bowzar] at Princeton to President Reed, Jan. 8, 1781.

11 Stillé, *Major General Wayne and the Pennsylvania Line*: 255, Gen. Wayne at Princeton to Joseph Reed, Jan. 8, 1781.

12 Wayne Papers, William Bowser, Sgt., Sergeants Response, Jan. 8, 1781 (two copies) and Stillé, *Major General Wayne and the Pennsylvania Line*: 255, Anthony Wayne at Princeton to Joseph Reed Jan. 8, 1781.

13 Ibid.

14 Wayne Papers, Joseph Reed to Anthony Wayne at Princeton, Jan. 8, 1781 and Stillé, *Major General Wayne and the Pennsylvania Line*: 259-260, Joseph Reed to the Mutineers, Jan. 8, 1781.

15 Brigadier General Cortlandt Skinner wrote a note to Oliver De Lancey that Francis King had arrived on January 8, 1781. De Lancey's Journal identifies his passage at the Blazing Star. Blazing Star Ferry is at Rossville and the New Blazing Star Ferry, also known as Long Neck, is at Travis once called Linoleumville, Staten Island, opposite Carteret, New Jersey.

16 CP 139:39, Cortlandt Skinner to Oliver De Lancey, Jan. 8, 1781.

17 CP 139:38, Isaac Ogen to Oliver De Lancey, Jan. 8, 1781 at 2:00 p.m.

18 CP Frederick Mackenzie to Oliver De Lancey, Jan. 9, 1781.

19 Burgoyne, *Journal of the Hesse-Cassel Jaeger Corps*: 134.

20 Gruber, *John Peebles' American War*: 424.

21 Ibid.

22 Sabine, *William Smith's Historical Memoirs 1778-1783*: 375, Jan. 8, 1781.

23 New-York Historical Society Collections 1882, von Kraft's Journal: 129. and Diary of George Nelson: Jan. 9, 1781.

24 Livingston Papers Microfilm Edition , John Sullivan at Trenton to William Livingston, Jan. 9, 1781.

25 JCC, 1774-1789, Wednesday, Jan. 24, 1781: 82.

26 Jonathan Richmond was the barrack master at Trenton in 1779. Richmond's tavern was located on the east side of South Broad Street. It was destroyed in a fire in 1843 when it was known as the True American Inn.

27 Smith, *St. Clair Papers*: 535 Gen. St. Clair at Morristown to Brigadier Gen. Wayne, Jan. 9, 1781.

28 Gruber, *John Peebles' American War*: 424, Jan. 9, 1781.

29 CP 144: 12, Oliver De Lancey's Journal.

30 Gruber, *John Peebles' American War*: 424, Jan. 9, 1781.

31 CP 139:35 Andrew Gautier's Report, Jan. 8, 1781.

32 CP 139:44, Intelligence by Joseph Clark. Jan. 9, 1781.

33 The *New Jersey Gazette* of Jan 17, 1783 col. 3 states the raid was the 10th. However Nathaniel Heard in a January 10 letter to William Livingston says the raid was "yesterday morning" being the 9th.

34 Stryker: 327. There is an Ensign Asher Fitz-Randolph of the Middlesex County New Jersey Militia. On p. 456 there is a Ensign Lewis Fitz-Randolph in Captain Asher Fitz-Randolph's company. Both are listed on p. 329.

35 Gruber, *John Peebles' American War*: 424; Gruber says it was twelve men and Peckham (*Toll of Independence*: 79) says it was ten men.

36 CP 139:54, William Phillips to Oliver De Lancey, Jan. 9, 1781.

37 Quibbletown is now the New Market section of Piscataway, New Jersey. The two men who were intercepted on Friday going to the British could not have been in response to the proposal from General Clinton as Mason and Ogden had not delivered the proposal till Saturday night.

38 CP 139:41 Captain Charles Stirling to General William Phillips, Jan. 8, 1781.

39 Gruber, *John Peebles' American War*: 424.

40 Burgoyne, *Journal of a Hessian Grenadier Battalion*: 156.

41 Ibid.: 134.

42 CP 144: 12 Oliver De Lancey's Journal.

43 CP 139:48, Sir Henry Clinton's note, Jan. 9, 1781. Van Doren in *Mutiny in January* lists this person as Blank, who was sent out on the 5th. Van Doren, as everyone else, had a problem reading Clinton's shorthand and handwriting. In the British headquarters documents of Sir Henry Clinton there are only two names that match his shorthand, Brink and Frink. Nathan Frink was asking to be sent out to the mutineers on the 7th. This was two days after the courier had already left. CP 139: 32, Vandycke to Oliver De Lancey, Jan. 7, 1781. I believe the name should be Alexander Brink.

44 CP 141:1 Intelligence by William Boyce with Clinton's endorsement.

45 CP Major General William Phillips to General Henry Clinton, Jan. 10, 1781.

46 CP 139:54, William Phillips to Oliver De Lancey, Jan. 9, 1781.

47 *Diary of George Nelson*: Jan. 9, 1781.

48 JCC, Jan. 24, 1781: 82.

49 Wayne Paper, Anthony Wayne to Council, Jan. 10, 1781.

50 GWP, General Correspondence. Washington to Health, Jan. 10, 1781. The original is in the Massachusetts Historical Society.

51 GWP, Varick Transcripts, Letterbook 2: 161-162, George Washington to Philip J. Schuyler, Jan. 10, 1781.

52 Gruber, *John Peebles' American War*: 424.

Chapter 10

1 Wayne states that he did not see him again. Wayne Papers, Anthony Wayne to George Washington, Jan. 12, 1781.

2 *Diary of George Nelson*: Jan. 11, 1781.

3 Where the four roads merged would be Green Street in Morrisville, Pennsylvania.

4 GWP, General Correspondence, Philemon Dickinson to George Washington, Jan. 12, 1781.

5 Depending on which source you want to believe the hanging took place at either at 9:00 a.m. or noon. The hanging may have been scheduled for 9:00 a.m. but with the delays involved noon is the more likely time of actual execution. JCC, Jan. 24, 1781: 82, execution at noon.

6 Stevens, *Facsimiles*, Vol. 17 #1632: 37-38, Lafayette to Comte de Vergennes, Jan, 30, 1781.

7 CP 140:21 Andrew Gautier's Report, Jan. 12, 1781. Isaac Ruggles reported to British Headquarters on the 15th that on Saturday the two men were still hanging at Colvin's Ferry.

8 CP 140:34 SW to DC (Samuel Wallis to Daniel Cox), Jan. 13 and 19, 1781.

9 Wayne Papers, Gov. Reed at Bloomsbury to Unknown (Wayne), Jan. 11, 1781.

10 JCC, 1774-1789, Wednesday, Jan. 24, 1781, Page 83.

11 Prince, *Papers of William Livingston*, Vol. 4: 122, James Burnside to William Livingston, Jan. 11, 1781. He is most likely the James Burnsides of the 4th Artillery Regiment.

12 Prince, *Papers of William Livingston*, Vol. 4: 124, William Livingston at Trenton to Sarah Jay (his daughter and wife of John Jay), Jan. 14, 1781 and William Livingston at Bordentown to Philip Schuyler, Jan. 18, 1781.

13 JCC, Volume 19: 79-83, Committee of Congress Report written by Jonathan Witherspoon, Jan. 24, 1781.

14 PCC, No. 20, II, folio 101, report, in the writing of John Witherspoon.

15 CP 187:20, Message to Andrew Gautier, Jr., Jan. 12, 1781.

16 Gruber, *John Peebles' American War*: 424, Jan. 12, 1781

17 CP 144: 12 Oliver De Lancey's Journal.

18 CP 140:17 Uzal Woodruff's Deposition, Jan. 11, 1781.

19 CP 140:24 Stewart Ross on the Neptune to Oliver De Lancey, Jan 12, 1781 at 2:00 p.m.

20 *Pennsylvania Magazine of History and Biography*, Vol. XLI No. 4 (1917): 401, Journal of Samuel Rowland Fisher.

21 Wayne Papers, Anthony Wayne to George Washington, Jan. 12, 1781.

22 *Proceedings of the New Jersey Historical Society*, 64:34, Diary of William S. Pennington, Jan. 1, 1781.

23 GWP, Varick Reanscripts, Letterbook 13: 62-63, George Washington to Arthur St. Clair, Jan. 12, 1781.

24 GWP, Varick Transcripts, Letterbook 13: 62-63, George Washington to Arthur St. Clair, Jan. 12, 1781.

25 GWP, Varick Reanscripts, Letterbook 13: 62-63, George Washington to Arthur St. Clair, Jan. 12, 1781.

26 *Proceedings of the New Jersey Historical Society*, 64:35 Diary of William S. Pennington, Jan. 12 and 13, 1781.

Chapter 11

1 CP 140:39 Oliver De Lancey to John Stapleton, Jan. 14, 1781.

2 CP 140:41 John Stapleton to Oliver De Lancey, Jan. 14, 1781.

3 Captain Crowell could be either Captain Joseph Crowell from Sussex County, New Jersey, of the 1st Battalion New Jersey Volunteers or Captain Thomas Crowell of Monmouth County, New Jersey, of Militia and Warden of the Port of New York.

4 CP 141:8 Elisha Lawrence to Oliver De Lancey (?), Jan. 15, 1781.

5 On June 24, 1776, Thomas Oakerson was in the Burlington County jail.

6 Cortlandt Skinner Papers, New Jersey Loyalists Schedule of Commissions and Warrants, Feb. 24, 1778.

7 *New Jersey Gazette*, April 1778.

8 He was transferred to Colonel Robert Roger's Rangers. He and his family settled in Granville, Nova Scotia. He was given half pay as a pension in 1792.

9 Monmouth Courthouse is now known as Freehold, New Jersey.

10 Diary of George Nelson: Jan. 14, 1781, the snow changed to rain between 8:00 and 9:00 a.m.

11 *Pennsylvania Magazine of History and Biography*, Vol. XLI No. 4 (1917): 404 Journal of Samuel Rowland Fisher.

12 The date is the most probable. Document in the Wayne Papers only says "Friday Morning." Reed busy borrowing money on the 11th and Dean is busy with the other auditor starting the 13th. Gov. Reed to Anthony Wayne, no date but marked Friday Morning.

13 Wayne Papers Joseph Reed at Bloomsbury to Joseph Dean, Jan. 13, 1781 and J. B. Smith and Joseph Dean at Bloomsbury near Trenton, Jan. 13, 1781.

14 Wayne Papers, Colonel F. Johnston to Anthony Wayne, Jan. 13, 1781 and Heitman: 305 and 322.

15 Wayne Papers, Col. A. Butler at Major Trent to Gen. Wayne, Jan. 14, 1781.

16 Wayne Papers, Joseph Borden to Anthony Wain [Wayne], Jan. 14, 1781.

17 Wayne Papers, General Wayne at Trenton to Council, Jan. 15, 1781.

18 Ezekiel Yeomans had been recruiting men for the British army until he was identified by a deserter from the Orange Rangers. He then went into New York on Sept. 1, 1777.

19 CP Uzal Woodruff of Elizabethtown Report Jan. 9, 1781 and CP 141:16 Woodruff Intelligence, Jan. 15, 1781. No other source was found to confirm the statement that two Pennsylvania soldiers carrying letters were going to meet with Sir Henry Clinton.

20 Burgoyne, *Journal of the Hesse-Cassel Jaeger Corps*: 135.

21 Sabine, *William Smith's Historical Memoirs 1778-1783*: 379, Jan. 17, 1781.

22 GWP, Varick Transcripts, Letterbook 5: 426-427, George Washington to John Sullivan, Jan. 16, 1781.

23 *Diary of George Nelson*: Jan. 18, 1781.

24 *Pennsylvania Archives First Series*, VIII: 701, Joseph Reed to Merchants and Citizens of Philadelphia, Jan 18, 1781.

25 Diary of George Nelson: Jan. 18, 1781.

26 Wayne Papers, War Office, Richard Peters to Anthony Wayne, Jan. 18, 1781.

27 Wayne Paper, General Wayne at Trenton to Gentlemen, Jan. 15, 1781.

28 Wayne Papers, General Irvine at Philadelphia to Anthony Wayne, Jan. 22, 1781.

29 *Nathanael Greene Papers* 16:11 Chevalier de Luzerne at Philadelphia to Nathanael Greene, Jan. 21, 1781.

30 Wayne Papers and GWP Gen. Correspondence, Anthony Wayne to George Washington, Jan. 28, 1781.

31 *Pennsylvania Gazette*, Jan. 24, 1781, p. 3, c. 1-2.

32 CP 141:38 McFarlane's [McFarlan] Report. Jan. 20, 1781.

33 Ibid.

34 Heitman, *Historical Register of Officers of the Continental Army*: 175.

35 Ibid.: 149.

36 Recruiting sergeants and musicians were not furloughed.

37 Wayne Papers and GWP Gen. Correspondence, Anthony Wayne to George Washington, Jan. 28, 1781.

38 Wayne Papers, Colonel Farmer, Jan. 26, 1781.

39 Wayne Papers, Anthony Wayne to Colonel Nelson, Jan. 29, 1781.

40 Wayne Papers and GWP Varick Transcripts, Letterbook 13: 90-91 George Washington to Anthony Wayne, Jan 27, 1781.

41 Wayne Papers and GWP Varick Transcripts, Letterbook 13: 108-109 George Washington to Anthony Wayne, Feb. 2, 1781.

42 Jacob Hyer's house built in 1780 was on Nassau Street and was moved in 1875 to 19 Vandeventer Street, Princeton. Hyer was the owner of the Hudibras Tavern.

43 Prince, *Papers of William Livingston*, Vol. 4: 162, William Livingston Court Martial Sentence, Mar. 23, 1781.

44 Gruber, *John Peebles' American War*: 426, Jan. 24, 1781

CHAPTER 12

1 *Pennsylvania Archives First Series,* Vol. VIII: 701, General Arthur St. Clair to Joseph Reed, Jan 7, 1781.

2 GWP General Correspondence, Massachusetts 2nd Regiment to Ebenezer Sprout, Jan. 17, 1781.

3 *William Livingston Papers*, Vol. 4: 130-131 fn 2.

4 Ibid.

5 CP 139:36 Unknown to Peter Dubois, Jan. 8, 1781.

6 CP 139:43 copy of handbill that was hung on the fences, Jan. 9, 1781.

7 *Pennsylvania Archives First Series,* Vol. VIII: 701, General Arthur St. Clair by a Mr. Donaldson to Joseph Reed, Jan. 7, 1781.

8 CP 141:16 Uzal Woodruff Report Jan. 15, 1781.

9 Hatfield–CP 144: 12, Oliver De Lancey's Journal, Mr. H [Cornelius Hatfield].

10 CP 141:25 William Bernard Gifford to Oliver De Lancey, Jan. 18, 1781.

11 GWP General Correspondence, Israel Shreve to George Washington, Jan. 20, 1781.

12 Ibid.

13 Ibid.

14 *Pennsylvania Gazette*, p.2 c.1, Article by David Gilmore, sergeant, and John Tuttle, private, of the 1st wrote that 160 soldiers were lead by the sergeants on their trip to Chatham.

15 Lieutenant John Shreve son of Col. Israel Shreve says the commissioners along with his father met with the mutineers. *Magazine of American History with Notes and Queries*, Vol. III (1879), p. 575, Personal Narrative of the Services of Lieut. John Shreve of the New Jersey Line of the Continental Army.

16 GWP, Varick Transcripts, Letterbook 13: 78-79, David Humphreys to William Heath, Jan. 21, 1781.

17 GWP, Varick Transcripts, Letterbook 13: 81-82, David Humphreys to Benjamin Throop, Jan. 21, 1781.

18 GWP, Varick Transcripts, Letterbook 13: 80 and Gen. Correspondence, George Washington to Frederick Frelinghuysen, Jan. 21, 1781.

19 GWP, Varick Transcripts, Letterbook 13: 79, George Washington to Israel Shreve, Jan. 21, 1781.

20 GWP, Varick Transcripts, Letterbook 5: 402, George Washington to John Sullivan, Jan. 21, 1781 and Gen. Correspondence, George Washington to Continental Congress Pennsylvania Committee (John Sullivan), Jan. 21, 1781.

21 GWP, Varick Transcripts, Letterbook 13: 83-84, George Washington to Robert Howe, Jan. 22, 1781.

22 GWP, Varick Transcripts, Letterbook 4: 75-76, George Washington to William Livingston, Jan. 23, 1781.

23 At this point in the circular to New York the following was added: "With flour we are fed only from day to day."

24 GWP, Varick Transcripts, Letterbook 4: 209-210, George Washington to Meshech Weare, et al, Jan. 22, 1781, Circular Letter on New Jersey Line mutiny.

25 GWP, Varick Transcripts, Letterbook 5: 402, George Washington to Continental Congress, Jan. 23, 1781.

26 GWP, Gen. Correspondence, George Washington to Governor Abner Nash of North Carolina, Jan. 23, 1781.

27 *Proceedings of the New Jersey Historical Society*, 64: 35, Diary of William S. Pennington, Jan. 22, 1781

28 De Lancey was in New York City on the 22nd and the mutineers left Chatham on the morning of the 24th.

29 For his report to be true, he would have to have left very early on the morning of the 24th, which was possible. He would have also arrived and departed Chatham very early in the morning, which could have happened. If he had stayed at Chatham for any length of time, he would have seen the mutineers march out bound for Pompton.

30 O'Callaghan, *Documents Relative to the Colonial History of the State of New York*, VIII: 810-811, General Robertson at New York to William Knox, Jan. 29, 1780 from New York.

31 Emmett Collection, New York Public Library, Private Intelligence: 8-9, Major McKenzie to Oliver De Lancey at Staten Island, Jan. 26, 1781.

32 Gruber, *John Peebles' American War*: 425-426 and *Proceedings of the New Jersey Historical Society*, 64: 35, Diary of William S. Pennington, Jan. 23, 1781.

33 *Proceedings of the New Jersey Historical Society*, 64: 35, Diary of William S. Pennington, Jan. 24, 25 and 26, 1781.

34 The Forest of Dean is now part of the West Point Military Reservation.

35 Thatcher, *A Military Journal During the American Revolutionary War*: 244-245.

36 GWP, Varick Transcripts, Letterbook 13: 86, David Humphreys to Artillery Detachment Commanding Officer, Jan. 23, 1781 and Van Doren: 217.

37 U.S. Naval Observatory, Sun and Moon Data for Saturday Jan. 27, 1781 at Pompton, New Jersey.

38 GWP, Varick Transcripts, Letterbook 13: 83-84, George Washington to Robert Howe, Jan. 22, 1781. Sources are not consistent with John Tuttle's first name. It is recorded as

John, Israel, and "J." or "I." It is difficult to distinguish between a capital J and I in eighteenth-century script.

39 Thatcher, *A Military Journal During the American Revolutionary War*: 245-246.

40 Ibid.

41 *Proceedings of the New Jersey Historical Society*, 64: 36, Diary of William S. Pennington, Jan. 27 and 28, 1781.

42 Gordon, *History of the Rise*, Vol. 4: 22.

43 *Magazine of American History with Notes and Queries*, X: 331 fn 2. There is no documentation as to why he turned the documents over to the American officers. One possible reason was to save Joseph Nichols, second in command of the mutineers and his cousin from arrest and execution. I have not found any documentation of his being a double agent till after this event.

44 *Diary of George Nelson*: Jan. 25, 1781.

45 CP 143:4 Oliver De Lancey to Sir Henry Clinton, Jan. 26, 1781.

46 GWP Gen. Correspondence, Anthony Wayne to George Washington, May 26, 1781, GWP, Gen. Correspondence, Courts Martial, May 20 and 22, 1781 and Pennsylvania Packet May 29, 1781.

47 There are several different accounts of what transpired at York, Pennsylvania. This version seems to have the most validity.

CHAPTER 13

1 GWP, Varick Transcripts, Letterbook 12: 245-267, George Washington at Tappan to Nathanael Greene, Oct. 6, 1780.

2 GWP, Varick Transcripts, Letterbook 5: 315-321, George Washington at Paramus to Congress, Oct. 7, 1780.

3 GWP, Varick Transcripts, Letterbook 12: 265-267, George Washington at Passaic Falls to Nathanael Greene at West Point, Oct. 14, 1780 and GWP, Microfilm, Samuel Huntington to George Washington, Oct. 6, 1780.

4 GWP, Microfilm, John Mathews at Philadelphia to George Washington, Oct. 6, 1780.

5 GWP, Varick Transcripts, Letterbook 12: 265-267, George Washington at Passaic Falls to Nathanael Greene at West Point, Oct. 14, 1780.

6 *Nathanael Greene* 53:41 Nathanael Greene to John Mathews Feb. 2, 1782.

7 JCC, Vol. XXI: 1085, Oct. 29, 1781.

8 The High Hills of the Santee is more a state of mind than a geographic feature. The area lies just east of the Wateree and Santee Rivers on a modern topographic map you can see the hills around Stateburg, South Carolina. These are the true "high hills," but the area called by the locals during the American Revolution as the "high hills" extended south about 20 miles. They are high only in relation to the river flood plane swamps.

9 Gordon, *The History of the Rise*, Vol. 4: 172-173.

10 JCC, July 26, 1779.

11 *Nathanael Greene* Vol. IX: 459 Death Warrant for Timothy Griffin Oct. 21, 1781.

12 GWP, General Correspondence, Virginia Line Officers to Christian Febiger, Nov. 17, 1781.

13 GWP, Varick Transcripts 4:272-273, George Washington to Benjamin Harrison, Jan. 10, 1782.

14 GWP, Varick Transcripts, Letterbook 14:361-363, George Washington to Christian Febiger, Jan. 12, 1781.

15 GWP, General Correspondence, Christian Febiger to George Washington, Mar. 14, 1782.

16 Calendar of Virginia State Papers, III:73-74, Febiger to Harrison, Feb. 23, 1782.

17 Ibid.

18 McKissack, "Colonel Thomas Posey and the Last Virginia Battalion" in *Southern Campaigns of the American Revolution*: 40-46

19 GP 56:57 Nathanael Greene to John Mathews Mar. 30, 1782.

20 *Nathanael Greene* Vol. X: 573-574, General Greene's Orders April 2, 1782.

21 The opposition to General John Barnwell was so great that he was forced to resign in mid-May 1782. His troops were incorporated into General Francis Marion's corps.

22 GP 57:19 Mathews to Greene April 5, 1782. The Horseshoe is probably the creek in modern Colleton County just north of Parker's Ferry Road on the Ponpon or Edisto River, near which Col. Isaac Hayne lived and was captured. Greene camped his army at Parker's Ferry, Round O, and Jacksonboro, all of which are in this area of South Carolina.

23 GP Nathanael Greene to George Washington April 13, 1782.

24 Both Gill and White had been prisoners of war and were exchanged in October, 1780.

25 *Nathanael Greene* Vol. X: 590-591 Nathanael Greene to General Anthony Wayne April 6, 1782.

26 GP 57:29 and *Nathanael Greene* Vol. XI: 4-5 Col. Edward Carrington at Philadelphia to Nathanael Greene April 7, 1782.

27 GP 57:49 and *Nathanael Greene* Vol. XI: 25-26 Gen. Anthony Wayne at Ebenezer, GA to Nathanael Greene April 9, 1782.

28 Mordecai Gist Papers, Letterbook, Mordecai Gist to John Sterett, April 22, 1782.

29 *Nathanael Greene* Vol. XI: 32 Greene's General Orders April 12, 1782).

30 GP 58:3 and *Nathanael Greene* Vol. XI: 32-34 Nathanael Greene to John Hanson, President of Congress April 12, 1782.

31 GP 58:4, 58:2, and *Nathanael Greene* Vol. XI: 50-51 Nathanael Greene to John Hanson and pp. 51-52 Greene to General Benjamin Lincoln, Secretary of War April 13, 1782.

32 GP 58:2 and *Nathanael Greene* Vol. XI: 51-52 Nathanael Greene to Benjamin Lincoln April 13, 1782.

33 *South Carolina Historical Magazine*, Vol. 98 # 2: 136, Walter Finney Diary.

34 Moultrie, *Memoirs of the American Revolution*: 297-298.

35 *Nathanael Greene* Vol. XI: 181-182 Major Roxburgh (Roxburg) of the 4th Maryland to General William Smallwood.

36 *Nathanael Greene* Vol. XI: 80 General Orders April 20, 1782 and *Nathanael Greene* Vol. XI pp. 199-200 Nathanael Greene to John Hanson May 18, 1782).

37 GP 58:66 and *Nathanael Greene* Vol XI: 103-104 Col Francis Mentges to Nathanael Greene April 22, 1782.

38 The name appears as Gosnell, Gornell, and Goznell. A return of the Second Pennsylvania Regiment that appears in the *Pennsylvania Archives Fifth Series* 2 (1906): 871 as George Goznall who enlisted in September 1778 and reenlisted in 1781.

39 Bray, *Diary of a Common Soldier*: 252, June 1782 Story as told to Jeremiah Greenman who was opposite West Point, New York.

40 *Nathanael Greene* Vol. XI: 81 Col. Josiah Harmar to Nathanael Greene April 20, 1782).

41 O'Kelley, *Nothing but Blood and Slaughter: The Revolutionary War in the Carolinas*, 4: 56-57. O'Kelley gives his sources as Garden: 365-368; Ripley: 237; Seymour: 35; Simms: 179; Moultrie: 298; Lee: 546-549; *Penn Gazette*, June 5 1782; Public Record Office, Treasury Office, Class 50, Vol. 2, folio 327; Crow: 78; and Pancake: 480.

42 *Nathanael Greene* Vol. XI: 82 General Orders April 21, 1782 and Col. Josiah Harmar to Gen. Mordecai Gist April 21, 1782.

43 Great Britain, Public Record Office, Treasury Office, Class 50 Vol. 2, folio 372, Abstract of pay for the Black Pioneer troop from July 1 to Sept. 30, 1782.

44 *Pennsylvania Magazine of History and Biography*, VIII, No. 4: 389, A Journal of the Southern Expedition 1780-1783 by William Seymour

45 Ibid.

46 Accounts differ as to the Americans losses. One source says three or four men killed and nine men and fifteen horses captured; another says eight men were lost and six horses, while still another says five or six men lost. *South Carolina Historical Magazine*, 98 No. 2:137, Walter Finney Diary.

47 *Pennsylvania Magazine of History and Biography*, VIII, No. 4: 389, A Journal of the Southern Expedition 1780-1783 by William Seymour.

48 GP 58:49 Gen. Mordicai Gist to Nathanael Greene April 21, 1782 at 10:00 a.m.

49 *Nathanael Greene* Vol. XI: 87 General Orders April 22, 1782.

50 Pempan River: I believe he means the Ponpon (sometimes written as Pon Pon) River, the Indian name for the Edisto River.

51 Balach, *Papers Relating Chiefly to the Maryland Line*: 175, Edward Dyer to Gen. Smallwood April 24, 1782.

52 Collections of the New-York Historical Society for the Year 1875: 502, Lewis Morris Jr. to Jacob Morris, April 24, 1782.

53 Mordecai Gist Papers, Letterbook, Mordecai Gist at Camp Bacons Bridge to John Sterett, April 22, 1782.

54 Captain Ferdinand O'Neill's name is sometimes spelled O'Neal.

55 Lee, *Memoirs of the War in the Southern Department*: 400-401.

56 GP 58:50 and *Nathanael Greene* Vol. XI: 82 Nathanael Greene to Anthony Wayne April 21, 1782.

57 *Nathanael Greene* Vol. XI: 139-140 Anthony Wayne to Nathanael Greene April 28, 1782.

58 Lee, Memoirs of the War in the Southern Department: 399.

59 GP 58:59 and *Nathanael Greene* Vol. XI: 94-95 Nathanael Greene to John Moylan April 22, 1782.

60 *Nathanael Greene* Vol. XI: 199-200 Nathanael Greene to John Hansen May 18, 1782 and 212-213 Nathanael Greene to George Washington May 19. 1782.

61 *Nathanael Greene* Vol. XI: 117 Nathanael Greene to Counte de Rochambeau April 25, 1782, 125-126 Nathanael Greene to Gen. Benjamin Lincoln April 26, 1782, and GP 59:1 Nathanael Greene to Richard Henry Lee April 25, 1782.

62 GP 59:40 Capt. Nathan Pendleton to General Griffith Rutherford May 1, 1782; *Nathanael Greene* Vol. XI: 117 Nathanael Greene to Counte de Rochambeau April 25, 1782; pp 125-126 Nathanael Greene to Gen. Benjamin Lincoln April 26, 1782 and GP 59:1 Nathanael Greene to Richard Henry Lee April 25, 1782.

63 *Nathanael Greene* Vol. XI: 217-218 Nathanael Greene to Gen Henry Knox May 20, 1782.

64 *Nathanael Greene* Vol. XI: 260, fn 2. *Virginia Gazette* of May 25, 1782.

65 GP 61:26 and *Nathanael Greene* Vol. XI: 258-259 Col Christian Febiger to Nathanael Greene May 28, 1782.

66 GP 61:36 Nathanael Greene to Benjamin Lincoln and 61:38 Nathanael Greene to George Washington May 31, 1782.

67 *Nathanael Greene* Vol. XI: 306 Nathanael Greene to Col. Peter Horry, June 8, 1782.

CHAPTER 14

1 Heath, *Memoirs of the American War*: 358.

2 GWP, Varick Transcripts, Letterbook 2: 391-393, George Washington to Joseph Jones, Dec. 14, 1782.

3 Ibid.

4 Quincy, *Journals of Major Samuel Shaw*: 99-100, Maj. Samuel Shaw at West Point to the Rev. Mr. Eliot, Dec. 22, 1782.

5 JCC, Volume 24: 291-293, memorial December 1782, read April 29, 1783.

6 GWP, Varick Transcripts, Letterbook 6: 363-364, George Washington to Gen. Benjamin Lincoln, December 11, 1782.

7 Knox Manuscripts (New England Genealogical Society, Boston), XI:36.

8 Quincy, *Journals of Major Samuel Shaw*: 99-100, Maj. Samuel Shaw at West Point to the Rev. Mr. Eliot, December 22, 1782.

9 Sparks, *Life of Gouverneur Morris*: 249.

10 Ibid.

11 GWP, Varick Transcripts, Letterbook 3: 9-12, George Washington to John Armstrong, Jan. 10, 1783.

12 JCC, Vol. 25: 851, Jan. 13, 1783.

13 Ibid.

14 Ibid.

15 Dempsey, *Washington's Last Cantonment*: 100, Col. John Brooks to Col. Henry Jackson, Jan. 19, 1783.

16 Ibid.

17 Ibid.

18 GWP, Varick Transcripts, Letterbook 3: 38-39, George Washington to David Rittenhouse, Feb. 16, 1783.

19 GWP, Gen. Correspondence, Joseph Jones to George Washington, Feb. 27, 1783.

20 GWP, Varick Transcripts, Letterbook 3: 49-53, George Washington to Alexander Hamilton, Mar. 4, 1783.

21 The Conway Cabal was intrigue to remove George Washington as commander in chief of the Continental Army. Washington had been defeated at Brandywine and Germantown. General Horatio Gates was the victor at the Battle of Saratoga. General Thomas Conway wrote a letter to Gates severely criticizing Washington. A phrase purportedly from this letter was leaked to Washington who sent it to General Gates without comment. Gates sent a reply to Washington through Congress. The scheme was over.

22 The phrase "on the tapis" means to be under consideration or discussion.

23 GWP, Varick Transcripts, Letterbook 3: 49-53, George Washington to Alexander Hamilton, Mar. 4, 1783.

24 *United States Magazine*, Vol. 1, No. 1, review of William Johnson's Sketches of the Life and Correspondence of Nathanael Greene: 40 footnote.

25 Ibid.

26 John Armstrong Jr. admits in *United States Magazine*, Vol. 1. No. 1, review of William Johnson's Sketches of the Life and Correspondence of Nathanael Greene that he did write the anonymous letters.

27 GWP, Gen. Correspondence, Anonymous to Continental Army Officers, Mar. 10, 1783.

28 Dempsey, *Washington's Last Cantonment*.

29 GWP, Varick Transcripts, Letterbook 3: 58-61, George Washington to Alexander Hamilton, Mar. 12, 1783.

30 GWP, Varick Transcripts, Letterbook 7: 83-84, General Orders, Mar. 11, 1783.

31 Dempsey, *Washington's Last Cantonment*: 183, from Armstrong to Gates from New-York Historical Society, m. r. 13.

32 Dempsey, *Washington's Last Cantonment*: 141-142, quoted from Jacob Judd ed., *Revolutionary War Memoir of Philip Van Corlandt*, 2 Vols. Tarrytown, New York, Sleepy Hollow Productions, 1976: 1:68.

33 GWP, Varick Transcripts, Letterbook 3: 54-57, George Washington to Joseph Jones, Mar. 12, 1783.

34 GWP, Varick Transcripts, Letterbook 7: 29-30, George Washington to Continental Congress, Mar. 12, 1783.

35 Quincy, *Journals of Major Samuel Shaw*: 101-104, Maj. Samuel Shaw at West Point to the Rev. Mr. Eliot, April 1783.

36 JCC, 24: 310-311.

37 GWP, Varick Transcripts, Letterbook 7: 36-37, George Washington to Continental Congress, Mar. 18, 1783.

CHAPTER 15

1 JCC, 24: 203, Mar. 20, 1783.

2 JCC, 24: 364-365, May 26, 1783.

3 *State Papers of North Carolina*, 16: 852-855, Benjamin Hawkins and Hugh Williamson at Princeton to Gov. Martin, Aug. 1, 1783.

4 *Transactions and Studies*: 134, Col. Richard Butler to John Dickinson and William Henry, gunsmith at Lancaster to John Dickinson, June 16, 1783.

5 Emmet Collection, Horatio Gates Papers microfilm, John Armstrong Jr. to Horatio Gates, June 16, 1783.

6 JCC, 24: 389 fn 2.

7 *Elliot's Debates*, 5: June 19, 1783.

8 Smith, *St. Clair Papers*, I: 587, Elias Boudinot to Major Jackson, June 19, 1783 at 2:00 p.m.

9 Smith, *St. Clair Papers*, I: 587, Major Jackson to Gen. St. Clair, June 19, 1783 at 2:30 p.m.

10 Smith, *St. Clair Papers*, I: 588-590, St. Clair to George Washington, July 2, 1783.

11 *Elliot's Debates*, 5: June 20, 1783.

12 *State Records of North Carolina*, XVI: 836-837 Benjamin Hawkins to Gov. Martin, June 24, 1783, Hawkins says the mutineers numbered 280.

13 Smith, *St. Clair Papers*, I: 588, St. Clair to George Washington, July 2, 1783.

14 *Pennsylvania Council Minutes*, 13: 540 and 605.

15 *State Records of North Carolina*, XVI: 836-837 Benjamin Hawkins to Gov. Martin, June 24, 1783, Hawkins says the mutineers only gave fifteen minutes for a reply.

16 Smith, *St. Clair Papers*, I: 587, John Byers to General Irvine, July 1, 1783.

17 JCC, 25: 973, June 21, 1783.

18 A tippling-house is a building where liquors are sold in drams or small quantities, to be drunk on the premises.

19 JCC, 25:974, June 21, 1783.

20 *Papers of Henry Laurens*, XVI:252 fn 8.

21 GWP, Gen. Correspondence, George Washington to Robert Howe, June 25, 1783.

22 GWP, Varick Transcripts, Letterbook 7: 103-106 George Washington to Continental Congress, June 24, 1783.

23 JCC, 24: 411, June 30, 1783.

24 *Rush Papers*, 29:120, Dr. Benjamin Rush to John Adams, 1812.

25 John Sullivan tried in 1786 to get his pay and commutation. Congress denied him any money. They stated the reason for the denial was, "John Sullivan having withdrawn himself from the United States without leave obtained before the conclusion of the War." JCC, 30: June 27, 1786.

26 Smith, *St. Clair Papers*, I: 588-590, St. Clair to George Washington, July 2, 1783.

27 GWP, Gen. Correspondence, Continental Congress to George Washington, July 3, 1783.

28 Virginia State Library, Virginia Governor Letters Received, Theodorick Bland, Arthur Lee and John T. Mercer to Benjamin Harrison, Aug. 14-15, 1783.

29 JCC, 25: 565 Sept. 13, 1783.

CHAPTER 16

1 JCC, 24: 254 April 17, 1783.

2 *The Papers of General Nathanael Greene* 12: 652, Major Joseph Eggleston Jr., to Nathanael Green, May 12, 1783.

3 GWP, Varick Transcripts, Letterbook 7: 101-103, General Orders, Mar. 28, 1783.

4 *The Papers of General Nathanael Greene*, 12: 659-660, Nathanael Greene to Major Joseph Eggleston Jr., May 17, 1783.

5 *The Papers of General Nathanael Greene*, 13:3, Major Joseph Eggleston Jr., to Nathanael Greene, May 22, 1783.

6 *The Papers of General Nathanael Greene*, 13: 4, Col. Francis Mentges to Nathanael Greene, May 22, 1783.

7 *The Papers of General Nathanael Greene*, 12: 659-660, Nathanael Greene to Major Joseph Eggleston Jr., May 17, 1783.

8 *The Papers of General Nathanael Greene*, 12: 661, Nathanael Greene to Benjamin Lincoln, May 17, 1783.

9 *The Papers of General Nathanael Greene*, 12: 673, Nathanael Greene to General Charles Scott, May 20, 1783, and PCC M247 r100 i78 V17: 159, Baylor's Regiment non-commissioned officers to Gov. Nelson, May 22, 1783.

10 *The Papers of General Nathanael Greene*, 12: 652-653, Major Joseph Eggleston Jr., to Nathanael Greene, May 12, 1783.

11 *The Papers of General Nathanael Greene*, 12: 660-661, Nathanael Greene to Gen. Benjamin Lincoln, May 17, 1783.

12 *The Papers of General Nathanael Greene*, 12: 673, Nathanael Greene to General Charles Scott, May 20, 1783.

13 *The Papers of General Nathanael Greene*, 12: 675-676, Nathanael Greene to Col. George Baylor, May 21, 1783.

14 *The Papers of General Nathanael Greene*, 12: 676, Nathanael Greene to Gov. Benjamin Harrison, May 21, 1783.

15 PCC, M247 r100 i78 V17 p159, Baylor's Regiment non-commissioned officers to Gov. Nelson.

16 Virginia, Council of State, Journals, 3: 261.

17 *The Papers of General Nathanael Greene*, 13: 61-62, Nathaniel Pendelton to Nathanael Greene, July 17, 1783.

18 Madison, Papers, 7:97.

19 JCC, 24:389, June 11, 1783.

20 JCC, 24:400-401, Report of the Superintendent of Finance and Secretary at War on the letter of 22 May from the non-commissioned officers of Baylor's regiment who have mutinied, June 17, 1783.

21 *The Papers of General Nathanael Greene*, 13:4-5, Captain John Watts to Nathanael Greene, May 22, 1783.

22 *The Papers of General Nathanael Greene*, 3:9-10, Nathanael Greene to Captain John Watts, May 25, 1783; and 11, Nathanael Greene to Gov. Benjamin Harrison of Virginia, May 27, 1783.

23 *The Papers of General Nathanael Greene*, 13:13-14, General Benjamin Lincoln to Nathanael Greene, May 28, 1783.

24 *The Papers of General Nathanael Greene*, 13:19-21, Nathanael Greene to General Benjamin Lincoln, June 3, 1783. The advertisement for the sale of the horses in the *South Carolina Gazette* and *General Advertiser* of May 24, 1783.

25 Ibid.

26 *The Papers of General Nathanael Greene*, 12:639, Colonel Josiah Harmar to Nathanael Greene, May 3, 1783.

27 *South Carolina Historical Magazine*, 98, 2 (April 1997), Finney Diary: 150-151.

28 *The Papers of General Nathanael Greene*, 13:56-58, Nathanael Greene to Gen. Benjamin Lincoln, Secretary of War, July 11, 1783 and 60 Nathanael Greene to George Washington, July 11, 1783.

29 Nathanael Greene Vol. 13: 44-45 Nathanael Greene's Farewell at Charles Town, South Carolina to the Southern Army, June 21, 1783.

CHAPTER 17

1 Of the British crew on board the *Mercer*, three were from Whitehaven, one from Workington, one from Harrington, and three from Newcastle.

2 The mutiny occurred at 47°N, 27°W.

3 PBF, 26: 399, Nathaniel Dowse to the American Commissioners, May 5, 1778

4 The commissioners discovered a plot among "persons from London, Manchester, Liverpool, Newcastle, etc. who had planned a scheme for buying this cargo for an old song." The local paper reported the commissioners were able to keep the bidding honest with the help of several Whitehaven gentlemen. "It was pleasant to hear that some went away without tobacco, and others were furnished at second hand. We trust, when another ship comes in here, they will learn more wisdom and bid with more candor." Fustic is the wood from a tropical American tree *Chlorophora tinctoria* which is from the mulberry family. It produces a light yellow dye.

5 Naval, 8: 855 fn 2 from *The Public Advertiser*, London, May 30, 1777, and the *Cumberland Chronicle* or *Whitehaven Public Advertiser* at www.pastpresented.info/cumbria/chronicle1776.htm taken from microfilm at Library of Congress, May 24, July 5, July 26, and Dec. 6, 1777.

6 Naval, 8: 946, Charles Carroll to Charles Carroll Sr., May 10, 1777 from Carroll Papers, 5, Maryland Historical Society.

7 Naval, 8: 840, Minutes of the British Navy Board, Public Record Office, Admiralty 106/2595.

8 The management practice referred to as "passing the trash," that is sending your problem person to someone else, was also practiced in the eighteenth century.

9 The armed boat *Eagle* was mounted with a four pound cannon.

10 *Pennsylvania Colonial Records*, X: 296, Minutes of the Pennsylvania Committee of Safety, Aug. 1, 1775 and also in Naval, 1: 1031 and 3:1322.

11 The Officers and Men of the Pennsylvania State Navy 1775 – 1781 Taken from the *Pennsylvania Archives Third Series*, XVII, 1897 Pennsylvania Packet Feb. 12, 1776, List of Ships) The armed boat *Terror* was mounted with a four pound cannon.

12 JCC, 3: 381-382, Nov. 28, 1775.

13 Naval, 6: 274, Aug. 22, 1776 advertisement for deserters from *Scorpion*.

14 Purdie, *Virginia Gazette*, p. 1 c. 1, Aug 23, 1776 Supplement.

15 The *Congress* had one large cannon in its bow.

16 *Pennsylvania Colonial Records*, X: 405.

17 JCC, 3: 443, the Committee reports the vessels are the *Alfred*, *Andrew Doria*, named after the Genoese admiral, *Cabot*, and the *Columbus*, Dec. 22, 1775 and Naval, 2, 1305, Autobiography of John Adams.

18 Cabot was a Brigantine that was 189 tons, length 74′ 10″, beam 24′ 8″, beam 11′ 4″, complement 120, and armament was fourteen 6-pounders.

19 JCC, 3: 443, Dec. 22, 1775.

20 Reedy Island is in the Delaware River 50 miles below Philadelphia and 20 miles from Bombay Hook. It is 3 miles long, 1/2 of a mile wide and is overflowed with the high tide.

21 JCC, 4: 103, Jan. 30, 1776.

22 Naval, 3: 1305-1307 Captain Nicholas Biddle to his sister Mrs. Lydia Mc Funn in Third St., Philadelphia and 1236. The letter also is in the *Pennsylvania Magazine of History and Biography*, 1950: 378-381.

23 Naval, 4: 716-719, Round Robin of the Crew of the Continental Brig *Cabot*.

24 GWP, Varick Transcripts, Letterbook 1: 29-32, George Washington to Nicholson Broughton, Sept. 2, 1775 and *Dictionary of American Naval Fighting Ships*, Hannah. Broughton signed his first name as Nicholas, Nicholson, and Nicholasson.

25 GWP Microfilm film 36 reel 34, Nicholas Broughton to George Washington, Sept. 7 and 9, 1775.

26 Clark, *George Washington's Navy*: 8-10 and GWP, General Orders, Sept. 22, 1775.

27 Ibid.

28 *Dictionary of American Naval Fighting Ships*, Harrison I.

29 Clark, *George Washington's Navy*: 43-44.

30 *Dictionary of American Naval Fighting Ships*, Washington I.

31 Clark, *George Washington's Navy*: 84-85 and Great Britain, Admiralty, Class I, 485, Mandide's Journal.

32 GWP, Letterbook 7: 141-144, George Washington to Continental Congress, Dec. 4, 1775.

33 Norton, *Orderly Book of Captain Ichabod Norton*: 54.

34 Allen, *Naval History of the American Revolution*, 1: 198-199 and *Dictionary of American Naval Fighting Ships*.

35 Peckham, *Toll*: 116 and 118.

36 A firkin is a small wooden barrel usually equal to about 1/4 of a barrel or 9 gallons (34 liters).

37 The tierce is an old English unit of casks. The container holds about 159 liters.

38 The mutiny occurred at latitude 44°10′ and longitude 27°20′.

39 Naval, 8: 784 and 801, quoted from the *London Chronicle* April 19 to 29, 1777.

40 The mutiny occurred at latitude 36°32′ north and longitude 51°41′ west.

41 Naval, 8: 869-870 Captain James Worth to Philip Stephens, May 27, 1777.

42 "Deseada" appears on old maps as "La Désirade," an island dependency of Guadeloupe, east of Grand Terre, See the map between pages 196 and 197 in Volume 1 of Gardner Allen's *A Naval History of the American Revolution*.

43 Naval, 8: 575, Extract from Glasgow Feb. 10, 1777 from *London Packet or New Lloyd's Evening Post* Feb. 17 to 19, 1777. Mr. Thompson of Greenock, carpenter, was part of the crew of the *Ronals*.

44 *Magazine of American History with Notes and Queries*: 175-176, Narrative of Lieutenant Luke Matthewman of the Revolutionary Navy from the *New York Packet* Aug. 24, 1787.

45 PBF, 23: 617 Lambert Wickes to the American Commissioners, April 27, 1777.

46 Naval, 3:553 fn2.

47 Naval, 3:47 Manly Song sheet music.

48 Naval, 8: 925 Captain Hector Mc Neill to Captain John Paul Jones, May 7, 1777 and *Dictionary of American Naval Fighting Ships*.

49 Naval, 8: 572-573 American Commissioners at Paris, France to Lord George Germain Feb.7, 1777 and Franklin Papers Series (2), 18: No. 335.

50 Naval, 8: 576 *Public Advertiser* Monday Feb. 10, 1777.

51 *Papers of Henry Laurens*, 15: William Livingston to Henry Laurens, July 25, 1778

52 Naval, 8: 922 Letter from St. Kitts from London Chronicle June 26 to 28, 1777.

53 One source says it was the 71st Regiment but another says they were on the Crawford transport.

54 *New England Historical and Genealogical Register*, CXII (July 1958):210 fn 3, Departure was scheduled for April 15 quoted from CO 5/123: 80 and 5/124: 37. A list of the transports in the fleet can be found in the *London Public Advertiser* of Sept. 16, 1776.

55 *New England Historical and Genealogical Register*, CXII (July 1958): 200.

56 Naval, 9 Appendix C: 1007-1011 Account of Officers and Men belonging to the brigante *Andrew Doria*.

57 The *Cranford* and *Oxford* were northward of the *Andrew Doria* at latitude 42° longitude 55°.

58 Naval, 5: 564 Capt. Nicholas Biddle to Charles Biddle from Historical Society of Pennsylvania, Capt. Nicholas Biddle Papers.

59 The squall continued until 11:00 a.m.

60 Naval, 5: 565-566 Capt. Nicholas Biddle to Charles Biddle June 16, 1776, HSP, Nicholas Biddle Papers.

61 Lieutenant John Trevett's Journal is at the Newport (Rhode Island) Historical Society.

62 Naval, 5: 293 Journal of Continental Brig *Andrew Doria*, May 29, 1776 (Journal Appendix C Vol. 4); 565-565 Captain Nicholas Biddle to Charles Biddle June 16,1776 from Captain Nicholas Biddle Papers 1771-1778 at HSP; 586 *New York Gazette* June 24, 1776 report from Newport June 17; 638 Commodore Esek Hopkins to Brig. Gen. Nathanael Greene June 20, 1776 from Hopkins Letter Book Rhode Island Historical Society; 642-643 George Washington to John Hancock, June 20, 1776 Fitzpatrick, *Writings of Washington*, V, 160-161; 658-659 Richard Henry Lee at Williamsburg, Virginia, to Landon Carter June 22, 1776 from Philip Lee Folder Virginia Historical

Society; Boyd, ed. *Jefferson Papers*, I, 406 William Fleming to Thomas Jefferson June 22, 1776; 686-687 Journal of the Virginia Convention, Williamsburg, Virginia, June 22, 1776; 687-688 *Pennsylvania Evening* Post July 2, 1776. Extract of a letter from Williamsburg date June 22; 688 *Virginia Gazette* Saturday June 22,1776; 756-758 Lord Dunmore to Lord George Germain June 26, 1776; 166 New York Provincial Congress II; 283 Capt. John Smith at Esopus to New York Convention Aug. 13, 1776: Vol. 6; 534 *Public Advertiser* Aug 7, 1776; and 601 *Public Advertiser* Sept. 16, 1776.

63 Fusee also spelled fuzee, now written fusil, is a short barreled lightweight flintlock musket.

64 One source said the mutiny occurred at longitude 16° West Latitude 47° while another gave the location at between longitude 20° and 21° and between latitude 47° and 48°.

65 Naval, 8: 547-548 Capt James Worth to Philip Stephens Jan 28, 1777; 555 Williamson's *Liverpool Advertiser*, Jan. 31, 1777 and 559 *London Chronicle* and *Public Advertiser* Jan 30-Feb 3, 1777.

66 Beaumarchais was also the author of two well known plays: *The Barber of Seville* and *The Marriage of Figaro*.

67 *Pennsylvania Magazine of History and Biography*, Vol. LXXX (80): 112, A British Editor Reports the American Revolution.

68 BFP, 23: 320-321, Agreement between the American Commissioners and Jacques Boux, Jan. 1777.

69 Naval, 8: 582-583 Agreement between the American Commissioners and Jacques Boux, Feb. 12, 1777 quoted from Yale University, Benjamin Franklin Papers.

70 Historic Manuscript Commission, Manuscripts of the Earl of Dartmouth, American Papers, II: 230, John Powell's note, after Oct. 18, 1774; 232, Oct. 1774, Lord Dartmouth to the Lords of the Admiralty; and 233, Nov. 18, 1774, Sir Joseph Yorke to the Earl of Suffolk.

71 Wright, *Franklin of Philadelphia*: 289.

72 Renault, *Le Secret Service de L'Amirauté Britannique au temps de la Guerre d'Amérique*.

73 Texel is pronounced as Tessel.

74 Lewis, *Neptune's Militia*: 10.

75 JCC, 9: 978-979, Nov. 28, 1777.

76 JCC, 10: 298, Mar. 31, 1778.

77 She traveled at the rate of three miles a day.

78 *Magazine of American History with Notes and Queries*, 2 (1878):183 Narrative of Luke Matthewman of the Revolutionary Navy.

79 Lewis, *Neptune's Militia*: 25.

80 Ibid.: 33.

81 Bruijn, *Dutch Navy*: 206.

82 Lewis, *Neptune's Militia*: 36.

83 Ibid.: 17 and Great Britain, Public Record Office, HCA 32/392 Declaration of John Joyner at Plymouth, July 7, 1778.

84 Lewis, *Neptune's Militia*: 44.

85 *Royal Gazette* July 3, 1782 and *Pennsylvania Packet* July 25, 1782.

86 Stiles, Henry R., *History of the City Brooklyn*, 1: 337.

87 Thomas Dring stated that it held 1,000 prisoners in the summer of 1782. *Recollections of the Jersey prison-ship; taken, and prepared for publication, from the original manuscript of the late Captain Thomas Dring . . . one of the prisoners* (1829) Published by H. H. Brown.

88 Ashe, *Biographical History of North Carolina*: 145.

89 *Calendar of Virginia State Papers*, Volume III: 506.

90 Shipton, *Rhode Islanders Record the Revolution*: 103-104.

CHAPTER 18

1 The frigate *Alliance* was abandoned on Petty Island, New Jersey across the Delaware from Philadelphia. At low tide, some of her timbers could be seen in the sands there until her remaining hulk was destroyed during dredging operations in 1901.

2 JCC: 484, May 9, 1778.

3 Kapp, *The Life of Frederick William Von Steuben*: 75-76 and 94.

4 JCC: 625 June 15, 1778

5 *Independent Chronicle*, William Murray' testimony, April 29, 1779.

6 PBF, 28: 589, Benjamin Franklin to Captain Landais, Feb. 22, 1779.

7 Marine Committee Letter Book: 236, Sept. 17, 1779 Letter to Franklin, Wharton Vol. III, p. 188, *Boston Gazette* April 19 and 26, 1779, *Independent Chronicle* April 22 and 29, 1779, and PBF, Vol. 28: 486, Landais to Benjamin Franklin, Feb. 7 (8), 1779.

8 PBF, 28: 486, Landais at Brest to Benjamin Franklin, Feb. 26, 1779.

9 PBF, 29: 615, Benjamin Franklin to the Marine Committee of Congress, June 3, 1779.

10 Diary of John Adams, May 9, 1779.

11 Diary of John Adams, May 12, 1779.

12 Ibid.

13 PBF, 29: 518, Benjamin Franklin to Chaumont, May 19, 1779.

14 The *Serapis'* forty-four guns were composed of twenty 18-pounders, twenty-two 9-pounders and two 6-pounders.

15 The *Bonhomme Richard* had six 18-pounders, twenty-eight 12-pounders and six 9-pounders.

16 Brody, Commodore Paul Jones: 175-228; Thomas, John Paul Jones: 168-205.

17 Sabine, *Notes on Duels and Duelling*: 226-227.

18 PBF, 32: 506, Benjamin Franklin to John Paul Jones June 12, 1780.

19 PBF, 32: 525, Samuel Wharton to Benjamin Franklin June 14, 1780.

20 PBF, 32: 544, Benjamin Franklin to John Paul Jones June 17, 1780.

21 PBF, www.franklinpapers.org/ John Paul Jones to Matthew Parke, June 20, 1780.

22 PBF, 32: 565, John Paul Jones to Benjamin Franklin June 21, 1780.

23 PBF, 32: 578, John Paul Jones to Benjamin Franklin June 23, 1780.

24 Library of Congress, Benjamin Franklin at Passy to Landais, June 24, 1780.

25 PBF, 32: 586, Benjamin Franklin to Jean Daniel Schweighauser, June 24, 1780.

26 PBF, 32: 613, Benjamin Franklin to Captain Landais, June 27, 1780.

27 PBF, 33: 43, Captain Landais at Groix to Benjamin Franklin, July 7, 1780.

Library of Congress, Benjamin Franklin at Passy to Francis Lewis (Board of Admiralty), Aug. 10, 1780.

28 PBF, 33: 160, Benjamin Franklin to Samuel Huntington, Aug. 9, 1780.

29 Lieutenant James Degge assumed command at latitude 40° 31′ north and longitude 59° west.

30 Paullin, *Out Letters of the Board of Admiralty*: 260-261, Board of Admiralty to Commissioners of the Navy Board of the Eastern Department, Sept. 5, 1780.

31 The *Alfred* was also the scene of a court martial held on October 22, 1776 at Newport, Rhode Island where Captain John Paul Jones was present. Jones had received orders from Esek Hopkins, Commander in Chief to attend at 2:00 p.m. the trial of Samuel Halm or Einom James Robinson and John Robinson for mutiny. Naval, 6: 1361, Samuel Lyon, Secretary at Newport, Rhode Island, to Captain John Paul Jones, Oct. 22, 1776 from the Papers of John Paul Jones, Library of Congress.

32 PBF, 34: 96, Benjamin Franklin to Samuel Cooper, Dec. 2, 1780.

33 There is a discrepancy in the date of placing the men in irons. The ship's log says March 31 while Kessler's narrative says March 30, 1781.

34 Griffin, *Commodore John Barry*: 134.

35 John Kessler narrative.

36 Griffin, *Commodore John Barry*: 181. The three men who were approached signed a sworn statement on October 3, 1782.

37 Library of Congress, John Atwood petition to John Paul Jones The names of the mutineers were John Atwood, John Balch, Thomas Barnes, Nathaniel Bonner, William Carmichael, Thomas Cole, Alexander Cooper, William Hanover, Christy Hertley, George Johnston, John Layton, James Louis, Elijah Middleton, Thomas Richards, John Rumley, Andrew Thompson, and Richard Watson.

38 Allen, *Naval History of the American Revolution*, 2: 449.

39 Ibid.: 534.

CHAPTER 19

1 Historic Manuscript Commission, the 14th Report Part X, Manuscripts of the Earl of Dartmouth, Vol. II, *American Papers* (1895): 318 Cabinet Minutes June 21, 1775. Document is in Dartmouth's handwriting. At the meeting it was decided that General Clinton was to raise 2,000 Canadians to be employed as light infantry under Gage, Highlanders to be sent to American and regiments from Gibraltar and Minorca to join them.

2 Clark, A Letter to the Right Honourable Charles Jenkinson, Esq., Secretary of War: 10.

3 Walcott, *Sir Archibald Campbell*: 12.

4 Arthur's Seat is the main peak of the group of hills which form most of Holyrood Park in the center of the city of Edinburgh. Its name stems from a legend that King Arthur watched his army's defeat of the Picts from there.

5 Frey, *British Soldier*: 74 Add. Mss 42,071, Copy of the Conditions entered into the

General Officers in Scotland with the Mutineers of the Earl of Seaforth's Regiment, September 1781.

6 Great Britain, Warwickshire County Record Office, Feilding family of Newnham Paddox, CR 2917/C244, p. 183 Letter Book of the 6th Earl of Denbigh, To the Earl of Loudoun from Newnham, Oct. 7, 1778 and Prebble, *Mutiny*: 120-134.

7 Burntisland is a town on the Firth of Forth with the 15th Century Rossend Castle and the Binn.

8 Firth of Forth is the estuary or firth of Scotland's Forth River where it flows into the North Sea.

9 Prebble, *Mutiny*: 148-153.

10 It was on September 30, 1779 after tattoo. U.S. Naval Observatory information indicates that the end of civil twilight was 18:30 hours.

11 Prebble, *Mutiny*: 188-198.

12 Ibid.: 198-204 and 208.

13 Ibid.: 159.

14 Forbes, *The Black Watch*: 115-117 and Prebble, *Mutiny*: 156-170.

15 *Four Excellent New Songs*, 1780.

16 Prebble, *Mutiny*: 241.

17 Ibid.: 228-248.

18 Michie, *Deeside Tales or Men and Manners on Highland Deeside since 1745*: 70-75.

19 Prebble, *Mutiny*: 247.

20 Clowes, *The Royal Navy A History*, IV: 50.

21 The ship was under the command of John Carter Allen: 2 April 1779-11 Mar. 1780 Suffolk Record Office, Lowestoft Branch Navel Log Books of the Aldous Family 15/2 Journal of the proceedings on board HMS *Egmont* under the command of John Carter Allen, kept by Aldous Charles Arnold, midshipman, 2 April 1779-11 Mar. 1780.

22 Clowes, *The Royal Navy A History*, IV: 50 fn2 and Hannay, Naval Courts Martial: 128-130.

23 *St. Eustatius* and *Etna* were also in port.

24 Guttridge, *Mutiny, a History of Naval Insurrection*: 10 quoting from T. H. Wintringham, *Mutiny being a Survey of Mutinies*, 1936.

25 Hannay, *Naval Courts Martial*:131-135.

26 *Historic Manuscript Commission*, the 14th Report (1896): 43 Lord Robert Manners to his brother (the Duke of Rutland), July 1781.

27 Guttridge, *Mutiny, a History of Naval Insurrection*: 10 quoting from T. H. Wintringham, *Mutiny being a Survey of Mutinies*, 1936 *Janus* had forty-four guns.

28 PBF, 32: 358, Admiralty Board to Benjamin Franklin May 6 1780.

29 Naval, 3: 689, Captain Andrew Snape Hamond, R.N. to Vice Admiral Samuel Graves, Jan. 9, 1776, Hamond Letter Book, 1771-1777, University of Virginia Library.

30 Naval, 4: 814-815, Philip Stephens, Admiralty Office to Vice Admiral Molyneux Shuldham, May 3, 1777.

31 Hannay, *Naval Courts Martial*:123-125.

32 Clowes, *The Royal Navy A History*, IV: 110.

33 Ibid.: 46 and 110 and Hannay, *Naval Courts Martial*: 125-127.

34 The *Raisonnable* had sixty-four guns.

35 Sheerness is located on the northwest corner of the Isle of Sheppey in North Kent. It is near the Thames River Estuary and the Medway River. It was the site of a Royal Dockyard from 1665 to 1960.

36 Clowes, *The Royal Navy A History*, III: 339.

37 Margrave is the English translation of the German Margraf. In heredity peerage it is higher than a count but lower than a duke.

38 Chadwick, *The Climate and Diseases of America*: 6, quoting *Der Soldatenhandel deutscher Fürsten nach Amerika* by Friedrich Kapp, Berlin, 1874.

39 Burgoyne, *A Hessian Diary of the American Revolution by Johann Conrad Döhla*: 4

40 Lowell, *The Hessians and the Other German Auxiliaries*: 47

41 Ochsenfurt translates to Oxford in English. Today it is in the northwest part of Bavaria and was sometimes spelled Ochsenfurth in the documents of the period.

42 Ochsenfurt, at that time, belonged to the bishop of Würzburg who was also the Prince of Bamberg.

43 Rosengarten, Joseph P. Popp Journal in the *Pennsylvania Magazine of History and Biography*, Vol. 26: 27 (1902).

44 Döhla: 5.

45 Ibid.

46 Burgoyne, *A Hessian Officer's Diary, Prechtel*: 283.

47 Döhla: 5.

48 Ibid.: 8.

49 Burgoyne, *Diaries of Two Ansbach Jaegers, Diary of Lieutenant Heinrich Carl Philipp von Feilitzsch*: 5

50 Burgoyne, *A Hessian Diary of the American Revolution, An Anonymous Ansbach-Bayreuth Diary*: 3 indicates 8:30 a.m. while Burgoyne, A Hessian Officer's Diary, Prechtel: 101 indicates 9:00 a.m.

51 Burgoyne, *A Hessian Officer's Diary, Prechtel*: 283.

52 Burgoyne, *A Hessian Officer's Diary, Prechtel*: 101 There is a story that Prince Alexander sat in his boat with a cocked rifle ready for future deserters. It does not appear to be true.

53 Nijmegen is known in French as Nimègue and in German as Nimwegen.

54 Döhla: 10, 10n and British Museum Additional Manuscripts, Rainsford Papers, vol. 23, 651, ff 122-123.

55 Lowell, *The Hessians*: 50.

56 PBF Vol. 24: 8, Ben Franklin to John Winthrop, May 1, 1777.

57 Lowell, *The Hessians*: 38-41, Journal of Johann Gottfried Seume, from *Archenholtz's Magazine*, 1789.

58 The battle is known both as Hunt's Bluff and Mars Bluff.

59 Great Britain, Public Record Office, Headquarters Papers of the British Army in

America, PRO 30/55/2949, Cornwallis to Sir Henry Clinton, dated Charlestown, 6 Aug. 1780.

60 Lacoursière, *Histoire Populaire du Québec*, 1: 440.

61 Siebert, *The Legacy of the American Revolution*: 11 quoted from The Report on American Manuscripts in the Royal Institutions of Great Britain, IV: 90 and 165.

CONCLUSION

1 McCrady, *History of South Carolina in the Revolution*: 333-335.

2 *Nathanael Greene*, Vol. 9: 148-149, Captain Nathaniel Pendleton to General Griffith Rutherford, May 1, 1782 (spelling corrected).

3 GWP, Varick Transcripts, Letterbook 8: 86-88, GW to John Sullivan, Feb. 14, 1779.

4 GWP, Gen. Correspondence, Israel Putnam to GW, Jan. 5, 1779.

5 GWP, Varick Transcripts, Letterbook 8: 25-27, GW to Israel Putnam, Jan. 18, 1779.

Bibliography

Manuscript Collections

British Museum Additional Manuscripts
    Rainsford Papers, vol. 23651

Connecticut Historical Society, Hartford, Connecticut:
    Oliver Wolcott Sr. Papers

Gilder Lehrman Collection on deposit at the New-York Historical Society, New York,
New York
    James Morrison Papers

Great Britain, Public Record Office
    Audit Office
    Headquarters Papers of the British Army in America
    Treasury Office

Great Britain, Warwickshire County Record Office
    Feilding family of Newnham Paddox

Historical Society of Pennsylvania, Philadelphia, Pennsylvania
    Anthony Wayne Papers
    Diary of George Nelson
    Nicholas Biddle Papers 1771-1778

Library of Congress, Washington, D. C.
    Cortlandt Skinner Papers
    George Washington Papers
    Papers of John Paul Jones

Maryland Historical Society, Baltimore, Maryland
    Mordecai Gist Papers

Massachusetts Historical Society, Boston, Massachusetts
    Adams Family Papers: An Electronic Archive at www.masshist.org/digitaladams/

New Jersey Historical Society, Newark, New Jersey
    William Peartree Smith Copybook, Nov. 1780

New York Public Library, New York, New York
    Emmet Collection on Microfilm
    Philip John Schuyler Papers

Pennsylvania State Archives, Harrisburg, Pennsylvania
    Revolutionary War Military Abstract Card File

Rhode Island Historical Society, Providence, Rhode Island
    Hopkins Letter Book

U. S. Naval Observatory, Astronomical Applications Department, Washington, D.C.
Sun and Moon Data

Virginia State Library, Richmond, Virginia
Virginia Governors Letters Received

William L. Clements Library, University of Michigan, Ann Arbor, Michigan
Henry Clinton Papers
Herbert S. Smith Collection, 2 Naval Affairs
James S. Schoff Collection
Nathanael Greene Papers
Shelburne Papers
Thomas Gage Papers

Printed Materials

Allen, Paul. *A History of the American Revolution Comprehending All the Principal* *Events in the Field and in the Cabinet*, Vol. 2. F. Betts, Baltimore, Maryland, 1822.

Archives of Maryland Series.

Armbruster, Eugene L. *Long Island its Early Days and Development*. Brooklyn Daily Eagle, Brooklyn, New York, 1914.

Ashe, Samuel A., editor. *Biographical History of North Carolina: from Colonial Times to the Present* (8 Volumes). C. L. Van Noppen, Greensboro, North Carolina, 1905.

Balch, Thomas, editor. *Papers Relating Chiefly to the Maryland Line during the Revolution*. The Seventy Six Society, Philadelphia, Pennsylvania, 1857.

Bancroft, George. *History of the United States from Discovery of the American Continent*. Little, Brown and Company, Boston, Massachusetts, 1856-1874.

Bangs, Edward, editor. *Journal of Lieutenant Isaac Bangs, April 1 to July 29, 1776*. John Wilson and Son, University Press, Cambridge, Massachusetts, 1890. Reprinted by the New York Times & Arno Press, New York, New York, 1968.

Berg, Fred Anderson. *Encyclopedia of Continental Army Units*. Stackpole Books, Harrisburg, Pennsylvania, 1972.

Bland, Theodorick. *The Bland Papers: being a selection from the manuscripts of Colonel Theorrick Bland Jr.* (2 Volumes). E. & J. C. Ruffin, Petersburg, Virginia, 1840-1843.

Boston Gazette, Boston, Massachusetts.

Bray, Robert C. and Bushnell, Paul E., editors. *Diary of a Common Soldier in the American Revolution 1775–1783, An Annotated Edition of the Military Journal of Jeremiah Greenman*. Northern Illinois University Press, De Kalb, Illinois, 1978.

Brody, Cyrus Townsend. *Commodore Paul Jones*. D. Appleton & Co., New York, 1900.

Brooke, T. H. *A History of the Island of St. Helena from its Discovery by the Portuguese to the Year 1806*. Black, Parry and Kingsbury, London, England, 1808.

Bruijn, Jaap R. *The Dutch Navy of the Seventeenth and Eighteenth Centuries*. University of South Carolina Press, Columbia, South Carolina, 1993.

Burgoyne, Bruce E., translator. *A Hessian Diary of the American Revolution by Johann Conrad Döhla*. Heritage Books Inc, CD Version 2005 reprint of 1990 book.

Burgoyne, Bruce E., translator. *A Hessian Officer's Diary of the American Revolution, Prechtel*. Heritage Books Inc, CD Version 2005.

Burgoyne, Bruce E., translator. *Diaries of Two Ansbach Jaegers: Diary of Lieutenant Heinrich Carl Philipp von Feilitzsch*. Heritage Books, Bowie, Maryland, 1997.

Burgoyne, Bruce E., translator. *Journal of the Hesse-Cassel Jaeger Corps*. Heritage Books, Bowie, Maryland, 2005.

Burgoyne, Bruce E., translator. *Revolutionary War Letters Written by Hessian Officers*. Heritage Books, Bowie, Maryland, 2005.

Butterfield, Consul Willshire, editor. *Washington–Irvine Correspondence. The Official Letters Which Passed Between Washington and Brig.-Gen. William Irvine and Between Irvine and Others Concerning Military Affairs in the west from 1781 to 1783*. David Atwood, Madison, Wisconsin, 1882.

Calendar of Virginia State Papers, Volumes 1, 11 and 111. James R. Goode, Printer, Richmond, Virginia, 1875, 1881, and 1883.

Carp, Wayne E. *To Starve the Army of Pleasure: Continental Army Administration and American political culture, 1775-1783*. University of North Carolina Press, Chapel Hill, North Carolina, 1984.

Chawick, James Read, translator. *The Climate and Diseases of America by Dr. Schoepff, Johann David*. H. O. Houghton and Company, New York, 1875.

Clark, John. *A Letter to the Right Honourable Charles Jenkinson, Esq., Secretary of War. Animadverting on the Late Mutinies in the Highland Regiments*. Charles Elliot and T. Cadell, London, England, 1780.

Clark, William Bell. *George Washington's Navy*. Louisiana State University Press, Baton Rouge, Louisiana, 1960.

Clayton, W. Woodward, editor. *History of Union and Middlesex Counties with Biographical Sketches of Many of their Pioneers and Prominent Men*. Everts & Peck, Philadelphia, Pennsylvania, 1882.

Clowes, William Laird. *The Royal Navy A History from the Earliest Times to 1900, Volumes III and IV*. Chatham Publishing, London 1997 reprint of Sampson Low Marston & Co., 1899.

Coldham, Peter Wilson. *American Migrations 1765-1799*. Genealogical Publishing Company, Baltimore, Maryland, 2000.

Cumberland Chronicle or Whitehaven Public Advertiser at www.pastpresented.info/cumbria/chronicle1776.htm taken from microfilm at Library of Congress, 1776.

Dann, John C. *One Hundred and One Treasures from the Collections of the William L. Clements Library*. Clements Library, Ann Arbor, Michigan, 1998.

Dann, John C. *The Revolution Remembered*. University of Chicago Press, Chicago, Illinois, 1980.

Dawson, Henry B., Editor. *New York City During the American Revolution*. The Mercantile Association of New York City, New York, New York, 1861.

Dempsey, Janet. *Washington's Last Cantonment: High Time for a Peace*. Library Research Associates Inc., Monroe, New York, 1987.

Dewey, Adelbert, editor. *Life of George Dewey, Rear Admiral U.S.N. and Dewey family History*. Dewey Publishing Company, Westfield, Massachusetts, 1898.

Dictionary of American Naval Fighting Ships at www.history.navy.mil/danfs/

Dring, Thomas. *Recollections of the Jersey Prison Ship, from the manuscript of Capt. Thomas Dring*. Corinth Books, New York, 1961.

Eckenrode, Hamilton James. *The Revolution in Virginia*. Houghton Mifflin Co., Boston & New York, 1916; also, Archon Books, Hamden, Connecticut, reprinted 1964.

Elliot, Jonathan. *The Debates in the Several State Conventions on the Adoption of the Federal Constitution*. J.B. Lippincott & co., Philadelphia and Taylor & Maury, Washington, DC 1836-1859.

Enoch Poor's Valley Forge Order Book: Jan. 28 – Feb. 20, 1778.

Faust, Albert Bernhardt. *German Element in the United States, Vol. I*. Arno Press & the New York Times, New York, 1969.

Field, Edward, editor. *Diary of Colonel Israel Angell Commanding the Second Rhode Island Continental Regiment during the American Revolution 1778-1781*. Preston and Rounds, Providence, Rhode Island, 1899.

Fischer, David Hackett. *Paul Revere's Ride*. Oxford University Press, New York, New York, 1994.

Forbes, Archibald. *The Black Watch: The Record of an Historic Regiment*. Cassell and Company, Ltd, London, England, 1896.

Force, Peter. *American Archives*. Johnson Reprint Corp., New York, 1972 reprint of 1837-1853 editions.

Ford, Chauncey Worthington, editor. *General Orders Issued by Major-General Israel Putnam, when in Command of the Highlands, in the Highland in the Summer and Fall of 1777*. Historical Printing Club, Brooklyn, New York, 1893.

Four Excellent New Songs, 1. A song in praise of the Honourable Lord Seaforth's regiment, II. A new song in praise of the scots heros, III. The plundering of the bonny house of Airley, IV. The Power of Love. Edinburgh, Scotland, 1780 Online Gale Group, http:galenet.galegroup.com/servlet/ECCO

French, Allen. *General Gage's Informers*. University of Michigan Press, Ann Arbor, Michigan, 1932.

Frey, Sylvia R. *The British Soldier in America: a Social History of Military Life in the Revolutionary Period*. University of Texas Press, Austin, Texas, 1981.

Friedman, Steve Morgan. *A Brief History of the University of Pennsylvania*. University Archives and Records Center University of Pennsylvania's website www.archives.upenn.edu/histy/genlhistory/brief.html

Garden, Alexander. *Anecdotes of the Revolutionary War in America*. A. E. Miller, Charleston, South Carolina, 1822.

Gibbes, Robert Wilson. *Documentary History of the American Revolution, 1764-1776*. D. Appleton & Co., New York, 1855.

Gordon, William. *The History of the Rise, Progress and Establishment of the Independence of the United States of America*. London, England, 1788.

Great Britain, Suffolk Record Office, Lowestoft Branch. Naval Log Books of the Aldous Family 15/2 Journal of the proceedings on board HMS *Egmont* under the command of John Carter Allen, kept by Aldous Charles Arnold, midshipman.

Greene, Evarts B. and Harrington, Virginia D. *American Population Before the Federal Census of 1790*. Genealogical Publishing Company, Baltimore, Maryland, 1981 reprint of 1932 edition.

Greene, Nathanael. *Papers of General Nathanael Greene*. 13 Volumes (1976-2005). University of North Carolina Press, Chapel Hill, North Carolina.

Griffin, Martin Ignatius Joseph. *Commodore John Barry, "the Father of the American Navy," the Record of His Services for Our Country*. Philadelphia, Pennsylvania, 1903.

Gruber, Ira D., editor. *John Peebles' American War The Diary of a Scottish Grenadier, 1776-1782*. Stackpole Books, Mechanicsburg, Pennsylvania, 1998.

Guttridge, Leonard F. *Mutiny, a History of Naval Insurrection*. Naval Institute Press, Annapolis, 1992.

Hall, Charles S. *Life and Letters of Samuel Holden Parsons*. Otseningo Publishing Company, Binghamton, New York, 1905.

Heath, William. *Heath's Memoirs of the American War*. A. Wessels Co., New York, New York, 1904, a reprint of *Memoirs of Major-General Heath*, I. Thomas and E. T. Andrews, Albany & Worcester, 1798.

Heitman, Francis B. *Historical Register of Officers of the Continental Army during the War of the Revolution, April, 1775 to December, 1783*. The Rare Book Shop Publishing Company, Inc., Washington, D.C., 1914.

Historic Manuscript Commission, the 14th Report (1896): 43 Lord Robert Manners to his brother (the Duke of Rutland).

Historical Manuscript Commission, *Manuscripts of the Earl of Dartmouth, American Papers*, Vol. II, 14th Report, Appendix, Part X, 1895, reprinted Gregg Press, Boston, Massachusetts, 1972.

Huchinson, Thomas. *Diary and Letters of His Excellency Thomas Hutchinson, Esq., Vol. 1.* Burt Franklin, New York reprinted 1971.

Independent Chronicle, Boston, Massachusetts.

Johnston, Henry Phelps. *The Campaign of 1776 around New York and Brooklyn: Battle of Long Island, Loss of New York etc.* Long Island Historical Society, Brooklyn, New York, 1878.

Johnston, Henry Phelps. *The Record of the Connecticut Men in the Military and Naval Service during the War of the Revolution 1775-1783*. Clearfield Co., Inc. Baltimore, Maryland 1997; reprint. Originally published as pages 1-780 of *Record of Service of Connecticut Men in the I.-War of Revolution. II.-War of 1812. III.-Mexican War.* (Hartford, Connecticut, 1889).

Jones, Charles Henry. *History of the Campaign for the Conquest of Canada in 1776.* Porter & Coates, Philadelphia, Pennsylvania, 1882.

Jones, Joseph Seawall. *A Defense of the Revolutionary History of the State of North Carolina: From the Aspersions of Mr. Jefferson.* Turner & Hughes, Raleigh, North Carolina, 1834.

Journals of the Continental Congress, 1774-1789, ed. Worthington C. Ford et al., Washington, D.C., 1904-37.

Journals of the Council of the State of Virginia, Virginia State Library, Division of Purchasing and Printing, Richmond, Virginia (1931-).

Kapp, Frederich. *The Life of Frederick William Von Steuben: Major General in the Revolutionary Army.* Mason Brothers, New York, 1859.

Lacoursière, Jacques. *Histoire Populaire du Québec, Des Origines à 1791.* Sillery, Quebec: Septentrion, 1995.

Laurens, Henry. *Papers of Henry Laurens.* University of South Carolina Press, Columbia, South Carolina.

Lederer, Jr., Richard M. *Colonial American English.* Verbatim Book, Essex, Connecticut, 1985.

Letters of Delegates to Congress, 1774-1789, 25 volumes, Smith, Paul H., et al., eds. Washington, D.C.: Library of Congress, 1976-2000.

Lewis, James Allen. *Neptune's Militia: the Frigate South Carolina During the American Revolution.* Kent State University Press, Kent, Ohio, 1999.

London Chronicle and Public Advertiser, London, England.

Lossing, B. J. *Pictorial Field Book of the Revolution.* Harper Brothers, New York, New York, 1851 Volume I and 1852 Volume II.

Lowell, Edward J. *The Hessians and the Other German Auxiliaries of Great Britain in the Revolutionary War*. Corner House Historical Publications, Gansevoort, New York, 1997 reprint of Harper & Brother, New York, 1884.

Madison, James. *Writings of James Madison*, ed. by Gaillard Hunt. G. P. Putnam & Sons, 1900-1910.

Martin, Joseph Plumb. *Private Yankee Doodle*. Eastern Acorn Press, Yorktown, Virginia, 1962.

Massachusetts Historical Society. *Collections of the Massachusetts Historical Society*, 7th Series, Volume 2, Boston, Massachusetts, 1902.

Mackenzie, Frederick. *Diary of Frederick Mackenzie*. Harvard University Press, Cambridge, Massachusetts, 1930.

Magazine of American History with Notes and Queries Series.

Massachusetts Archives Series.

Massachusetts Soldiers and Sailors of the Revolutionary War, 1775-1782, Vol. XII, CD edition.

McCrady, Edward. *The History of South Carolina in the Revolution, 1775-1780*. Russell & Russell, New York, 1969 reprint of 1901 edition.

McDonald, Bob, transcriber. *Diary of Pvt. John Smith, 1st Rhode Island Regiment: July 18, 1777–January 9, 1778*, appearing at www.revwar75.com/library

Mickie, John Grant. *Deeside Tales or Men and Manners on Highland Deeside since 1745*. D. Wyllie & Son, Aberdeen, Scotland, 1908.

Mississippi Valley Historical Review, 20: 247-270, "Sergeant John Smith's Diary of 1776."

Moore, Frank. *Diary of the American Revolution*. New York Times, New York, 1972; reprint of 1860 edition.

Moore, Horatio Newton. Life and Service of General Anthony Wayne. John B. Perry, Philadelphia, Pennsylvania, 1845.

Moultrie, William. *Memoirs of the American Revolution*, Volume II. David Longworth, 1802 and reprinted by the New York Times & Arno Press, New York, New York, 1968.

Naval Documents of the American Revolution. 11 Volumes (1964–). United States Naval History Division, U. S. Government Printing Office, Washington, D.C.

Neagles, James C. *Summer Soldiers: a Survey and Index of Revolutionary War Courts-martial*. Ancestry, Inc., Salt Lake City, Utah, 1986.

New England Historical & Genealogical Register, CXII (July 1958).

New Hampshire Provincial and State Papers, Vol. 17. (1889). John B. Clarke, Manchester, New Hampshire (1867-1943).

New Jersey Gazette, printed by Issac Collins, Burlington, New Jersey (1777-1786).

New York Gazette and Weekly Mecury, printed by Hugh Gaines, New York, New York (1768-1783).

New York-Historical Society. Collections of the New-York Historical Society for the Year 1872, Lee Papers, Vol. II and 1875, 1878, 1882.

Norton, Ichabod. *Orderly Book of Captain Ichabod Norton of Colonel Mott's Regiment.* Keating & Barnard, Fort Edward, New York, 1898.

O'Callaghan, E. B., Editor. *Documents Relative to the Colonial History of the State of New York,* VIII. Weed, Parsons and Company Printers, Albany, New York, 1857.

O'Callaghan, E. B., editor. *Marriage Licenses issued by the Secretary of the Province of New York Previous to 1784.* Weed, Parsons and Company, Albany, New York, 1860.

O'Kelley, Patrick. *Nothing but Blood and Slaughter: Military Operations and Order of Battle of the Revolutionary War in the Carolinas.* Volume 4. Booklocker.com, Bangor, Maine, 2005.

Papers of Benjamin Franklin. Yale University Press, New Haven, Connecticut, 1959– and www.franklinpapers.org/franklin/

Papers of the Continental Congress both published and microfilm.

Parsons, John C. *Letters and Documents of Ezekiel Williams of Wethersfield, Connecticut.* The Acorn Club of Connecticut, Stinehour Press, Lunenburg, Vermont, 1976.

Paltists, Victor Hugo, editor. *Minutes of the Commissioners for Detecting and Defeating Conspiracies in the State of New York.* State of New York, Albany, New York, Volume I 1778-1779 (1909), Volume II 1780-1781 (1909), and Volume III Analytical Index (1910).

Paullin, Charles Oscar. Out-Letters of the Continental Marine Committee and the Board of Admiralty; August 1776 – September 1780. De Vinne Press, New York, 1914.

Peckham, Howard Henry, editor. *Memoirs of the Life of John Adlum in the Revolutionary War.* The Caxton Club, Chicago, Illinois, 1968.

Peckham, Howard Henry, editor. *The Toll of Independence - Engagements & Battle Casualties of the American Revolution.* University of Chicago Press, Chicago, Illinois, 1974.

Pennsylvania Archives.

Pennsylvania Colonial Records.

Pennsylvania Council Minutes.

Pennsylvania Gazette, Philadelphia, Pennsylvania.

Pennsylvania Magazine of History and Biography, Historical Society of Pennsylvania, Philadelphia, Pennsylvania (1877-)

Pennsylvania Packet, Philadelphia, Pennsylvania.

Prince, Carl E., editor. *The Papers of William Livingston*, 5 Volumes. New Jersey Historical Commission, Trenton, New Jersey, 1979. Also Microfilm edition for unpublished papers on the Pennsylvania Line Mutiny.

Proceedings of the Massachusetts Historical Society, 1858-1860.

Proceedings of Lehigh County Historical Society, Vol. 21. Jacob Weiss Letter Book of 1778-1781.

Proceedings of the New Jersey Historical Society, New Jersey Historical Society, Newark, New Jersey.

Quincy, Josiah. *Journals of Major Samuel Shaw: The First American Consul at Canton*. William Crosby and H. P. Nichols, Boston, Massachusetts, 1847.

Rankin, Hugh F. *North Carolina Continentals*. University of North Carolina Press, Chapel Hill, North Carolina, 1971.

Renault. *Le Secret Service de L'Amirauté Britannique au temps de la Guerre d'Amérique.*

Richards, Samuel. *Diary of Samuel Richards: captain of Connecticut line, War of the Revolution 1775-1781*. Press of the Leeds & Biddle Co., Philadelphia, Pennsylvania, 1909.

Roberts, Kenneth. *March to Quebec*. Doubleday, Doran & Co, New York, 1939.

Rosengarten, Joseph P., Translator. Popp's Journal, 1777–1783. *Pennsylvania Magazine of History and Biography*, 16, 1902.

Royal Gazette, London, England.

Sabine, Lorenzo. *Notes on Duels and Duelling*. Crosby, Nicholas and Company, Boston, Massachusetts, 1859.

Sabine, William H. W., editor. *Historical Memoirs of William Smith 1763-1778*, Vol. 2. New York Times & Arno Press, New York, New York, 1969.

Salley, Alexander Samuel Jr. *History of Orangeburg County, South Carolina*. R. Lewis Berry, Orangeburg, South Carolina, 1898.

Shipton, Nathaniel N. and Swain, David, editors. *Rhode Islanders Record the Revolution, The Journals of William Humphrey and Zuriel Waterman*. Rhode Island Publication Society, Providence, Rhode Island, 1984.

Siebert, Wilbur H. *The Legacy of the American Revolution to the British West Indies and Bahamas*. The Ohio State University Bulletin, Columbus, Ohio April 1913.

Smith, William Henry. *The St. Clair Papers*, Volume I. Robert Clarke & Co., Cincinnati, Ohio, 1882.

South Carolina Historical Magazine, Volume 98, Finney Diary, South Carolina Historical Society, Charleston, South Carolina.

Southern Campaigns of the American Revolution Journal at www.southerncampaign.org/

Southern Literary Messenger (1838).

Sparks, Jared. *Life of Gouverneur Morris with Selections from his Correspondence and Personal Papers, Volume I.* Gray and Bowen, Boston, Massachusetts, 1832.

State Records of North Carolina Series. Nash Bros. Book and Job Printers, Raleigh, North Carolina.

Steadman, Charles. *History of the Origin, Progress, and Termination of the American War,* 2 vols. London and Dublin, 1794.

Stevens, Benjamin F. *Facsimiles of Manuscripts in European Archives Relating to America 1773-1783,* 25 Volumes, 1889; reprint by Mellifont Press, Inc., Wilmington, Delaware, 1970.

Stiles, Henry R. *History of the City Brooklyn,* Vol. 1. Brooklyn, New York, 1867

Stillé, Charles Janeway. *Major General Wayne and the Pennsylvania Line.* J. B. Lippincott Co., Philadelphia, Pennsylvania, 1893.

Thacher, James A. *A Military Journal During the American Revolutionary War from 1775 to 1783.* Richardson and Lord, Boston, Massachusetts, 1823.

Thomas, Evan. *John Paul Jones: Sailor, Hero, Father of the American Navy.* Simon & Schuster, New York, 2003.

Todd, Charles Burr. *History of Redding, Connecticut.* John Gray, New York, 1880.

Transactions and Studies of the College of Physicians of Philadelphia, 4th Series Vol. 13 # 3 (Dec. 1945). Benjamin Rush Terminates a Post-War Mutiny among Troops Demanding Their Discharge by James Gibson.

Tussell Jr., John B. B. *The Pennsylvania Line Regimental Organization and Operations, 1776-1783.* Pennsylvania Historical and Museum Commission, Harrisburg, Pennsylvania, 1977.

United States Magazine and Literary and Political Repository, Vol. 1 No. 1, review of William Johnson's Sketches of the Life and Correspondence of Nathanael Greene. Charles Wiley, New York, 1823.

Valley Forge Muster Roll at www.valleyforgemusterroll.org/

Virginia Gazette, Williamsburg, Virginia.

Waddell, Joseph A. *Annals of Augusta County, Virginia.* C. R. Caldwell, Staunton, Virginia, 1902.

Walcott, Charles H. *Sir Archibald Campbell of Inverneill Sometimes Prisoner of War in the Jail at Concord, Massachusetts.* Beacon Hill, Boston, Massachusetts, 1898

Williamson's Liverpool Advertiser.

Wilson, Joseph Lapsley. *Book of the First Troop, Philadelphia City Cavalry, 1774–1914.* Hallowell Company, Philadelphia, Pennsylvania, 1915.

Wright, Esmond. *Franklin of Philadelphia.* Belknap Press of Harvard University Press, Cambridge, Massachusetts, 1986.

Index

Acknowledgements

No ONE COMPLETES A BOOK WITHOUT the help of friends. I have had the assistance from many sources and I am extremely grateful. I want to thank the staff of the William L. Clements Library at the University of Michigan who have gone beyond what could reasonably be expected at such a research facility. John C. Dann, Director, who always provided ideas of where else to look when I encountered dead ends in my research; Donald Wilcox, Book Curator, who was always willing to go the extra mile in assisting me find that rare book that I needed; Brian Leigh Dunnigan, Head of Research, who was always willing to help me interpret some bad eighteenth century handwriting; Barbara DeWolfe, Manuscript Curator, who was helpful in so many ways with all of my requests to see all of the Clinton, Gage, Germain, Greene, Shelburne, etc., papers; and Clayton Lewis, Graphics Curator, for his cooperation in locating the prints for this work. I want to thank Janet Bloom, Laura Daniels, John Harriman (deceased), and Cheney Schopieray for their extra effort. To the rest of the staff at Clements, thank you for your all help.

One library does not provide enough research material for any book and this one was no exception. I want to thank Greg Johnson and Katherine Ludwig at the David Library of the American Revolution in Washington Crossing, Pennsylvania; Sarah Heim and Dan Rolph at the Historical Society of Pennsylvania; Michael J. Crawford, Head, Early History Branch of the United States Naval Historical Center; Glenn F. Williams, United Staes Army Center of Military History, Thomas Crew of the Virginia State Library; John McClure, Reference Department Manager, Virginia Historical Society, Matthew J. Schumann, Eastern Michigan University, Gregory J. W. Urwin, Temple University, Georgiana Ziegler at the Folger Shakespeare Library, Washington, D.C., with her help in clarifying General Anthony Wayne's quote of Shakespeare's Apothecary; the Library Company of Philadelphia; Special Collections and University Archives at the Archibald Stevens Alexander Library at Rutgers University; Department of Special Collections at the Van Pelt-Dietrich Library at the University of Pennsylvania; and the Mount Laurel, New Jersey, Township Library for accomplishing all my interlibrary loan requests which were numerous.

I would like to thank Todd Braisted, who has been willing to share his vast knowledge of loyalists; Charles Baxley of the Southern Campaigns American Revolution Round Table who answered numerous questions on the war in the south; Charles F. Price, who pointed me in the right direction to where I could find information on the mutiny of Baylor's Dragoons.

There was a cadre of people who willingly shared their knowledge: John L. Bell, Bruce E. Burgoyne, Don H. Hagist, Bob McDonald and John U. Rees. I also would like to thank Doug MacGregor of the Fort Pitt Museum with help on the mutinies at Pittsburgh, and Joseph Becton of the Independence National Historical Park and diligent researcher of the 1st Rhode Island Regiment.

I would like to than the William L. Clements Library, Independence National Historical Park, and the Rhode Island Historical Society for permission to publish the images that are in this book. I would also like to thank the staff of Westholme Publishing, including publisher Bruce H. Franklin and Tracy Dungan for his work on producing the maps.

I appreciated the encouragement from the members of the American Revolution Round Table of Philadelphia, Thomas Fleming, Willard Stern Randall and fellow alumni of Saint Francis University, Loretto, Pennsylvania. I also would like to thank Ida Marie Nagy, Jennifer Ann Nagy, Lisa Marie Nagy, and Debra Springer for help with the typing.

Finally I would like to thank Lisa Marie Nagy for taking the pictures used in this book.